T
If y

Design and Layout
of Foodservice Facilities

Design and Layout
of Foodservice Facilities

Third Edition

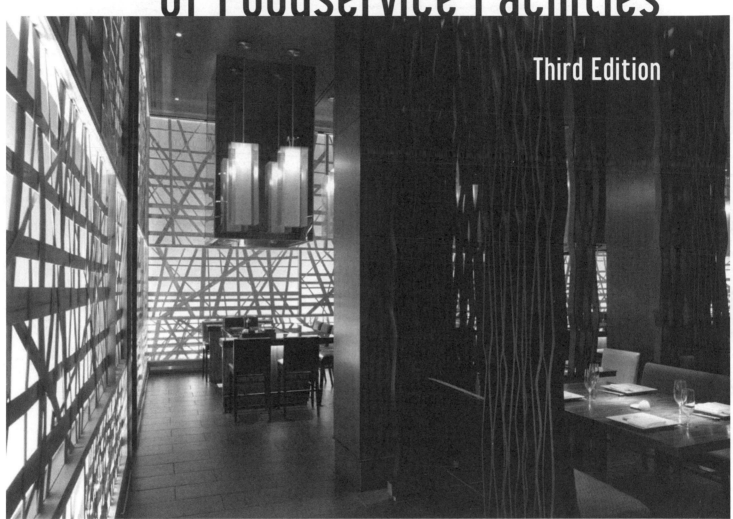

John C. Birchfield

BICENTENNIAL
1807
WILEY
2007
BICENTENNIAL

JOHN WILEY & SONS, INC.

Copyright © 2008 by John Wiley & Sons, Inc. All rights reserved.

Published by John Wiley & Sons, Inc., Hoboken, New Jersey.

Published simultaneously in Canada.

Anniversary Logo Design : Richard Pacifico.

For general information on our other products and services or for technical support, please contact our Customer Care Department within the United States at (800)-762-2974, outside the United States at 317-572-3993 or fax 317-572-4002.

Wiley also publishes its books in a variety of electronic formats. Some content that appears in print may not be available in electronic formats.

For more information about Wiley products, visit our Web site at http://www.wiley.com.

Library of Congress Cataloging-in-Publication Data

Birchfield, John C.
    Design and layout of foodservice facilities/John C. Birchfield. – 3rd ed.
        p. cm.
    Includes bibliographical references and index.
    ISBN 978-0-471-69963-7 (cloth)
    1. Food service management.   2. Food service–Equipment and supplies.
3. Restaurants–Design and construction.   I. Title.
    TX911.3.M27B57 2008
    647.95068—dc22
                                                                    2007021011

Printed in the United States of America.

10 9 8 7 6 5 4 3 2 1

Dedication

The third edition and revision of *Design and Layout of Foodservice Facilities* involved the skills and talents of many people including the great folks at John Wiley, equipment representatives, architects, engineers, and teachers who have used this book in the classroom.

This book is dedicated to the two people who assisted the author in more ways than I can recount, John C. Birchfield, Jr. and Robert Jacobs, Principals of Birchfield Jacobs Food Systems, Inc., Baltimore, Maryland.

Contents

CHAPTER 4

Space Analysis   83

CHAPTER 5

Equipment Layout   119

CHAPTER 6

Foodservice Equipment, Part I   147

Preface

The foodservice industry is evolving rapidly to keep pace with changes in consumer needs and expectations. In the commercial sector, new restaurant concepts are emerging to satisfy an increasingly discriminating market. In the off-site sectors of the industry (formerly known as noncommercial sectors), such as health care, education, and business and industry, foodservice is becoming increasingly market driven. These changes occurring throughout the industry call for the creation of new foodservice facilities as well as the renovation of existing facilities. The professional foodservice manager is likely to be involved in the design of a new or renovated facility several times during his or her career.

Design and Layout of Foodservice Facilities is intended to be a resource for hospitality professionals involved in a design project, for college and university students preparing for careers in foodservice management, and for design professionals who wish to know more about the foodservice design process, beginning with market research and financial feasibility studies and including design principles, equipment selection, and engineering.

NEW TO THIS EDITION

Many changes and additions have been made to *Design and Layout of Foodservice Facilities, Third Edition*, including:

- ❏ New pedagogical features incorporated throughout the text, including Key Terms, Review Questions, and Discussion Questions
- ❏ Significant expansion of chapters 6 and 7, Foodservice Equipment Parts I and II, with detailed descriptions of 65 pieces of equipment, many of which are new to this edition
- ❏ Updated and reorganized equipment chapter featuring new images
- ❏ Information on the expanding industry use of cook/chill technology in large foodservice design projects
- ❏ Additional examples of layouts of foodservice facilities
- ❏ Updated bibliography reflecting the most recent foodservice facilities publications
- ❏ Revised appendices that include web references for additional information
- ❏ Expanded and updated glossary

INSTRUCTOR'S MATERIALS

An *Instructor's Manual* (978-0-470-13505-1) is available. It includes:

❏ Suggestions for using the textbook in a 15-week semester

❏ Background information for each chapter that is useful in preparing lectures

❏ Student homework assignments for each chapter, many using Internet resources

❏ Examination questions and answers for each chapter

❏ Guidelines for assigning and evaluating a student design exercise as a major project

Please contact your Wiley sales representative to get a copy of the *Instructor's Manual*. If you do not know who your representative is, please visit www.wiley.com/college click on "Instructors", and click on "Who's My Rep". The *Instructor's Manual* is available to qualified instructors on the companion website at www.wiley.com/college. PowerPoint slides are also available for download on the web site.

Acknowledgments

The author wishes to recognize and thank John Birchfield Jr. and Bob Jacobs of Birchfield Jacobs Foodsystems, Inc. He is also grateful to the Nestlé Library at Cornell University's School of Hotel Administration for providing the information for the bibliography. At John Wiley & Sons, Melissa Oliver, Tzviya Siegman, and Richard DeLorenzo have been helpful editors.

The author would also like to acknowledge these reviewers for their insight and recommendations throughout the manuscript preparation process: John Bandman of The Art Institute of New York City, Paul J. Cannamela of Erie Community College, Robert Hertel of Saint Louis Community College, and William D. Thornton of San Antonio College.

The foodservice facility plans in this book are provided courtesy of Birchfield Jacobs Foodsystems, Inc., Baltimore, Maryland, unless otherwise noted.

About the Author

John C. Birchfield is the founder of Birchfield Foodsystems (now Birchfield Jacobs Foodsystems, Inc.), a foodservice consulting and design firm with offices in Baltimore, Maryland. Mr. Birchfield was an associate professor of hotel, restaurant, and institutional management at Michigan State University and has operational experience in hotels, clubs, restaurants, and colleges. In 1973 Mr. Birchfield won the International Foodservice Manufacturer's Association Silver Plate Award as Foodservice Operator of the year. He is a past president of the National Association of College and University Food Services and the Foodservice Consultants Society International. A graduate of Cornell University's School of Hotel and Restaurant Management, Mr. Birchfield also holds a master's degree from Rutgers University in the field of institutional management and nutrition.

Mr. Birchfield is the author of many articles and two books on foodservice and management, *The Contemporary Quantity Recipe File*, published by Cahners Books, and the comprehensive *Foodservice Operations Manual*, published by Van Nostrand Reinhold. He served on the advisory board of Cahners Publishing Company for three years and has been a guest columnist for *Food Management Magazine*.

Mr. Birchfield has designed numerous foodservice facilities and has served as an operations consultant to many institutions, hotels, and clubs in the United States and Europe.

Design and Layout
of Foodservice Facilities

CHAPTER 1

Preliminary Planning

THIS CHAPTER

☑ Assists the reader in determining the scope of a project, which in turn will determine the complexity of the planning process

☑ Explains the process of concept development for hotels, chains, restaurants, and institutions

☑ Guides the person who is contemplating a design or equipment replacement project through the decision-making process regarding menu, market, management, money, and method of execution

☑ Introduces the elements of a feasibility study and outlines the different kinds of feasibility research that are necessary before designing a foodservice facility

SCOPE OF A PROJECT

Scope refers to the size and complexity of a foodservice facility design project. The scope of the project influences the design approach taken by the owner or manager. If the project involves only the layout of a new hot-food production area for an existing restaurant, the approach used and the planning process will be fairly simple. If the project entails the construction of a new restaurant or the complete renovation of an existing facility, the planning process becomes more difficult. And if the project includes the construction of a new facility that is to serve as the prototype for a chain or franchise, the planning process is even more complex.

Scope can be divided into four levels of complexity, each of which requires the involvement of different individuals and different amounts of planning time. Determining the scope of the project is an important first step before the planning begins.

Level I Scope

Projects of level I scope involve no more than the selection of a major piece of equipment or the replacement of a small area of a foodservice facility. Examples of level I projects include:

❑ Replacement of a dish machine and dish tables in a school cafeteria

❑ Replacement of the display refrigerator and service counter in a delicatessen

	Level of Scope			
	I	II	III	IV
Owner	✓	✓	✓	✓
Foodservice Design Consultant	✓	✓	✓	✓
Architect		✓	✓	✓
Engineer	✓	✓	✓	✓
Interior Designer		✓	✓	✓
General Contractor		✓	✓	✓
Subcontractor		✓	✓	✓
Equipment Dealer	✓	✓	✓	✓
Manufacturer's Representative	✓			
Banker			✓	✓
Lawyer			✓	✓
Accountant			✓	✓
Realtor			✓	✓

Figure 1.1. Professionals Involved in Projects of Different Levels of Scope.

❏ Purchase and installation of an outdoor walk-in freezer in a nursing home

❏ Replacement of the range section in a country club

Projects of level I scope typically can be carried out under the leadership of the owner or manager, assuming that he or she is familiar with foodservice equipment and has a good grasp of the workings of the food facility. If the owner does not have a working knowledge of equipment, a food facilities design consultant may be needed. The owner also will require the assistance of the kitchen equipment dealer and/or manufacturer's representatives in selecting and installing the equipment. Figure 1.1 compares the professionals involved in projects with different levels of size and complexity.

Figure 1.2 compares the time requirements of typical projects at each of the four levels of scope.

Level II Scope

Level II scope projects involve the renovation of a significant portion of an existing foodservice facility. Examples of level II scope projects include:

❏ Renovation of the entire service area in a university foodservice facility

❏ Replacement of all of the walk-in coolers and freezers in a country club

Task	Level I	Level II	Level III	Level IV
Planning	1 week	4 weeks	6 weeks	3 months
Equipment selection	1 week	2 weeks	1 month	2 months
Design and engineering	1 week	4 weeks	2 months	4 months
Preparing bid documents	2 days	4 weeks	2 months	2 months
Equipment delivery	4–6 weeks	2–3 months	4–6 months	4–6 months
Installation	3–5 days	2–6 weeks	1–3 months	1–3 months

Figure 1.2. Timelines for Projects of Different Levels of Scope.

❏ Replacement and relocation of the warewashing system in a hospital

❏ Addition of banquet rooms and serving kitchens in a hotel

The professionals likely to be involved in level II scope projects include the owner, an architect, mechanical and electrical engineers, a foodservice facility design consultant, a construction company or general contractor, and a kitchen equipment contractor. (The roles of these individuals are described in Chapter 2.) A full complement of professionals is necessary at level II because such projects are complex and require expertise in construction, engineering, and foodservice equipment layout and design.

Level II scope projects require a much longer time to complete than level I projects. Figure 1.2 shows a typical timeline for a level II renovation project.

Level III Scope

Level III scope projects involve the complete renovation of an existing foodservice facility or the design and construction of a new foodservice facility. Examples of level III scope projects include:

❏ Renovation of the dictary department of a hospital

❏ Construction of a new theme restaurant

❏ Renovation of the kitchen, service, and dining areas in a country club

❏ The development of foodservices for a new hotel

The planning process for the renovation of a foodservice facility often is even more complex than designing a new facility because of the difficulty of dealing with existing walls, structural members, utilities, and space and the demolition of parts of the existing structure. Moreover, in renovation projects, decisions must be made about which pieces of existing equipment should or could be used in the newly renovated facility.

The professionals likely to be involved in level III scope projects include the owner, an architect, mechanical and electrical engineers, a foodservice facility design consultant, an interior designer, a general contractor, and a kitchen equipment contractor.

Level III scope projects may take from one to three years from design to completion. Figure 1.2 shows a typical timeline for a level II renovation project.

Level IV Scope

Level IV scope projects involve the development of a chain or franchise prototype. Chain or prototype foodservice facilities require intense planning and design efforts because they will be constructed in multiple locations. Inefficiencies in design or inadequacies in equipment could be repeated hundreds of times and thus will be exceptionally expensive to correct. Such projects, in addition to the requirements of level III scope projects, involve a corporate strategy, a well-researched marketing plan, complex financial planning, and a strong management team. The food facility design at level IV must fit the needs of the menu, market, strategy, and financial package that are being developed by the corporation.

Professionals likely to be involved in level IV projects include investors and/or owners of the corporation, marketing consultants, financial planners, bankers, and corporate staff specialists as well as the design team, consisting of an architect, engineers, a foodservice design consultant, an interior designer, and general contractors.

The time required for a level IV scope project is longer than for a level III project in the design phases but may be shorter in the construction phases. Figure 1.2 shows the typical amount of time required for level IV scope projects. Level III and IV should not proceed unless a budget matching the expectations of the scope is prepared.

Once the scope has been determined and the budget has been approved, the owner can move forward with the project. In level I and level II scope projects, moving forward means going directly to the design process. However, when the scope of the project involves a major renovation of an existing facility or the development and construction of a new foodservice facility, the next step in the process is concept development.

CONCEPT DEVELOPMENT

The *concept* of a foodservice operation is the overall plan for how it will meet the needs and expectations of its intended market. A foodservice operation's concept is expressed in many ways, including its menu, decor, form of service, pricing, and location. *Concept development* means developing a plan for the success of the operation in its market in advance of actually designing—let alone building—the facility.

It is not unusual for a person to consider a new restaurant or, in fact, to open a new restaurant without knowing what type of food facility will have the best chance of succeeding. The potential entrepreneur may have some investment money, a location or a theme in mind, and a great amount of enthusiasm for the food business, but may not really have thought through the total concept of the operation. Unfortunately, enthusiasm and great food products are only half of the success equation. The other half of the equation is the market.

Concept development precedes the actual design of a foodservice facility because the foodservice design team must know what the menu, demand, hours of operation, and mode of service will be.

Single-Unit Restaurant Concept Development

The client who most frequently comes to the food facilities design consultant for help with concept development is the individual restaurant owner. The restaurant owner typically organizes a corporation comprised of a small number of local businesspeople and then begins to develop a concept that will eventually become a freestanding restaurant. The success or failure of the venture often depends on how well the concept was planned and how well the plan was followed.[1]

Numerous concepts are possible for single-unit restaurants. Commonly found concepts often are described in terms of these general

[1] Adapted from K.S. Chan and R.T. Sparrowe, *Welcome to Hospitality: An Introduction*, 2nd ed. (Albany, NY: Delmar, 2000) 210–215.

categories:

- *Fine-dining restaurants*. Fine-dining restaurants are distinguished by fine cuisine prepared by celebrity chefs, attentive service, stylish decor, and high prices.
- *Theme restaurants*. Theme restaurants offer a dining experience that evokes special times, places, or events, such as English pubs, restaurants owned by sports celebrities, and re-creations of diners from the 1950s.
- *Casual dinner houses*. Casual dinner houses emphasize a comfortable and contemporary decor as well as high value. Well-known casual dinner houses are not single-unit restaurants, but chains such as Chili's, T.G.I. Friday's, and Outback Steakhouse.
- *Ethnic restaurants*. Ethnic restaurants are closely tied to the cultures or foodways from which they originated. They include Mexican, Italian, French, German, Thai, and Indian restaurants, to name but a few.
- *Family restaurants*. Family restaurants specialize in relatively inexpensive fare and are kid-friendly.
- *Fast casual*. Fast casual restaurants generally combine quick service with higher-quality food, a more upscale environment, and an emphasis on fresh ingredients. They include chains such as Panera Bread, Chipotle Mexican Grill, and Baja Fresh.
- *Quick-service restaurants*. Quick-service restaurants specialize in convenience and fast service and include fast-food operations as well as delis, bagel shops, and sandwich shops.

Each of these categories of foodservice concept involves differences in menu, decor, mode of service, and price. However, not all of these factors are equally important within a given concept. Price is a critical factor in the success of quick-service, family, and casual dinner restaurants, where customers are value-conscious. However, price may not be as important in fine-dining restaurants, where customers expect to pay top dollar. Similarly, location is crucial for quick-service restaurants because their clientele depends on convenient access. But for some fine-dining and theme restaurants, location is not critical. Concept development for a single-unit restaurant is thus a complex process.

Chain Restaurant Concept Development

When Dave Thomas, who is now deceased, was chairman of the board of Wendy's, traveled around the country with Colonel Sanders in the mid-1950s trying to promote a chicken franchise, he learned many of the dos and don'ts of food franchise marketing. Thomas certainly picked up good ideas about concept development for chain restaurants and franchises, as the success of Kentucky Fried Chicken (known as KFC) and then Wendy's demonstrates. The basic objectives he developed, which led to the formation of Wendy's, were:

- Produce a "Cadillac" hamburger with a large number of available condiments.
- Limit the menu to the smallest number of items possible, as most restaurants can prepare only a few food items extremely well.

❏ Create an image different from major competitors. In the case of Wendy's, distinctive features included an old-fashioned, nostalgic theme, carpet on the floor, marketing directed at adults, and a larger hamburger than the competition.

Concept development for Wendy's was more comprehensive than that for a single-unit restaurant. The franchise strategy was carefully thought out to create a balance between company-owned stores and franchised stores. In 1970, only two stores were open, both of them owned and operated by the company. By 1975, 83 company-owned stores and 169 franchised stores were in operation. A ratio of 30 to 40 percent company-owned stores to 60 to 70 percent franchised stores permitted a balance of control and greater financial return. The strategy entailed rapid expansion of the franchise and heavy promotion of the Wendy's name through national advertising. Wendy's now has over 9,900 stores worldwide.

Multiunit casual dinner houses and theme restaurants, such as Chili's, T.G.I. Friday's, and the Olive Garden, follow a similar pattern in concept development. Their emphasis is on identifying the key characteristics of their target markets and then locating restaurants where there is a high concentration of individuals who have those characteristics. Key characteristics may include income, age, education, and home ownership.

What gives multiunit restaurants a competitive advantage over single-unit restaurants is the opportunity to learn from experience with multiple examples of the same concept. When a chain restaurant firm has 500 virtually identical restaurants, it can analyze the factors that differentiate its high-performing restaurants from its low-performing restaurants, and make changes as necessary before opening additional units.

Multitheme Restaurant Concept Development

A particular form of multiunit restaurant for which concept development is critical to success is the restaurant organization that opens and operates restaurants whose concepts are not identical but different. Brinker International and Lettuce Entertain You are two examples of successful restaurant chains that have developed multitheme restaurant concepts. These two companies each use several different themes, and each restaurant is promoted with its theme rather than by using the corporate name. Lettuce Entertain You, for example, operates Papagus (a Greek concept), foodlife (a multitheme marketplace concept), Ben Pao (an Asian concept), and Cafe Ba-Ba-Reeba! (a tapas bar). Through excellent marketing, well-planned menus, and good design, a very sophisticated management team has developed these restaurant concepts.

Hotel Food and Beverage Concept Development

The development of foodservice concepts for hotels has evolved in recent years from the traditional view that considered the food and beverage department as a necessary evil to the modern idea that the food and beverage department is an important profit center. Some large hotels have food and beverage sales of over $35 million per year, an amount that exceeds room sales and creates in management a high expectation of profit from these two departments.

The Hilton Hotel in Atlanta, Georgia, has developed a concept for its first-class rooftop restaurant that goes beyond the idea of a foodservice facility as a profit center. The restaurant, called Nikolai's Roof, was conceived as a luxury dining room and is marketed to the city of Atlanta as well as to hotel guests. The decor is exquisite, the food is served with flair and showmanship, and the entire theme captures the imagination of the city's residents. The concept was developed with such success that the hotel's own guests had great difficulty getting reservations to dine. A hotel restaurant so overcrowded that it could not serve the guests of the hotel would have been unthinkable in earlier days of hotel keeping in the United States. Nikolai's Roof is an excellent example of the execution of a hotel dining concept that complements the hotel itself as well as draws a significant number of guests from the community.

Hotel managers have known for many years that hotel restaurants must have certain desirable features if they are to be successful. These features include:

❏ Availability of parking

❏ Unique theme or decor (differing from the decor of the hotel itself)

❏ Strong promotion to the community

❏ A menu and a method of service that are distinctive

The developers of hotel properties, and in some cases hotel chains, have used outside foodservice facilities and interior design consultants to create unique specialty restaurants that can be marketed successfully to both hotel guests and the community.

Institutional (Noncommercial) Foodservice Concept Development

Institutional foodservice is usually conceived as a service to an organization and often has a not-for-profit philosophy. Most institutional food operations are expected to break even, and all are expected to budget and operate within well-defined ranges of costs so that they do not become a financial burden on the organization they serve. In some cases, the institutional food operation is expected to make a profit and to pay for all of its direct and indirect operational costs.

Often the development of an operational concept for the institution is ignored, and this is usually a serious mistake. The institution must accurately interpret its market and must "sell" its products, even when the food is indirectly paid for by the customer. For instance, in hospital foodservice, an unattractive meal presentation will cause dissatisfaction and complaints on the part of the patient and possibly adverse health effects as well if he or she does not eat a meal and thus does not get sufficient nourishment. In a college or university dining hall, a comprehensive concept of service and decor can greatly influence financial success. Attractive food court service or a marketplace design, for example, can increase the popularity of a college foodservice operation and generate additional profit. The electronic industry has had a tremendous impact on institutional foodservices, especially in the college and university sector. The use of an institution-issued identification card that identifies the student/customer and that contains a dollar amount of funds for the purchase of food can

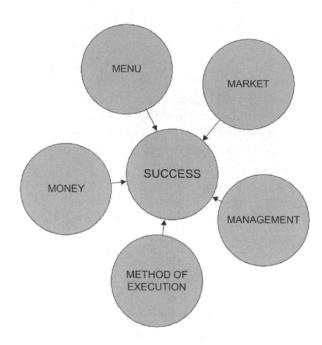

Figure 1.3. Five *M*'s of Concept Development.

significantly increase sales. The card often can be used in dining halls, vending machines, snack bars, convenience stores, or for a late-night pizza delivery. Parents like the idea of a "food-only" card for their students away at college while students enjoy the flexibility of the card and the cash-free transactions.

A dining facility operated by a corporation for its employees should also have a well-planned concept and decor. The ability of corporate food-service operations to attract employees may influence the degree of subsidy that a company is willing to contribute to the operation. Keeping employees within the building or corporate campus has also been shown to increase their productivity, thus benefiting the corporation.

FIVE *M*'s OF CONCEPT DEVELOPMENT

The successful foodservice operation combines these elements of concept development: market, menu, money, management, and method of execution (Figure 1.3).

Market

The importance of conducting market studies before proceeding with the construction of a food facility cannot be stressed too heavily. The basic marketing questions that must be answered are:

- ❏ To whom is the food operation being marketed?
- ❏ Is the market large enough to generate sales and produce a profit?
- ❏ How will the market be identified?
- ❏ What level of competition exists in the market?

❏ What method will be used to communicate to this market?

❏ Will the potential customer want or need the food product?

❏ Will a quality assurance plan be developed that will encourage the customer to return because of superior service and/or product quality?

❏ Will internal marketing successfully sell the customer additional services or products after he or she arrives at the food facility?

A classic mistake made by both large corporations and individual restaurant operators is to conduct the market analysis and then fail to act on the basis of the information obtained. There are several cases in which extensive marketing feasibility studies were conducted by outside marketing firms but the owners and managers made their decisions on gut feelings rather than from the hard data derived from the study.

Even owners (or potential owners) of food operations who have no marketing background can conduct their own market research, with a small amount of guidance and a large amount of energy and common sense. Do-it-yourself marketing and the limitations of this approach are discussed later in this chapter.

Menu

The importance of the menu to the design of the food facility cannot be overemphasized. The subject of menu writing is too broad to be addressed adequately in a book on foodservice facilities design. The owner or manager is encouraged to seek additional sources of information as a part of the process of developing a menu for a new or renovated food operation.

The menu has a tremendous influence on the design and success of a food operation. From a design and layout perspective, these are just some of the factors determined by the menu:

❏ *Amount of space required.* A complex menu requires more space to prepare than a limited or simple menu because separate workstations and additional equipment are necessary.

❏ *Service area size and design.* The greater the number of menu items, the more area required for service. For example, in a cafeteria each beverage requires a dispenser and each entrée a point of service.

❏ *Dishwashing area size and dish machine capacity.* Complex menus often require multiple plates, dishes, and utensils, so the dishwashing area and machine capacity will need to be greater than in the case of simple menus.

❏ *Types of cooking equipment.* Complex menus require multiple types of equipment, especially in the final preparation area, where it may be necessary to steam, fry, bake, broil, and sauté.

❏ *Equipment capacity.* Limited menus may require relatively few pieces of equipment but with large capacities. Complex menus may require many different types of equipment with relatively small capacities.

❑ *Size of dry and refrigerated storage areas.* Complex menus may require larger storage areas to maintain the par stocks necessary to meet demand.

❑ *Number of employees.* Simple menus require fewer employees than complex menus.

❑ *Amount of investment required.* When large or complex menus require more equipment, space, and employees, costs rise.

Money

Successful capitalization of a food facility includes funds for:

❑ Planning costs

❑ Building construction or renovation

❑ Equipment (fixed)

❑ China, glassware, utensils

❑ Furniture and fixtures

❑ Decor

❑ Start-up and operating costs

These funds must be identified and committed before serious planning can begin. Yet in concept development, the commitments may not be made in the early planning stage because the costs are not yet known. Therefore, planning for capital funds is a two-step process: First the financial needs are estimated and sources of financial support are contacted to determine the possibility of obtaining investment funds; then, after concept development has taken place, preliminary designs and construction estimates have been made, and market research is completed, financial commitments are made by lenders and investors.

Management

The quality of the management of the foodservice operation will be the most important element in achieving success. Following are typical questions to be addressed by the owners:

❑ Who will operate the foodservice facility?

❑ What kind of food experience and educational background must this person have?

❑ Who will assist this person in covering the long hours that are usually required to operate a foodservice facility?

❑ What level of pay will this person receive?

❑ Will this person be rewarded in some way for excellent sales and profit results?

❑ How will the owners set operational policies and communicate these to the management staff?

The answer to these questions will determine the organizational structure and the kind of management team that will be used to operate the food facility. The successful restaurant often is owned and operated by one individual whose personality becomes a part of the guests' dining experience. In contrast, the management of the food and beverage department of a hotel may be under the control of more than one person and usually is part of a more complex organizational team. In this case, the policies and procedures of the food facility should be described in an operations manual to ensure consistent implementation of management policy. From the point of view of the investor or the institutional administration, the management of a food facility must follow traditional management principles of good communication, strong controls, and sound personnel relations regardless of the number of people operating the facility. The operational philosophy and specific management guidelines to be used in foodservice operations must be carefully considered by the investors in a foodservice facility. Failure to develop management guidelines will very likely lead to the financial failure of the operation.

Method of Execution

The last step in concept development involves operational matters. Although the opening date might seem to be in the distant future to the person planning a food facility, decisions about operating methods must be made during the concept development phase on matters such as production methods, control systems, and personnel.

PRODUCTION METHODS

Will convenience foods or traditional "from scratch" cookery be used? This decision will have a great influence on the size of refrigerated and dry storage areas and on the size of the kitchen. Production methods will also determine the number of employees in the kitchen and the skill level of these employees.

CONTROL SYSTEMS

Food and beverage controls involve many different parts of the facility, and planning for these controls before the project is under construction is strongly recommended. These areas of control should be carefully considered:

- ❏ Cash control
- ❏ Sales analysis
- ❏ Guest check control
- ❏ Food production forecasting
- ❏ Storeroom and refrigeration control
- ❏ Back door security
- ❏ Labor control
- ❏ Purchasing and receiving control
- ❏ Quality control
- ❏ Portion control

PERSONNEL

The development of financial feasibility studies cannot begin until the amount of labor required is known. The employee schedules, hours of operation, staffing patterns, staff benefits, skill levels, and level of supervision of employees must all be determined before serious development of the food facility begins. As part of its concept development, the fast-food industry based its low labor costs on the use of hourly unskilled labor, scheduled to work short periods of time. When the food operation is busy, part-time employees are scheduled to work. The traditional eight-hour day is seldom used in the fast-food industry, except for supervisors and managers. The use of part-time employees in fast-food restaurants has also significantly reduced the cost of benefits, and was an important part of concept development in the fast-food industry.

FEASIBILITY

Many terms are commonly used in the hospitality industry to describe the process of determining whether a food facility is likely to return a profit to its owners. A partial list of these terms follows.

- ❑ Market or marketability study
- ❑ Market segmentation analysis
- ❑ Market and operations analysis
- ❑ Appraisal report
- ❑ Economic study
- ❑ Time-share feasibility study
- ❑ Feasibility study, report, or analysis
- ❑ Financial feasibility study
- ❑ ROI (return on investment) analysis
- ❑ Sales/performance study

Although each term has a slightly different meaning or involves a slightly different approach, they all share the goal of determining the potential of a facility to generate sales and a profit. In the case of the financial feasibility or ROI (return on investment) analysis, the emphasis is on financial matters, such as capital needs, operating funds, cash flow, and return on investment. However, even financial feasibility reports have as their primary focus the determination of whether a facility under good management can give investors or owners a return on their investment. For purposes of explaining the feasibility studies and of guiding the owner, manager, or student into a commonsense approach to these studies, the studies are classified here into two general categories: those that deal with market feasibility and those that attempt to determine financial feasibility. The two forms of feasibility study can be understood in relation to the financial statements for the operation. The *market feasibility study* focuses on the income statement and is conducted to determine whether revenues are sufficient to generate a profit. The *financial feasibility study* focuses on the balance sheet and is conducted to determine whether retained earnings (derived from net income) will be sufficient to satisfy the owners' expectations for a return on their investment.

The primary question addressed in the market feasibility study is: What level of sales revenues can the operation be expected to generate? The answer to this question really cannot be known until the operation has opened; however, building a new restaurant only to find that the sales are insufficient to generate a profit is an expensive lesson. The market feasibility study attempts to project the sales level for the operation before investors have committed their funds to purchase property, construct a building, and hire a team of employees.

Market Feasibility Study

The sales revenue for a foodservice facility is a function of two factors over an appropriate period of time: the number of customers and the price they paid.

$$\text{Sales} = \text{Price} \times \text{Quantity}$$

Market feasibility studies thus have to formulate sales estimates from two separate projections: How many customers will there be? How much will each customer spend? These two estimates are interrelated through the simple economic principle that demand (quantity sold) is more or less a function of price.[2]

Market feasibility studies can be conducted either to test the feasibility of an established foodservice concept or to develop new foodservice concepts that would be appropriate for a given market. Chain restaurant organizations interested in expansion usually want to determine whether, or where, in a given market area their concept would enjoy the greatest opportunity for success. Independent restaurateurs, as well as chain restaurant organizations, who are interested in developing a new restaurant use the market feasibility study to develop and refine the concept.

Because the market feasibility process is complex and time-consuming, often it is conducted by specialized consultants. Independent restaurateurs may find that the cost of engaging a market feasibility consultant is prohibitive. However, it is possible—and certainly advisable—for entrepreneurs to conduct an abbreviated market feasibility study. Resources and guidelines for conducting a restaurant feasibility study are available from the National Restaurant Association. (Consult Appendix 1 for information on contacting the National Restaurant Association.)

Market feasibility studies generally follow the process presented—in simplified and shortened form—in Figure 1.4. *Demographic data* and *economic factors* for the community are analyzed to determine the potential market for the restaurant. *Traffic counts* and proximity to *demand generators* are used to assess the viability of possible sites for the restaurant. A *competitive analysis* is performed to determine whether the market can sustain another restaurant at each potential site. Based on these analyses, sales projections are formulated. Each of these steps in the market feasibility study is described in greater detail in the sections that follow.

---

[2] The term "more or less" refers to the price elasticity of demand, a concept that goes beyond the scope of this book.

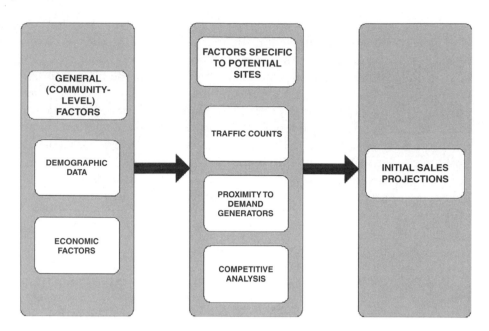

Figure 1.4. Market Feasibility Process.

DEMOGRAPHIC DATA

Demographic data include information about the population near the proposed location of the restaurant, including age, income, gender, occupation, number of children at home, home ownership, the use of automobiles, and similar information. These data about individuals are relevant because target market segments for restaurants are often described in terms of the same factors. Demographics thus are known to predict restaurant behavior. For example, the developers of a casual dinner restaurant believe that their concept will attract young, single professionals between the ages of 26 and 34 who have incomes in the $35,000 to $50,000 range and who pay monthly rents between $1,000 and $1,600. Obviously, the restaurant should be located where there is a high concentration of individuals who fit the profile of the target market. Gathering demographic data enables the developers to detect the presence of the proposed restaurant's target market segment.

The most comprehensive demographic data are gathered in the decennial U.S. Census. Until recently, using census data involved either extensive library research or access to a mainframe computer. Now, however, detailed census data are available to the public on CD-ROM at a reasonable cost. Also, in the interest of promoting economic growth, many local municipalities have developed extensive databases combining demographic data with information about businesses, organized on detailed maps of the area. This kind of database, called a GIS (geographic information system), gives restaurant developers immediate access to information about the market and the competition.[3] GIS software and databases also are increasingly available for desktop computers, bringing the resources of high-priced market consultants to the fingertips of entrepreneurs.

---

[3] M. Muller and C. Inman, "The Geodemographics of Restaurant Development," *Cornell Hotel and Restaurant Administration Quarterly* 35 (3) (1994): 88–95.

ECONOMIC FACTORS

The prevailing economic climate in a community has a significant impact on the market feasibility of a foodservice operation. The health of the restaurant industry in a local area is closely related to the disposable income of its residents. Generally, when disposable income rises in boom times, restaurants prosper. In bust times, disposable income falls and restaurants suffer. However, the effects of economic prosperity and depression affect various restaurant concepts differently. Concepts that offer a high degree of perceived value for the price will suffer less than restaurants with high prices. Also, restaurants that draw customers from a particular industry or from a few large, nearby firms may be protected from broader economic fluctuations if the industry or the large firms prosper during down times. Economic projections for a local area often are available from the chamber of commerce or the local economic development council.

New housing developments are an important indicator of economic growth, especially when they are located on the fringes of existing communities. New restaurants often follow new housing developments. County planning commissions usually are quite willing to share information about planned housing developments, new roads, and zoning issues.

TRAFFIC COUNTS

Restaurants are usually developed along major thoroughfares. Determining market feasibility requires an estimate of the number of cars that pass by each potential location, and traffic counts are used in determining which site is optimal. Traffic counts can usually be obtained free of charge from the local chamber of commerce, highway department, mayor's office, tourism agency, or other municipal offices.

Some fast-food chains have developed very exact specifications for locating a good site for the foodservice facilities. For instance, one of the guidelines for placement of a Kentucky Fried Chicken (KFC) outlet is that it be located on the "going-home side of the street," for obvious reasons. Other chains have minimum community size, minimum traffic count, and minimum average income standards that must be met before consideration will be given to building or franchising on a particular site.

DEMAND GENERATORS

Demand generators are destinations that draw extensive traffic, such as shopping malls, recreation and sports facilities, and public facilities such as museums, zoos, and parks. Restaurants located near demand generators benefit from the traffic they produce—as, for example, when shoppers have lunch after visiting the local mall.

For some foodservice concepts, proximity to other restaurants enhances rather than hurts market feasibility. Fast-food concepts, for example, often locate in clusters along interstate highway interchanges. Similarly, cities and suburbs often have a "restaurant row" in commercial areas.

COMPETITIVE ANALYSIS

A competitive analysis is crucial to the market feasibility study because the local market potential for a given concept must be shared among all of the competitors. If demographic research identifies an area that has a sales potential of $6 million to $8 million for casual dinner houses, it is important to know how many already are in operation. Moreover, when the restaurateur identifies an area that appears to be ripe for development, he or she should assume that the competition will soon arrive. Most chain restaurant organizations have access to GIS market data, and many of them use those data extensively to identify prime development opportunities.

An independent restaurant entrepreneur who is conducting a market feasibility analysis should identify all the similar concepts within the geographic area, compare menus and prices, and count seats. More important, he or she should count customers at various times during the week at the restaurants that would be the closest competition. If patrons are lined up outside the doors to get a seat on Monday or Tuesday night, that is good news. However, if there is no waiting at the competition on Friday or Saturday night, the independent restaurateur should look elsewhere. It is also important to take seasonal factors into account. Counting cars and customers at the competition during the summer months will bias estimates upward, just as counts taken during the winter when two feet (610 mm) of snow are on the ground may bias estimates downward.

Sales Projections   Sales projections are affected by the information gathered about demographics, economic factors, traffic patterns, demand generators, and competitive analysis. Recall that sales projections are composed of estimates about quantity (number of customers) and price. Demographic data indicate the relative size of the local population and thus are useful in projecting the number of customers (quantity). Income information may also be found in demographic data and may thus assist in estimating the price range people are willing to accept. Economic factors are especially important in projecting price. Entrepreneurs often make the mistake of basing their sales estimates on data gathered during boom times and find themselves suffering during bust times. Traffic pattern data are crucial in estimating customer counts, as is the presence of demand generators. Competitive analysis helps the entrepreneur determine his or her share of the customer market and predict price points against the competition.

The weakness in many market feasibility studies can be found within the sales projection section. This part of the feasibility report is often the first place that a banker will look to determine the accuracy of the financial forecast. Bankers always appreciate conservative sales projections that reflect the restaurateur's planning for sales fluctuations during difficult periods. Restaurant entrepreneurs also often overestimate the dining patterns and price sensitivities of the local market. Sometimes this is the result of wishful thinking, but other times it is the result of insufficient planning and preparation. A valuable way for the entrepreneur to check his or her assumptions about the market is to develop a questionnaire and distribute it to those who reside or work in the area. A questionnaire is helpful in determining such things as:

- ❑ Detailed demographic data about age, income, and family size
- ❑ Eating-out patterns (frequency, meal preferences)
- ❑ Price sensitivity and the average price paid for lunch and dinner at competing establishments
- ❑ Favorite eating places for various occasions

For a hotel, the sales pattern would be influenced by the house count (number of persons who occupy the guest rooms). The calculation, therefore, should be based on the projected occupancy. Data on hotel occupancy levels are available from leading hospitality industry accounting firms. PricewaterhouseCoopers and Pannell, Kerr, Foster, for example, regularly publish hotel operations data from all parts of the country and different segments of the hotel field (resorts, transient hotels, and motels).

By utilizing these resources, one should be able to make accurate sales projections that will be credible to the lending institution or investor.

Projections for hospitals and nursing homes are based on patient room occupancy data, but in the health care field a feasibility study usually does not include any data on sales. Foodservice in hospitals and other health care institutions is a service and support arm of the facility, with the primary management and financial considerations focused on the quality of the service and cost containment of the operation.

Once relevant market data have been gathered, a complete sales forecast should be prepared. Figure 1.5 describes the basic steps involved in preparing the sales forecast and illustrates how it is done in a hypothetical college foodservice operation.

This overview of marketing feasibility studies should give the manager, owner, investor, or student a basic understanding of the process, as well as the confidence to conduct such a study if the project is not too large in scope. The associations that represent segments of the foodservice industry are excellent sources of more detailed information on the subject.

Financial Feasibility Study

The lending institution, investor, owner, and manager will all want to know the financial projections for the planned new or renovated food facility. Each of these persons will, of course, have a different set of reasons for seeking the projections, and each will want data from the projections presented in a different manner. For instance, the banker will be looking in part for the ratio of invested capital to borrowed capital. The banker may also want to know the amount of operating cash and the cash flow from sales that will be involved in the operation. The manager needs to know what his or her budget is and what the expectation of the owners is concerning profit and loss. The manager and the banker probably will not be using the same financial reports and projections, but they certainly will be getting their information from the same original source, which probably will be the financial feasibility study. In the financial feasibility study, two basic documents—the projected balance sheet and the pro

The projected sales revenue for a foodservice facility is a function of customer count and the average check for a given period of time. Sales equal customer count multiplied by average check.

Step 1: Customer Count (Projected)
The market research should indicate the total number of seats necessary for the new or renovated facility. During any meal period, each seat is likely to turn over, or be used by more than one customer. How often a seat turns over is a function of several factors, including how long the meal period is and how long it takes a customer to finish his or her meal. Seat turnover between 11:30 A.M. and 1:30 P.M. in a fast-food restaurant may be relatively high compared to a fine-dining restaurant.

To determine the total potential customer count, the number of anticipated seats is multiplied by the seat turnover to determine the customer count for each meal during a given period of time, such as a week. It is essential to make separate calculations for each meal during the week, because the total number of seats needed for the new or renovated facility derived from market research should represent the optimal capacity during peak demand periods—for example, Friday and Saturday evenings in a fine-dining restaurant. Other meal periods are likely to have a lower demand (expected customer count). The next example shows projected customer counts for a college dining facility.

	Sun.	Mon.	Tues.	Wed.	Thurs.	Fri.	Sat.	Total
Breakfast	Closed	200	225	250	250	220	100	1,245
Lunch	Closed	300	350	375	375	300	200	1,900
Dinner	Closed	320	350	350	300	200	150	1,670

Step 2: Average Check (Estimated)
Determine the average check by using the actual average check if the operation already exists or the prices from the new menu if one is anticipated. If a new operation is being planned, check the questionnaire results and the average check for similar operations or restaurants in the area. Check averages will be different for breakfast, lunch, and dinner. In the college dining facility next example, the estimates are in the far right column.

	Sun.	Mon.	Tues.	Wed.	Thurs.	Fri.	Sat.	Total	Price
Breakfast	Closed	200	225	250	250	220	100	1,245	$2.75
Lunch	Closed	300	350	375	375	300	200	1,900	$4.00
Dinner	Closed	320	350	350	300	200	150	1,670	$5.00

Step 3: Multiply Projected Customer Count by Estimated Average Check
The sales estimate for a week is the sum of the project sales for each meal period (far right column).

	Sun.	Mon.	Tues.	Wed.	Thurs.	Fri.	Sat.	Total	Price	Sales
Breakfast	Closed	200	225	250	250	220	100	1,245	$2.75	$3,423.75
Lunch	Closed	300	350	375	375	300	200	1,900	$4.00	$7,600.00
Dinner	Closed	320	350	350	300	200	150	1,670	$5.00	$8,350.00
										$19,373.75

Step 4: Prepare a Sales Projection for the Year
Sales projections for an entire year are computed by multiplying the weekly sales estimate by the number of weeks the operation is open during the year. It is necessary, however, to correct for seasonal fluctuations in demand. A restaurant with an outdoor patio seating seventy-five is likely to have greater sales during the summer months. For the college dining example, the yearly sales are calculated in this way: 30 weeks of full operation @ $19,373.75 = $581,212.50, plus 10 weeks of summer school (50 percent sales potential) @ $9,686.88 = $96,868.75, for a total of $678,081.25.

Figure 1.5. Calculation of Projected Sales.

JOE'S GRILL PROJECTED COMPARATIVE BALANCE SHEET		
	January 1, 2008	**January 1, 2009**
ASSETS		
Current assets		
Cash	$12,000	$14,000
Food inventory	6,000	7,000
Total	$18,000	$21,000
Fixed assets		
Building	$220,000	$220,000
Furniture and fixtures	60,000	65,000
Land improvements	10,000	10,000
Total	$290,000	$295,000
Total assets	$308,000	$316,000
LIABILITIES		
Current liabilities		
Accounts payable	$8,000	$13,000
Note to bank	40,000	35,000
Total	$48,000	$48,000
Long-term liabilities		
Mortgage, building	$180,000	$175,000
OWNER'S EQUITY		
Capitalization	$80,000	$93,000
Total liabilities and equity	$308,000	$316,000

Figure 1.6. Example of a Projected Balance Sheet.

forma profit-and-loss statement—usually are prepared, along with other supporting reports and schedules. A good outline of the kind of information that must be projected can be made by examining the line items on each of these documents.

PROJECTED BALANCE SHEET

A simple comparative balance sheet, like that shown in Figure 1.6, illustrates the kind of data that must be determined. This balance sheet is a simplification of the projected comparative balance sheet that should be developed under the guidance of an accountant. Note that the balance sheet shows a projected comparison between the assets, liabilities, and capital for a 12-month period. The balance sheet illustrates a number of projections that must be made by the person or firm preparing the financial feasibility study.

On the asset side of the balance sheet:

❑ Amount of cash needed as operating funds

❑ Amount of cash tied up in food inventory

❑ Investment in land and building

❑ Cash needed for a down payment on land and building

❑ Cost of furniture, fixtures, equipment, and utensils

❑ Cost of parking lots, driveways, lighting, and other improvements to the property

On the liabilities and equity side of the balance sheet:

❑ Necessary short-term funds that must be borrowed

❑ Amount of payables

❑ Amount of long-term mortgages on building and land

❑ Amount of funds that will represent the owner's equity (capitalization)

Decisions regarding the type of business organization (proprietorship, partnership, corporation, etc.) and control of ownership (closely held, limited number of investors, the sale of common stock, etc.) are made prior to preparing the projected balance sheet.

PRO FORMA PROFIT-AND-LOSS STATEMENT (INCOME STATEMENT)

The pro forma profit-and-loss (P&L) statement should be prepared by the owner, manager, or other persons who will be involved in the management of the food facility. This statement projects the income and expense for a particular period of time. For the financial feasibility study, a three-to-five-year projection would be considered sufficient. The format for the P&L should follow the Uniform System of Accounts developed for hotels and restaurants for income and expense categories that fit the needs of the food operation. An example of a pro forma P&L is found in Figure 1.7.

JOE'S GRILL
PRO FORMA STATEMENT OF PROFIT AND LOSS

	2008	2009	2010
Revenue			
Food sales	$400,000	$500,000	$600,000
Cost of food sales (40%)	(160,000)	(200,000)	(240,000)
Beverage sales	200,000	300,000	400,000
Cost of beverage sales (30%)	(60,000)	(90,000)	(120,000)
Gross profit on sales	**$380,000**	**$510,000**	**$640,000**
Controllable expenses			
Salaries	$60,000	$70,000	$80,000
Wages	120,000	140,000	160,000
Benefits	3,600	5,200	6,000
Supplies	2,000	3,000	4,000
Insurance	3,000	3,500	4,000
Entertainment	4,000	4,500	5,000
Utilities	30,000	32,000	34,000
Maintenance	10,000	15,000	20,000
Replacement china and glass	3,000	7,000	8,000
General	2,000	3,000	4,000
Total	$237,600	$283,200	$325,000
Fixed expenses			
Real estate taxes	$15,000	$15,000	$15,000
Lease on land	12,000	12,000	12,000
Total	$27,000	$27,000	$27,000
Total controllable and fixed expenses	**$264,600**	**$310,200**	**$352,000**
Net profit before taxes	**$115,400**	**$199,800**	**$288,000**

Figure 1.7. Pro Forma Statement of Profit and Loss.

Menu Item: Ham and Cheese Sandwich			
Ingredient	Portion Size	Cost ($)	Total ($)
Ham	2 oz	2.00 lb	.25
Swiss cheese	2 oz	2.40/lb	.30
Rye bread	2 slices	.80/loaf, 20 slices/loaf	.08
Mustard	1/4 oz	3.60/gal	.01
Mayonnaise	1/2 oz	4.80/gal	.02
Lettuce	1/20 head	.80/head	.04
Pickle chips	2 slices	4.00/gal	.02
		Total	$.72

Figure 1.8. Calculating Standard Recipe Cost.

Several supporting schedules are prepared to supplement the P&L statement. Because food and labor costs combined typically run between 60 and 80 percent of sales revenue, schedules providing detailed information on how the cost of food sales and the cost of personnel and related expenses were calculated are often provided.

Cost of Sales   A schedule detailing how the amount shown on the cost-of-sales line of the P&L statement was calculated often is prepared. Because the cost of sales for the menu equals the selling price minus the cost of the ingredients used in preparation, two closely related steps are involved in preparing the schedule: determining the portion cost for each menu item and estimating the price for each menu item.

The portion cost for each menu item is determined by examining the recipe and costs for each ingredient. Figure 1.8 illustrates the costing process for a menu item. The form provides this information:

❏ List of all food ingredients

❏ Portion size of each ingredient

❏ Cost of each ingredient

❏ Total portion cost

If the menu price includes the meat, vegetable, dessert, and beverage, then the example would necessarily include a complete list of all foods that are a part of this meal. A small amount ($.05) might be added to cover the cost of seasonings and other condiments.

The two traditional methods for determining the selling price for menu items are (1) to divide the portion cost by a set percentage (the desired food cost percentage for the operation) and (2) to add a set dollar amount to the cost. Using the first pricing approach, a manager who seeks to have a 32 percent food cost percentage would divide the food cost of a menu item by the desired percentage. For example, a food cost for a ham sandwich of $1.40 would be divided by 0.32, and the selling price would be $4.38. Using the second approach, the manager would add a fixed amount to the cost of each menu item. Adding $3 to the cost of the ham sandwich would result in a selling price of $4.40.

A third approach to setting prices involves looking not at each item but at the menu and *menu mix* (the quantity sold of each menu item) as a whole. The goal of this approach is to set prices so that the *contribution*

Menu Item	Selling Price ($)	Portion Cost ($)	Contribution Margin ($)	Item Food Cost Percentage (%)	Item Quantity	Total Sales ($)	Total Cost ($)	Total Item Contribution ($)
1	8.95	3.11	5.84	34.75	240	2,148.00	746.40	1,401.60
2	7.95	2.74	5.21	34.47	225	1,788.75	616.50	1,172.25
3	11.95	3.88	8.07	32.47	85	1,015.75	329.80	685.95
4	6.95	3.05	3.90	43.88	280	1,946.00	854.00	1,092.00
5	9.95	3.18	6.77	31.96	160	1,592.00	508.80	1,083.20
6	11.95	4.01	7.94	33.56	110	1,314.50	441.10	873.40
7	8.95	2.77	6.18	30.95	220	1,969.00	609.40	1,359.60
8	5.95	2.43	3.52	40.84	315	1,874.25	765.45	1,108.80
						13,648.25	4,871.45	8,776.80
					Food Cost Percent		35.69%	

Figure 1.9. Spreadsheet for Determining Cost of Sales.

margin (the amount of revenue remaining when the cost of sales has been subtracted from revenue) is sufficient to pay all expected fixed expenses and satisfy the owner's expectations for a return on investment.

A spreadsheet like that shown in Figure 1.9 can be used to estimate the overall cost of sales by building from the cost of each menu item.[4] It shows columns for the projected price, the portion cost, the contribution margin (price minus cost), the menu item cost percentage (cost divided by price), the projected quantity sold (the menu mix), the total sales (price multiplied by quantity), the total cost (portion cost multiplied by quantity), the total cost (cost multiplied by quantity), and the total contribution (contribution multiplied by quantity) for each menu item. The total cost, $4,871.45, when divided into $13,648.25, the total sales, gives an overall cost percentage of 35.69 percent given the projected prices, costs, and menu mix.

Using a spreadsheet like that shown in Figure 1.9 allows the owner to evaluate the effects of different pricing strategies on the overall food cost percentage for the operation. The advantage of the spreadsheet approach over traditional strategies to pricing, such as simply marking up the cost by a given percentage or dollar amount, is that prices can be set to generate the maximum contribution margin. In foodservice, profits come not from minimizing the food cost percentage but from maximizing the contribution margin. However, for the purposes of preparing the pro forma profit-and-loss statement, the overall food cost percentage derived from the spreadsheet can be used to estimate the cost of sales.

Finally, it is essential to check the competition in setting prices for each menu item, because an operation that is not competitively priced will suffer.

Once the menu pricing and preferred menu mix have been established, the calculation of the cost of food sales is simple: The projected sales revenue is multiplied by the overall food cost factor, and the result is shown on the pro forma P&L statement. In Figure 1.9, the cost factor is

---

[4] The spreadsheet is based on the "menu engineering" process developed by Kasavana and Smith. For further information, see M. Kasavana and D. Smith, *Menu Engineering: A Practical Guide to Menu Analysis* (Lansing, MI: Hospitality Publications, 1981).

Position	Number of Persons	Hours per Week	Weekly Cost
Manager	1	40–50	$800.00
Assistant manager	1	40–50	600.00
Chef	1	40	600.00
Cook	2	80	960.00
Cook's helper	1	40	400.00
Dishwasher	3	120	840.00
Server	4	160	960.00
Total weekly cost			$5,160.00
Weekly labor	$5,160 × 52 weeks		$268,320
Overtime at 10%			26,832
Benefits at 25%			73,788
Total labor and benefits			$368,940

Figure 1.10. Calculating the Cost of Personnel and Related Expenses.

40 percent of food sales. For the years shown, the cost of food sales is estimated to be 40 percent of the sales revenue.

Cost of Personnel and Related Expenses   The method of projecting the total labor costs for the pro forma P&L statement is to decide on the number of persons needed in each job category and then prepare an employee schedule. Salary and wage levels should be estimated and the annual cost of labor computed. A small amount, perhaps 10 to 12 percent, should be added for overtime. The labor schedule might appear as shown in Figure 1.10.

The examples illustrated are very simple to construct and take a commonsense approach to providing the backup data that often are required for a financial feasibility study. Other major costs, such as utilities and taxes, should be obtained from local utility and government agencies, to be sure of accurate projections. The estimates of other expense categories should be made by using comparative data from the National Restaurant Association or any of the professional associations shown in Appendix 1.

The Go/No-Go Decision

After completing the market and financial feasibility studies and presenting them to bankers and potential investors, the owners can make a good judgment as to the potential success of the food facility project. Further contacts with zoning boards, liquor license agencies, and other municipal groups will bring the project to a point of decision. The accumulation of the data contained in the feasibility studies together with encouragement or discouragement from lenders, investors, and municipal agencies will lead the owner to the first go/no-go decision. In other words, if the project looks financially sound, the market is identified, a need for the foodservice exists, and the capital is obtainable, the decision to go ahead can be made. If one or more elements of the go/no-go decision are uncertain, there are three alternative courses to explore. The first is to correct the problem area that has been identified. Is the facility too large? Are the labor costs too high? Is the menu wrong for the market? Is the competition too strong in the immediate trading area?

The second option is to abandon the project and look for another place to invest the funds. The third alternative is to delay the decision until the final go/no-go decision point. This alternative is financially risky, because to progress from this point means incurring costs for foodservice facilities design consultants, architects, lawyers, accountants, and other professionals.

Chapter 2 describes some of the outside assistance that will be needed to ensure a successful foodservice project. The biggest mistake that could be made at this point in the process is to try to do the planning without the help of professionals.

SITE SELECTION AND PLANNING

E. M. Statler's famous quote, "The three most important things for the success of a hotel are location, location, and location," is certainly true for many foodservice facilities. A poorly located restaurant will certainly experience a low level of sales, and a coffee shop in a hotel may miss a significant amount of business unless it has easy access both to the hotel guests and to street traffic. On a college campus, students typically will select convenience as the primary reason for eating in a particular food facility. Avoiding high rent by selecting a location that is inconvenient or out of the mainstream of foot or automobile traffic is usually a bad decision. A location on the immediate left or right of an entrance to a shopping mall is often considered a poor location for a food facility, because the typical mall customer needs first to enter the mall and then look around for interesting places to shop and/or eat.

Site selection has been discussed in the feasibility section of this chapter. It includes the calculation of foot traffic, automobile counts, and distance to travel as a part of the feasibility study process. Other considerations for site selection are:

❏ *Visual recognition.* Can the food facility be seen easily by potential customers? Will the appearance of the outside of the facility communicate the character and concept of the dining experience inside?

❏ *Convenience.* The developers of a destination restaurant, in which the customer has previously made a decision to dine, must consider parking, an attractive entrance, valet parking, and safe surroundings as important site selection criteria. Coffee shop, deli, and fast-food entrepreneurs must depend on impulse buying as the primary market, and therefore site selection must focus on signage, ease of entry, and drive-in windows and/or take-out service.

❏ *Code restrictions.* Site selection may involve local code requirements for setback from the street, parking capacity, street access, or the acceptability of a food facility in a particular neighborhood. Usually these code requirements are available from the engineering or city planning office of the municipality where the food facility will be located.

❏ *Environmental issues.* In suburban areas, the development of an attractive site for a foodservice facility may encroach on wetlands or adversely affect water runoff in nearby neighborhoods. In older, urban areas, sites may have previously been used for industrial and manufacturing processes that left dangerous materials in the ground. Environmental factors such as these are increasingly important to the site selection process because they present additional costs.

OBTAINING NECESSARY APPROVALS FROM AGENCIES

The approval process for a new or renovated foodservice facility is typically long and complicated, involving many different agencies. Developers often experience the approval process—and the inevitable delays that occur—as frustrating because they are eager to get the facility open and operating so that it can generate a positive cash flow. In defense of those agencies and departments that must be satisfied before proceeding, it is worthwhile to recall that the project needs to be controlled so that it does not create an unsanitary, unsafe, or unattractive addition to the community. Each municipality has a different group of agencies that must approve the food facility, and each has a definite sequence in which the approvals are given. For example, a health department may require preliminary approval of the equipment layout before construction begins and a final inspection after the facility is built and the equipment is in place.

The solution to obtaining necessary approvals for a complex project (new construction or major renovation) is to develop a comprehensive checklist, in which each member of the planning team (architect, engineers, foodservice consultant, financial advisors, lawyers, etc.) submits a list of necessary agencies and deadlines. After dates are recorded, one person (usually the architect) serves as the coordinator of the approval process.

Typical approval agencies involved in foodservice projects include:

❑ Zoning board
❑ Health department
❑ Municipal engineers (water, sewer, gas, and electrical)
❑ City planner
❑ Fire marshal
❑ Liquor control board
❑ Telephone company
❑ State or federal agencies (on state or federal projects)

SUMMARY

A food facilities design project, regardless of its scope and complexity, must start with a preliminary plan. If the owner or manager follows the planning method suggested in this chapter, a successful food facility is not necessarily guaranteed, but the chances of its success are greatly enhanced. The preliminary planning process should include:

❏ *Careful consideration of the scope and complexity of the project.* This will enable the selection of an appropriate planning team. If the project is simply a replacement of equipment, the team will be small or perhaps consist of only the food facilities design consultant and the owner or manager. If the scope involves major renovation or construction, a larger group of professional people would be drawn into the project.

❏ *Concept development.* For hotels, restaurants, and institutions, this is now recognized as an important planning stage. It includes consideration of menu, market, money, management, and the method of execution of the plan.

❏ *Feasibility studies.* Marketing and financial feasibility studies often are requested by bankers, investors, and others before financial commitments can be made. For large projects these may be conducted by professional accounting firms; in other instances the owner or manager may want to undertake it him- or herself. A go/no-go decision on the project should be made only after the marketing and feasibility studies have been completed.

❏ *Site selection.* Site selection will have much to do with the success of the facility. The best location may have higher rent or capital costs, but these costs will be covered through increased sales.

❏ *Agency approvals.* Agency approvals are often long and frustrating to obtain, but they are helpful in avoiding safety or architectural problems for the protection of the community.

KEY TERMS

Scope	Demographics
Five *M*'s	Go/No Go
Feasibility	Approval agencies

QUESTIONS

1. How could the scope of a level IV project be reduced? How could the planning time be reduced?

2. Menu limitation is one of the most effective management methods for increasing profits; why is this true?

3. This chapter mentions 10 control systems. Describe 5 of them.

4. How many of the control systems involve electronics?

5. Can the planning for a foodservice facility proceed before a feasibility is complete? Could you do a feasibility study without professional help?

6. What does *pro forma* mean? Does it apply to both the profit and loss statements and the balance sheets?

DISCUSSION QUESTION

If a prospective client, who had solid foodservices management experience and excellent marketing skills but limited financial resources, sought to use your consulting services, how would you decide whether to take him or her as a client?

CHAPTER 2

Foodservice Design

THIS CHAPTER

- ☑ Explains the role of each member of the foodservice facility design team
- ☑ Describes the sequence of steps involved in the design of a foodservice facility
- ☑ Illustrates the work typically done by a food facilities design consultant
- ☑ Describes the method of compiling a cost estimate for a food facility project

PROJECT TEAM

The development of a new foodservice facility is guided by a project team consisting of the owner and various design and construction professionals. The size and composition of the project team depend on the complexity of the project, but the team typically includes the owner (or owner's representative), an architect, engineers, a foodservice design consultant, an interior designer, a general contractor, and a foodservice equipment dealer.

Smaller projects (level II in scope), such as a 40-seat delicatessen built in a space leased in a strip mall, may require only the services of an architect, engineers, and a general contractor. Large projects (level III or IV in scope), such as a university cafeteria serving 2,500 hundred students at each meal, may require the services of all the members of the design team.

Owner's Representative

In small projects, the owner's interests are represented on the project team by the owner him- or herself. Thus independent restaurateurs usually are deeply involved with the project team throughout the design and construction process. In most larger projects, however, the owner is not a single individual but is instead a corporate entity. Or the owner may be a single individual, but he or she chooses not to be directly involved in the project. In such cases the owner's interests will be represented by a person or persons who have been assigned to the project team.

The use of an owner's representative is common in large and institutional foodservice design and construction projects. When a hospital renovates its foodservice operation, the hospital's board of directors may be represented on the project team by the director of dietary services.

When a new hotel is built, the corporate director of food and beverage services may represent the owner's interests with respect to the foodservice facilities, and the corporate director of rooms may represent the owner's interests with respect to guest rooms.

Although the foodservice operator entrusts the design process to professionals trained in architecture, engineering, and construction, the role of the owner's representative is crucial to the overall success of the project. Design professionals rely on the owner's representative for the information they need to develop a facility that meets its intended objectives. Architects, engineers, and foodservice design consultants do not create masterpieces out of thin air; instead, they rely on the owner's representative for direction and guidance throughout the project.

The specific responsibilities of the owner's representative vary from organization to organization and from project to project. Depending on the scope of the project, the responsibilities of the owner's representative are likely to include:

❑ Selecting design professionals (architect, engineers, etc.), establishing the scope of their services, and negotiating fees

❑ Determining the operational objectives of the project to guide the design

❑ Setting the budget for the project

❑ Evaluating the designs prepared by the project team in light of the operational objectives for the project

❑ Accepting (or rejecting) the selections of furniture, fixtures, and finishes recommended by the design professionals

When the owner's representative plays an active role on the project team by fulfilling these responsibilities, the outcome is likely to be a successful project that fulfills the owner's expectations. If, however, the owner's representative plays a passive role in the process, the design team is forced to make assumptions based on their professional experience about what the owner requires. Their assumptions may be good ones, but they may not be the right ones for the owner's unique needs.

Architect

On most building projects, the architect serves as the overall leader of the design and construction process. The architect coordinates the work of all of the design professionals on the project team and supervises the work of the contractors who build and equip the facility. Because of the leadership role played by the architect, she or he often is the first member of the design team to be selected by the owner. Once selected, the architect identifies the other design professionals to serve on the project team, including, as necessary, the engineers, interior designer, and foodservice consultant. Foodservice facility design projects often are an exception to this practice, as the foodservice design consultant may be retained before the architect. We explain this exception later in the section describing the role of the foodservice design consultant.

The architect guides the design process through a sequence of steps (described later in this chapter) that begins with planning and ends when the owner's representative has accepted the new facility. The architectural work for small projects may be performed by a single individual.

Most projects generally involve several architects from a single firm. Depending on the size of the project and the size of the architectural firm, the roles that follow may be combined to a team appropriate to the project:

❏ *Principal in charge.* Responsible for negotiating the terms of the design contract and ultimately responsible for successful completion of the project.

❏ *Design architect.* Works closely with the owner's representative in the early stages of the project, guiding the planning and design process. The design architect is primarily responsible for taking the owner's operational objectives and designing functional spaces through which those objectives can be fulfilled.

❏ *Project manager.* Responsible for the day-to-day workings of the design and construction process. The project manager coordinates the team's work and schedules the sequence of design activities necessary to complete the project.

❏ *Site architect.* Coordinates the work of the contractors and their tradespeople throughout the construction process. The site architect inspects the progress of the work and resolves problems before they become too expensive to correct.

The selection of the architectural firm for the project is an important decision because of the key role the architect plays in coordinating the entire project. Several important factors, outlined next, should be considered in the selection process.

EXPERIENCE WITH SIMILAR PROJECTS

Most, though not all, architecture firms specialize in certain building types, such as educational facilities, health care facilities, or hospitality facilities. Selecting an architectural firm with experience designing similar buildings brings the benefit of their experience to the project.

EXPERIENCE WITH FOODSERVICE FACILITIES

Although an architectural firm may have experience with a specific type of project, such as educational or health care facilities, that does not mean that the firm has experience designing the foodservice facilities found in hospitals, schools, or colleges. Experience designing foodservice facilities in similar buildings is an important factor in the success of the project. The foodservice facilities in large institutions (hospitals, colleges, large corporate buildings) are complex and present a number of design and engineering challenges. Architectural firms lacking experience in comparable foodservice facilities may not be well prepared to anticipate the needs of complex food production systems.

PERFORMANCE ON PAST PROJECTS

Architectural firms provide prospective clients with lists of past projects. It is a good idea to contact past clients and ask for a frank assessment of the architectural firm's performance. Important questions include: Did the firm understand the needs of the operation? Was the project completed on schedule? Were there many changes to the design after construction had begun? Did the architect overlook anything or fail to follow through? How did the final cost of the project compare with the architect's estimates?

EXPERIENCE OF THE ARCHITECT'S TEAM

The success of the project depends not only on the skill and experience of the architectural firm but also on the abilities and experience of the engineers, interior designer, and consultants. In larger projects it is important to evaluate the credentials of everyone on the team.

CHEMISTRY

Large projects (level III or IV in scope) require extensive teamwork between the owner and the architect. Chemistry, although it is a vague term, is an important factor in selecting an architect. Face-to-face interviews are helpful to determine whether the members of the architectural firm are the people the owner wants to work closely with throughout the duration of the project.

Engineers

Which engineering disciplines will be represented on the project team depends on the scope and requirements of the project. Foodservice facilities are often engineering-intensive because commercial kitchen equipment requires extensive electrical and mechanical services. This is why virtually all foodservice projects require the assistance of electrical and mechanical engineers. Depending on the scope of the project, however, civil and/or structural engineers may also be required.

Structural engineers design systems to support the structure of the building and to protect its integrity. They determine how floors will support the fixtures that are required, and they ensure that the roof system will withstand the weight of equipment located there. *Electrical engineers* design the systems that supply electricity as needed in the facility. They determine the overall electrical load in the building, assign circuits, locate panels and receptacles, and determine the route wiring will take throughout the building. *Mechanical engineers* design the plumbing, heating, ventilation, and air-conditioning systems within the facility. Plumbing systems supply hot and cold water and remove waste through drains. Heating and air-conditioning systems temper the air within the facility so that the occupants are comfortable. Ventilation systems circulate air; in the kitchen, specialized ventilators located above cooking equipment remove grease, vapor, and heat from the kitchen. Mechanical engineers also design systems that supply energy in the form of natural gas or steam to the facility. Both gas and steam are frequently used sources of energy in commercial kitchen equipment. *Civil engineers* typically design roads, bridges, and similar structures. They are involved in foodservice projects only when the building site must be developed and made ready for new construction. For example, a restaurant built on an undeveloped site may need the services of a civil engineer to prepare site plans showing what grading must be done and how access to the site will be gained from adjoining roadways.

Owners and architects often call on the specialized expertise of a foodservice facility design consultant to assist in the design of foodservice facilities. This is done because an effective design for a foodservice facility demands knowledge of operations, layout and design, engineering, and equipment. Few architects possess the in-depth knowledge of foodservice systems necessary to design complex kitchens. While experienced in operations and knowledgeable about equipment, rarely do most owners have sufficient in-depth knowledge of layout, engineering, and equipment to design a complex foodservice facility without professional assistance. There are more than 700 established manufacturers of foodservice equipment, and each manufacturer offers multiple products, models, and options. Knowing which product and options are best for a specific application is not a simple matter. The owner of a poorly designed foodservice facility suffers for years: initially by having to pay the heavy investment required in equipping a facility that fails to meet his or her needs, and year after year through higher labor, utility, and maintenance costs.

Certain kinds of projects may not require the specialized expertise possessed by a foodservice facility design consultant. Small facilities, such as independent sandwich shops, quick-service diners, and family restaurants, often are simple and straightforward in operation, so specialized design expertise may be unnecessary. Small, independent restaurateurs often seek the assistance of their foodservice equipment dealer for layout and equipment selection. Chain restaurant firms and large foodservice management companies may not retain a foodservice facility design consultant because they possess the necessary expertise in design, layout, engineering, and equipment in house.

The architect may select his or her own foodservice consultant, or the client may need assistance for early planning before naming the architect. The food facilities design consultant should become involved with the project at the beginning—ideally, even before the architect is named. The reason for the early selection of a design consultant is to seek assistance with concept development and feasibility studies.

The services most often provided by foodservice consultants are discussed next.

COMPREHENSIVE PLANNING AND CONCEPT DEVELOPMENT

Approaching the development of a foodservice facility haphazardly, without making a careful study of the long-range objectives, can lead to inefficient operations and waste capital funds. Noncommercial foodservice operations often are large and far more complex than typical restaurants. A university foodservice operation, for example, may feed thousands of students three times per day from as many as 20 different foodservice facilities, maintain a commissary (central production facility), and operate a warehouse. These factors lead institutions to seek expert assistance in

Foodservice Facilities Design Consultant

determining the long-term direction for all facilities to determine what kinds of foodservice concepts, systems, and technologies will best serve their markets. This assistance helps ensure that the concept and planning of the facility to be designed in the short term fits into the long-term program.

Some colleges and universities, for example, find themselves with foodservice facilities that were designed to meet the menu preferences and dining habits of students 30 years ago. Through the comprehensive planning process, the consultant assists the university by determining what combination of new foodservice concepts would best meet the needs of the students, faculty, and staff. The plan may indicate where new facilities should be located and estimate the amount of space required for each. The plan may also describe the production, storage, and service systems that would be necessary to support the new foodservice facilities.

Using the comprehensive plan or feasibility study (described earlier), the team can develop the concept. The concept (described in Chapter 1) forms the basis for space planning and the design process that follows.

PROGRAM

A foodservice facility program, often called an architectural program, translates the concept into a description of the functional spaces and systems required. A *program* is a narrative presentation of the way a particular projected foodservice facility is intended to operate. The consultant's specific objective is to highlight space and room usage and to define the flow of people and material through the proposed facility. The form and content of an architectural program for foodservice are described in detail in Chapter 4. *Systems* are defined as a series of interacting parts (subsystems) that must be evaluated to achieve the most satisfactory and efficient result. The decisions that foodservice operators make about how to store food, clean vegetables, cook hamburgers, serve guests, and wash dishes all involve systems. A small deli may serve food on disposable plates, just as a hospital might use specialized trays and a fine-dining restaurant bone china. The difference between a small and large facility lies in the complexity of the system. A warewashing system in a deli may involve no more than running pots, pans, and utensils through a small dish machine and returning them to their storage places. In a hospital, however, warewashing may involve transporting soiled dishes back from patient rooms on large carts, scraping food waste into a disposer, separating out dishware and placing it in the appropriate racks, sorting silver, feeding dish racks through a dish machine, stacking clean dishes in specialized carts, and returning the carts filled with clean dishes and silver to the tray makeup line to be used again at the next meal. Transport carts are moved into a cart washing area, where they are cleaned and sanitized using a high-pressure system; when dry, they are returned for use during the next meal. It is typical that such systems and subsystems are discussed at length during the initial stages of the design process to ensure that proper amounts of space and a description of the system are included in the program.

FOODSERVICE FACILITY EVALUATIONS

A service often provided by foodservice consultants in conjunction with planning and design services is the evaluation of an operation's existing facilities and equipment. A facilities evaluation assesses the strengths and weaknesses of an operation in relation to its intended objectives. Facilities evaluations frequently are conducted when an owner suspects that the existing facility no longer is adequate to the needs of a changing market.

Master planning and programming, systems analysis, and facilities evaluations are services provided by foodservice consultants that are closely related to the actual design process. Often they are provided in preparation for the construction of a new facility or the renovation of an existing facility.

Foodservice consultants, like other design professionals, may belong to a professional organization, the Foodservice Consultants Society International (FCSI). Consultants who are members of FCSI subscribe to a code of ethics that ensures a high level of professional service and integrity in client relations. FCSI consultant members receive payment for their services and do not sell foodservice equipment, materials, or supplies in contrast to foodservice designers who are employed by equipment dealers or manufacturers. FCSI consultant members are prohibited from receiving "any monetary benefit or other consideration from the sale of equipment or other product" (FCSI By-Laws, Section IVa).

Interior Designer

Working with the owner's representative and the other members of the design team, the interior designer gives the foodservice operation its distinctive visual character and theme through the design of interior spaces, the selection of colors, and the specification of furniture and finishes. The interior designer thus focuses on the public or customer parts of the facility rather than on the kitchen or storage areas.

In competitive markets, the success of a restaurant depends on a distinct identity or theme that shapes the customer's expectations and contributes to a memorable dining experience. The guest's perceptions of the dining facility itself—apart from the quality and presentation of the food—create the environment in which the food and service are experienced. How the light falls and the colors, textures, and shapes within the dining area all affect customer perceptions. Many restaurants use interior design to create a dining experience that transports the guest to another place or time, such as a French café or a 1950s diner. Interior designers often are involved in projects of this kind, where the success of the concept depends on the execution of a distinct dining experience.

General Contractor

When the architect, engineers, foodservice consultant, and interior designer have completed the work of drawing up plans and specifications for the foodservice facility, the project is put out for bid to general contractors. The general contractor who is awarded the contract then becomes a member of the project team. The general contractor's role is to build the facility as it was designed by the architect, engineers, foodservice consultant, and interior designer. The general contractor works with a series of building tradespeople including, for example, plumbers, electricians, roofers, and tile setters. These employees, working for the general contractor, are subcontractors (often referred to simply as subs). The general contractor schedules, coordinates, and oversees the work of his or her subs and thus is accountable for building, equipping, and furnishing the facility in accord with the intentions of the owner and designers.

Two other approaches to organizing the project team for the construction of the facility are common in the building industry. The first involves using a construction manager rather than a general contractor. In this approach, the construction manager becomes involved much earlier in the design process and gives input into design decisions based on potential construction costs. The construction manager, unlike the general contractor, is involved in the preparation of the contract documents. Like the general contractor, however, the construction manager coordinates the work of the building tradespeople.

The second approach involves using a design-build firm that has architectural, engineering, and construction capabilities all within one organization. The design-build approach has been used by governmental organizations to develop large public works projects where strict adherence to the budget is essential. Several large restaurant chains also use the design-build approach by employing in-house architects, engineers, designers, and contractors.

Foodservice Equipment Contractor

The foodservice equipment contractor, often known in the industry as the KEC (kitchen equipment contractor), is the firm that provides the foodservice equipment for the project. The KEC may be involved in the project through a contract directly with the owner or as a subcontractor under the general contractor. The foodservice equipment contractor, like the general contractor, typically is selected through a competitive bidding process for large projects. On smaller projects, the owner may negotiate the engagement of the foodservice equipment contractor.

The qualifications of the foodservice equipment contractor have a direct and immediate effect on the overall quality of the equipment installation. Foodservice facilities, large or small, often require custom-fabricated equipment (dish tables, chef's counters) that necessitates precise manufacture and installation, as well as complex systems (ventilation hoods, walk-in coolers and freezers, conveyor systems) that are built for the project and must be assembled at the job site. Not all restaurant suppliers have the experience and expertise necessary to complete a large foodservice installation. The experience of a foodservice design consultant on multiple previous installations often proves helpful in identifying and evaluating the qualifications of potential foodservice equipment contractors.

DESIGN SEQUENCE

The overall development of a new or renovated foodservice facility proceeds through a series of steps, one leading to the next. The design sequence used by both architects and food facilities design consultants is

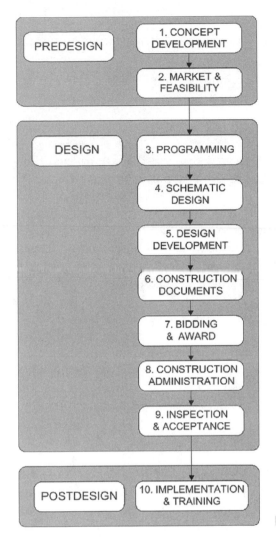

Figure 2.1. Foodservice Facility Design Sequence.

an integral part of the overall process of developing a new or renovated foodservice facility. The overall foodservice facility development process follows 10 steps, which are illustrated in Figure 2.1.

Step 1, concept development, and step 2, market and feasibility, often are referred to as predesign planning processes. These steps may not require the services of architects and engineers; however, owners often retain a foodservice consultant for assistance in these functions. Step 10, implementation and training, is a postdesign service often important in foodservice facilities where the employees need training in using new equipment and new production processes. This function often is provided by foodservice consultants.

Steps 3 through 9 define the sequence of the design process itself, through which the new or renovated facility moves from idea to reality. Architects and other designers often reduce these seven steps to five phases:

Phase I: Schematic design (includes programming and space analysis)
Phase II: Design development
Phase III: Construction documents

Phase IV: Bidding and contract award

Phase V: Construction administration (includes inspection and acceptance)

Chapter 1 discusses concept development and market and feasibility, the predesign steps in the development process.

Space Analysis and Programming

The objectives of space analysis are to determine the size of each functional area and the relationships among functional areas, according to the owner's operational objectives.

The analysis of the space required for each of the functional areas in a facility is based both on the particular needs of the owner and on generally accepted standards. For example, the space needed for the dining area is computed by multiplying the number of seats needed to generate adequate revenues by a factor reflecting the square footage needed for each seat. That factor may range from 11 square feet (1.0 square meters [sq m]) per seat for banquet seating to 16 square feet (1.5 sq m) per seat (or more) for a fine-dining restaurant; the actual factor selected is determined by the concept and the owner's preferences. If a restaurant requires 160 seats, at 15 square feet (1.4 sq m) per seat, then the dining room would require 2,400 net square feet (224 net sq m) exclusive of support areas. Space analysis proceeds to identify each of the necessary areas, and the space required by each, for the foodservice facility. Chapter 4 discusses space analysis in greater detail and provides guidelines for each of the primary functional areas in a foodservice facility.

Space analysis also involves establishing the physical relationships among each of the functional areas in the facility. One technique used to determine physical relationships, the adjacency matrix, is illustrated in Figure 2.2. The owner's representative and the foodservice design consultant evaluate the cells in the matrix pair by pair. They determine the importance of any two areas being located adjacent to each other by assigning a priority from 0 (unnecessary) to 3 (essential). Figure 2.2 shows a 3 in the cell where "Refrigerated Storage" and "Pre-preparation Area" intersect, indicating that it is essential for the coolers to be in close proximity to the pre-preparation area. There is a 0 in the cell where "Customer Entrance" and "Trash Holding" intersect, showing that it is unnecessary—indeed, undesirable—for these areas to be located next to each other.

In completing the adjacency matrix, the owner and the design team evaluate the relationship between every one of the functional areas in the planned facility. This process helps ensure that all members of the project team are working from the same set of fundamental assumptions about the owner's objectives and needs.

A related approach in space analysis is the bubble diagram, such as the relatively simple example shown in Figure 2.3. Designers sketch bubble diagrams to show the relative sizes and relationships among functional areas early in the design process. These diagrams are particularly helpful to the owner's representative in identifying design problems. In Figure 2.3, the position of the ballroom—between the preparation area, the dining room, and the warewashing area—clearly must be changed. The

	Receiving	Dry Storage	Refrigerated Storage	Pre-preparation	Final preparation	Service	Warewashing	Trash Holding	Offices	Customer Entrance
Receiving										
Dry Storage	1									
Refrigerated Storage	0	1								
Pre-preparation	0	2	3							
Final preparation	0	0	2	3						
Service	0	0	0	1	3					
Warewashing	0	0	0	1	1	3				
Trash Holding	3	0	0	0	0	0	0			
Offices	1	0	0	2	2	1	0	0		
Customer Entrance	0	0	0	0	0	0	0	0	0	

The numbers in this diagram show how important it is for two spaces to be adjacent to each other in a foodservice facility. Importance ranges from "0" (not at all important) to "3" (extremely important).

Figure 2.2. Adjacency Diagram (Simplified).

preparation area should conveniently serve the main dining room; proximity to the ballroom should be viewed as a secondary consideration.

Space analysis provides the data necessary for the preparation of the architectural program for the facility. Among design professionals, an architectural program or program statement is a specific kind of document that describes in a narrative the requirements of each functional area. It states the function of each space in a building, how that space will be used most frequently, and the number of square feet needed to serve these needs. A program statement for a foodservice facility is the same as an architectural program, except that the focus is on specific functional areas,

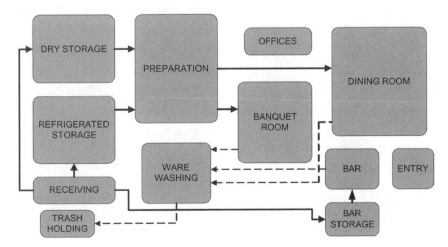

Figure 2.3. Example of a Bubble Diagram (arrows show the flow of food products).

Room Number: 103

Room Name: Dishroom

Relationship to Other Rooms: Near dining room, for self-busing of dishes, and adjacent to kitchen. Easy access to service lines, so that clean dishes can be returned to serving area.

Description of Use: This room will be used to wash all utensils, serving pans, china, glassware, and cafeteria trays. The space must be well ventilated but need not be air-conditioned. The pot sink will be located in this room, as well as space for the storage of utensils and dishes on portable carts. Utility requirements will include provision for drains, hot and cold water, electrical power in single and three phase, and a high level of ventilation (air turnover).

Square Footage Needed: 420 (39 sq m)

Finishes: Walls must be structural glazed tile for ease of cleaning and resistance to wear. Floors must be quarry tile with slip-resistant qualities. Ceiling should be moisture-resistant and approved for use in commercial foodservice establishments. Lighting should be at 50–60 foot-candles, or at a level acceptable to the local health department.

Figure 2.4. Example of a Section of a Foodservice Facility Program Statement.

such as receiving, storage, pre-preparation, final preparation, service, and warewashing. An example of a program statement for a dishroom is found in Figure 2.4.

Space analysis and programming make it possible for the design team to estimate the total size, the basic construction approach, and the kinds of finishes necessary for the building. This information is essential before the architect, engineers, and foodservice consultant begin the process of actually generating plans for the facility. Figure 2.5 shows an example of a summary program statement that identifies the total space required for a restaurant.

The total space required for the facility is calculated first, by summing all of the space requirements for the functional areas as determined through space analysis and programming. That figure, however, is only the net amount of square feet required for the facility. Often the estimates reflected in the program statement do not include the space required for walls and wall thickness, chases for pipes and other utility services, stairwells, corridors, fire escapes, or rooms for mechanical equipment, such as elevator machinery or telephone equipment. The square footage calculated from the program statement is increased to reflect the space required for these functions, and the resulting estimate is the gross square footage required for the facility.

The gross square footage can be used by the design team in preparing a preliminary estimate of the cost of construction for the facility. Industry reference publications provide data on current costs for various types of construction on a per-square-foot basis. These data can be used to generate a rough estimate of the construction cost of the project. It is not uncommon to discover that the amount of space and the quality of construction necessary to create a facility that fulfills the owner's objectives exceeds the resources he or she has to invest. In such cases, the owner's representative and the design team must evaluate their previous

Functional Area	Net Square Feet (Meters)
Receiving Dock	64 (5.9)
Receiving Area	80 (7.4)
Trash Holding	60 (5.6)
Cleaning Supplies Storage	80 (7.4)
Dry Storage	240 (22.3)
Cold Storage (Walk-in Cooler)	160 (14.9)
Frozen Storage (Walk-in Refrigerator)	120 (11.1)
Liquor/Beverage Storage	80 (7.4)
Pre-Preparation	320 (29.7)
Final Preparation	280 (26.0)
Bakery	120 (11.1)
Servers' Stations	160 (14.9)
Bar Service	200 (18.6)
Bar Seating	320 (29.7)
Maitre d' Station	40 (3.7)
Dining Seating	2600 (241.5)
Table/Chair Storage (Dining Area)	160 (14.9)
Warewashing	220 (20.4)
Foodservice Offices	180 (16.7)
Foodservice Rest Rooms/Lockers	240 (22.3)
Total Foodservice	5724 (531.8)

Figure 2.5. Example of Summary of Space Estimated from a Program Statement.

work in concept development, feasibility, space analysis, and programming to determine how the requirements of the program can be reduced without adversely affecting the financial feasibility of the project. Usually this is a difficult process, because those involved may feel very strongly about the size or function of a given space. For example, the chef may be committed to a large receiving dock, the owner to the maximum number of seats in the dining room, and the architect to a particular configuration for the entry, coat check, and host/hostess station. Examples of the kinds of questions and issues that often are raised at this point follow.

❏ *Can the number of seats in the dining room be reduced?* This is generally an undesirable option in commercial restaurants because sales revenue is a function of the number of available seats.

❏ *Can the size of the walk-in refrigerators be reduced?* This option may be feasible if fresh meats, produce, and dairy items can be delivered daily.

❏ *Is it necessary to have a room dedicated to washing garbage cans?* Perhaps this space is not necessary for the long-term success of the facility.

❏ *Is there a less expensive alternative to finishing the kitchen walls in ceramic tile?* Other materials may offer a lower initial investment cost, but they may be less durable and more difficult to keep clean and sanitary.

The one word that describes this space and cost-cutting exercise is *compromise*. After the program is approved in writing by the client, then and only then should the design process begin.

Schematic Design

The primary purpose of the schematic design is to show the shape of the building, the entrances and flow patterns, and the location of the dining rooms, kitchen, and other major components of the foodservice facility. The architect's drawings at this stage will show elevations of the outside of the building, site plans for the building lot, and the location of roads, sidewalks, and parking lots. The foodservice design consultant's drawings show the shape, size, arrangement, and major equipment items for all of the foodservice and related areas. Schematic designs often are used to gain preliminary approval from zoning officials, or for public relations purposes in selling stock to potential investors. For institutions, schematic designs are used to seek approval from the board of trustees or other governing board.

The architect and foodservice design consultant typically revise and present schematic designs several times before gaining the approval of the owner's representative. In some cases, they may present several schematic designs, each illustrating a different approach to the program.

The architect's schematic designs for the entire building are usually presented in small scale ($^1/_{16}$ inch or $^1/_{32}$ inch = 1 foot), so that the entire facility and the surrounding property will fit on a single large (often 42 inches long by 30 inches high) sheet of paper. The foodservice design consultant's schematic designs usually are prepared at a scale of $^1/_8$ inch = 1 foot so as to fit the storage, preparation, service, and dining areas of a large facility on a single sheet. Figure 2.6 is a schematic design for the service level of a café (the storage and pre-preparation areas are located on a lower level of the building and so are not shown). Note: In many countries, the scale would be expanded in metrics.

A cost estimate for the project is prepared at the end of the schematic design phase. This estimate, in contrast to the rough estimate prepared with the program statement, is based on more specific information about the project. This estimate often is a joint effort by the architect, engineers, and foodservice design consultant. The architect will gather information from the building program (step 3) as to the quality of finish of each space and will then use more detailed price-per-square-foot data available from outside commercial publications. The engineers will examine the size of the space, the type of HVAC (heating, ventilation, and air-conditioning) system needed, and the amount and kind of equipment needed in the foodservice areas. The foodservice design consultant will determine the general kinds of foodservice equipment needed in the project and prepare a cost estimate, even though the actual equipment items have not yet been selected. The consultant relies on his or her experience with projects of similar size and scope in generating estimates at the schematic design phase of the project. The foodservice design consultant submits to the engineers an estimate of the electrical load, steam requirements, and special ventilation needs for the foodservice equipment so that the cost of all utilities for the foodservice area

Figure 2.6. Schematic Design for a Production Kitchen.

can be calculated. The final cost estimate, compiled by the architect, includes:

- ❑ Land acquisition
- ❑ Site preparation
- ❑ Building construction
- ❑ Electrical, plumbing, and other mechanical systems
- ❑ Foodservice equipment
- ❑ Interior design and furnishings
- ❑ Construction loan interest costs
- ❑ Professional fees and other costs that will occur during planning and construction

This phase of the design sequence continues until the owner's representative is satisfied with the design and the projected cost of the project. At that point, he or she provides written acceptance of the design team's work, thus concluding the schematic design phase. Acceptance of the schematic design should be made in writing by the owner's representative and the architect on an actual floor plan of the building or food facility. Acceptance of the schematic design by the owner's representative does not mean that changes in the design of the facility cannot be made. Changes can be—and often are—made in subsequent phases of the project. On occasion, those changes take the project all the way back to the point of concept development. The owner's acceptance does not prevent changes; it only provides fair compensation for the design professionals involved in the project if their work must be done again.

Design Development

Design development is the phase of the project when the owner's representative, architect, engineers, foodservice design consultant, and interior designer flesh out the design of the project through increasingly detailed drawings. The design development phase leads up to, but does not include, the preparation of actual working drawings from which general contractors will bid the project.

The design development phase of the design sequence allows the project team to investigate different approaches and alternative systems for meeting the owner's functional needs. This phase thus involves what is called value engineering, in which the project team evaluates the projected operational costs of major equipment systems over their expected lifetimes. For example, the owner may be interested in a power potwashing system that circulates hot water and detergent over soiled pots and pans in a large wash tank rather than relying on an employee to scrub them clean. However, the power system might cost $12,500 to purchase and install as compared to $2,500 for a traditional three-compartment pot sink. Applying value engineering to this decision, the labor savings for the power system over its life expectancy would be evaluated against its higher purchase price as well as its greater utility and maintenance costs.[1] It is possible that the long-term savings from reduced labor requirements of the power potwashing system would make up for its higher purchase price and utility and maintenance costs.

In the design development phase of the project, the foodservice design consultant typically prepares:

❑ *Detailed floor plans showing the location of each piece of equipment.* This work is done in close coordination with the architect to ensure that, for example, equipment will fit as shown on the plan, columns will not interfere with production processes, and ceiling heights will be adequate for ventilation systems. Figure 2.7 is an example of a detailed floor plan for a conference center foodservice facility.

❑ *Utility plans (electrical, plumbing, ventilation) showing the location of each utility connection and the load imposed by each piece of equipment.* This work is done in close coordination with the engineers to ensure that, for example, the dish machines have adequate hot water, drains flow freely, electrical circuits do not fail when a banquet cart is plugged into a nearby wall outlet, and ventilation hoods do not pour cold air on the head of the chef during cold

---

[1] The actual financial calculations used in value engineering are more complex than is suggested in this simple example because they take into account factors such as the cost of capital and the reinvestment of cash flows.

Item	Description	Existing	New
K-1	Hot Food Cabinet	1	0
K-2	Convection Oven	1	0
K-3	Fryers	2	0
K-4	Steam Jacketed Kettle	1	0
K-5	Range with Griddle	1	0
K-6	Range with Burners	1	0
K-7	Reach-in Refrigerator	1	0
K-8	Reach-in Freezer	1	0
K-9	Hand Sink	1	3
K-10	Walk-in Cooler and Freezer	1	0
K-11	Fryer Filter and Dump Station	0	1
K-12	Slicer on Table	0	1
K-13	Pot Rack	3	0
K-14	Pot Sink	0	1
K-15	Prep Table with Sink	0	1
K-16	Prep Table with Sinks	0	1
K-17	Disposer (2 HP) with Prerinse	0	1
K-18	Disposer (3 HP) with Prerinse	0	1
K-19	Walk-in Shelving	22	0
K-20	Dry Storage Shelving	6	16
K-21	Dunnage Racks	0	6
K-22	Ice Machine on Bin	1	0
K-23	Receiving Table	0	1
K-24	Scale	0	1
K-25	Racks	3	?
K-26	Mixer 30 Qt	0	1
K-27	Dish/Tray Carts	0	8
K-28	Clean Dish Table	0	1
K-29	Dish Machine with Side Loader	0	1
K-30	Soiled Dish Table	0	1
K-31	Trough-Veyor	0	1
K-32	Worktable	0	1
K-33	Worktable w/Sink	0	1
K-34	Hood	0	1
K-35	Pant Leg Hood	0	1
K-36	Salad Bar	0	1
K-37	Hot Food Counter	0	2
K-38	Hot Food Inserts	0	8
K-39	Frost Top and Display Case	0	2
K-40	Milk/Beverage Dispenser	0	2
K-41	Tray/Silver Counter	0	2

Figure 2.7. Design Development for a Conference Center Kitchen.

winter weather. Figures 2.8 and 2.9 show examples of electrical and mechanical utility connection drawings like those prepared during design development.

❑ *A book of catalog sheets (often called cut sheets or buyout brochures) for each equipment item to be purchased from a manufacturer.* This work is done in close coordination with the owner's representative to ensure that, for example, each piece of equipment will have the kind of features, accessories, and controls desired by the owner; each manufacturer selected offers the quality and durability necessary for long-term value; and no important items will be overlooked. Figure 2.10 shows an example of a foodservice equipment catalog sheet.

❑ *Elevations, sections, and/or detail drawings for each piece of custom-fabricated equipment.* This work is done in close coordination with the owner's representative to ensure that, for example, worktables, chef's counter, scrapping and dish tables, service counters, and bars all meet the owner's functional needs.

FOODSERVICE EQUIPMENT SCHEDULE

Item	Description	Quantity	Existing/New	Quantity
FE-01	Banquet Cart	1	New	1
FE-02	Reach-in Refrigerator, 1 Compt	2	New	2
FE-03	Hot Food Inserts	1	New	1
FE-04	Coffee Urn	1	New	1
FE-05	Service Counter	1	New	10
FE-06	Roll-in Refrigerator, 2 Compt	2	New	2
FE-07	Sandwich Prep Table	1	New	4
FE-08	Work Table with Sink	1	New	1
FE-09	Conveyor Oven, Single	1	New	1
FE-10	Hood - Pizza Oven	1	New	1
FE-11	Retail Sandwich Display	1	New	14
FE-12	Pizza Merchandiser	1	New	1
FE-13	Hot/Pizza/Italian Counter	1	New	35
FE-14	Pizza Prep Table	1	New	1
FE-15	Hot Food Inserts	1	New	1
FE-16	Cold Food Inserts - 2 Well	1	New	1
FE-17	Hot Food Holding Cabinet	2	New	2
FE-18	Reach-in Freezer, 2 Compt	1	New	1
FE-19	Reach-in Refrigerator, 2 Compt	1	New	1
FE-20	Fryers with Filter System	1	New	1
FE-21	Griddle, 36"	1	New	1
FE-22	Charbroiler, 36"	1	New	1
FE-23	Hood - Grill	1	New	1
FE-24	Grill Prep Rail (Condiment)	1	New	1
FE-25	Plate Lowerator	8	New	8
FE-26	Salad Bar	1	New	15
FE-27	L-Shaped Work Table w/Sinks	1	New	16
FE-28	Dishmachine - Undercounter	1	New	1
FE-29	Cashier Counter	2	New	16
FE-30	Condiment Counter	1	New	16
FE-31	Condiment Dispenser	4	New	2
FE-32	Toaster	2	New	2
FE-33	Condiment Containers	8	Existing	0
FE-34	Bottled Beverage Display	1	New	8
FE-35	Soft Serve Machine	1	Existing	0
FE-36	Soup Inserts	2	New	2
FE-37	Dish/Bowl Lowerators	4	New	4
FE-38	Soda & Ice Dispenser	1	New	1
FE-39	Beverage Counter	1	New	24
FE-40	Milk Dispenser	1	New	1
FE-41	Glass/Cup Lowerators	24	New	24
FE-42	Coffee Brewing System	1	Existing	1
FE-43	Ice Cream Freezer	1	Existing	
FE-44	Unused Item Number		New	
FE-45	Retail Snack Counter	1	New	24
FE-46	Hand Sink	4	New	4

Figure 2.8. Design Development Detailed Floor Plan (Part) for a Small Scramble Servery.

46

ELECTRICAL SYMBOLS

α 120/1 Duplex Receptacle
☐ 120/1 Service
☒ 120/1 120/1 Junction Box
⊕ 208/1 Receptacle
⊕ 208/1 Service
⊠ 208/1 Junction Box
⊕ 208/3 Service
⊞ 208/1 Junction Box

FOODSERVICE EQUIPMENT ELECTRICAL REQUIREMENTS

Conn	Item	Description	Volts	Phase	Amps	KW	HP	AFF	Connection
E1	FE-01	Banquet Cart	120	1	10.4	1.25		60	NEMA 5-15
E2	FE-02	Reach-In Refrigerator	120	1	8.6	0.87	1/4	72	Wire to JB on Unit
E3	FE-04	Coffee Urn	208	1	18	3.8		24	Bring service to JB under counter
E4	n.a.		120	1	15			52	DR in wall above counter
E5	FE-06	Roll-in Refrigerator	120	1	16.2	1.04	1/2	72	Wire to JB on Unit
E6	FE-07	Sandwich Prep Table	120	1	20		1/2	18	NEMA 5-20
E7	FE-09	Conveyor Oven	120	1	15		1/12	36	NEMA 5-15
E8	FE-11	Retail Sandwich Display	208	1	10		1		
E9	FE-13	Hot/Pizza/Italian Counter	208	1				6	Stub service up from base to JB in Counter
	FE-15	Hot Food Inserts	208	1		2.4			Connect to JB (E8) in Counter
	FE-03	Hot Food Inserts	208	1		3.2			Connect to JB (E8) in Counter
E10	FE-13	Hot/Pizza/Italian Counter	120	1				6	Stub service up from base to JB in Counter
	FE-12	Pizza Merchandiser	120	1	10.2				Connect to JB (E10) in Counter
	FE-16	Cold Food Inserts	120	1	2.3		1/5		Connect to JB (E10) in Counter
E11	FE-13	Hot/Pizza/Italian Counter	120	1				6	Stub service up from base to JB in Counter
	FE-24	Grill Prep Rail (Condiment)	120	1	2.4		1/5		Connect to JB (E11) in Counter
	FE-26	Salad Bar	120	1	15				Connect to JB (E11) in Counter
E12	FE-14	Pizza Prep Table	120	1	20		1/2	18	NEMA 5-20
E13	FE-17	Hot Food Holding Cabinet	120	1	17.6	2.11		60	NEMA 5-20
E14	FE-18	Reach-in Freezer	120	1	11	1.26	3/4	72	Wire to JB on Unit
E15	FE-19	Reach-In Refrigerator	120	1	8.1		1/3	72	Wire to JB on Unit
E16	FE-20	Fryers w/Filter System	120	1	4.8	0.55		48	DR for food warmer
	FE-20	Fryers w/Filter System	120	1			1/2	48	and for filter motor
E17	FE-21	Griddle, 36"	120	1	15			48	Power for electronic burner ignition
E18	FE-13	Hot/Pizza/Italian Counter	208	1				6	Stub service up from base to JB in Counter
	FE-36	Soup Inserts	208	1		1.2 (2)			Connect to JB (E18) in Counter
E19	FE-29	Cashier Counter	120	1	15			12	Dedicated circuits for cash computers
E20	FE-32	Toaster	208	1	9.62	2		52	Mount two (2) receps in wall above Counter
E21	FE-34	Bottled Beverage Display	208	1	11.5		1		NEMA L14-30
E22 (2)	FE-35	Soft Serve Machine	208	1	9 (2)		1 1/2 (2)	60	Two circuits: 22 Ampacity each
E23	FE-44	Dishmachine Undercounter	208	1	43.6			30	Connect to Dishmachine
E24	FE-39	Beverage Counter	120	1				6	Stub service up from base to JB in Counter
	FE-38	Soda & Ice Dispenser	120	1	11				Icemaker (1)
	FE-38	Soda & Ice Dispenser	120	1	11				Icemaker (2)
	FE-38	Soda & Ice Dispenser	120	1	7				Soft Drink Dispenser
	FE-40	Milk Dispenser	120	1	6				Milk Dispenser
E25	FE-39	Beverage Counter	208	1				6	Stub service up from base to JB in Counter
E26	FE-45	Retail Snack Counter	120	1				6	Stub service up from base to JB in Counter
E27	FE-45	Retail Snack Counter	208	1				6	Stub service up from base to JB in Counter

Figure 2.9a. Design Development Utility Drawing (Electrical) for a Small Scramble Servery.

MECHANICAL CONNECTION SYMBOLS

○ CW (Cold Water) 1/2"
● HW (Hot Water) 1/2"
◑ 3/4 CW (Cold Water) 3/4"
◐ 3/4 HW (Hot Water) 3/4"
● Drain 2"
◉ Funnel Type Floor Drain (Indirect Waste)
○ Floor Drain (Flat)
▣ Floor Sink with Grate, 12" x 12"
⊕ Gas Connection

FOODSERVICE EQUIPMENT MECHANICAL CONNECTION SCHEDULE								
Conn	Item	Description	Water	Drain	Gas	Steam	AFF	Notes
M1	FE-04	Coffee Urn		FTFD			6	Stub up in base.
M2	Varies			FD				
M3	FE-05	Work Table w/Sink	1/2" HW, CW	2"			24	
M4	FE-46	Hand Sink	1/2" HW, CW	2"			24	
M5	FE-08	Work Table w/Sink	1/2" HW, CW	2"			24	
M6	FE-04	Coffee Urn	1/2" CW				6	Stub up from base into Counter
M7	FE-09	Conveyor Oven			80,000 BTU		24	
M8	FE-13	Hot/Pizza/Italian Counter		FTFD			6	Stub up from base into Pedestal
M9	FE-13	Hot/Pizza/Italian Counter	1/2" CW				6	Stub up from base into Pedestal
M10	FE-20	Fryers w/Filter System			165,000 BTU		24	
M11	FE-21	Griddle			40,000 BTU		24	
M12	FE-22	Charbroiler			105,000 BTU		24	
M13	FE-27	L-Shaped Table w/Sinks	1/2" HW, CW	4"			24	
M14	FE-28	Dishmachine, Undercounter	3/4" HW 140 D				4"	Hose Bib Connection
M15	FE-26	Salad Bar		FTFD			6	Stub up in Base
M16	FE-39	Beverage Counter	1/2" CW				6	Stub up in Base
M17	FE-38	Soda & Ice Dispenser		FTFD				Set in Notch in Base
M18	FE-45	Retail Snack Counter		FTFD			6	Stub up in Base
M19	FE-45	Retail Snack Counter	1/2" CW				6	Stub up in Base
M20	FE-44	Dishmachine, Undercounter		2"			6	
M21	FE-39	Beverage Counter	1/2" CW				6	Stub up in Base

Figure 2.9b. Design Development Utility Drawing (Mechanical) for a Small Scramble Servery.

Figure 2.10. Example of a Foodservice Equipment Catalog Sheet.

Figure 2.11 shows an example of a foodservice equipment elevation drawing.

❑ *Detail drawings of any special construction required for foodservice equipment.* The foodservice design consultant may prepare detail drawings showing, for example, how walk-in coolers and freezers are constructed in depressions in the floor or how trench drains for kettles and braising pans are to be fabricated.

❑ *Preliminary specifications.* Written specifications describe in narrative form the general conditions, quality standards, materials, products, and execution of the installation. The foodservice design consultant prepares a preliminary set of specifications for review by the owner's representative and other members of the project team so that they can be revised and refined.

Another cost estimate is prepared near the conclusion of the design development phase of the project. This estimate is more accurate than previous estimates because the architect, engineers, and design consultant will have substantially completed the design of the entire project. All of the materials and products will have been selected, and the techniques for construction of the project will have been identified. The actual cost of new construction projects should vary from the design development cost

Figure 2.11. Examples of Elevation Drawings.

estimate by only a small amount due to changes in prices, labor costs, or other conditions.

The design development phase of the sequence concludes with the owner's acceptance of all the materials prepared by the design team. The owner's acceptance of this phase of the design work authorizes the design team to proceed to the preparation of actual construction documents. Changes made from this point forward are relatively time-consuming to incorporate into the plans and specifications because a single change may have to be reflected on multiple drawings as well as at several points in the specifications.

Construction Documents

The construction documents phase of the design sequence involves the preparation, in final form, of:

❏ *Drawings* showing construction of the new or renovated facility, including all site work, structural systems, rooms and other spaces, utility systems, equipment, finishes, and details

❑ *Specifications* describing the materials and products, the standards of workmanship, the methods of fabrication and construction, the applicable code requirements, and the methods of installation, cleaning, and testing

❑ *General conditions of the contract* defining terms, assigning responsibility, establishing payment schedules, describing how changes are to be handled, and listing the specific project conditions

The specifications and general conditions are bound together to form the project manual, which, combined with the drawings, comprises the contract documents for the project.

A large building project, such as a hotel or hospital, may require a stack of drawings two inches (51 millimeters) thick and a 900-page project manual. To prevent misunderstanding of the designers' intent, construction documents follow specific standards and a uniform format. Drawings are prepared in accordance with architectural standards that describe the organization, appearance, and annotation of graphic materials. Specifications are written according to guidelines and organized into divisions based on the format recommended by the Construction Specification Institute. The standards for drawings and specifications are widely accepted in the construction industry and so prevent costly misunderstandings by the general contractor.

There are three basic types of specifications:

1. *Descriptive specifications* completely identify all the important characteristics of the material or product.
2. *Proprietary specifications* identify the product by reference to a manufacturer and model number, and require the contractor to provide that item and no other.
3. *Performance specifications* establish performance criteria that are relatively independent of the specific description of the item.

Foodservice equipment specifications usually are descriptive and include the materials, construction, components, utility requirements, dimensions, features, and options necessary to identify the product completely and unambiguously to the bidder. Figure 2.12 provides an example of a foodservice equipment item specification for manufactured equipment, and Figure 2.13 provides an example of an item specification for fabricated equipment.

Specifications for manufactured equipment also usually include a reference to a specific manufacturer and model number. The purpose of naming a specific manufacturer and model is to establish, by way of example, the quality of workmanship, materials, and features desired by the owner. Reference to a specific make and model is not intended, in most cases, to exclude comparable products manufactured by other companies. However, the burden of proof that another product is equal to or better than what was named in the reference specification lies with the foodservice equipment contractor.

In some cases, the owner will not accept anything but the manufacturer and model named in the specification. This form of specification is called *proprietary* because it requires the foodservice equipment contractor to furnish a product manufactured by a single firm (a proprietary product). Proprietary specifications are thought to reduce competition during

Item D-2   Dish machine, carousel type

Quantity:	One (1)
Dimensions:	14′8″ long
Manufacturer:	Stero of Petaluma, CA
Model:	SCT-94
Utility Requirements:	208/3/1 125 amps/45 KW one 3-wire feed for booster heater

208/3/1 3-wire feeder to machine panel for:

Scrapper motor	2 HP/5.9 amps
Wash pump motor	2 HP/5.9 amps
Rinse pump motor	2 HP/5.9 amps
Conveyor motor	$\frac{1}{4}$ HP 1.1 amps
208 to 115 control circuit	5 amps
Wash tank heat	20 KW/55.6 amps
Rinse tank heat	20 KW/55.6 amps
Disposer	3 HP/8.9 amps

CW, HW $\frac{1}{2}$″ to hand sink and cleaning hose
HW 1″ 140°F 20 PSI to booster heater
CW $\frac{3}{4}$″
Drain, floor sink for machine waste
Drain, 2″ for scrapper waste
Drain, 2″ for disposer waste
Drain, 2″ for sink waste
Vent: 1,000 CFM exhaust to $11\frac{7}{8}$″ × $17\frac{1}{8}$″ duct at 69″ AFF

Featuers:

1. Stainless-steel construction
2. Automatic fill with water level control
3. Door safety switches
4. Cleanup hose (25′)
5. Interplumbed
6. Interwired with circuit breaker panel with breakers for each motor
7. Kit 55
8. Isolated final rinse with inspection door; final rinse saver
9. Stainless-steel conveyor drive with reversing switch
10. Thermostatically controlled electric tank heat
11. C-45 booster heater
12. Oval 12-gauge stainless-steel tables
13. Scrap trough 12-gauge stainless steel; provide disposer (item D-4) and interwire
14. Glass rack shelf 3′ 6″
15. All-purpose overhead shelf 6′
16. Richlite stacking shelf 12′ 0″
17. Drying hood (90 degree) with vent and inspection door
18. Mount doors in-facing
19. Hand sink with hardware
20. 14-gauge stainless-steel wheeled interconnected carriers with all-purpose racks
21. Cold-water aquastat
22. Bus box that supports two remote start/stop stations
23. Two-rack rotating rack shelf
24. Supervision of installation by factory-approved representative

Figure 2.12. Foodservice Equipment Specification for Manufactured Equipment.

D-5   Clean-dish table

Quantity: One (1)
Dimensions: As shown on detail drawings
Manufacturer: Fabricated
Model:
Features:

1. Construct in conformance to Part 2.03 and as shown on plans and detail drawings
2. Provide 10″ backsplash joining dish rack unloader
3. Close end of backsplash at end opposite dish rack unloader
4. Provide table limit switch and connect to dish machine
5. Understructure of cross members and spreaders as shown on detail drawings (omit front cross member and spreaders for placement of hot-water booster heater)
6. Provide overshelves of length shown on detail drawings and attach securely to wall at height selected by owner's representative at time of installation
7. Table and rolled edge (1¼″ radius) to be of 12 gauge stainless steel polished to a #4 finish

---

Figure 2.13. Foodservice Equipment Specification for Fabricated Equipment.

the bidding phase of the project because they specifically permit one manufacturer and exclude all others. When named in a proprietary specification, the manufacturer has little incentive to bargain. For this reason, most public works (government-funded) construction projects allow proprietary specifications only after a stringent set of requirements has been fulfilled.

Privately funded foodservice projects may—and often do—use proprietary specifications for manufactured equipment. This may be done for a number of reasons:

❏ The owner may have had an exceptionally positive experience with the manufacturer named in the specification.

❏ The item named in the proprietary specification may be the only one available with the precise combination of features desired by the owner.

❏ There may be advantages in maintenance and service with a particular manufacturer, as when the owner already possesses several units from the named manufacturer.

❏ Complex equipment systems, such as ventilation hoods, conveyor systems, or walk-in refrigerators and freezers, require significant coordination among the architect, engineers, and foodservice design consultant. These systems are often designed and engineered around a specific manufacturer's components. Changing to a different manufacturer would entail significant redesign and reengineering that would cost more than any price advantage.

Performance specifications are rarely used in the foodservice industry. Performance specification wording, however, does frequently appear in equipment catalog materials. For instance, specifying that a fryer "must be capable of preparing 100 pounds of french fries per hour" clearly sets a performance criterion. The problem with performance specifications is that the criteria often are very difficult to measure or judge. When the fryer is installed, how can the consultant or owner measure the actual results? Frying 100 pounds of french fries in one hour might be possible, but to what degree of doneness? Are the french fries frozen or fresh? How large is each fry? A specification that explicitly describes the materials or products to be furnished is less likely to be misinterpreted.

Although foodservice equipment specifications can be written in several different ways, the most important consideration is whether the exact requirements for the equipment are clearly described.

Bidding and Contract Award

When the contract documents are complete, they are made available to interested bidders. This process is colloquially referred to as "putting the project on the street." The architect (or construction manager, if there is one on the project) coordinates this process. Small foodservice projects involving equipment only, with little or no architectural work, may be bid by the owner.

Bid packages (copies of the contract documents) may be mailed directly to interested bidders identified by the project team. Bid packages also may be made available by construction industry organizations that have "reading rooms" where contractors can review and order bid packages. The foodservice design consultant often identifies foodservice equipment contractors who, on the basis of previous project experience, are qualified to bid.

Contractors are given a set period of time (usually between two and six weeks) to prepare their bids. On large renovation projects, the architect may schedule a mandatory site visit, during which time interested bidders can examine the existing facility and obtain clarification on project conditions.

The bidding process often raises questions that require clarification or necessitate changes to the contract documents. Such clarifications and changes are communicated to the bidders in the form of an addendum. All of the addenda become part of the formal contract.

At the time specified, the bids are opened. In some cases, such as public works projects, the bids are opened in the presence of the bidders, and their quotations are read aloud. Bidders do not attend private bid openings.

The foodservice design consultant also evaluates any substitutions or alternates proposed by the bidders and included with their bids.

❑ *Substitutions* are proposals to provide materials, products, equipment, or systems from a manufacturer other than the one named in the specifications (the base bid). In proposing a substitution, the foodservice equipment contractor is claiming that what he or she proposes to furnish and install is equal to or better than what was specified in the contract documents. The bidder may propose to offer the substitution at a lesser price. However, it is more common for the bidder simply to seek approval for the substitution at the same price as the base bid.

❑ *Alternates* are proposals to provide materials, products, equipment, or systems different from what was described in the specifications, generally at a significantly lower price. The project team may have included several alternates in the contract documents that it required contractors to bid. Or the foodservice equipment contractor may have voluntarily proposed one or more alternates. In proposing an alternate, the bidder claims that the alternate performs comparably (provides similar results), but does not claim that it is equal to or better than what was originally specified as would be the case for a substitution.

Proposals for substitute or alternate engineered systems, including kitchen ventilation, walk-in refrigeration, and conveyors, are especially problematic. Although there is a large variation in both the cost and quality of these systems, the differences in quality are more difficult for operators to see than the differences in cost. One manufacturer's ventilation system may cost only 60 percent of what another manufacturer's system costs, but both systems are made of shiny stainless steel and both move air around over the cooking equipment. The engineering and performance differences may appear only in the winter months, when cold air supplied to the inexpensive hood meets hot air rising from the cooking equipment and it begins to "rain" (drip condensation) over the range section.

The evaluation of bids determines the *lowest qualified bidder*, who is then awarded the contract. After the contract has been awarded, and necessary permits and approvals obtained, construction can begin.

Construction Coordination

The actual work of construction is performed by the general contractor and his or her subcontractors from the building trades. During this phase of the design sequence, the architect assumes primary responsibility for monitoring the progress and quality of the work. On large building projects, this responsibility is carried out by a field architect, who establishes an office at the job site and works closely with the trades.

During the construction phase, the foodservice design consultant performs these tasks:

❑ *Submittal review.* The foodservice equipment contractor prepares plans of the foodservice facility, obtains shop drawings for all custom equipment from the fabricator, and assembles a book of catalog sheets showing all the equipment to be provided. The foodservice design consultant reviews these submittals to ensure that they conform to the contract documents. He or she notes deviations from the requirements of the contract directly on the submittals. When there are substantial errors or omissions in the submittals, the foodservice design consultant will require that they be redone and resubmitted. Small deficiencies may be accepted as noted.

❑ *Coordination.* Questions about the foodservice equipment installation may arise from the foodservice equipment contractor, the general contractor, or the plumbing, electrical, or HVAC contractor. The foodservice design consultant responds to these questions, keeping a written record of the questions and responses.

❑ *Review changes to the work.* Project conditions or other factors may require a change in the work from what originally was specified. For example, a foodservice equipment manufacturer may discontinue the specified model after the bid was awarded but before the item was ordered by the foodservice equipment contractor. The foodservice design consultant reviews the rationale for such changes and, if acceptable, communicates his or her acceptance to the architect. The architect, in turn, prepares a *change order,* a formal contract document that authorizes the foodservice equipment contractor to proceed with the change.

❑ *Attend job site meetings.* On some projects, the foodservice design consultant may attend job site meetings, especially at crucial points in the installation of the foodservice equipment. Participation in job site meetings can help to prevent problems in execution of the installation. Not all subcontractors read the entire project manual carefully, and some may overlook important points affecting their work. For example, tile-setting contractors remove excess grout from tiles using muriatic acid. Unfortunately, unless proper precautions are taken, using muriatic acid on quarry tile installed on the floor of a walk-in cooler can damage the finish on its walls. The consultant's participation in job site meetings can reinforce important provisions of the specifications that affect various trades.

Inspection/Acceptance

During construction, the facility is under the possession and control of the general contractor, and he or she is responsible for the progress of the work as well as for protection of the building and its contents. Prior to turning the completed facility over to the owner, the architect, engineers, foodservice design consultant, and interior designer examine their parts of the project to determine whether the work meets the requirements of the contract documents. A punch list is prepared by each member of the design team, describing all work that remains to be done to complete the project according to the plans and specifications. The foodservice consultant prepares the punch list for the foodservice equipment installation and submits it to the KEC and to the owner. The completed facility is turned over to the owner only when the project team is satisfied that the work is complete and fulfills the requirements of the contract.

Because the installation of the foodservice equipment is complex, the foodservice design consultant will review the progress of the work several times during the final phase of construction. The first site visit may occur when the walk-in systems have been erected, the hoods have been hung from the ceiling, and the rough-in connections for utility services are complete. The purpose of this visit is to check the installation of the hoods and the walk-ins, since any rework of these systems will surely be time-consuming. Checking the locations of the utility rough-ins may pinpoint a problem when it is relatively easy to make corrections.

The second visit may occur after all the equipment has been set in place and most of the pieces are connected to their respective utility services. This site visit usually is arranged so that the foodservice design consultant, the foodservice equipment contractor, and the architect can go over the progress of the installation in detail. Any problems

```
Project Memo
Date:      February 5, 2008
To:        David West, AIA
           Design Space International
           6400 Tuttle Road
           Dublin, Ohio 43017
From:      John Birchfield, FCSI
           Foodservice Consultant
CC:        Richard Albright, Dublin Center Retirement Village
           Bill Davis, Davis Foodservice Equipment
Project:   Kitchen renovation
           Dublin Center Retirement Village
           Phase I
```

On February 2, 2008, we examined the work on the foodservice equipment for this project. Items needing correction are as follows:

All stainless-steel tables and pot sink: Grind and polish rough welds on understructure joints to a smooth #4 finish.

Item D-11	Spray system remote stations: Furnish and install on the wall a bracket to hang the spray wand when not in use.
Item H-1	Hoods: Furnish extractor wand for hood cartridges.
Item K-3	Refrigerator: Gauge shows 41.4°F. Verify that unit is holding temperatures below 38°F. Adjust or repair as necessary.
Item K-5	Existing mixer: Relocate where shown on plan.
Item K-9	Proofer cabinet: Specified unit was FWE PHU-1826. Unit delivered is FWE P-72-XL. Replace unit with item as specified.
Item K-10	Hand sink: Provide HW to sink in pot wash area.
Items K-11, K-12, and K-13	Range, charbroiler, griddle: Locate these items under hood where shown on plan to ensure proper operation of fire suppression system.

Figure 2.14. Part of a Punch List.

observed during this site visit are noted and compiled into what is termed a preliminary punch list by the foodservice consultant. The items on the list must be corrected by the foodservice equipment contractor before the final site visit is made. Figure 2.14 is an example of part of a punch list.

The final site visit is made after all equipment has been connected and tested and is ready for food preparation. A second punch list is prepared by the foodservice consultant, usually much shorter than the first. The foodservice design consultant prepares a letter to the owner's representative and the architect in which he or she recommends acceptance of the food facility.

The submission of the letter recommending acceptance of the project by the owner is often the final step in the design sequence.

Implementation and Training

In foodservice facilities projects, equipment demonstration and training sessions often provide immense benefit to the employees. If the proper use of new equipment is demonstrated to the kitchen staff at the outset, they will be far better prepared to come up to speed in the new facility quickly. Equally important is an explanation of how the design and layout are intended to work. Employees often do not have the opportunity to participate in planning and design sessions and so find themselves in a new facility whose operating principles and design rationale they may not fully understand. In outmoded and poorly designed kitchens, the staff had to find ways to work around the problems. Over time, their work-arounds became habits, and the habits become the accepted way of doing things. When the old kitchen is replaced by a new one, the accepted and habitual ways of doing things no longer make sense. Employees need guidance and support in learning how to use the new kitchen and its equipment efficiently.

One approach that was taken by a successful director of foodservice in training employees for opening a new food court utilized teams of employees. A detailed description of each of the food concepts that was to be in the new facility was prepared. The first team to be established was the menu team, who developed the menus for each station. They researched and tested standard recipes and suggested ways of merchandising the products. Then an equipment team was created, with a head cook as leader and with other cooks, a maintenance person, a dishwasher, and a salad prep person as team members. This team evaluated equipment descriptions and catalog sheets and determined ideal production techniques, cleanup procedures, and maintenance schedules for each of the food stations. A third team was charged with public relations and marketing. This team recommended the decor for each station, researched menu board systems, and prepared a plan and budget for advertising in the local paper.

When each team completed its work, the foodservice director held meetings in which the team leaders presented their reports to the entire staff of the operation. As a result, employees were well prepared to operate the new facility. They knew what to expect.

The approach just described is, of course, only one of many that are possible. The key to successful training for a new facility is employee involvement. Employees who are involved in the planning process gain a sense of ownership, and ownership leads to commitment to the success of the new facility.

Opening Day

The key to a successful opening day is *planning*. The first impressions guests have of a new facility are critical. Preopening planning is so important that many restaurant chains and hotels employ specialists who spend weeks or months preparing a new facility for opening day. After the facility has been in operation for several weeks, they turn over the reins to the regular management and go on to the next facility.

A good discipline for opening-day planning is to list everything that has to be in place when the first guest arrives. One way to make that list is to go through an existing operation, noting everything that is there: silver, napkins, menus, employee uniforms, telephones, and so on. Then determine what has to be done to get that item in place in the new facility. It is a good idea to work backward on a calendar. For example, if opening day is August 1 and menus take two weeks for printing and laminating, with another two weeks added for safety, when must the menus be ordered? If menus must be ordered by July 1, and the graphic designer needs six weeks to prepare camera-ready copy, when must prices be finalized? Working backward in time through each item that must be prepared before opening day will result in a schedule that lists each critical deadline.

SUMMARY

The project team for the development of a foodservice facility can work together most effectively if each member understands the roles of the others. This chapter clarifies the functions of the various team members, including the owner's representative, architect, engineers, foodservice design consultant, interior designer, general contractor, and foodservice equipment contractor. The design sequence is the chronology of events that typically occur when a project is being planned and constructed. The architect and food facilities design consultant work together during many stages in this sequence. Two of the steps, however—feasibility, and implementation and training—are frequently the sole responsibility of the design consultant. Contract documents establish the legal relationship between the client and the contractor and frequently are used to interpret the quality of work that must be accomplished by the contractor. Specifications that are a part of the contract documents must be written carefully so that the quantity and quality of each piece of equipment is clearly understood. A standard format for writing the specifications provides clarity and assists all persons who must read and interpret the contract documents.

The manager or other foodservice professionals can obtain maximum benefit from the food facilities design consultant if the role of the consultant is clearly understood.

KEY TERMS

Foodservice facilities design
   consultant
Foodservice facility program
Facilities evaluation
Systems analysis
Foodservice equipment contractor
Predesign planning process

Architectural program
Schematic design
Design development
Value engineering
Project manual
Lowest qualified bidder

QUESTIONS

1. What are the responsibilities of the owner's representative? How does project size and scope affect these responsibilities?
2. Explain the differences between the design architect and the site architect.

3. For what types of projects is a foodservice facilities design consultant considered essential?

4. What are the duties of each member of the project team?

5. Why is it important to do cost estimates as part of the space analysis, the schematic design, and the design development phases?

6. What are some benefits to using proprietary specifications?

7. What are contract documents, and why are they important?

8. Why is a team approach in employee training for a new facility a good idea?

9. What is a punch list?

DISCUSSION QUESTION

At Level IV, conflict is common on new construction projects. Discuss how the conflicts might be resolved under these circumstances:

a. The equipment layout is unacceptable to the new chef.

b. The architect has gotten "carried away" by the architectural design of the project and the cost now exceeds the budget.

c. The two lowest bids for the foodservice portion of the project are from companies that do not have a good reputation for quality work.

CHAPTER 3

Principles of Design

THIS CHAPTER

☑ Explains the impact of design on efficiency and safety

☑ Describes the basic principles of design for all food facilities

☑ Focuses on human engineering in design

IMPACT OF DESIGN ON EFFICIENCY AND SAFETY

Labor costs and food costs consume between 60 percent and 80 percent of the income of most food operations, and the control of these two costs determines the difference between profit and loss. It follows, then, that the efficiency of a food facility can be judged by how well the design limits the cost of labor.

Designing a food facility to achieve maximum labor productivity requires the collaboration of the foodservice consultant, the owner (operator), and the architect. In other words, getting the design right, and using the best professional talent available, pays significant dividends. For example, consider the savings of one second cook (or cook's helper) and one server, accomplished by good design.

Cook's helper @ $21,000/year	= $32,000
Server @ $6.50/hour × 40 hours × 50 weeks	= $13,000
Total	= $45,000
Benefits @ 18%	= $ 8,100
Uniforms, 2 persons @ $4/day each	= $ 2,000
Employee meals @ $5/meal	= $ 1,500
Total annual cost of two employees	= $56,600
Three-year savings	= $169,800

The savings from good design that made unnecessary two low-to-medium-wage employees over a three-year period ($169,800) would more than pay for the services of highly skilled design professionals.

A good design incorporates certain principles, which are described in this chapter. These principles can be applied to any food operation, with the ultimate goal of satisfying the customer and achieving a profit. If the food operation is designed with the needs of the guests and employees as a major consideration, then high food quality, good sanitation, the smooth flow of materials and people, and good supervision will follow. Poor standards of design yield cross-traffic patterns for guests and employees, backtracking that results in wasted effort, difficult-to-clean surfaces, and poorly thought out work and dining spaces. Employee safety is likely to be compromised in poorly conceived designs, bringing the risk of higher insurance costs and exposure to litigation.

BASIC DESIGN PRINCIPLES

Although there are significant differences in the physical layout, menu, and method of service of various foodservice facilities, food facilities designers follow underlying design principles in virtually all situations. These principles lead to efficiency and a pleasant environment for the worker and customer but do not result in one particular layout. Prototype restaurants of the three leading hamburger chains are quite different in layout, each for its own reasons, but all follow a common set of design principles.

A common misconception about design is that there is only one "right" way to lay out the equipment and arrange the space. There are, in fact, many design solutions that would be acceptable and workable for the same facility. A competent designer will approach a facilities design project knowing that in each project a different set of variables will prevail. Each foodservice facility is treated as unique, with its own design problems to be solved.

The reader should understand the difference between design and layout. Design encompasses the entire facility, with all the considerations that were discussed in Chapter 1 on concept development. Layout involves a consideration of each small unit or work space in a foodservice facility. In the fields of architecture and foodservice facilities design we speak of "designing" a building or a foodservice operation and of "laying out" a range section or a bakery.

Each design professional has a set of guidelines that he or she has found helpful in approaching the design of a food facility. Thus while certain principles are universally accepted, there is no standard set of design rules for all professionals working in the foodservice field. The principles that follow, which are based on the author's experience as a foodservice facilities design professional, are intended to provide a general framework for approaching the design process.

Efficient and effective designs should:

❏ Consider hazard analysis and critical control point

❏ Be flexible and modular

❏ Enhance the customer's experience

❏ Show simplicity
❏ Create an efficient flow of materials and personnel
❏ Facilitate ease of sanitation and promote food safety
❏ Create ease of supervision
❏ Use space efficiently

Hazard Analysis and Critical Control Point

The U.S. Food and Drug Administration has adopted hazard analysis and critical control point (HACCP, pronounced ha-sip) as the basic standard by which food service facilities are evaluated. In is simplest definition, HACCP is the process by which food temperatures are monitored and corrected in a foodservice facility. This process includes the entire system from receiving through waste removal. There are seven basic principles of HACCP:

Taken from the FDA Center for Food Safety and Applied Nutrition Web site www.cfsan.fda.gov

❏ *Analyze hazards.* Potential hazards associated with a food and measures to control those hazards are identified. The hazard could be biological, such as a microbe; chemical, such as a toxin; or physical, such as ground glass or metal fragments.

❏ *Identify critical control points.* These are points in a food's production—from its raw state through processing and shipping to consumption by the consumer—at which the potential hazard can be controlled or eliminated. Examples are cooking, cooling, packaging, and metal detection.

❏ *Establish preventive measures with critical limits for each control point.* For a cooked food, for example, this might include setting the minimum cooking temperature and time required to ensure the elimination of any harmful microbes.

❏ *Establish procedures to monitor the critical control points.* Such procedures might include determining how and by whom cooking time and temperature should be monitored.

❏ *Establish corrective actions to be taken when monitoring shows that a critical limit has not been met*—for example, reprocessing or disposing of food if the minimum cooking temperature is not met.

❏ *Establish procedures to verify that the system is working properly*—for example, testing time-and-temperature recording devices to verify that a cooking unit is working properly.

❏ *Establish effective record keeping to document the HACCP system.* This would include records of hazards and their control methods, the monitoring of safety requirements, and actions taken to correct potential problems. Each of these principles must be backed by sound scientific knowledge: for example, published microbiological studies on time and temperature factors for controlling food-borne pathogens.

HACCP is a complex subject that applies primarily to the operator, and the reader is encouraged to research this subject thoroughly. However, designers must consider how the design and layout ease the process of monitoring food temperatures and assist with food temperature control. For example, if walk-in refrigeration is too far from food production areas, the food sits in the nonrefrigerated environment longer. Thus the design has negatively affected a critical control point. In the selection of equipment, the designer may want to consider equipment that documents the internal temperatures of the food throughout the cooking process. This assists with the effective record keeping principle of HACCP.

Flexibility and Modularity

Menus change to respond to changes in consumers' tastes and preferences. New preparation techniques and new equipment may be necessary if an operation is to keep abreast of consumer trends. If changes in preparation and equipment require substantial modifications to the facility, they are likely to be very expensive—perhaps prohibitively so.

The use of heavy-gauge stainless steel in the construction of kitchen equipment is almost universally accepted by the foodservice industry. Stainless steel does not rust, is easy to clean, is not porous, and does not easily wear out. However, stainless steel has the major fault of being very inflexible. A stainless-steel table in the kitchen cannot be modified easily to accommodate a change in the design. If, for instance, a work area 14 feet (4.27 meters [m]) in length is required, the principle of flexibility would lead the designer to specify two tables, one 6 feet (1.83 m) long and one 8 feet (2.44 m) long. These two lengths would permit rearrangement of the kitchen without the necessity of buying new tables to accommodate a new design.

Foodservice operators often find that a new menu item requires an additional piece of cooking equipment. However, the total cost of the installation may be as much as two or three times greater than the purchase price of the equipment because another hood has to be added and new utility services provided. Adding an additional few feet of ventilation hood when a foodservice facility is built is relatively inexpensive when compared to the cost of extending the hood three years after the operation has opened.

An inflexible construction method that was popular in the past was the use of concrete pads as a base for kitchen equipment. These bases were used in place of legs for refrigerators, ovens, or other heavy pieces of equipment because they eliminate the difficult chore of cleaning under the equipment. The problem with concrete bases is that when the equipment requires replacement or needs to be rearranged, the bases may then be the wrong shape or in the wrong location. A concrete base is difficult to eliminate and impossible to move. Concrete bases are now seen infrequently in commercial kitchens.

The principle of flexibility requires components that can be rearranged to meet changing conditions, such as new management, different methods of service, a new menu, or a new preparation method. Designing for change is the primary means of achieving flexibility.

In the dining area, flexibility can be achieved by the use of movable walls (room dividers) as well as other partitions, such as planters or screens. In the service area, the space can be divided to accommodate both table service and buffet service.

Modularity in design provides standardized sizes and functions of space and equipment. For example, in the construction industry, doors are modular because they are sized according to an industry standard. Modularity means that a given equipment item can be replaced easily with a comparable item from the same or another manufacturer, rather than having to rely on a custom design available from only a single manufacturer. Much of the equipment manufactured for use in commercial kitchens, such as ranges, refrigerators, carts, and racks, is modular.

In a free-flow or scramble cafeteria, the service components should be modular, so that the service lines can be shifted easily as the menu and customer tastes change. Modular range sections, which are commonly used, permit the designer to select from many types of equipment and to arrange these in a smooth and continuous lineup. The modular pieces can be designed for off-the-floor installation, with the entire range section mounted on legs for ease in cleaning. In future years, if a piece of equipment needs to be replaced, the modular unit can be removed without disturbing other pieces of equipment.

Simplicity

In the designing of a foodservice facility, striving for simplicity offers a great many advantages. Food facilities seem to invite clutter, and clutter leads to poor sanitation, confusion, and inefficiency in the work areas, as well as to an environment that customers may find uncomfortable and overcrowded.

The principle of simplicity can be incorporated into the design of foodservice components and systems in various ways. Several examples of simplicity are:

❏ Clean, uncluttered lines for range sections
❏ Simplifying and reducing the number of menu items in order to simplify the kitchen and allow for greater consistency and quality of food items being prepared
❏ The elimination of utility connections that penetrate the floor (rather than the wall behind the equipment), creating dirt pockets and clutter
❏ The selection of a piece of equipment without unnecessary accessories
❏ Convenient server stations near the serving area in the dining room
❏ The arrangement of tables in the dining room to create natural and comfortable aisle space for servers and guests

Flow of Materials and Personnel

The movement of food through a foodservice facility should follow a logical sequence beginning with receiving and ending with waste disposal. Since both receiving and waste disposal usually occur at the back dock of

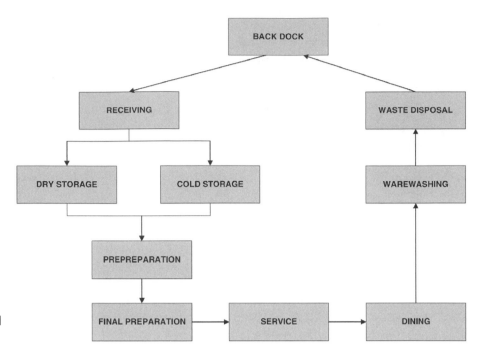

Figure 3.1. Flow of Materials and Personnel in a Foodservice Operation.

a foodservice operation, the food moves through the facility in a circle, as illustrated in Figure 3.1.

If the food does not move through the production cycle in the order shown, then backtracking by the personnel will occur, resulting in lower productivity and wasted labor.

Flow is an important consideration in efficient design throughout a foodservice facility. Some flow considerations in design are:

❑ The movement of employees from one section of the kitchen to another

❑ The flow of dishes through the dishwashing system and back to the service area

❑ In a restaurant, the flow of customers from the entrance to the cocktail lounge and/or to the main dining room

❑ In a cafeteria, the flow of customers from the entrance through the service cafeteria to dining and then the dish drop-off point

❑ The flow of raw food ingredients through the main traffic aisles of the kitchen to the preparation area

❑ The flow of all materials to minimize cross traffic of dirty items and clean items

It is helpful for the designer to diagram the flow patterns on the preliminary floor plan, showing the movement of customers, food, dishes, trash, and garbage. Color-coding the flow lines makes the patterns easier to distinguish and assists the designer in arriving at a design solution that accommodates the proper flow of materials and personnel.

In virtually every type of foodservice facility, more employee labor hours are spent cleaning than are spent preparing the food. A facility designed with sanitation in mind can be cleaned more quickly and easily and thus requires fewer labor hours for this aspect of the operation. Some examples of sanitation design considerations:

Ease of Sanitation

❑ *Building finishes that are durable and easy to clean.* Structural glazed tile on the walls is the most desirable building finish because of ease of cleaning and resistance to damage. Ceramic tile is easy to clean and can be purchased in colorful patterns that make the kitchen a pleasant place to work. Epoxy paint on cement block is the least expensive wall finish but will turn brown around areas that are exposed to high heat. The painted surface is also easily chipped by rolling equipment. The use of bright colors in the kitchen will improve the general appearance of the space and encourage cleanliness. Quarry tile is the standard floor finish for the industry because it does not wear, is grease-resistant, and is less slippery than other floors when wet.

❑ *Equipment racks with a minimum number of legs.*

❑ *Garbage disposals in work areas to facilitate waste disposal.*

❑ *Shelf storage design.* Portable storage shelving systems and open shelving under tables can be cleaned easily.

Many hotels and foodservice institutions built during the 1920s and 1930s had vegetable preparation areas that were remote from the main kitchen or separated by partitions and therefore were difficult to supervise. The open type of design, which is now preferred, allows the supervisor to oversee the production areas more efficiently. The elimination of walls and partitions also permits workers to move and communicate with each other more easily and tends to reduce the number of people needed.

Ease of Supervision

The separation of production areas by floor level not only violates the ease-of-supervision principle by increasing the amount of supervision needed but also creates cumbersome flow patterns between the floors. The designer should avoid separating the production areas by floor whenever possible.

It is often desirable to put a half wall under hoods and between work departments. A 4-foot (1.2m) half wall provides separation and defines work space but does not block the view of the supervisor, who needs to maintain contact with production workers. A half wall is also very useful as a sanitary site for utility connections, and a containment device for spilled water (around stock kettles).

As costs of building construction and maintenance rise, designers are constantly striving to incorporate space-saving ideas into their work. In this case, necessity can be turned to advantage—space saving is translated into space efficiency in the design of a small, well-equipped work area.

Space Efficiency

The principle of space efficiency can, of course, be carried to the extreme. Small, efficient kitchens are a pleasure to use, but kitchens that are too small can be most unpleasant for cooks and other kitchen workers. How can the designer know the difference between small and efficient, on one hand, and too small, on the other? Providing these components will help ensure that each section of the kitchen has the necessary equipment and storage space to enable employees to work efficiently:

❏ A work surface (table)
❏ A food prep sink
❏ A hand wash sink (must be separate from the food prep sink)
❏ A cutting surface
❏ Storage for utensils
❏ Storage for pans
❏ Storage for raw ingredients
❏ Storage for the finished product
❏ Proper aisle space for movement

If each work area includes the listed features, and the work area is arranged efficiently and is adequate for their utilization, the food facility will be space-efficient. (Space efficiency and the proper layout of work areas are developed more fully in Chapters 4 and 5.)

Lifetime Value

Commercial foodservice equipment can be expensive and certainly represents a significant part of the cost of a construction project. Often the foodservice operator is faced with a limited budget for the purchase of equipment, and it is therefore understandable that price becomes a primary factor in the selection process. In the not-for-profit sector of the food industry (hospitals, schools, the military, colleges), many times selecting the lowest price is required; for projects funded by federal, state, and local governments, often this is written into the law.

With carefully written specifications for the purchase of a piece of equipment, it is possible to consider the lifetime value of equipment rather than its initial purchase price. For example, a basic exhaust hood can be purchased for a typical cooking battery for $8,000 to $10,000. A more efficient hood designed to operate effectively with far less exhaust would cost more—perhaps $14,000 to $16,000. However, the more efficient design would dramatically cut down on heating and air-conditioning costs for the building. The savings in energy in this example would easily pay for the more expensive hood in two years or less.

The true cost of any foodservice equipment item is not the purchase price alone; rather, it is the purchase price plus:

❏ Operational costs
❏ Maintenance costs
❏ How long it will last
❏ Labor efficiency

A piece of equipment that is attractive because of its lower purchase price may, in the long run, prove to be a very expensive investment if it requires more maintenance or more labor or is not energy-efficient.

Compromise

In every design project, conflicting needs will give rise to a series of compromise conditions that the owner and design team must resolve. Ideally, if the conceptual design and planning phases of the project were conducted thoroughly, the number of compromises should be minimal. However, the need to compromise at some points in the design process is virtually inevitable. For example, in the design of a dining area, it might be highly desirable to include a private dining room that could be closed off for special groups. Should this room be near the customer entrance for easy public access or near the kitchen for convenience to the hot-food production area? The answer might be both. However, if placing the private dining room near both the entrance and the kitchen interferes with other major components of the design, the best alternative may be to move it to another part of the facility. Conflicting needs always arise in the design process, and only the skilled and experienced person will be able to balance priorities so that the resulting compromises are logical and defensible. Since the owner's priorities may not be the same as the designer's, often frank discussion and give-and-take by all parties are needed to create a satisfactory working relationship.

The designer will be basing the design on a set of principles that should be clearly described to the client before the project begins. If the client insists on making choices that depart from principles of good design, the designer has three choices:

1. Formally express the concern and give in to the client's demand. The change should be put in writing for all to see, but not in such a way that the client would be embarrassed.
2. Formally express the concern, then seek a design solution that will satisfy the client and will preserve the principles of good design.
3. As a last resort, resign and bill the client for the work completed as of the day of the disagreement.

Resubmission is quite common, and it is not unusual to resubmit at least four to six times for the design of a major project. Resubmission should be viewed as a healthy approach to the idea that a good design represents the best thinking of many people.

HUMAN ENGINEERING

A work environment that is designed with the comfort and safety of the workers in mind will have a tremendous effect on worker productivity. If workers have a pleasant place to work, with the proper equipment and tools at hand, they will be likely to enjoy the job and function more efficiently. An additional benefit is employee retention. Reduced training costs and increased consistency and reliability of long-term employees greatly benefits the operation.

Human engineering (or industrial engineering) is a discipline that addresses how working conditions affect employee satisfaction, safety, and productivity. The primary factors that influence the quality of the workplace are:

❏ Efficient work space

❏ Sufficient aisle space

❏ Construction, height, and arrangement of work surfaces

❏ Equipment properly designed for the range of motion of the human body

❏ Materials-handling tools and utensils

❏ Temperature and humidity

❏ Control of noise levels

❏ Adequate lighting to perform the task

Each of these factors is described in greater detail in the sections that follow.

Efficient Work Space

Many different work spaces must be considered in the overall design of a food facility. The amount of space needed by a dishwasher is far different from that needed by a server at a beverage station. In the dishwasher's situation, the worker needs to move back and forth, stooping, gathering carts and racks, and performing other tasks that require a considerable amount of space. The server may need only enough room to pass by a beverage station and pick up a coffeepot or glass of milk en route to the dining room.

The information that follows on work space can be used as a general guideline. It is no substitute, however, for a commonsense evaluation of the unique requirements of any given foodservice facility. The amount of space that an individual worker needs is influenced by the:

❏ Number of people working in the space

❏ Amount and type of equipment

❏ Clearance required for equipment doors

❏ Type of food being processed

❏ Amount of space needed for storage

Adequate Aisle Space

The aisle space needed for different types of work areas is listed next.

An example of a double aisle with protruding equipment is shown in Figure 3.2.

As noted, the width of major traffic aisles should range between 4 and 6 feet (1.2 and 1.8 m). A major traffic aisle is used for the movement of people and material from storage to production areas or from production areas to the point of service. A piece of equipment with a protruding door should never be located in a major traffic aisle that is only 4 feet (1.22 m) wide. An aisle 6 feet (1.83 m) wide can accommodate a refrigerator door or other protruding equipment.

Description of the Space	Aisle Width Needed
Single aisle with limited equipment	2 feet 6 inches to 3 feet 0 inches (0.76 to 0.91 m)
Double aisle with limited equipment	3 feet 6 inches to 4 feet 6 inches (1.1 to 1.4 m)
Single aisle with protruding equipment	3 feet 6 inches to 4 feet 6 inches (1.1 to 1.4 m)
Double aisle with protruding equipment	4 feet 6 inches to 6 feet (1.4 to 1.8 m)
Aisle with little traffic	3 feet 0 inches to 4 feet 0 inches (0.9 to 1.2 m)
Aisle with major traffic	4 feet 0 inches to 6 feet 0 inches (1.2 to 1.8 m)

It is important that aisles be the proper size, because they have a significant influence on the total size of the food facility and on operating efficiency. If the aisle is too narrow, employees will have a difficult time working in the space. If the aisle is too wide, employees will be required to take many extra steps during the day, and fatigue and low productivity will result.

Work Surfaces

Work surfaces should be arranged within easy reach of the worker. Table-tops are often 30 inches (760 mm) wide in production areas, because the average worker can reach out only 30 inches (760 mm) from a standing position. The height of the work surface should permit the worker to chop or to do other hand work without stooping over. A thick cutting board, for instance, will raise the surface height by 1¾ to 3 inches (45 to 76 mm).

The standard used by most designers for the height of a work surface is 34 to 37 inches (864 to 940 mm) (see Figure 3.3). If a work area will be used for heavy, bulky objects, a lower height should be selected. Some

CONVECTION OVEN

MIXER

6'

Figure 3.2. Double Aisle with Protruding Equipment.

Figure 3.3. Worktable Surface Height.

height variations can be created for the worker by the use of mats on the floor, cutting boards on the table, or adjustable table feet.

The amount of space needed from one side of a work surface to the other will depend on the size of the materials used and the layout of the work area. For example, if standard 18-by-26-inch sheet pans (460-by-660 mm) are used as trays for holding individual tossed salads, space would be needed for:

❏ Empty bowls

❏ Bulk tossed salad

❏ Empty sheet pans

❏ Sheet pans filled with salads

In this example, 6 linear feet of space is provided, even though the worker cannot reach that far from one position (see Figure 3.4).

The most important guideline for good workplace layout is to think through the steps in a process and provide a space for the food and equipment needed to carry out these steps. For instance, a sandwich makeup table in a cold-food production area needs:

❏ Storage for plates

❏ Refrigerated storage for food

❏ Storage for bread

Figure 3.4. Adequate Work Space for Salad Preparation.

❏ Utensil drawer or rack

❏ Cutting surface

❏ Toaster

❏ Refrigerated compartments for condiments

❏ Sink with hot and cold water

❏ Garbage disposal or can

❏ Pickup area for servers

The National Sanitation Foundation (NSF) lists three types of surfaces used for foodservice equipment: food contact surfaces, splash contact surfaces, and nonfood contact surfaces. NSF describes the materials that may be used in this way:

❏ *Food contact surfaces.* Surface materials in the food zone shall be smooth, corrosion resistant, nontoxic, stable, and nonabsorbent under use condition. They shall not impart an odor, color, taste, or contribute to the adulteration of food.

❏ *Splash contact surfaces.* These surfaces shall be smooth, easily changeable, and corrosion resistant or rendered corrosion resistant with a material which is noncracking and nonchipping.

❏ *Nonfood contact surfaces.* These surfaces shall be smooth, corrosion resistant or rendered corrosion resistant.

Properly Designed Equipment

The design of equipment from the human engineering point of view is also a consideration of the professional food facilities design consultant.

The NSF has established standards for constructing foodservice equipment that are primarily concerned with safety and sanitation. The reader can consult NSF publications, which are available at a small cost from NSF in Ann Arbor, Michigan.

A checklist (see Figure 3.5) can be used as a guide to human engineering in equipment design. Although it is not intended as a comprehensive guide to all design features that should be in a food facility, the list does contain items that are often overlooked in designing a foodservice facility. The use of the checklist will help ensure a food operation that is engineered for comfort, safety, and sanitation.

Appropriate Tools and Utensils

The lifting of heavy objects by foodservice workers can lead to accidents and personal injury. Materials-handling tools and equipment that can greatly reduce or eliminate worker injury include:

❏ Carts

❏ Forklift trucks

❏ Hand forklift trucks (mules)

❏ Hand trucks

❏ Portable receiving ramps

❏ Skate wheel conveyors

Floors

❏ Adequate number of floor drains to keep floors dry
❏ Carborundum chips in quarry tile in slippery or wet areas
❏ Slip-resistant wax on vinyl floors
❏ Ramps and handrails in receiving area and storage space for carts and hand trucks
❏ Floor mats for comfort of workers who must stand in one place for long periods of time
❏ Kitchen floor level with walk-in refrigerator floor
❏ Heavy slope of floor around steam-jacketed kettles to encourage quick drain-off of hot liquids to floor drains
❏ Coved corners of floors where they meet the wall, for ease of cleaning

Materials Handling

❏ Hand trucks and carts for moving all foods
❏ Strong, easy-to-clean shelving
❏ Portable shelving
❏ Ladders for reaching stored goods on high shelves
❏ Carts for the movement of processed foods from production area to refrigeration and then to service area

Utensil Handling

❏ Knife racks
❏ Easy-to-clean utensil drawers with removable inserts
❏ Utensil drawers at every workstation and table
❏ Overhead utensil racks

Food Production Equipment

❏ Compliance with NSF standards
❏ Compliance with ADA requirements
❏ Portable equipment, if needed in more than one department
❏ Portable bins for flour, sugar, and salt
❏ Wall-hung or mounted on legs for ease of cleaning
❏ Free of burrs, sharp edges, or difficult-to-reach areas
❏ Safety equipment and guards on equipment, such as shields for mixing machine
❏ Disposals in all production areas (if permitted by local codes)
❏ Open rail-type undershelving that will permit crumbs and small particles of food to fall to the floor
❏ Marine edge on all tables with sinks (to prevent water from spilling on floor)
❏ Adequate space for parking equipment from other departments (bread racks, raw ingredients from stores, etc.)

Warewashing Equipment

❏ Pot storage racks beside potwashing station and in or near each work area
❏ Storage containers for soiled linen
❏ Box, glass, and metal can container in each major work area
❏ Utensil sorting table
❏ Paper and bone container at dishwashing station
❏ Prerinse, power or hand
❏ Cleaning supply storage
❏ Hose reel
❏ Cart wash-down area

Service and Dining

❏ Condiments and support service equipment available near the point of service
❏ Convenient dish drop-off
❏ Easy-to-clean chairs with absence of cracks that accumulate crumbs
❏ Minimum number of steps from food pickup to point of service

Figure 3.5. Human Engineering Checklist for Foodservice Facilities Design.

A simple cart is the materials-handling tool most frequently used for assembling ingredients in the kitchen. Workers often abuse such carts, through heavy use and the dropping of full cases of food onto the top shelf. The designer should specify the heaviest cart possible to prevent damage and abuse.

Forklift trucks normally are reserved for large foodservice warehouses, but the hand-operated forklift is frequently used in the storerooms and kitchens of medium-size and large foodservice operations. Hand-operated forklifts raise pallets of food a few inches off the floor, permitting easy transport to a freezer or storeroom. Hand trucks are simple L-shape two-wheeled devices that permit the worker to balance a stack of case goods on two wheels and to move it in or out of storage.

Receiving ramps and skate wheel conveyors permit the movement of materials from one level to the next without lifting. Receiving docks are the wrong height for many of the different types of delivery truck that bring goods to the receiving area. A portable receiving ramp, constructed of lightweight aluminum, is very helpful in solving the height variation problem. Motorized load leveler devices often are designed into the ramp to solve this same problem. Motor-driven belts, dumbwaiters, and elevators are also used to transport materials from one level to the next.

Adequate Lighting

Adequate lighting is essential in food preparation and service. Employees need sufficient light to observe the quality of the food products they are handling and to monitor the cleanliness of their work areas. The standard measure of light is the foot-candle, which is equivalent to the amount of light from a standard candle that strikes a 1-foot-square surface from a distance of 1 foot. The farther away a light is placed from the surface to be lighted, the lower the number of foot-candles. For this reason, lighting needs to be spaced at frequent intervals in a food production area. Figure 3.6 can be used as a guide in selecting the proper light levels for food facilities.

Space	Foot Candles
Kitchen Work Area	30–40
Storeroom	10–20
Cashier	50–60
Loading Platform	20–25
Building Entrance	10–20
Rest Room	20–30
Hotel: General Guest Areas	10–20
Accounting and Bookkeeping Offices	100–150
Dining Rooms	
Quick Service	40–50
Casual Dining	10–20
White Tablecloth	5–15

Figure 3.6. Lighting Levels for Foodservice Areas.

Figure 3.7. Lighting for Food Display.

In service areas that will be seen by the public, one very effective means of lighting is to provide a high intensity of light on the food and low intensity for the main part of the room. Low- and high-intensity lighting for food display is illustrated in Figure 3.7.

Temperature and Humidity

The relationship among temperature, humidity, and air movement is a technical subject that is the responsibility of the engineer on the design project. However, the food facilities design consultant needs to be aware of this aspect of environmental design, which affects the comfort of building occupants. The range of temperature and humidity in which most of the people who use the building will be comfortable is referred to as the comfort zone. In the winter, if the temperature is too high and the humidity too low, an unpleasant dryness results. In winter, outside air usually contains very little moisture. When this air is drawn into a building and heated to 70°F (21.1°C), the humidity drops to a very low level. In the summer, the reverse condition often exists. Moist air from the outside is drawn in and cooled, resulting in high humidity. Air-conditioning reduces the amount of moisture in the hot, humid air and provides a comfortable combination of lower temperature and lower humidity in the summer.

In foodservice facilities, a limited number of kitchens or dishwashing rooms are air-conditioned. Air movement is therefore essential for comfort. If the temperature is slightly high but air movement is rapid, skin evaporation will usually keep the body cool enough for comfort. Dishwashing rooms and range sections of a food facility are usually the most difficult areas to keep comfortable. In the dishroom, the high humidity produced by the moisture from the automatic dishwashing equipment creates two problems: The workers are uncomfortable, and the dishes do not air-dry. The designer must work closely with the engineers to be sure that air movement is sufficient and that ventilation ducts are provided for both the feed (entrance) and discharge ends of the dish machine. Typical vent requirements recommended by commercial dishwasher manufacturers are 200 CFM (cubic feet per minute/5.66 cubic meters per minute) at the entrance to the machine and 400 CFM (11.32 cubic meters/minute) at the discharge of the machine. It is suggested that air movement be increased slightly above the recommended levels, since dishwashing rooms themselves often do not have enough room exhaust. The additional exhaust will keep the room more comfortable.

The range section of a kitchen is often uncomfortable for the cooks because of the heat generated by broilers, ranges, and other pieces of equipment that produce (and waste) large amounts of energy. The high heat condition is usually the result of inadequate exhaust ventilation by the hood equipment.

Noise Control

High noise levels are very unpleasant for the worker in a foodservice facility. It has been demonstrated in industrial settings that excessive noise causes fatigue, accidents, and low productivity in direct relationship to the volume of the noise. Some techniques that will help to reduce noise in a foodservice facility are:

❑ Sound-deadening materials sprayed onto the underside of all tables and counters.

❑ The separation of areas (other than production) in the food facility department, especially warewashing. The construction of walls between the kitchen and the warewashing area will restrict noise transmission.

❑ Designing conveyors to create a sound barrier between dish drop-off points and warewashing. An illustration of a sound barrier that might be used in a self-busing application for a restaurant or cafeteria is illustrated in Figure 3.8.

Figure 3.8. Controlling Sound Using Wall Construction to Create Barriers.

❑ Acoustic ceilings that are grease- or moisture-resistant.

❑ Carpeting in dining room seating areas.

❑ Carpeting on the walls in dining areas. This is an excellent wall finish because it not only absorbs sound but will take the punishment of chairs and tables that often scar wooden, papered, or painted wall finishes.

❑ Double doors between the dining room and the kitchen.

❑ Background music in both the public areas and the back of the establishment (kitchen, warewashing area, service areas).

❑ Remote refrigeration compressors.

FOODSERVICE DESIGN AND TITLES II AND III OF THE AMERICANS WITH DISABILITIES ACT

The Americans with Disabilities Act (ADA) became law on July 26, 1991. After January 26, 1992, alterations to existing places of public accommodation and commercial facilities must be accessible to the maximum extent feasible, and new construction must be accessible to individuals with disabilities to the extent that it is not structurally impracticable. Title II covers any state or local government and any of its departments, agencies, or other instrumentalities. Title III covers public accommodations, commercial facilities, and private entities that offer certain examinations and courses related to educational and occupational certification. Public accommodations include over 5 million private establishments, such as restaurants, hotels, and theaters. Sections 5.1 through 5.9 of Part III of the *Federal Register* (pages 35665–66) deal specifically with restaurants and cafeterias. Section 4.2 of Part III (pages 35620–21) and the corresponding charts deal with the heights of counters and the reach of customers with disabilities. For copies of the act, call the office of the Americans with Disabilities Act at (202) 514-0301, or access the Web site: www.ada.gov.

Following are some general provisions of the act, taken from the *Federal Register* (page 35665), that may be helpful in the planning process.

5.3 Aisle Width: All accessible fixed tables shall be accessible by means of an access aisle at least 36 inches (915 mm) clear between paralleled edges of tables or between a wall and the table.

5.4 Dining Areas: In new construction all dining areas, including raised or sunken dining areas, loggias, and outdoor seating areas shall be accessible.

5.5 Foodservice Lines: Foodservice lines shall have a minimum clear width of 36 inches (915 mm), with a preferred clear width of 42 inches (1065 mm) to allow passage around a person using a wheelchair. Tray slides shall be mounted no higher than 34 inches (865 mm) above the floor.

Entrance requirements and ramping are discussed in the *Federal Register* in great detail, and the reader is encouraged to review this material so that full compliance is achieved.

SUMMARY

The design of a foodservice facility will have a significant impact on its safety, efficiency, ease of maintenance, and long-term operating costs. Principles of design include:

❏ Flexibility and modularity make it feasible to change the design as consumer demand requires new and different menu items and preparation techniques.

❏ Simplicity in design leads to efficiency and long-term labor savings.

❏ A design that arranges work areas to facilitate the flow of products saves steps and therefore saves labor costs.

❏ A design that makes sanitation a simple process leads to greater food safety, thereby protecting the health of guests as well as the business.

❏ A design in which the manager can easily supervise and assist employees facilitates communication and coordination and leads to better employee relations.

❏ A design that maximizes lifetime value, rather than minimizing initial capital investment, leads to the long-term financial health and viability of the operation.

❏ All designs reflect some degree of compromise. The more informed the design team can be about the costs and benefits of each alternative, the better the outcome will be.

❏ Human engineering specifies the design factors that lead to efficient work as well as the prevention of work-related injuries.

❏ The Americans with Disabilities Act requires that foodservice facilities be designed to meet the needs of individuals with disabilities to the maximum extent feasible.

KEY TERMS

Flexibility	Lifetime value
Modularity	Compromise
Design simplicity	Human engineering
Work flow	Americans with Disabilities Act
Ease of supervision	

QUESTIONS

1. Does the flow of both personnel and food product always occur? How can you reduce the number of steps taken in this process?

2. Wall-mounted equipment (no legs) is seldom used in current kitchen design. Why?

3. Eight different components are listed in this chapter as the ideal work station. Can you name six of them?

4. What does "human engineering" mean?

5. Should a modern kitchen be air-conditioned? Will this create cold food (which is supposed to be hot)? What are some solutions that would keep employees comfortable and keep the food hot?

DISCUSSION QUESTION

In this chapter, in the event that the owner changes the layout and, in turn, violates the principles of good design, compromise is recommended. Discuss ways that a foodservice design consultant might resolve a conflict among the owner, the architect, and the future manager.

CHAPTER 4

Space Analysis

THIS CHAPTER

☑ Describes the space analysis process for these functional areas of a foodservice facility:

◆ Receiving
◆ Storage
◆ Office
◆ Pre-preparation
◆ Hot-food preparation, cold-food preparation, and final preparation
◆ Bakery
◆ Employee locker room and toilet
◆ Service areas
◆ Dining
◆ Bar
◆ Warewashing

CONDUCTING A SPACE ANALYSIS

How large should a food facility be? Should the kitchen be half the size of the dining room? How much space will be needed for warewashing and storage? These and related questions must be answered during the early phase of the design project, since the answers will determine the size and thus the total cost of the facility. By knowing space requirements in advance, the owner or architect can make realistic preliminary estimates of construction costs.

It is the foodservice design consultant's job to determine the space requirements for each section of the foodservice facility before the actual design can begin. This early but difficult estimate is achieved by gathering basic data about the nature of the planned food operation. Figure 4.1 shows the type of data that should be collected to determine space needs. Once this information has been obtained, the space requirements of each functional part of a foodservice facility are analyzed.

This chapter is devoted to discussing the space requirements of each of the functional areas of a foodservice facility. For purposes of easy reference, the description of each of these functional foodservice areas is divided into

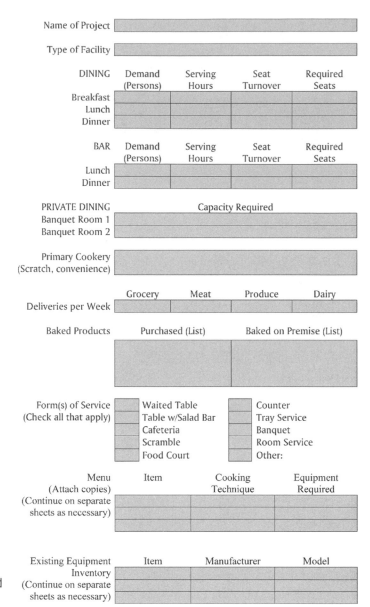

Figure 4.1. Data Used in Preparation for Foodservice Planning and Programming.

four sections:

1. General description of the space
2. Relationship to other areas
3. Amount of space needed
4. Special design features

BACK DOCK/RECEIVING

General Description of the Space The back dock and receiving area is located with easy access to driveways and street entrances to the property. Usually the architect decides where major ingress/egress for people, delivery trucks, and service vehicles will be located. The food facilities design consultant must work with the architect to be sure that sufficient space is allocated for the movement of large tractor-trailer trucks and other vehicles that need access to the receiving area. Consideration must be given to proper screening of the receiving dock and especially to trash and garbage storage containers so that persons looking out of the building windows or walking along the street will not have a full view of the receiving dock and garbage containers. In larger operations, a space internal to the building is often provided for checking in large orders and staging food for delivery to storage areas.

Relationship to Other Areas

The primary relationship of receiving is to the storage areas, which are often scattered and may in fact be located at different building levels. Regardless of the location of storage, easy access must be available for the movement of heavy materials from the receiving dock. The receiving dock must also be accessible to the kitchen for these reasons:

❏ Many food products will go directly from receiving to the production areas in the kitchen.

❏ Refrigerated storage areas are often located adjacent to the kitchen and will be stocked directly from the receiving dock.

❏ Since in small or medium-size foodservice facilities, supervisory personnel such as the chef, manager, or assistant managers will personally be responsible for receiving the food, easy access from the kitchen to the dock is highly desirable.

Other important relationships for the receiving area include access to trash containers, wash-down rooms, and cleaning equipment.

Amount of Space Needed

Space needs in the receiving area vary with the volume of food to be received, the frequency of delivery, and the distance between the receiving area and the storage spaces. If the receiving clerk must transport food products great distances before placing them in storage, additional space may be required on the back dock to temporarily store a quantity of food products. Often too much space is provided for the receiving dock, resulting in the accumulation of clutter. Figure 4.2 provides general guidelines for allocating the proper amount of space for the receiving area.

Special Design Features

The receiving dock can be designed as an elevated platform for tractor-trailer trucks, at street level, or at any level in between these two heights. The architect will make the decision on receiving dock height based on site development and the placement of the building on the property. The depth of the dock (distance from front to back) should permit a person to walk back and forth, with space for goods stored temporarily on wooden pallets. Usually 8 or 10 feet (2.4 to 3.0 meters [m]) is sufficient. The length of the dock should accommodate the number of delivery trucks that are likely to be unloading at one time. For most foodservice operations, a receiving clerk can check in only one or two trucks at a time, and a single or at the most a double truck width is usually sufficient. A third truck width for a trash/garbage vehicle is also desirable. A range of 10 to 15 feet of width (3.0 to 4.6 m) per truck should be used as a standard, depending on the angle for backing to the dock.

Type of Food Operation	Space Needed in Square Feet (Square Meters)	Number of Trucks
Fast food	**40–60 (3.72–5.58)**	1
Small restaurant (under 75 seats)	**60–80 (5.58–7.44)**	1
Medium restaurant (75–150 seats) *or* **Small institution** (300–1,000 meals per day)	**80–100 (7.44–9.30)**	1
Large restaurant (150–400 seats) *or* **Medium institution** (1,000–2,000 meals per day)	**120–150 (11.16–13.95)**	2
Large institution (over 2,000 meals per day)	**150–175 (13.95–16.28)**	2
Large hotel, restaurant, or institution with complex menu, catering facilities, snack bars	**175–200 (16.28–18.60)**	3

Figure 4.2. Space Required for Receiving.

CONTROL OF FOOD AND SUPPLIES

The control of food and supplies moving in and out of the receiving area will be of concern to the foodservice management staff. If the food facility is large enough to justify a receiving office, visibility of the receiving area from an office window is highly desirable. For a small food facility that does not have a receiving office, visual control from the kitchen or the manager's office should be a design consideration. It is often necessary to construct a stairway at the back dock for the use of employees coming and going from the workplace. This presents a serious control problem because it permits easy access to food and supplies by employees as they enter or exit the building. If possible, a separately controlled entrance for employees should be incorporated into the building design. If this is not possible, the next best solution is to design a separate door and corridor from the receiving area to the interior of the building.

PROTECTION FROM THE WEATHER

Receiving personnel must be protected from rain, cold, and excessive heat as they perform their duties on the back dock. Typical architectural solutions include a simple roof overhang, placement of the receiving dock in a recess behind the exterior wall of the building, or the enclosure of the entire receiving area with a heavy-duty folding door. Unless weather conditions are extremely severe, the enclosure of the entire receiving area is excessively expensive. The door from the receiving area should be 5 feet (1.5 m) wide when two doors are used and a minimum of 4 feet (1.2 m) wide for a single door entrance. Double entry doors should be used for proper screening to prevent flies and other insects from entering the food production area. Air curtains, which are simple centrifugal fans located over the door entrances, are somewhat effective in discouraging the entry of insects.

SCALES

Many foodservice managers often overlook the importance of scales adjacent to the receiving dock. Many products are prepackaged and weighed, with the weights clearly marked on the containers. It is often assumed—falsely—that these weights are always accurate. All foodservice facilities should have a scale for use by the receiving clerk to verify the weights of foods that are purchased by the pound or kilogram. The location of the scale should be in the breakout area (a small space just inside the receiving doors for checking in and separating foods before putting them into storage) inside the building, so that the scale is protected from the weather.

MATERIALS-HANDLING EQUIPMENT

Several types of materials-handling equipment are commonly used in foodservice receiving areas for efficient transport and to avoid stress and injury to employees. Hand trucks (two-wheeled vehicles for moving small stacks of case goods), platform hand trucks (four-wheeled flat vehicles) that are strong enough to hold the weight of 10 or 15 cases of food goods, and wooden or steel pallets are all part of the equipment needs for the receiving clerk. Large numbers of wooden pallets (skids) often accumulate in the receiving area because they are commonly used in the food distribution industry for holding and moving large quantities of case goods. Large foodservice operations may want to consider the design of storeroom spaces to hold these pallets, which must be moved with either a hand-operated forklift device or a forklift truck.

The need for a separate receiving office, breakout area, wash-down room, or garbage room will depend on the size and complexity of the foodservice operation. These functions are usually carried out in the receiving area, and if space is not provided, they may encroach on other space. Office space should be small (50 square feet/4.6 square [sq] m), and the wash-down area and garbage room should be limited in size (50–80 square feet [4.6–7.4 sq m] should be sufficient). A small area just inside the receiving door can be allotted for breakout space. Figure 4.3 can be used as a guideline in deciding whether special rooms are needed.

| | Approximate Space Needed (Net) | | |
Number of Seats	Office Square Feet (Meters)	Wash-down Square Feet (Meters)	Garbage Square Feet (Meters)
Under 50 or fast food	None	None	60 (5.75 m)
50–100	None	None	60 (5.75 m)
100–175	80 (7.43)	80 (7.43)	80 (7.43)
175–250	100 (9.29)	80 (7.43)	80 (7.43)
250–500	160 (14.86)	80 (7.43)	120 (11.15)
More than 500	240 (22.30)	120 (11.15)	120 (11.15)

Figure 4.3. Support Spaces for Receiving/Dock Area.

STORAGE

General Description of the Space

The amount of storage in a foodservice facility is primarily influenced by the number of meals per day served, the number of items that appear on the menu, the frequency of delivery, and the operating policies of the management. It is considered good management practice to turn the inventory over 12 times per year (once a month). Turnover for perishable products should, of course, be at least twice a week, and turnover for such items as paper and cleaning supplies may be infrequent. The attitude of management toward inventory turnover should always be discussed prior to beginning the design. A canned-goods storeroom, for instance, might be viewed by one manager as too small because he or she likes the idea of keeping a large par stock on hand. Another manager who prefers to keep the par stock very low, so that cash is not tied up in inventory, might see the same storeroom as too large. The use of computers in the foodservice industry has greatly enhanced the ability of managers to forecast the precise amount of food needed for each meal and, therefore, decrease the amount of food that must be kept on hand at any one time. Computers, more efficient distribution of food products by vendors, and high interest rates have all contributed to a trend toward smaller storage spaces.

The four categories of storage that must be available in all food facilities are:

1. Dry or canned food storage
2. Paper and cleaning supplies storage
3. Refrigerated storage
4. Utensil and cleaning equipment storage

Relationship to Other Areas

Storage areas should be well ventilated, dry, and constructed of easy-to-clean surfaces. Concrete or tile floors, cement block walls with epoxy paint, and acoustic ceilings are common for all storage areas except those that are refrigerated. Large access doors and a high level of security must be included as part of the design. The most important relationship in the design is easy access from the storage area to both food production and receiving. The number of trips that will be made to the production area from the storage area will far exceed the number made from the receiving dock. It is therefore important to be sure that the staff in food production areas have short distances to travel to refrigerated storage and canned-goods storage spaces. It is often possible to locate a walk-in refrigerator in the immediate vicinity of the cold-food preparation department, so that few steps are necessary to procure salad materials and other frequently used perishable items.

Amount of Space Needed and Special Design Features

DRY STORAGE

Calculating a standard amount of dry storage space is difficult because of the many variables that affect the need. The method that is often used is to consider the many variables that cause fluctuations in the quantity of food to be stored and simply make an educated guess. It is usually better

Type of Food Operation	Dry Storage Square Feet (Square Meters)
Fast food	50–125 (4.65–11.63)
Small restaurant	100–150 (9.30–13.95)
Medium restaurant or small institution	200–300 (18.60–27.90)
Large restaurant or medium institution	400–1,000 (37.20–93.00)
Large institution with simple menu	1,000–2,500 (93.00–232.50)
Large hotel, restaurant, or institution with complex menu, catering facilities, snack bars	3,000+ (279.00+)

Figure 4.4. Dry Storage Space Requirements.

to estimate space needs on the basis of the industry's experience with different types of facilities. Figure 4.4 provides guidelines for determining dry storage needs (assuming that deliveries are made twice per week and that cleaning supplies and paper are stored separately).

PAPER AND CLEANING SUPPLIES STORAGE

The storage of paper supplies can be a major space problem for food operations that use a large quantity of disposable cups, plates, napkins, and plastic ware. No standard space requirement is possible because the extent of the use of disposables and the frequency of delivery are different for each food operation. Paper supply companies tend to give significant price breaks for larger orders of paper goods, and therefore the food operator is forced to accept large quantities in order to purchase economically.

Cleaning supplies must be stored separately from food supplies to prevent contamination and accidental mixing of cleaning products with foods. A separate storeroom for cleaning supplies should be large enough to handle 55-gallon drums, cases of dish machine detergent, and other cleaning items. A space 6 to 10 feet (1.8 to 3.0 m) wide and 10 to 15 feet (3.0 to 4.6 m) deep will handle the storage needs of most small and medium-sized operations. Figure 4.5 provides a guide for cleaning supplies.

Type of Food Operation	Storage Area Square Feet (Square Meters)
Fast food	60–100 (5.58–9.3)
Small restaurant	75–120 (6.98–11.16)
Medium restaurant or small institution	120–175 (11.16–16.28)
Large restaurant or medium institution	175–250 (16.28–23.25)
Large institution with simple menu	250–300 (23.25–27.90)
Large hotel, restaurant, or institution with complex menu, catering facilities, snack bars	300+ (27.90+)

Figure 4.5. Space Required for Paper and Cleaning Supplies Storage.

REFRIGERATED AND FROZEN STORAGE

Space needed for bulk storage of frozen and refrigerated foods should be determined at this stage.

A bulk freezer should be selected based on the menu and frequency of delivery. For instance, if the menu contains a large number of items prepared from frozen food products, the need for freezer space will obviously increase. A fast-food restaurant or college cafeteria will usually use a significant amount of frozen french fries, and the college may also use large quantities of frozen vegetables. A seafood restaurant may use large quantities of frozen fish, french fries, onion rings, but perhaps no frozen vegetables at all. A hotel or large catering operation may use smaller quantities but might stock a wide variety of frozen foods.

Frozen foods are usually shipped in rectangular cartons that are easily stacked, and the height of the freezer is therefore an important part of the calculation. The size of a freezer should be determined based on cubic feet of space needed. Figure 4.6 presents freezer size calculations based on these assumptions:

❏ The facility is a small restaurant with delivery of frozen foods once per week.

❏ Frozen hamburgers, french fries, and onion rings are a significant part of the volume of the business.

❏ The menu contains five or six additional items that are purchased frozen.

❏ Ice cream, in six flavors, is a popular dessert.

Walk-in refrigerated storage space is very expensive because of the amount of building space that walk-ins occupy and because of the high cost of the equipment. A careful calculation of the amount of space needed is therefore strongly recommended.

Assuming a standard-size walk-in (7 feet 4 inches/2.2 m high) is used, it can be filled only to a height of 6 feet (1.8 m). In fact, less than 50 percent of the space in the walk-in is usable, as shown in Figure 4.7. Therefore,

Food Item	Pack	Volume Cubic Feet (Cubic Meters)	Quantity	Total Volume Cubic Feet (Cubic Meters)
French fries	Case	1.8 (.050)	25	45.0 (1.260)
Hamburgers	Case	1.2 (.033)	30	36.0 (1.008)
Onion rings	Case	2.0 (.056)	20	40.0 (1.120)
Vegetables	Case	1.5 (.042)	15	22.5 (0.630)
Hot dogs	Package	.2 (.006)	35	7.0 (0.196)
Roast beef	12–15 lb	1.0 (.028)	30	30.0 (0.840)
Ice cream	3 gal	1.5 (.042)	45	67.5 (1.890)
Miscellaneous	Case	1.0 (.028)	35	35.0 (0.980)
Total	283 cubic ft (7.924 cubic m)			

Figure 4.6. Calculating Volume Required for Refrigerated and Frozen Storage.

Figure 4.7. Walk-in Freezer Size Is Determined by Volume Calculations.

the total number of cubic feet (m) of storage per linear foot (m) of walk-in freezer is:

6 feet (height) × 2-foot shelves × 2 (one on each side)
= 24 cubic feet per linear foot

1.8 meters (height) × .6 meter shelves × 2 (one on each side)
= 2.16 cubic meters per linear meter

To determine the necessary length, divide the total cubic feet needed by 24. In the example shown, the length of the walk-in would be:

283 cubic feet ÷ 24 = 11.79 linear feet
8 cubic meters ÷ 2.16 = 3.7 meters

The walk-in should be 12 feet (3.7 m) long by 9 feet (2.75 m) wide in this example. The 9-foot (2.75-m) width provides space on both sides for shelving, an aisle space of 3½ to 4 feet (1.0 to 1.2 m), plus 8 inches (32 mm) for the insulated walk-in panels.

The size of a walk-in refrigerator is determined in a similar manner but is more difficult to calculate because the products stored are not in rectangular boxes. Milk, produce, fresh meats, foods that have been prepared, and other miscellaneous items that need to be stored under refrigeration are difficult to measure in cubic footage (m).

Small fast-food operations or restaurants with very limited menus may need only one walk-in refrigerator. Medium-size operations may wish to separate meat, produce, and dairy products. Large hotels, restaurants, or

Type of Food Operation	Walk-ins	Square Feet (Square Meters)
Fast food	1	90–120 (8.4–11.2)
Small restaurant	1	120–150 (11.2–14.0)
Medium restaurant or small institution	2	180–240 (16.7–22.3)
Large restaurant or medium institution	3	240–400 (22.3–37.2)
Large institution with simple menu	3	400–600 (37.2–55.8)
Large hotel, restaurant, or institution with complex menu, catering facilities, snack bars	4	600–900 (55.8–83.7)

Figure 4.8. Walk-in Requirements.

institutions may need three or four large walk-in refrigerators, located in different sections of the kitchen. The chart in Figure 4.8 may be used as a general guide for determining the amount of space needed for walk-in refrigeration.

UTENSIL AND CLEANING EQUIPMENT STORAGE

Food facilities that do not include a storage space for infrequently used utensils, backup supplies of utensils such as knives and serving spoons, and cleaning equipment such as buffing machines and steam cleaners often are plagued with a considerable amount of clutter in the work areas. For instance, a restaurant that occasionally serves buffets for private parties may want to keep chafing dishes, punch bowls, and serving platters in a utensil storage room.

The amount of space needed is so variable that a standard cannot be easily established. For the small or medium-size foodservice facility, a closet with built-in shelving that can be easily secured provides a sufficient amount of space. Country clubs that hold private functions, buffets, and receptions and need to store substantial quantities of Christmas decorations and other special-events materials may require an extremely large storeroom with movable metal shelving. For the large food facility, the separation of cleaning equipment storage from utensil storage is recommended for reasons of security.

OFFICE

General Description of the Space

Offices are needed for the manager, assistant managers, chef or food production manager, and clerical staff. The justification for these spaces is to provide a private environment for talking with employees, vendors, and other businesspeople and to be sure that the management staff has a reasonably quiet place to work.

Relationship to Other Areas

The offices of the general manager and catering manager should be accessible to the public without the necessity of having customers walk through the kitchen. Office space for managers and assistant managers who have infrequent contact with the public outside the dining room should be located in a highly visible and easily accessible part of the food facility. Small foodservice operations often have the office located near the receiving area so that the movement of employees and of food in and out of storage areas and the building can be observed. Office space for receiving clerks, storeroom supervisors, and service supervisors should obviously be located in their respective work areas. Often these office areas are simple enclosures or spaces set aside without doors or four walls.

Amount of Space Needed

Small office areas usually range from 60 to 80 square feet (5.6 to 7.4 sq m) and can be increased from this size as space and funds permit. Combination offices in which the clerical staff are adjacent to a manager's office and separated by a partition require additional space to accommodate door swings and extra office equipment, such as computers, copy machines, and word processors.

The number of office spaces that may be needed for supervisory and management personnel will depend on the complexity of the organization. For instance, in a fairly complex operation, office space may be needed for:

- ❑ Food and beverage director
- ❑ Accounting and payroll personnel
- ❑ Catering manager
- ❑ Sales manager
- ❑ Executive chef
- ❑ Production manager
- ❑ Dietitian
- ❑ Cash counting office
- ❑ Assistant manager
- ❑ Purchasing manager
- ❑ Receiving supervisor
- ❑ Maître d'hôtel

Special Design Features

Carpeted floors, light-colored walls with chair rails, and acoustical ceilings with fluorescent lighting are desirable surfaces in an office. The location of telephone, data, and electrical outlets on all four walls will permit maximum flexibility as personnel and space needs change. Management and supervisory personnel often prefer an office with many windows for purposes of supervisory control. Clerical employees, however, often dislike windows that create distractions from their work or that do not provide a sufficient amount of privacy.

PREPARATION AREAS

General Description of the Space

In a well-designed kitchen, the food preparation area is divided into four general areas. Although in a small kitchen these areas are often combined, recognition of each of the areas is an important part of the design. The four working areas of a kitchen are:

❏ Pre-preparation

❏ Hot-food preparation

❏ Cold-food preparation

❏ Final preparation

PRE-PREPARATION

The pre-preparation area of the kitchen is where foods are processed, mixed, combined, held, cleaned, or otherwise worked with before the meal period begins. Chopping celery, mixing meatloaf, simmering broth, peeling potatoes, and making salad dressing are all pre-preparation activities. Sinks, large work surfaces, and all of the other equipment necessary to accomplish food pre-preparation tasks are a part of this area of the kitchen.

The pre-preparation area usually includes all of the equipment needed to process foods before the meal begins. Typical equipment located in the pre-preparation area includes:

❏ Worktables with sinks

❏ Racks for storage of pots and pans

❏ Utensil storage (drawers, hanging racks)

❏ Choppers, vertical cutter-mixers, and food processors

❏ Mixers

❏ Ovens

❏ Steam-jacketed kettles

❏ Tilting braising pans

The amount of equipment in this area, and especially the amount of worktable surface needed, will be determined by the amount of hand preparation that is dictated by the menu and by the volume of food being processed. The layout and dimensions of a pre-preparation area for a small restaurant are illustrated in Figure 4.9. Note in the figure that the total space for pre-preparation is 13 feet by 17 feet 6 inches (4.0 by 5.3 m), or 227.5 square feet (21.2 sq m). The addition of an aisle on two sides of this would increase the amount of space needed by approximately 90 square feet (8.4 sq m), to a total of 317.5 square feet (rounded to 320), or 29.6 square meters (rounded to 30).

HOT-FOOD PREPARATION

The range section of a kitchen is usually considered the hot-food preparation area. Since this is where heat is applied to the food product, the space must be extremely resistant to soiling from grease and able to withstand

Figure 4.9. Preparation Area for a Small Restaurant.

high heat. Also necessary are elaborate (and expensive) ventilation systems above the cooking surfaces. The area must be designed to meet the demands of the menu, and equipment should be selected accordingly. The most frequent design error in the kitchen is to select generic equipment that is manufactured to cook all foods under all circumstances rather than pieces best suited to preparing the foods served in the particular facility.

COLD-FOOD PREPARATION

In small and medium-size kitchens, this area is where salads are assembled, desserts are dished up, and appetizers are made ready for service. For a large restaurant or hotel, a separate garde-manger department may be required for the preparation of cold appetizers, entrées, and beautifully decorated items for buffets. Typically most of the pre-preparation and final preparation for cold foods will occur in the same general area. Worktables and refrigerated storage should be accessible to all food preparation personnel located in this area. A pickup station designed as part of cold-food preparation allows the servers easy access. In European kitchens, the traditional layout included a cold-food kitchen as a separate area.

FINAL PREPARATION

The final preparation area is the space in which foods are prepared very close to and during the meal period. It is important in the design to define this space carefully and to be sure that all equipment located within it has to do with final preparation. Foods usually cooked in this area include steak, seafood, french fries, fried eggs, toast, hamburgers, frozen vegetables, and other similar items that can be prepared quickly and will deteriorate rapidly if cooked ahead of time. In a successful restaurant, the final food preparation area is the most carefully attended and supervised part of the entire kitchen. Foods prepared in this area can be held only a very short period of time before being presented to the guest. Successful fast-food chains have designed elaborate means to be sure that foods are not held more than five to six minutes in the final preparation area before being served. The final preparation area typically includes a range, grills, fryers, steamers, and broilers. Obviously, some small amount of pre-preparation also occurs in this area, but in an efficient operation it is kept to a minimum.

Relationship to Other Areas

The flow of people and materials from storage to pre-preparation to final preparation can best be illustrated by a simple diagram (see Figure 4.10). Although this diagram seems very simplistic, the concept that it illustrates is extremely important if good kitchen design is to be achieved. Frequently kitchens are laid out with steam-jacketed kettles (used in pre-preparation) in the final preparation area or fryers (used in final preparation) located in the pre-preparation area. Although these arrangements may save some duplication in equipment, they tend to cause congestion in the flow of materials and personnel.

Figure 4.10 also shows how preparation spaces relate to the service components of a food facility. The reader should also bear in mind the comprehensive picture of a facility, with the kitchen at the center of all the functional spaces. The design should always reflect these relationships and facilitate the movement of employees and food between functionally related areas. For instance, the distance between the final preparation area and the customer should be short because the time that it takes to move the food is critical. The relationship of the preparation area to the employee locker room is not critical, however, and these spaces could be a considerable distance away from each other.

Figure 4.10. Relationship among Storage, Pre-preparation, Final Preparation, and Service.

Vertical as well as horizontal space relationships must be considered. As a general guideline, when spaces must be located on different floors, these functional areas may be at a different level from the kitchen:

❏ Bulk dry storage

❏ Bulk frozen storage

❏ Paper and utensil storage

❏ Employee locker rooms

❏ Receiving

Warewashing, service areas, and dining areas should never be located on a different level from the kitchen. This guideline is often violated in large hotels and institutional kitchens, where it is quite common to see dishwashing located on a different level from the dining room. Architectural limitations at times make it necessary to violate this rule, but there is always a cost in labor, efficiency, and effectiveness of supervision.

Amount of Space Needed

A question frequently asked by the owner or architect at the beginning of a project is: What is the ratio of kitchen space to dining room space? The food facilities design consultant usually will answer that it depends. First of all, no clear standards exist for a ratio between the dining room and kitchen/support spaces, and second, different types of operations have different requirements. Space needs depend on:

❏ The number of items on the menu

❏ The number of different forms of final preparation required by the menu items (e.g., fry, sauté, steam)

❏ The use of convenience foods versus scratch cookery

❏ The complexity of the preparation required (e.g., fast food versus the cuisine found in expensive table service restaurants)

❏ The number of foodservice functions supported by a single kitchen, which may include banquet service, coffee shop service, and main dining room foodservice

Although there are rules of thumb regarding the size of the preparation areas relative to the size of the dining areas—such as 60 percent dining and 40 percent kitchen—such recommendations fail to take into account many important factors. On one hand, where the menu is simple, the kitchen might be only 25 or 30 percent of the size of the dining area. On the other hand, a restaurant with a complex menu and significant take-out business might need a kitchen as large as or larger than the dining area.

A comparison of kitchen sizes and dining room capacity can be made from Figure 4.11, which indicates the range of space requirements in different types of food facilities.

Because of the extreme variability in space needs, the owner or manager should look to the design consultant for professional advice before deciding on the amount of space to allot to the food production area.

The equipment in the final preparation areas of the kitchen is determined by the production requirements of the various menu items. Final

Type of Food Operation	Meals per Day	Kitchen Size Square Feet (Square Meters)	Dining Room Size Square Feet (Square Meters)
Restaurant, table service, 100 seats	1,000	1,400 (130.20)	1,300 (120.90)
Restaurant, table service, 175 seats	1,800	2,625 (244.13)	2,000 (186.00)
Country club, 200 seats	600	3,400 (316.20)	1,288 (119.78)
Hospital, cafeteria, and 200-bed tray service	1,400	2,250 (209.25)	2,300 (213.90)
College cafeteria, 350 seats	2,400	4,200 (390.60)	1,500 (139.50)
University cafeteria and catering department	4,000	5,625 (523.13)	2,530 (235.29)
Coffee shop, 100 seats	800	1,225 (113.96)	850 (79.05)

Figure 4.11. Kitchen Size in Relation to Dining Room Size.

preparation equipment often includes many of these items (see Chapters 6 and 7 for information on equipment):

❏ Convection, deck, and conveyor ovens
❏ Fryers
❏ Grills
❏ Tabletop steam-jacketed kettles
❏ Steamers
❏ Charbroilers
❏ Ranges with open burners or hot tops
❏ Reach-in refrigerators and freezers
❏ Worktables and "chef's tables"

Special Design Features

Since food production areas are continually subjected to heat as well as soiling from grease and spilled foods, damage-resistant, easy-to-clean surfaces are essential. Equipment surfaces of stainless steel are the most practical. Floors of quarry tile with Carborundum chips provide a slip-resistant, easy-to-clean surface. When made of ceramic tile or structural glazed tile, walls behind the equipment will withstand the combination of heat and grease. Ordinary epoxy paint on cement block is not recommended because the high heat will discolor the painted surface. To avoid sanitation problems, careful attention should be given to eliminating cracks and spaces around equipment.

Ventilation over final preparation equipment is a key consideration in the design of this area. The increased use in recent years of compensating hoods that bring a large percentage of makeup air (air that replaces exhausted air) into the hood itself does not eliminate the need for independent ventilation in the kitchen area. The kitchen must be well ventilated without complete dependence on the hood system to exhaust the air.

BAKERY

General Description of the Space

The bakery remains a popular production area in the foodservice facility in spite of the availability of a wide variety of fresh and frozen bakery products. The foodservice manager or owner must give the food facilities design consultant complete details concerning the volume of baking that is to be done on the premises.

A small or medium-size restaurant (under 150 seats) that plans to make only rolls, cobblers, sheet cakes from a mix, and a few specialty desserts may require only a small worktable, ingredient bins, a mixer, and access to an oven. However, a large institution planning to bake pies, cakes, rolls, loaf breads, Danish pastries, doughnuts, and extensive specialty products may require a very large bakery space and a sizable equipment budget. The long-range plans for the food facility need to be carefully considered. If the owner plans to have a bakery, these questions need to be addressed during the planning process:

- ❑ What products will be baked on the premises (versus bought from vendors)?
- ❑ What bakery products will be made from scratch or from mixes?
- ❑ What products will be baked from frozen or pre-prepared doughs?
- ❑ Will the products be delivered fresh from the bake shop to the service area, or will they be frozen and stored until needed?
- ❑ Will the bakery make products to be sold on a retail basis in addition to supplying all bakery products to the foodservice area?

Relationship to Other Areas

The bakery is one food production area that can be separate from the main activity of the foodservice facility. If sufficient space exists, however, the bakery should be near the main food production areas so that supervision is easier, equipment can be shared occasionally, and common storage spaces can be used. If the bakery is located at a remote point in the food facility, it should have easy access to receiving. Depending on size, it may need its own separate dry storage and walk-in refrigerator/freezer.

The movement of finished bakery products to the kitchen or service area should be accomplished in rolling closed cabinets. Ramping or the use of elevators should be planned if the bakery is not on the same level as the area where the product will be served or sold. The planning of central bakeries serving multiple dining facilities must include well-thought-out food transportation systems to ensure that the product is not damaged in transit and that the proper temperature (hot, cold, or room temperature) is maintained.

Amount of Space Needed

The information in Figure 4.12 can be used to make a rough estimate of the amount of space needed in a bakery, keeping in mind the many variables that can affect this determination.

Number of Seats in the Facility	Limited Baking Square Feet (Square Meters)	Extensive Baking Square Feet (Square Meters)
Under 50	40 (3.72)	80 (7.44)
50–100	100 (9.30)	150 (13.95)
100–175	250 (23.25)	400 (37.20)
175–250	300 (27.90)	600 (55.80)
250–500	400 (37.20)	800 (74.40)
More than 500	600 (55.80)	1,400 (130.20)
*Storage not included.		

Figure 4.12. Bakery Size Guidelines*.

Special Design Features

The floors of most bakeries quickly become covered with flour and other dry ingredients that are used in large quantities in the baking process. The flour sticks to the floor of the work area, especially when the area becomes damp, and is difficult to remove at the end of the workday. The floor should be constructed of quarry tile or other smooth masonry material (marble, tile, or terrazzo) that will not be damaged by frequent scrubbing and occasional scraping.

The mechanical engineers will need to provide an air supply and exhaust for the bakery, usually in the form of simple oven vents. From 30 to 45 air changes per hour should be sufficient for this space, exclusive of the air ventilated by the oven exhaust.

EMPLOYEE LOCKER ROOM AND TOILET

General Description of the Space

The employee locker room and rest rooms are too often given minimal consideration by those who are involved in the total design of a food facility. These facilities deserve careful attention because they affect sanitation, security, and employee attitude. The space, if properly planned, can be clean, orderly, and have a bright appearance that sets the tone for management's expectations of cleanliness and orderliness in other areas of the building.

Relationship to Other Areas

The locker rooms and rest rooms can be designed together so that space is efficiently used and control over uniforms is maintained. The area can be remote from the main food production areas, but the entrance and exit to the space should be arranged so that employees can be observed as they move from the work area to the locker room. Locker rooms can create food and utensil control problems if they are located near exits or are in remote locations that are difficult to supervise. Many local codes do not allow employee rest rooms to open directly into food production spaces; thus they are often located off of service corridors and back dock areas. Many employees no longer change clothes when coming to and/or

Number of Employees*	Space Required Square Feet (Square Meters)
5 or under	60 (5.58)
5–10	100 (9.30)
10–20	150 (13.95)
20–40	225 (20.93)
40–75	250 (23.25)
75–100	350 (32.55)

*Number of employees refers to the peak number on duty at one time, not the total number of employees on the payroll.

Figure 4.13. Space Required for Employee Locker Room and Toilet.

leaving work, thus formal locker rooms are often not required. Space to secure personal items (small lockers) often suffices.

Amount of Space Needed

The space needed for a combined locker room and rest room area is estimated in Figure 4.13.

Space requirements for rest room facilities should be checked with local codes to be sure that they comply with requirements for the handicapped and for the minimum number of employee toilet facilities.

Special Design Features

An employee locker room and rest room area can easily be made too large, which encourages loitering. The purpose of the space is to provide a place for changing clothes, using the toilet, and washing the hands before reporting for work. It should not be used for coffee breaks, card games, eating, and so on. The design should include locker room benches, double-stacked lockers to save space, and, for the larger food facility, a linen control system for exchanging soiled uniforms for clean uniforms.

Foodservice managers often disagree whether an employee dining room or coffee area is necessary. Some managers feel that these employee rooms encourage long breaks and that employees should eat in the main dining room before the meal period for customers. Large hotels and food operations, however, usually provide an employee lounge.

SERVICE AREAS

General Description of the Space

There are almost as many different types of service areas as there are types of foodservice establishments. Each of these types of food operations has a different kind of service area, and the list is certainly not complete: fine-dining restaurant, snack bar, lunch counter, fast-food restaurant, diner, cafeteria, and delicatessen.

The service area and the type of service planned for a food facility will be among the first decisions made during the concept development phase of the design process. For a small table service restaurant, the service area might be very limited because only a pickup station at the hot- and cold-food areas in the kitchen and a server station in the dining room

Type of Operation	Type of Delivery System
Table service restaurant	Kitchen pickup station
Snack bar	Service counter direct to customer
Fast food	Service counter direct to customer
Cafeteria	Straight-line cafeteria
Delicatessen	Deli counter
Buffet	Buffet line
Scramble	Separate food stations
Food court	Separate food locations around a common dining area
Tray service (health care)	Cold and hot carts rolled to patient room or dining area

Figure 4.14. Type of Foodservice Operation and Typical Delivery System.

are needed. A large institutional food facility using the scramble form of cafeteria service may need extremely large service areas in the range of 2,000 to 3,000 square feet (186 to 279 sq m). The service area in a table service restaurant provides an efficient means for the food production staff to get the food to the service staff, while the service area in self-service food operations offers a means for the food production staff to get the food to the customer. In both of these circumstances the time that it takes for the food to be delivered to the customer is critical and obviously should be as short as possible. The method for accomplishing this task is often referred to as a food delivery system.

The simplest food delivery system may involve holding a short-order meal for a few moments under a quartz heater at the server pickup station. A complex food delivery system in a large hospital might involve numerous employees and hundreds of thousands of dollars' worth of equipment. Regardless of the size of the food operation or its method of service, the importance of planning an efficient food delivery system cannot be overemphasized. As an illustration of the typical delivery systems used in foodservice facilities, Figure 4.14 presents a partial list of several types of service areas.

Relationship to Other Areas

The most important connection of the service area is to the hot- and cold-food production part of the food services. A small distance between these two functional areas will provide a reduced labor cost and a higher-quality food product. Conversely, a long distance between these two areas will increase the cost of labor and equipment significantly and make it much more difficult to keep foods at the proper serving temperature. Service areas also have a primary relationship to these spaces in the food facility:

❑ Warewashing

❑ Dining room

❑ Private dining rooms

❑ Customer entrances and exits

❑ Cashiers or other control systems

Other facilities that must be accessible to service areas are:

❑ Storerooms
❑ Refrigeration
❑ Bakery
❑ Office areas
❑ Cleaning supplies

Amount of Space Needed

Variations in the size and type of foodservice facility make it extremely difficult to develop a standard space requirement. As a guideline to the foodservice planning team, several types of service areas are listed in Figure 4.15 together with a range of sizes.

The figures for service area space needed indicate that as the level of service changes from table service to self-service scramble or food court,[1] the amount of space needed increases dramatically. The scramble cafeteria or food court requires the greatest amount of space of any of the forms of service because of the need for good circulation within the space. It is assumed that the cost of constructing the service area will be more than offset by the potential volume of customers who can be served and by an increase in the speed of service. The scramble cafeteria or food court also allows a wide range of menu items to be merchandised to the customer.

Special Design Features

Figures 4.16 through 4.19 show typical service area design features of several common types of foodservice facilities: a table service restaurant with bar, a fast-food counter, a scramble/food court cafeteria, and a health care tray-makeup system.

DINING ROOMS

General Description of the Space

The architect and interior designer typically give the appearance of the dining space the highest priority.

Obviously, an environment that is pleasant for the guests and that lends itself to an enjoyable dining experience should be a goal in designing the facility. The ease of cleaning floors, walls, and furnishings as well as the potential for food spillage must also be considered. Coverings such as carpeting, for example, are popular in table service restaurants but are inappropriate for dining rooms with a higher risk of soil from spilled foods and debris. Other factors in dining room planning include:

❑ Heating, ventilation, and air-conditioning
❑ View

---

[1] The terms "scramble" and "food court" are often used interchangeably to refer to a large area in which customers freely circulate from one point of service to another. There is, however, a slight difference. Commercial "food courts" typically have a cash register at each point of service, whereas "scramble cafeterias" typically have central cashier stations where customers pay for everything on their trays.

Number of Seats	Meals per Day*	Service Area† Square Feet (Square Meters)
Under 50	300	75 (6.9)
50–100	500	100 (9.2)
100–175	750	140 (12.9)
175–250	1,000	160 (14.7)
250–500	1,600	175 (16.1)
More than 500	2,400	200 (18.4)

*Breakfast not included.

†Includes chef's pickup station (excluding range and aisle spaces) and a server station.

Figure 4.15a. Service Area Space Requirements for Table Service Restaurants–Limited Menu.

Number of Seats	Meals per Day*	Service Area† Square Feet (Square Meters)
Under 50	200	100 (9.2)
50–100	300	120 (11.0)
100–175	600	160 (14.7)
175–250	700	200 (18.4)
250–500	1,000	250 (23.0)
More than 500	1,500	300 (27.6)

*Breakfast not included.

†Includes server stations, pickup stations for hot and cold food, and separate beverage stations.

Figure 4.15b. Service Area Space Requirements for Luxury Table Service Restaurants–Extensive Menu.

Number of Seats	Meals per Day*	Service Area† Square Feet (Square Meters)
100–175	800	350 (32.2)
175–250		
One line	1,250	475 (43.7)
Two lines	1,500	900 (82.8)
250–500	2,000	1600 (147.2)
More than 500	5,000	2000 (184.0)

*Breakfast not included.

†Size of the cafeteria line and aisle space in front of and behind the line.

Figure 4.15c. Service Area Space Requirements for Straight-Line Cafeterias.

Number of Seats	Meals per Day*	Service Area† Square Feet (Square Meters)
175–250	1,500	1,800 (165.6)
250–350	1,800	2,000 (184.0)
350–500	2,250	2,400 (220.8)
More than 500	5,000	3,000 (276.0)

*Breakfast not included.

†The service area of the scramble, including interior circulation space. Condiment and beverage stations located outside of the service area are not included.

Figure 4.15d. Service Area Space Requirements for Scramble or Food Court Cafeterias.

Figure 4.16. Kitchen and Bar for a Table Service Restaurant.

- ❑ Sound control
- ❑ Seating arrangement
- ❑ Server stations
- ❑ Sanitation
- ❑ Lighting
- ❑ Cashier or other control systems

The owner or manager of a food facility is encouraged to visit a variety of food operations during the early planning stage of a project and to consult some of the illustrated trade journals and reference volumes that are available. Gaining familiarity with the design of a variety of dining room interiors will aid in the selection of mood, color, texture, lighting, and other interior features.

Figure 4.17. Service Area Design for Fast-Food Concept.

Figure 4.18. Scramble Cafeteria.

ITEM K-07, HOT FOOD TABLE TO MOVE TO THIS LOCATION.

ITEM	QUAN	DESCRIPTION
K-01	1	TRAY CONVEYOR
K-02	1	PELLET HEATER (EXISTING)
K-03	1	TRAY DISPENSER
K-04	1	STARTER STATION
K-05	1	DISH DISPENSER
K-06	2	REFRIGERATOR
K-07	2	HOT FOOD TABLE
K-08	2	PLATE DISPENSER
K-09	1	HOT FOOD TABLE
K-10	1	TOASTER TABLE
K-11	1	TOASTER (EXISTING)
K-12	1	ICE CREAM DISPENSER
K-13	1	COFFEE STAND
K-14	1	COFFEE URN (EXISTING)
K-15	1	MILK/JUICE DISPENSER
K-16	1	LID RACK (EXISTING)

Figure 4.19. Health Care Tray-Makeup Design.

As the number of meals consumed at foodservice chain facilities and franchise operations has grown, hotel corporations, restaurant chains, and fast-food companies have become more sophisticated in their interior design plans. The restaurant owner who succumbs to the temptation of do-it-yourself decorating or who spends insufficient funds to create an attractive dining room will lose business to the more attractive and sophisticated chain operations. Similarly, the institutional cafeteria owner or manager who installs vinyl tile floors and institutional-looking chairs and tables will experience a loss of customers to dining facilities that offer a more pleasant setting.

Relationship to Other Areas

The dining room must be directly connected to service areas and to the kitchen. Remote dining rooms, such as hotel banqueting rooms or private meeting rooms that are located away from the kitchen, may require special equipment for food delivery. One solution for the remote banquet dining room is the use of specially designed service kitchens.

Vertical space relationships can be solved in part by the use of elevators or dumbwaiters. In one London eating establishment, an entire building of banquet rooms is serviced by a bank of dumbwaiters from a central kitchen on the first floor. The building is seven stories high, and the communication system is controlled by a series of hollow pipes that permit the staff to shout their needs back and forth through the pipes. The system is over 100 years old and continues to operate smoothly without the need for an electronic speaker. In spite of the success of this English banqueting hall, dumbwaiters are usually not a good solution for the vertical movement of food. Dumbwaiters do not transport people, and they must be attended by two persons. They are also difficult to clean, can cause excessive breakage of dishes, and create communication problems. Budget and space considerations permitting, service elevators are much preferred to dumbwaiters.

Amount of Space Needed

The proper size of the dining room can be calculated once it is decided how many customers the food facility will seat. Determining the proper number of seats is easy in an institutional foodservice operation if the number of persons to be fed is known. For a restaurant or commercial cafeteria project, however, where the number of customers is uncertain, determining the number of seats needed can be quite difficult. Forecasting the volume of business that might be anticipated for a commercial restaurant is often no more than an educated guess. In other instances, the number of seats planned into a restaurant is decided based on the available space or funds. The number of seats to be included in the design is a basic investment question and should be given careful consideration. Seating capacity affects dining room size, kitchen size, rest room capacities, parking lot size, and many other features of the building.

The number of persons who can be accommodated during a meal period is determined by the space occupied by the chairs and tables and by the seat turnover rate. Each type of service requires a different amount of space for tables and chairs. For instance, a snack bar that uses disposable ware can be designed with very small tables and utilitarian chairs without arms. However, a luxury table service restaurant would require a large dining room table with sufficient space for flowers, condiments, a variety of crystal glasses, and side dishes to accompany the main course. Chairs in luxury restaurants are often large because they are padded and have arms. Space in the aisles of such a restaurant needs to be sufficient to accommodate ice buckets for wine and the waiter's tray stand. The space requirements listed in Figure 4.20 are generally accepted industry standards for the various forms of service.

The amount of space needed in a dining area is also influenced by the number of seats turned over per hour. For example, in a luxurious restaurant, the seats may turn over once every two hours, whereas a snack bar or fast-food restaurant may turn over seats three times per hour. The estimates of seat turnover for different segments of the foodservice industry in Figure 4.21 should be used as a guide.

A typical calculation to determine the size of a dining area and support service area for a restaurant serving a moderately priced menu with 200 seats follows.

❏ Determine the size of the support area from the chart. A 200-seat restaurant would need 200 square feet (18.6 sq m) of server station space.

❏ Determine the size of the dining room. Multiply 200 seats by 13 square feet per chair, which equals 2,600 square feet (1.2 sq m per chair, equaling 240 sq m).

Form of Service	Square Feet (Square Meters) Service Area* per 100 Seats	Square Feet (Square Meters)† per Chair
Table service, moderate price	100 (9.3) of server station	12–14 (1.1–1.3)
Table service, high price	150 (13.9) of server station	13–16 (1.2–1.5)
Table service, luxury	200(18.6) of server station	16–20 (1.5–1.9)
Cafeteria service	500 (46.5) of straight-line cafeteria	12–14 (1.1–1.3)
Scramble cafeteria	600 (55.7) of servery	12–14 (1.1–1.3)
Booth service	100 (9.3) of server station	12–14 (1.1–1.3)
Banquet (private dining)	25 (2.3) of storage and service area	10–12 (0.93–1.1)
Fast food	50 (4.7) of counter area	9–11 (0.84–1.0)

*Service area is separate, not a part of the dining room.

†Square feet per chair (square meters per chair) includes space for aisles and general circulation.

Figure 4.20. Dining Area Space Requirements.

❑ Calculate the number of persons who could be served in one hour in this restaurant. Multiplying 200 seats by 1.5 turns equals 300 persons per hour.

In this example, the restaurant would make maximum use of the server station by keeping in the station as many of the accompaniments to the meal as possible. For instance, the station might contain:

❑ Silverware
❑ Linen (napkins)
❑ Condiments
❑ Coffee
❑ Soft drinks
❑ Ice
❑ Glasses
❑ Trash container
❑ Crackers

Form of Service	Seat Turnover
Table service, moderate price	1.0–2.0
Table service, high price	0.75–1.0
Table service, luxury	0.5–0.75
Cafeteria service	2.2–3.0
Counter service	2.0–3.0
Booth service	2.0–3.0
Fast food	2.5–3.5

Figure 4.21. Table Turnover Rates for Selected Forms of Service.

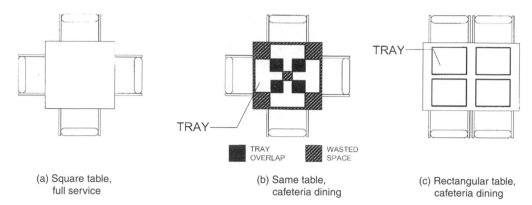

Figure 4.22. Saving Space in a Cafeteria or Food Court through Properly Designed Dining Tables.

(a) Square table, full service

(b) Same table, cafeteria dining

(c) Rectangular table, cafeteria dining

❑ Cups and saucers

❑ Bread

❑ Butter

❑ Cream

❑ Hot tea

❑ Cold tea

❑ Milk

❑ Point-of-sale terminal

❑ Soup

After determining the type of service, the amount of support space needed, and the seat turnover, the final consideration is the shape and size of the table. A dining room table in a fine restaurant might be shaped as shown in Figure 4.22a. This shape permits the service personnel to place side dishes, wineglasses, condiments, and other accompaniments to the meal on the table without crowding. This same shape for a cafeteria dining room would waste space and make it impossible for four people to place rectangular cafeteria trays on the table—note the black areas indicating where trays would overlap in Figure 4.10b. The wasted space in the example could be quite significant for a large cafeteria dining room. An estimate for a 400-seat cafeteria would be 4 square feet (0.37 sq m) of wasted space per table times 100 tables, or 400 square feet (37 sq m). The extra amount spent in construction for this wasted space, if the cost was $200 a square foot ($2,153 a sq m), would come to $80,000. One solution to the problem is to choose a rectangular table on which four trays fit properly, arranged so that a natural aisle is created on the two short sides of the table, as shown in Figure 4.22c.

Special Design Features

Two popular dining room styles that have been developed as alternatives to traditional table arrangements are fast-food or snack bar seating and booth seating.

FAST-FOOD OR SNACK BAR SEATING

The special design features developed by the fast-food industry can be incorporated into any food operation in which space efficiency, ease of

Figure 4.23. Booth Seating.

cleaning, and resistance to soiling is desirable. In these dining areas, table legs have been largely eliminated and seats are suspended from a table pedestal. The ease of sweeping and mopping the floors that this feature permits is important because of the large amount of food spillage and paper debris common in fast-food facilities. Another distinctive feature is the bevel or space that is often designed into the tabletop to encourage the sharing of the table with strangers. The division creates the impression of two tables when in fact there is only one.

BOOTH SEATING

The use of booths in foodservice establishments, which creates a visual break from traditional seating, is popular because of the sense of privacy that it provides. Early American and Victorian decor often featured booths with extremely high backs and side panels that almost completely enclosed the diners. Although booths are more expensive than traditional chairs and tables, they are extremely space-efficient; their higher cost is more than offset by a reduction in the size of the dining room. Space efficiency results from adjoining booths being placed back to back. Figure 4.23 illustrates a typical booth arrangement with standard dimensions.

BAR

The bar provides beverage service and bar and table seating for customers. Bars are of two basic types: customer bars and service bars. Customer bars provide beverage service to customers seated at the bar as well as to servers who take drinks to tables, whereas service bars are designed only for servers to pick up drinks. The major components of the bar space include the bar and bar equipment, the bar support area, and seating.

General Description of the Space

BAR AND BAR EQUIPMENT

A bar consists of beverage service equipment that is enclosed in attractive finishes, such as wood, brass, leather, decorative laminates, stone, and/or glass. The customer section of the bar provides high seating and a surface for beverage service. The employee's (bartender's) side of the bar provides:

- ❏ Display and storage space for bottled spirits
- ❏ Refrigerated storage for bottled beers, wines, specialty soft drinks, and mixes
- ❏ Dispensers for tap beer and mixers
- ❏ Glass storage and glass washing
- ❏ Ice storage and dispensing
- ❏ Blenders for specialty drinks
- ❏ Coffee making and dispensing
- ❏ Sinks
- ❏ Cash registers/point-of-sale terminals

The back bar, or equipment behind the bartender, may also provide for some of the functions just listed. Bars traditionally are built in two separate steps by specialists. The bar equipment is first set in place. Then the bar is built around the equipment and finished by the bar builder or contractor to give it its distinctive features and appearance.

BAR SUPPORT AREA

The bar support area provides storage for beverages. Spirits are stored in a locked storage room. Fine wines are stored horizontally in bins in a cool room (cellar); jug wines may be stored on storage shelves. Beer kegs and bottled or canned beers that need refrigeration may be stored in locked walk-in refrigerators. Beer taps (dispensers) may be mounted directly on a refrigerated unit in which the keg is placed once tapped. Or beer taps may be connected through a system of cooled tubes to a remote system located in the bar support area. Mix dispensers usually are supported by bag-in-a-box systems located in bar support areas. Carbon dioxide for mixes and soft drinks may be provided in interchangeable tanks or, in larger operations, by a single stationary tank that is filled directly from a supply truck. Ice makers also are located in the bar support area.

SEATING

Customer seating at the bar itself usually takes the form of stools or high chairs. Seating in the bar area also may be at tables where snacks or food can be served, or at small cocktail tables. Service bars, designed only for servers, do not have seating for customers.

Relationship to Other Areas

When the bar is used as a waiting area for guests who will be dining, it should be located adjacent to the reception area. If the bar is a destination in itself, it should be located near the main entrance. If customers in the bar can order food, then the bar should be located adjacent to the final preparation area of the kitchen. The bar support area should be located adjacent to the bar, be easily secured, and be accessible from the receiving area.

The amount of space needed for the bar area is a combination of the space needed for the bar itself, the bar support area, and the seating areas to be located in the bar. A bar in a restaurant is often designed as a holding area so that diners have a place to sit while waiting for a table. Designing this holding area so that it can generate revenue (and profit) is highly desirable. Many restaurateurs and investors consider the combination of a cocktail lounge and restaurant to be the most profitable arrangement. In this combination, the emphasis is on the food as well as the marketing of before-dinner cocktails, wine with dinner, and after-dinner cordials.

BAR

The space required for the bar itself is determined by the number of customers who need to be accommodated by the bar. Each seat at the bar requires between 28 and 36 inches (711 and 914 millimeters [mm]) of linear distance, depending on the actual width of the seats. The depth of the bar is dictated by the seating space (24 to 30 inches [in]/610 to 762 mm), the bar and underbar equipment (48 to 56 in/1220 to 1422 mm), the aisle (42 to 54 in/1067 to 1372 mm), and the back bar (30 to 36 in/762 to 914 mm). Long bars often are configured in rectangular patterns to minimize the number of steps the bartender has to take.

BAR SUPPORT AREA

The space required by the bar support area is a function of the complexity of the beverage menu. Bars with a full complement of spirits, multiple beers on tap, and a collection of fine wines that need to be cellared require substantially more space than a bar that serves primarily beer and inexpensive wines.

SEATING

Additional seating (beyond that provided at the bar) will require between 10 square feet (0.93 sq m) per person (at small cocktail tables) and 15 square feet (1.4 sq m) per person.

Figure 4.24 provides space estimates for several kinds of bars. These data are based on the assumption that the bar is an integral part of a restaurant operation. A bar in a cocktail lounge, brew pub, or other operation dedicated primarily to beverage service is likely to have a large bar. The data do not reflect an industry standard but do represent commonsense relationships.

The visual characteristics of the bar are important in creating an atmosphere that supports the owner's concept for the facility. The guidelines suggested earlier for dining areas apply to bar seating as well.

From the functional perspective, the area behind the bar needs to be designed for ease of cleaning and sanitation, especially beneath equipment.

Restaurant Dining Room Size		Suggested Cocktail Lounge and Bar Size*			
				Bar size†	
Seats	Square Feet (Meters)	Seats	Square Feet (Meters)	Length Feet (Meters)	Square Feet (Meters)
50	750 (69.7)	15	150 (13.9)	10 (3.0)	120 (11.1)
80	1,200 (111.5)	20	200 (18.6)	15 (4.6)	180 (16.7)
100	1,500 (139.4)	30	300 (27.9)	20 (6.1)	240 (22.3)
140	2,100 (195.0)	40	400 (37.2)	30 (9.1)	360 (33.4)
180	2,700 (250.8)	50	500 (46.5)	35 (10.7)	420 (39.0)
200	3,000 (278.7)	60	600 (55.7)	40 (12.2)	480 (44.6)

*A standard of 10 square feet (0.93 sq. meters) per seat (including bar stools) is used for this calculation.
† A bar with a 3′ 6″ (1.1 m) back bar, 4′ 0″ (1.2 m) aisle, and 4′ 6″ (1.4 m) front bar would have a total depth of 12′ (3.7 m). The length of the bar multiplied by 12′ (3.7 m) thus determines the total square footage.

Figure 4.24. Space Requirements for Bars in Restaurants.

Control of inventory and cash is an important issue with respect to bars. Secure storage of spirits, wines, and beer in the bar support area is crucial. The bar itself needs to be designed so that management can readily observe the activities of bartenders—particularly with respect to cash handling.

WAREWASHING

General Description of the Space

The one word that best describes the environment in the warewashing area is *wet*. With the exception of the hot-food preparation area, warewashing equipment and surrounding areas receive more wear and abuse than any other section of the food facility. Water on the floor, spilled food, steam and high humidity, and the striking of carts and utensils against the walls and equipment are often a common part of the warewashing environment. Food facilities designers, architects, and engineers should make every effort to eliminate the wet conditions while recognizing that the floor, walls, and ceiling must be constructed to withstand a large amount of moisture.

Health department standards for the equipment and interior of warewashing rooms have become increasingly stringent because of the potential for spreading food-borne diseases. In designing the warewashing area so that it is easy to sanitize and will withstand the wet conditions, the use of slip-resistant quarry tile floors, ceramic or structural glazed tile walls, and a moisture-resistant acoustic ceiling is recommended.

Relationship to Other Areas

The most important relationship of the warewashing space is to the dining room. The design should facilitate the movement of soiled dishes from the dining room to the warewashing area. In many institutions where self-busing of dishes is encouraged, the warewashing space must be located adjacent to the exit from the dining room. Without this convenient feature, customers are unlikely to cooperate in busing their own dishes. The primary problem with the close proximity of warewashing to the dining area is the noisiness of the former. Conveyor belts for soiled dishes, screening with masonry walls, or the use of double sets of doors to isolate the warewashing area are all common solutions to the noise problem.

Warewashing must also have a close working relationship with the main kitchen, especially if pots, pans, and utensils are cleaned in the warewashing area. The warewashing room may be designed with three-compartment pot sinks or potwashing machines, or it may be the practice of management to have most small and medium-size utensils washed by the standard dish machine. If pots and utensils are to be washed in this area, the primary food production spaces and the warewashing unit should be reasonably close.

Amount of Space Needed

Warewashing machine ratings are usually based on the number of standard 20-by-20-inch racks or the number of dishes per hour that can be processed through the machine. Since neither the machine nor the machine operator can operate at 100 percent efficiency, an efficiency factor of 70 percent is normally used. Figure 4.25 provides a range of square footage requirements for several different styles of dishwashing systems. The data were determined under the assumption that a three-compartment pot sink with drain boards is included in the warewashing space.

Special Design Features

Nowhere in the design of a foodservice facility is an understanding of time and motion in the work environment more important than in warewashing. A dishwasher usually works in a restricted area with a minimum amount of walking. Good warewashing design must include a study of each move that the dishwasher makes so that the dishes can be handled in the most efficient means possible. The basic steps that are normally taken in washing dishes are:

- ❑ Separation of dishes from paper, trays, and so on
- ❑ Scraping (prerinsing may be done in combination with this step)
- ❑ Stacking or accumulating
- ❑ Racking

Type of Dish System	Dishes per Hour	Square Feet (Square Meters)
Single-tank dishwasher	1,500	250 (23.3)
Single-tank conveyor	4,000	400 (37.2)
Two-tank conveyor	6,000	500 (46.5)
Flight-type conveyor	12,000	700 (65.1)

*Figures given include space for dish carts, empty racks, and potwashing. The size of the space will vary significantly on the basis of the layout of the soiled- and clean-dish tables. For instance, a single-tank dishwasher located along a wall in a small restaurant might only occupy 125 square feet (11.6 sq m).

Figure 4.25. Warewashing Area Space Requirements*.

❏ Prerinsing (if not done earlier)

❏ Washing

❏ Air drying

❏ Removing clean dishes

The design principle of simplicity discussed earlier is important to keep in mind when designing warewashing systems. Elaborate conveyor and bridge systems for soiled-dish tables often add to the clutter and expense of the warewashing area and create barriers that are difficult to move around. At the other extreme, designs that do not provide sufficient space for soiled-dish accumulation or warewashing rooms that have insufficient cart storage space for clean dishes are to be avoided.

Sound-absorbing materials on the ceiling, a high level of lighting (80 to 100 foot-candles), and the use of bright colors on the walls and ceiling are desirable design features. One frequent mistake in the engineering of warewashing areas is to provide inadequate circulation of air. The vents and small hoods required by the health department on dish machines often are not sufficient for the removal of moist air from the space. Supply and exhaust equipment that will accomplish 60 air changes per hour is recommended.

SUMMARY

A general description of the primary spaces of a foodservice facility has been included to provide the food facilities planner with basic guidelines concerning the spaces needed. Each of the spaces should work in harmony with other functional areas so that a high level of efficiency is achieved. The penalty for ignoring space relationships is an increase in labor and other operating costs. Food facilities owners and managers are encouraged to visit existing operations to familiarize themselves with a variety of design alternatives and to see how others have dealt with spatial relationships.

The amount of space needed for each area will vary. Some spaces may be squeezed and others made larger, depending on the special circumstances of the design or the desires of the owner or manager. The special design features presented for each of the spaces reflect solutions to problems that are frequently encountered in the process of planning and designing foodservice operations.

KEY TERMS

Programming	Delivery system
Tray makeup	Pre-preparation
Flight-type dishwasher	Materials handling

1. What data are needed before the design of a foodservice begins?
2. Name the primary determining factors needed in designing a receiving area.
3. What are the four categories of storage needed in all foodservice facilities?
4. Some refrigeration is needed in the receiving area, and some is needed in the kitchen. What type of refrigeration is needed in these two areas? Are there exceptions to your answer?
5. Draw a simple flow chart of people and materials, starting with receiving and ending with the dining room.
6. How can you increase aisle space in the dining room by careful design of the dining table?
7. Eighteen items that could be included in a dining room service station are listed. Name 10 of them.

DISCUSSION QUESTION

A typical foodservice facility has many different storage needs. Contemporary materials and packaging have influenced the need for storage. Discuss the different types of storage and suggest methods of reducing the storage space needs in each area of the facility based on the new types of packaging of both foods and materials.

CHAPTER 5

Equipment Layout

THIS CHAPTER

☑ Describes the desirable relationships between the component parts of a work area in a food facility

☑ Develops the methods for analyzing a layout and lists the features that should be included in each work area

☑ Illustrates typical layouts for each functional area of a foodservice operation

EFFECTIVE LAYOUT

Layout is the arrangement of equipment to create efficient, safe, and ergonomically correct work areas. As was discussed in Chapter 3, design focuses on the arrangement of functional areas in the entire facility, whereas layout focuses on the way equipment is placed within individual work spaces. When work areas are logically arranged according to the principles of good design and the equipment is carefully selected to meet the specific criteria of the operation, the space will yield a high level of efficiency and employee productivity. Effective layout thus depends on access to raw materials, attention to the flow of food and personnel in the production process, relationships to other departments, access to utensils and equipment, and ease of cleaning and sanitation.

Access to Raw Materials

In a typical factory setting, materials move down an assembly line past each employee's workstation. This is an ideal arrangement because the worker is not required to walk great distances, the raw materials are readily available, and the speed of the process (productivity) can be established by management. Often raw materials or parts are delivered to the factory at several points along the assembly line to eliminate double handling. The flow of materials in a factory assembly-line process is illustrated in Figure 5.1.

The idea of applying the factory assembly-line model to a foodservice operation has not had wide acceptance except in hospitals, where a conveyor belt is often used to move trays down an assembly line as food

Figure 5.1. Assembly-line Model.

items are added. Although a conveyor belt would have limited usefulness for other types of foodservice facilities, the principles underlying the factory layout can be adapted to the needs of any foodservice design.

Raw or unprocessed materials in a foodservice operation are usually stored in walk-in refrigerators and freezers or in the dry-goods storeroom. The materials for the final assembly of the meal are usually found in or on:

❑ Walk-in refrigerators
❑ Reach-in refrigerators
❑ Dish storage cabinets or carts
❑ Steam tables
❑ Slicing machines
❑ Food-holding cabinets
❑ Portable food racks
❑ Beverage containers and dispensers
❑ Utility or receiving carts

The raw materials must be available to each work area so that the worker has to take a minimum number of steps to obtain the ingredients, process them, and transfer them to the next work area or to storage.

Figure 5.2 illustrates a cold-food preparation area designed to provide access to raw materials. This example is taken from a large facility that often prepares food for banquets. A walk-in cooler has been located adjacent to the preparation area, where it provides convenient access to the raw ingredients needed for cold food (salad and dessert) preparation. Notice that the walk-in refrigerator is available for storage of both raw ingredients and the finished product, thus serving a dual purpose. Designers frequently make the mistake of placing the walk-in refrigerators in a row, with little consideration of the workers' need for easy access to raw materials. Access doors in the side wall of the cooler are far more convenient for employees than if they have to walk around to the front entrance of the cooler. When salads are prepared in this area, employees remove the raw ingredients from the cooler; clean, cut, and chop them as needed; and

Figure 5.2. Access to Raw Materials.

assemble them on individual plates set on sheet pans. The plated salads then are covered with food wrap and set on racks in the cooler. When the time has come for the salads to be served, the racks are removed and taken to the banquet staging area, and the salads are brought to the guests.

Figure 5.3 illustrates how access to raw materials is supported in the layout of a final preparation area. A single-compartment reach-in freezer is located to the right of the fryers so that frozen french fries can easily be reached. To the left of the fryers is a grill, next to which is a single-compartment refrigerator where hamburger patties, chicken breasts, and other grill items are stored.

Convenient access to raw materials is especially important in the final preparation area. Without refrigerated storage at hand, the cooks are likely to bring an entire pan of steaks, seafood, or poultry and set it somewhere on the range section to save them from having to make multiple trips. The temperature of the food in the pan, exposed to the heat of the cooking

Figure 5.3. Access to Raw Materials in Final Preparation.

equipment, soon rises into the danger zone, increasing the risk of food poisoning.

Flow

In discussing the design sequence (Chapter 3), it was stressed that the layout of each part of the food operation should follow a logical progression. If the raw ingredients and/or the finished parts of the meal are arranged in the order in which they will be used (as on a factory assembly line; see Figure 5.1), the food operation is likely to be more efficient.

The flow relationship in each work area is most efficient if the movement is in a straight line or L shape. If workers are frequently required to move materials across an aisle or to work around another person, inefficiency and worker fatigue will result.

Relationship to Other Departments

Each part of a foodservice operation is closely related to the other parts. In design, the word "system" is often used to describe a functional part of the facility—a regularly interacting group of elements that form a whole. Dishwashing, for example, is described as a system, because each part of the process relates to every other part (see Figure 5.4). At the same time, dishwashing relates to other functions or systems within the facility. For instance, in a cafeteria, the dishes might be moved in small dish carts from the dishwashing area to the cafeteria line. A good layout in the cafeteria area would permit the dish carts to roll under the steam tables, for use by the person who is dishing up the food. This feature of the service

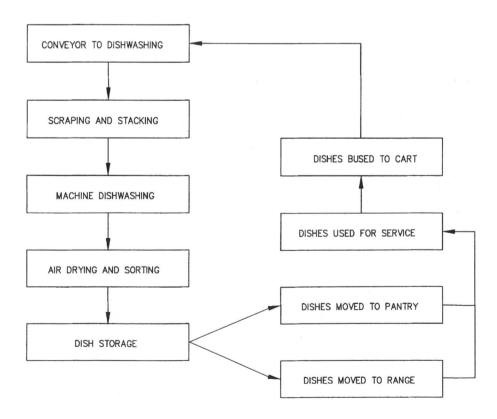

Figure 5.4. Dishwashing Process Flow.

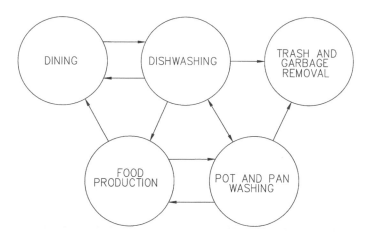

Figure 5.5. Relationship of Dishwashing to Other Functions.

system eliminates double handling of dishes and decreases labor and dish breakage.

The layout of one department must be carefully considered to make sure that it works well with other departments. A helpful tool in understanding how the departments interact is the bubble diagram (Figure 2.2) that illustrates departmental relationships. The interaction of dishwashing to other departments is illustrated in Figure 5.5. Notice in the illustration that some functions have simple relationships with one or two other activities, while others have complex relationships with three or more departments.

Certain pieces of equipment are needed in each work area of a food facility. For instance, all food preparation and service areas should have a sink with hot and cold water and a utensil storage area. Pieces of equipment that are used infrequently or are too expensive to duplicate, or both, cannot be located in each work area. A slicing machine, for example, is often placed on a portable stand so that it can easily be moved from one department to another to avoid unnecessary duplication. A mixer may be needed by the salad preparation workers for two hours a day and for three hours per day by the cooks in hot-food preparation. A single mixer could be located between the two departments, or each department could have its own high-speed food processor, since it is a small, inexpensive item.

Another factor that needs to be considered in the location of equipment is the availability of cart-parking space, which is often a problem in small kitchens. Two parking areas are needed in the food production area: a place to temporarily place carts containing raw ingredients and space for carts holding the finished product. A space 3 feet (0.91 meter [m]) deep by 4 feet (1.22 m) wide will accommodate most portable carts. Parking spaces in a typical salad preparation area are shown in Figure 5.6.

Often the difference between an excellent layout and a mediocre one is the amount of attention given to detail in each work area. A checklist of utensil storage criteria (see Figure 5.7) can be used to determine whether the layout of a food facility provides adequate working storage and access to utensils.

Access to Utensils and Equipment

PARKING SPACES

Figure 5.6. Spaces for Parking Partially Finished Products during Preparations.

Ease of Cleaning and Sanitation

Careful attention to the details of equipment layout is necessary to create work areas that are easily cleaned and sanitized. Ease of cleaning and sanitation is a function of several factors. In manufactured equipment, ease of sanitation results from:

❏ Use of easily cleaned materials, such as stainless steel

❏ Sealed food-contact compartments, so that food debris cannot fall into the inner workings of the equipment

> ❏ **Utensil drawer in each worktable**
> ❏ **Utensil drawer for each employee, or one drawer for each 4 linear feet (1.22 m) of worktable**
> ❏ **Utensil drawers in stacks of three for large workstations**
> ❏ **Overhead utensil racks (ceiling-hung) in hot-food and cold-food preparation areas**
> ❏ **Hooks or racks in immediate vicinity of steam-jacketed kettles for paddles or wire whips**
> ❏ **Shelving under each worktable or drain board for storage of larger utensils**
> ❏ **Wall-hung overshelf above each table that is against a wall**
> ❏ **Racks for mixer parts and bowls**
> ❏ **Large racks in bakery, hot-food preparation, and salad preparation areas for sheet pans, baking pans, and other large utensils**
> ❏ **Special storage racks for food processor blades and parts (these parts are easily damaged, and it is dangerous to store them in utensil drawers)**
> ❏ **Large rack or special storage room for catering supplies (chafing dishes, punch bowls, silver trays, etc.)**
> ❏ **Knife rack in each preparation area**

Figure 5.7. Working Storage and Utensil Checklist.

❑ Construction without ledges, crevasses, joints, and other areas that trap food debris and breed bacteria

❑ Simple disassembly and reassembly on equipment that has to be broken down for cleaning and sanitizing (e.g., slicers)

❑ Ready access to catch pans for grease and food debris (e.g., on griddles)

❑ Removable components that can be run through the dish machine, such as grease extractor cartridges in the hood system

❑ Mounting on 6-inch- (15-centimeter-) high legs or casters so that workers can clean under the equipment

❑ Enclosed and sealed controls that cannot be damaged by water in the cleaning and sanitizing process

Fabricated equipment, such as worktables and dish tables, also should be designed for ease of cleaning and sanitation. Important design features include:

❑ *Stainless-steel understructure.* Tables that are constructed with painted metal legs are less expensive than their stainless-steel competitors. However, painted legs have to be sanded and repainted regularly. Operators pay the small price difference of stainless-steel understructure many times over when employees have to sand and repaint the worktable legs every three years.

❑ *Backsplashes.* Where tables meet walls, stainless-steel backsplashes rising 10 inches (254 [mm]) above worktables to 16 inches (406 mm) above dish tables and pot sinks make work areas easy to clean (see Figure 5.8).

❑ *Coved radius corners.* Wherever food contact surfaces make 90-degree corners or edges, a cove with a minimum radius of ³/₄ inch (20 mm) allows thorough cleaning and sanitizing. Otherwise, food debris will become trapped in a sharp corner and grow bacteria. On sink bowls and the edges of dish tables, the radius often is as much as 1¹/₂ inches (38 mm). Figure 5.9 shows examples of the edge profiles used in the construction of dish tables and worktables.

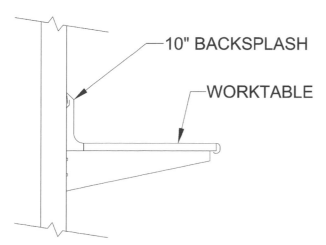

10" BACKSPLASH

WORKTABLE

Figure 5.8. Backsplash on Wall-Hung Worktable.

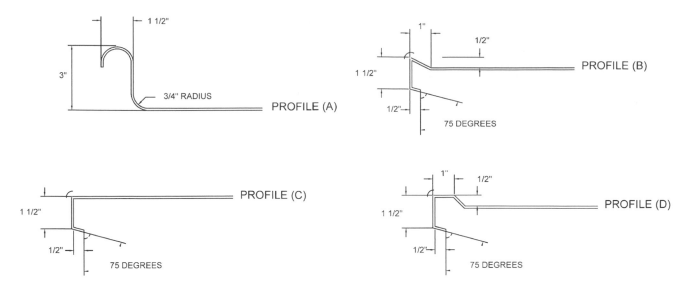

Figure 5.9. Edge Profiles for Stainless-Steel Tables and Countertops.

❏ *Spreaders under fabricated tables.* Worktables are often constructed with a solid lower shelf for storage. However, solid shelves collect dust, dirt, and food debris, and are often overlooked during the cleaning and sanitizing of the kitchen. A more sanitary solution is to design worktables with spreaders (stainless-steel tubes) running lengthwise on 6-inch (152-mm) centers. Large pots and pans can be stored readily on spreaders, but the open design forces food debris, dirt, and dust to fall to the floor, where they are more likely to be mopped up. Figure 5.10 illustrates a worktable with spreaders rather than a solid undershelf.

Ease of cleaning and sanitation also is affected by the location of utility connections, discussed in the next section.

Figure 5.10. Worktable with Spreaders.

PHYSICAL CHARACTERISTICS OF EQUIPMENT LAYOUT

The ability to assess a layout comes from experience as a food facility designer or from working for many years in a food operation. A layout can be planned in part on the basis of space allocation and desirable layout relationships, as already discussed in this text. Other characteristics in equipment layout are desirable if an efficient overall design is to be achieved. These characteristics are:

❏ Configuration (shape) of the layout

❏ Method for mounting the equipment

❏ Utility connection methods

Configuration of the Layout

The three most common shapes for work area layout are the straight line, the L, and the U. Each shape has advantages and disadvantages, but the straight line is usually considered the best arrangement from a time-and-motion-efficiency standpoint. Although warewashing layouts have been designed using every imaginable shape, more elaborate (and expensive) layouts tend to be inefficient. A straight-line layout, in which the dishes are unloaded, scraped, stacked, and placed directly into the dish machine, is usually the most efficient one. An example of such a layout is illustrated in Figure 5.11. The disadvantage of this layout for a high-volume food operation would be the limited dish drop-off area. It might, therefore, be desirable to create an L in this instance, as shown in Figure 5.12.

These and similar layouts, each with its particular advantages, can be used for food preparation areas. Several examples are shown in

Figure 5.11. Straight-Line Dishwashing Layout.

Figure 5.12. L-Shape Dish Drop.

Figure 5.13. Work Area Layouts.

Figure 5.13. The L-shape arrangement uses a limited amount of space and provides a very convenient work surface. This arrangement also creates a workstation that is out of the traffic aisle, which is a desirable feature if other equipment is likely to be parked in the work area. The U-shape layout offers a large amount of table surface area, but walking in and out of the U may add many steps to the employee's workday. The parallel and back-to-back parallel tables are very efficient as work areas and are frequently used in food production layouts for this reason. The tables shown are of a standard width, 2 feet 6 inches (762 mm), but, as can be seen in the illustrations, each shape uses a different amount of floor space.

Methods for Mounting Equipment

To design the area for efficiency, the layout of a work space must be considered from a three-dimensional perspective. The effective use of space above and below the table surface must be carefully considered by the food facilities consultant. Below the table surface, the most important consideration is the method for mounting the equipment. The most common mounting arrangements are:

- ❑ Small steel legs
- ❑ Equipment stands
- ❑ Casters

SMALL STEEL LEGS

The standard leg for kitchen equipment is 6 inches (152 mm) high. However, this height does not easily allow for thorough cleaning under the equipment. Six-inch (152 mm) legs on large pieces of equipment such as ranges or broilers make cleaning under the equipment especially difficult because of the distance from the front to the back of the equipment. Casters are thus the preferred mounting technique.

EQUIPMENT STANDS

The range section of a foodservice facility is traditionally mounted in a bank or row of equipment, one piece beside the other. This arrangement creates several problems:

❏ The grease that flows into cracks between pieces of equipment cannot be easily removed.

❏ The short legs on which the equipment is mounted make cleaning underneath it difficult.

❏ Utilities are connected from behind the equipment, making cleaning and repair difficult.

❏ Ovens are located close to the floor in many pieces of equipment, making it difficult to load and unload food being cooked.

A good design solution to these problems is to place this equipment on an equipment stand. Since equipment stands are sized to accommodate modular equipment in the range sections, the designer can specify the proper stand to fit each piece. Figure 5.14 shows a typical range section mounted on equipment stands.

CASTERS

The use of casters is a popular option in mounting foodservice equipment. Portability is often a desirable feature because the equipment can be easily moved for cleaning or shifted from one part of the food operation to another, permitting better utilization. Casters can be used on virtually any piece of foodservice equipment except for those that require permanent, rigid utility service connections, such as drains and ducts. Gas and water connections on caster-mounted equipment are made using flexible connectors (braided hoses) with quick-disconnect devices. A disadvantage of caster-mounted equipment is that employees may forget to disconnect the power cord, gas supply, or water hoses before rolling it away from the wall prior to cleaning. If so, the utility connection may be pulled right out of the wall by the inertia of, say, a double-stack convection oven. Restraining cables that are shorter than the utility connections should be installed on caster-mounted equipment to prevent this kind of damage.

The cost of a wall-hung kettle is more than double the cost of the same size kettle mounted on legs. Most owners of a food facility cannot afford the luxury of hanging large, heavy pieces of equipment. However,

Figure 5.14. Range Section on Equipment Stands.

many tables, shelves, and other smaller pieces of equipment can be hung using brackets attached securely to the wall.

LAYOUT OF FUNCTIONAL AREAS

To create an efficient layout, each area of the food facility must be considered according to its function. The layout of each of the major functional areas of a foodservice facility is discussed in this section. Because layout is closely related to space analysis and programming, the reader may find it helpful to review the corresponding sections in Chapter 4 for each of the primary functional areas in a foodservice facility.

Receiving

The primary components of the receiving area include the loading dock, access control (a locked door); space for staging food while it is being checked; a surface (worktable) on which cartons, lugs, flats, and other items can be set during inspection; and a scale. The primary considerations in the design and layout of a receiving area include providing:

❏ Adequate space for large trucks to maneuver while delivering products.

❏ A large enough dock. The width of the dock determines how many trucks can be parked at one time. Small foodservice operations typically need space for only one truck. However, larger operations may need space for two trucks, particularly if they do catering by truck.

❏ A controlled entry for foodservice, if the loading dock is shared by other functions in the building.

❏ Adequate aisle width so that products can be checked and weighed without blocking access to the dock.

Storage

The optimal layout of storage areas is one that maximizes usable storage area and minimizes unnecessary aisle space. The specific layout depends on the owner's operational priorities. If products are brought from receiving in cases or cartons on a hand truck, then standard shelving and dunnage racks separated by 3-to-4-foot (0.91-to-1.22-m) aisles will be adequate. If products are transported by forklift and stored on pallets, then industrial (warehouse) shelving may be used and aisles will need to be 6 to 8 feet (1.83 to 2.44 m) wide.

The majority of foodservice operations use hand trucks and standard shelving. Standard shelving depth for storage should be 24 inches (610 mm) because it permits most product containers to be stored without extending into the aisle, where they could be struck by a rolling rack and knocked to the floor. Narrower shelving requires food cartons to be stored lengthwise rather than back to back, which is less efficient. Shelving heights vary, but for most foodservice operations shelving higher than 72 inches (1.83 m) is rarely used except when storing cartons of light items, such as paper products.

(a)   (b)

Figure 5.15. (a) Dry Storage with 4-foot (.122 m) Aisles (b) Dry Storage with 3-foot (.91 m) Aisles.

Shelving should be laid out to minimize the amount of space used by aisles relative to actually storing products. Figure 5.15 shows two dry-storage rooms (interior dimensions 15 feet 3 inches by 14 feet 2 inches [4.65 m by 4.32 m]) of identical size. Figure 5.15a shows 4-foot (1.22-m)-wide aisles and a single row of center shelves, whereas Figure 5.15b shows 3-foot (0.91-m) aisles and a double set of center shelves. Using only the minimum necessary aisle width increases effective storage by 20 percent. Given the high cost of construction (often $150 or more per square foot [$1,615 per sq m]), efficient layout is a good investment.

In laying out the storage area for dry goods, the separation of cleaning supplies from food products is a health requirement in the United States. The reason for this requirement is to diminish the chances of accidentally mixing cleaning supplies with food. The separation of food products from paper supplies or uniforms is desirable in order to increase control over those products and to prevent employee pilferage. If a decision is made to issue partial cases of food to the kitchen, leaving the rest in the storeroom, then those partial cases probably would be stored in a separate section than the unbroken cases. Opened cases of foods require different types of shelving from whole cases, and they also invite pilferage. The separation of spices and broken cases into a special area of the storeroom equipped with solid shelving and secured by a special fence or "cage" is a common solution.

Maximizing shelving and minimizing aisle space is critical in the layout of walk-in coolers and freezers because of the high cost per square foot of these units. Figure 5.16 illustrates a minimum size for a combination (side-by-side) walk-in cooler and freezer unit. The interior width of the cooler and freezer sections is 7 feet 4 inches (2.24 m), allowing for 24-inch (610-mm)-deep shelves and a 38-inch (965-mm) aisle (the remaining 2 inches [51 mm] provide clearance between the shelving and the walls).

Figure 5.16. Minimum Efficient Size for a Walk-in Combination Cooler and Freezer.

Smaller walk-in units are available, but their space utilization is often very inefficient. For example, a walk-in that is wide enough for shelving only on one side—often called a step-in rather than a walk-in (Figure 5.17)—is functionally equivalent to a reach-in refrigerator but far more expensive because the operator is paying to refrigerate a 3-foot (0.91-m)-wide aisle.

Walk-ins are often designed so that the door to the freezer section opens from inside the cooler section in the belief that significant energy savings will result. Such savings are likely to be minuscule and not worth the loss of storage space in the cooler required to accommodate the door to

Figure 5.17. Step-in Cooler (Inefficient Use of space).

PRE-PREPARATION AREA

DISPOSER FOR REMOVAL OF FOOD WASTE

SINKS FOR CLEANING VEGETABLES

UTENSIL DRAWERS UNDER TABLE

REFRIGERATOR

SINK

FINAL PREPARATION AREA

Figure 5.18. Pre-preparation Area (Darker-line Area) for a 160-Seat Restaurant.

the freezer. However, other design considerations may make that approach unavoidable.

Pre-preparation

Depending on the size and complexity of the foodservice operation, pre-preparation areas can be as simple as a worktable with sinks or as complex as an entire room dedicated to producing ingredients in the exact weights and measures necessary for final preparation. Pre-preparation areas typically include worktables with sinks and a disposer, utensil storage, mixers, food processors and choppers, and parking spaces for racks. Pre-preparation areas also may include kettles, ovens, and similar equipment.

Figure 5.18 shows the layout of a basic pre-preparation area for a restaurant. It is designed for use by two or three employees. Figure 5.19 shows the layout of a pre-preparation area for a large institutional foodservice operation.

Cold-Food Preparation (Pantry)

In restaurants, clubs, and similar facilities, the cold-food area or pantry is dedicated to the preparation, assembly, and service of cold foods such as salads, sandwiches, desserts, and cold appetizers. In table service operations, the pantry is located as near as is feasible to the front of the kitchen, convenient to servers. Alternatively, some pantry functions may

Figure 5.19. Pre-preparation Equipment (Darker-line Area) for a Large Institutional Foodservice Facility.

be located in large server stations so that servers can obtain salads and desserts without going into the kitchen area proper. (This design approach is discussed in a later section of this chapter.) Foodservice operations that do not use table service often combine the cold-food preparation area with the final preparation area because both require access to raw materials stored in walk-in coolers.

Pantries typically include worktables with sinks, refrigerated storage for raw materials as well as for finished items, a refrigerated makeup area with cold pans, and a pickup station for servers. Depending on how the production processes are divided between the pre-preparation area and the pantry, pantries may also include small mixers, food processors, and/or slicers.

FINAL (HOT-FOOD) PREPARATION

The layout of the final preparation area is an especially critical part of the design and layout process in all foodservice concepts. This is so because errors in design, layout, and equipment selection in final preparation are most likely to have a direct impact on the satisfaction of the guest. Poorly laid-out final preparation areas may cause delays in service, over- or undercooked entrées, unattractive presentation, and mistakes in fulfilling orders. Further, poor layout reduces the productivity of the highest-paid employees in the back of the house (the chefs).

In restaurants, clubs, and other operations that feature cook-to-order food with table service, everything necessary to prepare the finished hot entrées must be immediately accessible to the chef and/or line cooks. For this reason, the owner and the foodservice consultant pay careful attention not only to the selection and layout of final preparation equipment but also to the design of the chef's table, where food is plated, garnished, and picked up by the server (or runner).

Customers in quick-service restaurants expect their food to be ready just a few minutes after placing their order. The layout of final preparation

Menu Item	Preparation Technique	Equipment Required	Servings/Hour*
Strip steak	Broil	Charbroiler	36
Swordfish steak	Broil	Charbroiler	16
Chicken breast	Broil	Charbroiler	44
Shrimp	Sauté	Open-burner range	12
Scallops	Sauté	Open-burner range	8
Calamari	Sauté	Open-burner range	4
Lobster tail	Steam with heat	Combi oven	12
Fried chicken	Deep-fat fry	Fryer	12
Home fries	Deep-fat fry	Fryer	32
Asparagus	Steam	Combi oven	24

* Servings per hour are shown as exact values to illustrate the concept of relating equipment selection to the anticipated demand for each menu item. In actuality, a range of estimate servings would be used to select and size equipment.

Figure 5.20. Sample Worksheet for Determining Final Preparation Equipment Requirements Based on Menu.

areas in these restaurants is critical for the success of the concept. Large chains carefully research the effects of even the smallest changes in the layout of the final preparation area and the design of each piece of equipment. Even the design of a utensil to scoop fries into a bag has been the focus of intense research and development.

A trend in institutional foodservices has been the shifting of final preparation from the back of the house to the servery, where the customer can see the food being prepared. Because institutional food facilities often feed large volumes of people in relatively short periods, the design of these final preparation areas is critical for operational efficiency and to prevent lengthy waits for menu items.

Equipment for the final preparation area should be selected for the desired cooking technique (e.g., sauté, charbroil, or steam) and should be sized to meet the anticipated demand for each item on the menu. Equipment that is specifically designed for the task is preferable to equipment that does many things but none of them well. Figure 5.20 is an example of a worksheet that can be used by the operator and the foodservice consultant to determine the kinds of equipment and capacities necessary for final preparation.

Figure 5.21 shows the final preparation line for a medium-size table service restaurant. Each piece of equipment has a specific function dictated by the menu.

Service Areas

The layout of the service areas depends on the concept of the food facility. Table service restaurants have far different requirements from quick-service restaurants, and quick-service restaurants are very different from institutional concepts.

The complexities of service areas in the dining room can range from a simple side stand to an elaborate server station. In a restaurant, the labor

Figure 5.21. Final Preparation Equipment Selected by Menu Requirements.

cost will be directly affected by the distance between the final preparation and the server stations. This distance can be altered significantly by the use of well-designed server stations. The importance of the server station for quick, efficient service cannot be overemphasized. If the service personnel must walk to the kitchen to pick up the typical table setup, this might result in the following trips:

First trip: Pick up linen, glasses, silverware, and condiments.
Second trip: Pick up water, ice, butter, crackers, and bread.

After the order is taken, these additional trips might be necessary:

Third trip: Pick up cocktail or wine order from the service bar.
Fourth trip: Place appetizer order and salad order.
Fifth trip: Pick up appetizer and salad.

After the cocktail and appetizers are served, these trips might occur:

Sixth trip: Place the entrée order.
Seventh trip: Pick up the entrée.
Eighth trip: Clear appetizer and cocktail (or combine this with the seventh trip).
Ninth trip: Clear entrée and place dessert order.
Tenth trip: Clear dessert, soiled linen, and all glassware and silverware.

Three or four of these trips to the kitchen can be avoided with a well-designed and properly located server station. Figure 5.22 lists 30 items that may be kept at the server station.

Eliminating four trips to the kitchen will provide these advantages:

❑ An increase in the speed of service

❑ A possible reduction in service personnel

❑ A less-crowded kitchen

❑ More attention to guests by the service personnel

One disadvantage of the use of well-designed server stations is some loss of control over the products that are located in the station. For this reason, the items listed are generally inexpensive and not the kind of food

1. Bread
2. Butter
3. Butter plates
4. Baskets for bread
5. Coffee machine
6. Coffee and filters
7. Coffee cups and saucers
8. Cream
9. Cream pitchers
10. Sugar
11. Silverware
12. Water and water pitcher
13. Glasses
14. Ice
15. Cold tea
16. Hot tea and Sanka
17. Boiling water
18. Linen napkins and tablecloths
19. Receptacle for soiled linen
20. Milk
21. Crackers
22. Tray stand or shelf for trays
23. Condiments (salad dressings, sauces, seasonings)
24. Sour cream
25. Soup
26. Precheck machine and/or space for writing out checks
27. Microwave oven
28. Soft drinks
29. Trash container
30. Pickup control board

Figure 5.22. Potential Items Located in a Server Station.

items that service personnel would steal or eat on the job. It would not be a good idea to place desserts, alcoholic beverages, or expensive appetizers on server stations. These items should be picked up from the cold-food area after being listed on the guest check.

An example of a redesigned kitchen in a country club, with a server station located near the dining area, can be seen in the before and after drawings of Figure 5.23. By exchanging the locations of the cooler and pantry areas in the before drawing, a server station could be created in the dining room that backs up to the pantry area of the kitchen. The pantry employees stock a pass-through refrigerator that opens to both areas with salads and desserts so that servers can pick them up for guests without going into the kitchen itself.

Quick-service restaurants involve the customer in the service process of taking the food to the table (or picking it up at the drive-through window). Although there is a great deal of similarity among quick-service restaurants, there also are important differences. These differences are illustrated in Figure 5.24a and 5.26b, which contrast two service areas. Figure 5.24a shows a counter with multiple service points where the customer receives his or her entrée, side order, and beverage. In this layout, the

Figure 5.23. Redesigned Kitchen in a Country Club, with a Server Station Located near the Dining Area (Upper Right Corner).

customer places the order and then stands in place waiting for the salesperson to assemble and bag it. Figure 5.24b, in contrast, shows a service counter where the customer places his or her order, waits while the order is assembled, and then moves along the counter to a point where the food is delivered. While the effects of these differences on the speed of customer service may be slight, chain foodservice firms seek even the slightest advantage—real or perceived—in the convenience they offer their guests.

Cafeteria service designs have changed dramatically over the past two decades. The traditional straight-line design has been replaced by a family of closely related approaches: the scramble, the scatter system, or the food court. Figure 5.25 shows a schematic design for a scramble cafeteria design with multiple food stations and a convenience store intended for corporate dining. A university foodservice with a scramble service concept is shown in Appendix 2.

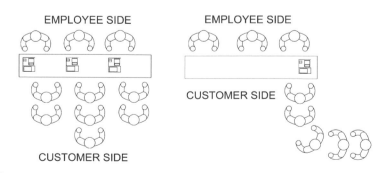

Figure 5.24. (a) Customers Served Simultaneously (b) Customers Served One at a Time.

(a)   (b)

HOT ENTREES

SOUPS

GRILL

WAREWASHING

PIZZA/CALZONES

DELI DISPLAY

SANDWICHES

SALADS

MENU DISPLAY

BOTTLED BEVERAGES

DESSERTS

BAKED GOODS

CONDIMENTS

CONVENIENCE STORE

BEVERAGES

CASH

BISTRO SEATING

CASH

CASH

DISH DROP

DINING AREA

Figure 5.25. Schematic Design for a Scramble. Courtesy of Maddox-NBD, Inc.

The change from straight-line to scramble designs has occurred for several reasons:

❑ Faster service

❑ Greater menu variety through multiple food stations

❑ Better merchandising

The principle behind the scramble (or scatter) design is to provide multiple stations from which the customer can freely select. Unlike the straight-line cafeteria service layout, in which the speed through the line is only as fast as the slowest customer, the scramble system can be designed so that each station serves at a predetermined rate. The only disadvantage of the scramble service layout is that it requires generous circulation space so that a large number of customers can move freely from station to station.

Warewashing

The overall approach taken to the layout of the dishwashing area is a function of these factors:

❑ *Concept of the foodservice operation.* The concept affects the type and volume of dishes that need to be washed. Fine-dining establishments use far more dishes and silverware on a per-customer basis than a simple family restaurant. Similarly, health care facilities need to wash specialized trays and containers, whereas schools may need only to wash a single tray.

❑ *Size of the operation.* The number of customers has a direct effect on the layout of a warewashing area.

❑ *Timing.* A foodservice operation that serves 600 covers in three hours places a different demand on the dish operation than an operation serving the same 600 covers in 45 minutes.

❑ *Operational approach to dishwashing.* There are several distinct approaches to organizing the warewashing process within the dishroom, especially in large operations. For example, a carousel dish machine requires a significantly different layout from a flight-type machine serving the same demand.

A representative dishroom layout for a small foodservice operation is shown in Figure 5.26. This design utilizes a single-tank, door-type dish machine that fits in a corner. Figures 5.27, 5.28, 5.29, and 5.30 illustrate

Figure 5.26. Dishroom for a Small Foodservice Operation.

Figure 5.27. Dishroom with a Two-Tank Dish Machine.

Figure 5.28. Dishroom with Flight-Type Dish Machine.

Figure 5.29. Carousel Dish Machine Layout.

Figure 5.30. Dishroom with Tray Acclmulator.

dishrooms using a two-tank dish machine, a flight machine, a circular (carousel) machine, and a corner dish machine with a tray accumulator, respectively.

Cart-Wash Room

The wash-down room is a space, usually located in the vicinity of the receiving dock, used for cleaning carts and trash cans. For a small or medium-size food operation, the room needs to be large enough to accommodate a hose reel, a large floor drain, and one or two parked carts. A space 6 feet wide by 10 feet long (1.83 m wide by 3.05 m long) would be adequate. Large hotel or hospital foodservice facilities would need a larger wash-down room because of the extensive use of carts. Wash-down rooms may be equipped with steam cleaners and foot-operated can washers, but these are usually not necessary.

Linen and Locker Room

Table linen is usually stored in a special storage space that is protected from moisture and convenient to the service personnel. Uniforms are usually issued to the employees on an exchange basis (each employee turns in a dirty uniform for a clean one). The use of a combination linen room/locker room/toilet is a good space-saving design for handling

Figure 5.31. Rest Rooms with Employee Lockers and Linen Storage Rooms.

uniform exchange (see Figure 5.31). Notice in the figure that linen is placed in the back side of the locker by the linen rental company or the person responsible for linen. The employee places his or her soiled uniform into the locker in exchange for a clean uniform. Separate lockers are provided for coats and street clothes.

Service Kitchens

Banquet halls and private dining rooms can best be served if a space is provided for holding the food prior to service. Service kitchens are not usually needed, if the banquet hall or private dining room is near the kitchen.

The amount of space needed for a banquet service kitchen will vary with the number of seats being served. Figure 5.32 lists guidelines for the square footage requirements of service kitchens based on the number of seats in the adjacent dining area.

Service kitchens can be equipped with support cooking equipment and elaborate hot and cold holding cabinets. An empty room that can accommodate portable equipment will serve the same function. A simple service kitchen with a minimum amount of equipment is preferred by most food facility design consultants. Figure 5.33 identifies equipment that should be considered for the service kitchen.

If space is needed for the storage of tables and chairs, this should be added to the listed space requirement figures. A formula that can be used

Number of Seats in Dining Area	Size of Serving Kitchen (Net), Square Feet (Square Meters)
50–100	75–100 (6.97–9.29)
100–250	100–150 (9.29–13.94)
250–500	150–300 (13.94–27.87)
500–1000	300–500 (13.94–46.45)

Figure 5.32. Guidelines for Serving Kitchen Area.

Necessary	May Be Desirable
Sink with hot and cold water	Dish machine
Ice machine	Refrigeration
Storage for china	Fryers, grills, or broilers
Table for holding service equipment	Steam table
Coffee urn	Storage for catering equipment
Electrical outlets for portable equipment	Heated cabinets
	Convection oven
	Three-compartment sink

Figure 5.33. Equipment Recommendations for Serving Kitchens.

as a guideline in calculating the space for storage of tables and chairs is to add 0.6 square foot (0.056 sq m) per seat for furniture storage.

Health care facilities, such as congregate care and retirement villages, often use serving kitchens for resident dining areas on the units or floors. These facilities often require larger serving kitchens in relation to the number of seats. To ensure that the food served to residents is fresh, final preparation equipment, such as a steamer to cook vegetables and a griddle for eggs, pancakes, and French toast, are added to the design. A serving kitchen for a large long-term-care community is shown in Figure 5.34.

SUMMARY

A foodservice facility must be designed with both space and function in mind. The work space will function best if attention in design is given to the interface between the employee and the foodservice equipment. The equipment must be laid out with due consideration to access to raw materials, the flow of raw materials and people, the relationship to other departments in the facility, and access to needed utensils and equipment.

Certain physical characteristics are desirable in all work areas. To determine the best physical arrangement, the designer must consider the shape of the layout, the best method for mounting the equipment, and the best means for connecting the utilities to each piece of equipment.

Design considerations are different for each area of the food facility, and therefore each area must be considered according to its function. Storage spaces, preparation areas, service areas in the dining room, and special support areas must have special design features if they are to be efficient.

KEY TERMS

System
Carousel-type dishwasher
Final preparation

Equipment stands
Garbage trough

Figure 5.34. Expanded Service Kitchen in Retirement Center.

QUESTIONS

1. Draw a simple flow chart for a dishwashing system. Label the parts.
2. Each kitchen employee needs a well-designed work area. The text lists 12 desirable features. Name 6 of these features.
3. Wall-hung equipment and concrete equipment bases are seldom used in modern kitchens. What has been used to ease cleaning under equipment?
4. Having garbage disposers in each work area is very convenient. Local plumbing codes often do not allow these. Why?
5. Where are service kitchens typically located?
6. How can you decrease the number of trips that a waitperson must make to the kitchen?

DISCUSSION QUESTION

Henry Ford designed the first efficient assembly line for making automobiles. How can the assembly-line design concept be applied in a foodservice facility for:

a. Hamburger/hot dog, french fry stand
b. A large table service restaurant
c. A cafeteria service for 1,000 students

CHAPTER 6

Foodservice Equipment, Part I

THIS CHAPTER

☑ Describes the basis for selecting foodservice equipment

☑ Outlines the standards of workmanship and common materials for constructing food-service equipment

☑ Provides an overview of the equipment specifications as they would appear in a set of contract documents

EQUIPMENT SELECTION

The purchase of a major piece of equipment is an important event for the manager or owner of a foodservice operation. A new piece of equipment may be selected for any of these reasons:

❏ The equipment is a part of a new food facility.

❏ Existing equipment needs to be replaced.

❏ Changes in the menu or variations in volume of business require an addition to the food facility.

❏ The equipment will reduce labor costs.

❏ The equipment will reduce maintenance costs.

❏ The equipment will produce savings in energy.

Trade journals and equipment shows in the foodservice industry offer a smorgasbord of interesting equipment that can be tempting to a prospective buyer. A careful evaluation of available alternatives is important in order to select the correct piece of equipment at the lowest possible total cost of ownership.

The total cost of ownership for a piece of equipment is a function of these factors:

❏ Initial purchase price

❏ Cost of installing the equipment

❏ Direct costs of operation

❏ Cost of maintenance and repair

❑ Labor costs required to operate the equipment

❑ Useful life of the equipment

Each of these factors is briefly discussed in the sections that follow.

Initial Purchase Price

Equipment purchasing decisions are often made strictly on the basis of the initial purchase price. For example, an oven costing $5,200 may be selected over one whose price is $6,500. Unfortunately, it is not always the case that the lower initial price represents the lowest total cost of ownership. An operation that serves three meals per day, 365 days per year, would probably be better off purchasing the more expensive oven—provided, of course, that the higher cost reflects better-quality components that will last substantially longer under heavy use. A facility that serves one meal per day only nine months of the year, such as an elementary-school kitchen, however, probably would be well served by the less expensive oven.

Foodservice equipment manufacturers recognize the tremendous variety of needs within the industry and offer products that are designed to address the full spectrum of operational requirements. Thus, the owner needs to clearly understand the specific requirements of his or her operation in order to select equipment that is appropriate. This knowledge is especially important because of the competitive nature of the foodservice equipment industry. Manufacturer's representatives are rewarded for selling their lines against those of the competition. Similarly, equipment dealers receive rebates for selling favored lines in quantity. These incentives can lead manufacturers' reps and dealers to push a favored product over a competitor's that may, in fact, be better for the application—especially when the product is less expensive. However, it also is true that many equipment manufacturers strive to bring products to market that genuinely offer higher quality at a lower price through new or improved technology.

How can the owner evaluate the relative merits of competitive brands of equipment? One important source of information is to talk to other people with similar operations regarding their experience with specific items. A second source of information is the foodservice facility design consultant because of his or her experience specifying equipment and inspecting its operation when it has been installed. A third source of information is industry trade shows, such as the North American Association of Food Equipment Manufacturers' show, www.nafem.org, where the features of competing equipment can be evaluated virtually side by side.

Although the initial purchase price is relevant to equipment selection, it is only one factor in the equation. The most important initial consideration for any piece of equipment is not how much it costs but how well it fulfills the needs of the operation.

Installation Cost

For many foodservice equipment items, the installation cost is a minor factor. A replacement slicer, for example, simply needs to be removed from the box, set in place, cleaned and sanitized, and plugged into the wall. Other equipment items can incur extraordinary installation costs. Consider these examples:

❏ Adding a charbroiler could require expensive modifications to a ventilation system or even a new hood.

❏ Adding a steam-jacketed kettle could require cutting into the floor to install a trench drain.

❏ Adding a steamer with an electric steam generator could require additional power circuits.

❏ Replacing a hood could require additional ductwork running from the kitchen to the roof. If the kitchen is on a lower floor of the building and a new chase needs to be built running through each floor, the expense could be substantial.

In addition, large equipment (dish machines, hoods, serving counters, conveyors) could prove very expensive to install due to limited access—narrow doorways, small elevators, and so on.

The total investment required in new or replacement equipment includes both the purchase price and the cost of installation. Identifying the costs of installation prior to purchasing the equipment will prevent expensive surprises.

Direct Operating Costs

Direct operating costs include the expenses associated with utilities, such as gas, electricity, steam, and water. Methods for evaluating relative utility costs are discussed in detail in Chapter 8. Here it is important to note that gas-fired equipment, such as kettles, steamers, or tilting skillets, often is more expensive to purchase than its electric-powered counterparts. However, depending on the relative costs of electricity versus gas in any given area, the higher initial investment could be returned through lower direct operating costs. Dish machines represent another important example because of their use of hot water.

The direct operating costs of equipment can be estimated using information provided by manufacturers' catalog sheets as well as local costs of electricity, gas, steam, and/or water.

Maintenance and Repair

The total cost of ownership of equipment also includes expenses associated with maintenance and repair. Maintenance requirements often can be determined by reading the operator's manual—for major equipment items, the owner should request copies of the maintenance sections of these manuals prior to making a final purchase decision. It is important to note whether the required maintenance can be done in-house or requires a service call from a service agency. In-house maintenance has a labor cost that should be estimated; similarly, the cost of a service call from an outside agency should be determined. Also important are the frequency and complexity of the maintenance required. A steamer with an enclosed, gas-fired steam boiler may seem to need relatively infrequent maintenance, but when it is time for it to be serviced, the boiler may need to be removed and partially disassembled. An electric steamer might need frequent maintenance, but all that is needed is to pour a deliming solution into the tank and run the unit through a cycle. Of course, the cost of the deliming solution for the electric steamer needs to be added to the estimated maintenance costs.

Repair costs are more difficult to estimate simply because equipment breakdowns are difficult to predict with any degree of accuracy. However, for major equipment items, the owner can contact a service agency to ask for typical repair prices and relative repair frequencies for the equipment being considered.

Labor Costs of Operation

When replacing old equipment with new pieces, labor costs of operation generally are not an important factor in the total cost of ownership if the replacement is functionally identical to the original. Often, however, new equipment is purchased that is substantially different in terms of how it functions. For example, replacing a manual slicer with an automatic slicer potentially has an impact on labor costs. Similarly, replacing a standard pot sink with one that circulates water in the soak compartment will reduce the time employees need to spend washing pots. In these examples, the labor savings actually reduce the total cost of ownership.

Useful Life of Equipment

How long will a piece of equipment last? When should an old piece of equipment be taken out in favor of a new piece? The answer to these questions depends mostly on the amount of maintenance given to the equipment and how heavily the equipment was used in the food operation. A steam-jacketed kettle that is well cared for and that does not have deep dents or scratches should last 25 years or more. The valves and piping to the kettle may need replacement before the useful life of this piece of equipment is over. In contrast, a poorly maintained convection oven that is used continuously during the day for baking, roasting, and grilling might have a useful life of only 5 years. Figure 6.1 shows estimated useful lives of major pieces of equipment.

What Figure 6.1 does not show are differences in the useful life of equipment based on the quality and durability offered by competing manufacturers. Recall the example of deciding whether to purchase an oven for $5,200 or $6,500. If the less expensive oven lasts five years under heavy use but the more expensive oven lasts eight years, then the higher initial purchase price is justified (all other factors being equal). Hard data regarding the useful life of competing manufacturers' equipment are difficult to obtain. As suggested, owners considering the purchase of major equipment items are well advised to check with operators in similar facilities and to contact a foodservice facilities design consultant.

Determining the total cost of ownership of an equipment item thus is the sum of the purchase price, installation costs, direct operating costs, and labor costs or savings, divided by the useful lifetime of the equipment.[1]

---

[1] Our computation of total cost of ownership is a simplification. For large equipment purchases, the cost of capital and the time value of money should be taken into account. However, a treatment of capital budgeting goes beyond the scope of this text.

Item	Useful Life (Years)
Convection ovens	8–10
Deck ovens	10–15
Rotary ovens	12–20
Mixers	15–25
Ranges	10–15
Steam-jacketed kettles	15–25
Food choppers	10–15
Vertical cutter-mixers	12–15
Tilting skillets	12–20
Grills	8–12
Fryers	8–12
Broilers	8–12
Steamers—high and medium pressure	10–15
Steamers—convection	8–12
Walk-in refrigerators/freezers	12–20
Reach-in refrigerators/freezers	8–12
Coffee urns	8–12
Dish machines	10–15
Stainless-steel worktables, sinks	25–40
Shelving—stainless steel	25–40
Shelving—galvanized wire	8–12
Ice machines	5–8
Hoods/ventilation systems	10–15

* These estimates assume: (1) two to three meals per day, (2) ongoing maintenance, and (3) typical industry conditions.

Figure 6.1. Estimated Useful Lives of Foodservice Equipment*.

FOODSERVICE EQUIPMENT STANDARDS AND SPECIFICATIONS

Foodservice equipment is manufactured or fabricated according to industry standards governing safety. Appropriate standards are determined by organizations, such as the National Sanitation Foundation (NSF), Underwriters Laboratories (UL), the American Gas Association (AGA), the American Society of Mechanical Engineers (ASME), and the Environmental Protection Agency's Energy Star® program. In addition, governmental agencies formulate standards that affect the construction and installation of foodservice equipment. The standards and approval processes of the National Sanitation Foundation are particularly relevant because they address food safety and sanitation.

NSF Standards and Seal

The NSF seal of approval is a recognized standard of acceptance for many pieces of equipment. This seal assures the buyer that the equipment meets certain construction standards of sanitation and safety. NSF is an independent, nonprofit organization dedicated to the improvement of public health. Equipment manufacturers can write to the NSF testing laboratory to describe the equipment that is being developed and can learn whether it will meet NSF standards of construction. The manufacturer pays a fee to NSF to arrange for a representative to visit the manufacturing plant to inspect and test the equipment. (In some cases the equipment is shipped to the NSF testing laboratories for inspection.) If the equipment passes the inspection and tests, the manufacturer is given permission to display the NSF seal of approval. The continued use of the NSF seal requires ongoing communication between the manufacturer and NSF to ensure that changes in the equipment continue to meet the organization's standards.

NSF carries on a variety of activities in pursuit of its objectives, including:

❏ Providing liaison services to strengthen communications between industry, the public health professions, and the general public

❏ Conducting basic research and establishing standards on health-related equipment, processes, products, and services

❏ Disseminating research results to educate industry, regulatory agencies, and the general public regarding health hazards and means of eliminating them

❏ Issuing official NSF seals for display on equipment and products tested and found to meet NSF standards

The NSF seal of approval and the food facilities design consultant's specifications containing the statement "Equipment must be constructed to NSF standards" imply two different things. In cases where the specifications state that the equipment must bear the NSF seal of approval, it is assumed that only those pieces of manufactured equipment that have been inspected and approved by NSF may bear this seal. For fabricated equipment, the consultant and fabricator follow the NSF handbooks containing the construction methods and standards that have been approved by NSF. The fabricator should be preapproved by the NSF so that the fabricated equipment can bear the NSF seal.

Energy Star®

The Energy Star® program was established by the U.S. Environmental Protection Agency (EPA) in 1992 for energy-efficient computers and has since grown to encompass more than 35 product categories for the home and workplace, new homes, and superior energy management within organizations. In August 2003 the Energy Star® label became available for commercial cooking equipment. The Energy Star program has dramatically increased the use of energy-efficient products and practices and is well positioned to promote more widespread efficiency improvements.

Equipment Specification

Recall, from Chapter 2, that the role of equipment specifications in the overall design process is to ensure that the products have exactly the features required by the owner and are installed in complete accordance with governmental requirements and industry standards. The standards for the specification of equipment are derived from four primary sources:

1. NSF, UL, ASME, AGA, EPA, and regulatory agencies such as health departments
2. Manufacturers' standards
3. Functional capabilities and features desired by the buyer
4. Industry standards, as reflected in the language of the consultant's specifications

Equipment specifications fall broadly into two categories: manufactured equipment, as selected from manufacturers' catalogs, and fabricated equipment, which is custom-built to meet the requirements of the project.

MANUFACTURED EQUIPMENT

The specifications for equipment that is selected from a catalog are less complex than for fabricated equipment. The specifier—whether the owner or a foodservice design consultant—examines the catalogs of all of the major manufacturers of the type of equipment desired, and, based on the functional needs of the operation, makes an equipment choice. (Many other factors, as discussed in the previous section, are also involved in the selection process.) The specification is then written in one of two forms, a performance-based spec or a specific-type spec.

The performance-based spec is then carefully written to include all of the required features and characteristics yet remains sufficiently general to allow bids from several competing manufacturers. The specification of characteristics and features depends on the kind of equipment being selected but often includes:

- ❏ Dimensions of the unit
- ❏ Quantity of units to be purchased
- ❏ Specific utility requirements of the equipment item
- ❏ Materials used in the construction of the equipment
- ❏ Specific construction techniques employed
- ❏ Any relevant performance criteria
- ❏ Desired features, accessories, and/or options
- ❏ Relevant industry, association, or governmental standards

Often the specifier names a manufacturer and model number. The purpose of doing so is not to exclude other manufacturers with competitive products but to set a reference standard whereby other products can be judged. Also, naming a specific manufacturer and model typically is necessary to establish the utility requirements needed for the proper engineering of the project. If a bidder prefers to provide a competitor's product, he or she must demonstrate that it is equal to or better than the reference standard, and must assume any cost involved in providing different utility services.

Chapter 7 discusses the major types of manufactured foodservice equipment.

FABRICATED EQUIPMENT

The buyer must write a complete and comprehensive specification for a piece of equipment that will be fabricated. Fabricated equipment, such as a soiled-dish table, must be described in complete detail so that the kitchen equipment contractor and the fabrication shop will know exactly how to build it. To assist the dealer and fabricator in understanding the appearance and general construction quality of the equipment, the food facilities consultant will prepare plan and elevation drawings. These drawings may also include detailed sections of the equipment so that the quality of the equipment and the way that it is constructed will be clearly understood. The fabrication shop will read the specification very carefully and prepare shop drawings, in large scale, showing all of the details of construction. The owner and/or foodservice design consultant will have an opportunity to approve the shop drawings before the equipment is actually built.

EQUIPMENT CONSTRUCTION MATERIALS

The most common materials for constructing a piece of foodservice equipment are:

❑ Stainless steel
❑ Aluminum
❑ Galvanized iron
❑ Plastics
❑ Wood

Stainless Steel

Specifications for stainless steel in foodservice facilities are usually type 302 or 304, with a U.S. Standard 18.8 composition (18 percent chromium and 8 percent nickel). The stainless is polished to a number 4 finish, and the thickness is specified by gauge. The gauge (or thickness) has a great impact on cost, and the specifier should use the minimum thickness needed for each part of the equipment. Figure 6.2 indicates typical applications for various gauges of stainless steel.

Stainless steel is usually shaped under pressure at a fabrication shop and then welded and polished. The weld should be of the same metal as the material being welded; usually spot welding, soldering, or bolting is not acceptable. If equipment pieces are to be attached to each other, bolting is acceptable; and the pieces should be tight enough to form a hairline seam. The seam should be sealed with silicone to prevent grease or moisture from flowing into the crack.

Aluminum

This lightweight rust-resistant metal is widely used for carts, portable racks, cabinets and the interior of reach-in refrigerators. Aluminum is less expensive that stainless steel, but is not as strong and is more difficult to clean. Aluminum cooking containers are seldom used in commercial kitchens because of staining problems and concern that the metal may

Gauge	Typical Use
8 and 10	Support elements for heavy equipment or at stress points
12	Heavily used tabletops, pot sinks, or other surfaces that will receive a great amount of wear
14	Tabletops, sinks, overshelves, and brackets that will receive frequent use or that will carry heavy weights
16	Equipment tops and sides that are small and that will carry little weight; shelves under equipment and heavily used side panels
18	Side panels that are not exposed to wear, equipment doors, hoods, and partitions
20	Covers for supported or insulated panels, such as refrigerators or insulated doors

Figure 6.2. Stainless-Steel Applications by Gauge (Thickness).

give off an undesirable residue. Bakeries use many aluminum sheet pans covered with paper pan liners.

Galvanized Iron

Galvanized iron and other types of galvanized sheet metal are frequently used in foodservice equipment construction. The obvious advantage of this material is that it has a significantly lower cost than stainless steel. A typical use of galvanized iron is a structure or underbracing for equipment; for example, iron is welded to the underside of stainless-steel tables and cafeteria lines.

Galvanized sheet metal is used for the construction of sinks, tables, and interior shelves in food facilities that have limited funds for kitchen equipment. Galvanized iron piping rather than stainless steel is frequently used for legs as an economy measure. Again, the advantage is lower cost, but the disadvantage is that a painted surface chips in a short period of time, and the legs and undershelving are difficult to clean and are not attractive.

Plastics

Thermoplastic cutting boards and tops have been approved by NSF because they do not warp or crack. Traditional maple cutting boards crack and separate in a short period of time, and the cracks harbor bacteria and soil. Thermoplastic tops and cutting boards should be used where cutting, chopping, or carving will occur. Typically, sandwich and salad makeup tables and occasionally the entire top surface of a worktable will be covered with this plastic material. The use of plastic as cutting boards also allows for color coding so that the boards can be returned to their respective work area to prevent the possibility of cross-contamination (i.e., raw uncooked meat in the kitchen prep area versus deli meat in the service area).

Plastic is now being used for the construction of carts and enclosed cabinets because of its strength, light weight, and ease of cleaning. Fiberglass and plastic are also being used as internal sides, bottoms, and tops of some reach-in refrigerators and transport cabinets.

Plastic laminates, which have been used for many years for dining room tables, are also frequently used to cover vertical and horizontal surfaces in foodservice equipment, particularly in serving areas. Cafeteria counters, server stations, snack bars, condiment stands, dish enclosures, and some worktables are often covered with plastic laminates. In addition to the cost advantage over stainless steel, the use of plastic laminates permits inexpensive changes to be made to the equipment. However, plastic laminates have a relatively thin wear surface that can easily become scratched and damaged through everyday use. Exposed corners and edges on serving counters are especially vulnerable because of frequent contact. "Solid-surface" materials (i.e., as Corian™, granite, and other stone surfaces) are more durable alternatives to plastic laminate for many high-wear surfaces.

Wood

Hard rock maple and pecan cutting tops are frequently used for dining room tables and bakery production tables in food operations. Many bakers prefer the maple top because the surface is easy to clean and dough and flour do not stick to it. Separation of the wooden top does not normally occur in a bakery because the fats from the dough keep the wood from being saturated with water. A well-cared-for maple table or countertop in a bakery should last for many years.

Wood finishes in service areas and on cafeteria counters are used primarily for decorative purposes. Wood may not be used in places where it can come into direct contact with food, but it is appropriate for cafeteria slides, decorative sneeze guards, edging for display shelves, and enclosures for dining room server stations.

Other Materials Used in Equipment Construction

Many different types of materials are used to build foodservice equipment. No list of materials can be considered complete, because imaginative designers are continually developing and experimenting with new surfaces and textures. The surfaces that need the most careful scrutiny, if they are to be built to NSF standards, are those that come in contact with the food or the food handler. These surfaces should be smooth and nonporous and should resist chipping and wear under frequent use. They should also be resistant to the corrosive effect of salt, food acids, and oils. Some alternative materials used in construction include:

❏ Glass
❏ Solid-surface materials, such as Corian™
❏ Ceramic tile
❏ Stone, such as granite
❏ Rubber
❏ Copper
❏ Brass
❏ Cast iron

FOODSERVICE EQUIPMENT SPECIFICATIONS: AN OUTLINE

Following the standards of the design and construction process, foodservice equipment specifications for a new or renovated foodservice facility are contained in Section 11400 of the project manual. Equipment specifications follow a generally accepted outline. The three major divisions of Section 11400 are "General," "Products," and "Execution."

Part 1—The "General" section of the foodservice equipment specifications typically:

❏ Refers the bidder to other parts of the contract documents that are necessary for understanding all of the project requirements.

❏ Describes the specific responsibilities of the foodservice equipment contractor and of the electricians, plumbers, and other tradespeople in connecting the equipment.

❏ Indicates who will provide the hardware necessary for plumbing connections—the plumber or the foodservice equipment contractor.

❏ Discusses how the foodservice equipment contractor is to deal with removal, storage, repair, and reinstallation of existing equipment that is to be used in the new or renovated facility.

❏ Establishes the requirements for submittals, such as shop drawings, catalog sheets, and samples, to be provided by the foodservice equipment contractor for review and approval.

❏ Instructs the foodservice equipment contractor how to handle deviations from the requirements of the contract documents. Such changes occur as a result of many factors. For example, a manufacturer might change the utility requirements for a piece of equipment. Such changes must be "conspicuously noted" in correspondence so that all members of the project team are aware of the new requirements.

❏ Sets standards designed to ensure a quality installation. Such standards are necessary to ensure that the bidder has the financial resources, physical capabilities, and workforce necessary to complete a major equipment installation.

❏ Sets standards for the manufacture and installation of the foodservice equipment. A "reference standard" essentially means that by referring to the standard in the specifications, that standard becomes a part of the project requirements—just as if the entire text of the standard were typed into the project manual. Standards address sanitary construction techniques, approved electrical components and construction, fire protection, safe steam boiler construction, quality standards for architectural millwork, and installation that conforms to health department regulations.

❏ Provides information to the foodservice equipment contractor regarding storage, delivery, and handling of the foodservice equipment. These contract provisions are necessary to prevent complications during the installation of the equipment.

❑ Requires the foodservice equipment contractor to check that the utility services are appropriate before actually installing the equipment.

❑ Specifies that all foodservice bids should be itemized. Each item bid must match bid document item numbers and be inclusive of all labor and materials required to provide the item fully furnished, assembled, and set in place.

Part 2—The "Products" section of the foodservice equipment specification typically:

❑ Sets standards for the composition and quality of the stainless steel used in manufactured and fabricated equipment.

❑ Sets standards for other raw materials used in the construction of foodservice equipment.

❑ Describes the requirements for the components to be used in the foodservice equipment, including plumbing (faucets, drains) and electrical components (junction boxes, receptacles).

❑ Sets standards for workmanship in stainless-steel fabrication, such as how joints are to be made and the quality of the arc welding.

❑ Sets standards for the fabrication and installation of stainless-steel sinks, drainboards, utensil drawers, work surfaces (tabletops), legs, shelving, and other fabricated items.

❑ Sets standards for architectural millwork, including the grade and type of materials and specific construction techniques.

❑ Provides a brief description of each item of foodservice equipment to be provided.

Part 3—The "Execution" section of the foodservice equipment specifications typically:

❑ Requires the foodservice equipment contractor to verify that the utility rough-in connections provided by the electricians and plumbers are located where required for the equipment.

❑ Requires the contractor to "field-measure" to determine that dimensions are as required for the equipment installation.

❑ Provides specific instructions for the installation of walk-in coolers and freezers.

❑ Describes how field joints in equipment are to be made. This is done because proper field joints enhance the quality and sanitation of the installation, whereas poor joints collect dirt and food waste, promote the growth of dangerous bacteria, and offer passageways for insects.

❑ Establishes the requirements and describes the procedures for ensuring the quality of the installation of the equipment in the field, including inspection—and rejection if necessary—of the work of the foodservice equipment contractor.

❏ Requires the foodservice equipment contractor to set up and test each item of equipment, adjust it as necessary, and replace equipment that is not functioning to specifications.

❏ Requires the foodservice equipment contractor to clean and sanitize the equipment prior to turning it over to the owner.

❏ Requires the foodservice equipment contractor to demonstrate the use of the equipment and clearly instruct the owner in proper maintenance procedures.

❏ Sets the requirements for product guarantees and warranties.

SUMMARY

Foodservice equipment should be selected on the basis of many factors, including the overall cost of ownership. The total cost of ownership is a function of several factors, including: initial purchase price, cost of installing the equipment, direct cost of operation, cost of maintenance and repair, cost of the labor required to operate the equipment, and useful life of the equipment.

Standards for the construction of foodservice equipment are important, especially with respect to sanitation. The National Sanitation Foundation promotes safe equipment construction materials and methods. The differences between manufactured and fabricated foodservice equipment were pointed out, and the primary materials used in the construction of foodservice equipment were identified. Finally, the chapter outlined the contents of a typical set of foodservice equipment specifications.

KEY TERMS

Galvanized

Gauge of steel

NSF

Useful life

Energy saving

Standards of workmanship

Energy Star

QUESTIONS

1. Which of the following are the two most important factors in determining the cost of a piece of equipment:
   a. Initial price
   b. Cost of installing the equipment
   c. Labor cost to operate the equipment
   d. Energy consumed
   e. Maintenance and repair over useful life

2. Rank the useful life of the equipment by "short," "medium," or "long" (S, M, L).

   Convection oven
   Dish machine
   Hood
   Ice machine
   Steam-jacketed kettle
   Walk-in refrigerator

3. What is the difference between manufactured and fabricated equipment?

4. What determines the desirability of the material used to manufacture equipment?

5. What is a specification? Why are they so important?

DISCUSSION QUESTION

A foodservice consultant specified 25 stainless-steel shelving units for a large walk-in freezer and separate refrigerator. After the shelving units had been approved by the owner and were ordered, the owner requested that each unit be fitted with casters for ease of cleaning. When the shelving arrived, the shelving units were 2 inches higher than the freezer and refrigerator doors. The late request for the casters was responsible for this very serious problem. Discuss how it would be determined who was ultimately responsible for the error and who would bear the cost of correcting the mistake.

CHAPTER 7

Foodservice Equipment, Part II: Manufactured Equipment

THIS CHAPTER

☑ Introduces the major kinds of manufactured foodservice equipment, discussed under six functional categories:

- ◆ Receiving and storage
- ◆ Preparation
- ◆ Cooking/Production
- ◆ Bakery
- ◆ Service and cafeteria
- ◆ Beverage equipment
- ◆ Warewashing
- ◆ Waste removal

☑ Describes the characteristics of the equipment as well as its primary use in a foodservice operation. When selecting equipment, consideration should be given as to what type of production is to be used. The current methods include:

- ◆ Cook-serve
- ◆ Cook-hold-serve
- ◆ Cook-chill-store-reheat-serve (known as cook/chill)

Receiving, preparation, and cleanup options typically do not vary enough to warrant detailed discussions.

The cook-serve method of production is typically used in a restaurant setting, although it can also be used in an institutional setting when display cooking is introduced. After a meal order has been received, the food is cooked on the appropriate piece of cooking equipment and then immediately served to the customer. In a restaurant setting, the completed meal may sit on a chef's counter for a short period of time waiting for the waitstaff to pick it up, but holding time should be negligible.

The cook-hold-serve method incorporates an extended period of holding, up to 60 minutes, between the cooking time and service to the customer. This type of production typically occurs in a cafeteria-type setting.

The food can be held in several different pieces of equipment where customers may or may not be able to see and select their food choice. Selecting the appropriate piece of holding equipment is critical to the quality, appearance, and nutritional value of the food.

Finally, the cook/chill production method involves cooking the food then rapidly chilling and storing for later use. This method is also known as cook/chill or advanced food production. When this type of food production was first introduced into the industry over 25 years ago, its primary application was for centralized kitchens. Cook/chill and cook/freeze technology make it possible to cook to inventory and extend the shelf life of the finished product from five days to six weeks for cook/chill products and six months or more for cook/freeze products. Cook/chill and cook/freeze technology maximizes the advantages of centralized food production through:

❏ *Reduced labor costs.* Labor costs are less, since production is occurring in one central location rather than multiple cooks cooking the same product in multiple locations. Also, high-level and high-paid personnel can be eliminated. This is the major cost savings when implementing a cook/chill operation.

❏ *Reduced food costs.* Reduced food costs are achieved through increased food yields, reduced waste by eliminating over-production of cook-hold-serve methods, and procurement savings occur since food is delivered to a single central kitchen instead of multiple locations.

❏ *Reduced equipment operating and maintenance costs.* Since food production is occurring in a single location with cook/chill technology, the traditional cooking equipment in the satellite receiving kitchens is used far less, thus increasing the life cycle of the equipment and reducing the maintenance costs.

❏ *Reduced utility costs.* The overall utility costs will also be reduced since production occurs at a single location rather than at multiple locations.

❏ *Consistent quality and production control.* Since production is occurring in one central location rather than with multiple cooks, quality control is maintained.

❏ *Improved food safety.* The sanitation controls on advanced food production equipment systems are much easier to enforce.

The advanced food production's primary application for centralized kitchens or central production units has encouraged the development of equipment that can be used on a smaller scale while still realizing the same benefits. Tumble/chill systems continue to become downsized while blast chillers are commonplace. Cook/chill has been implemented in chain and single-store restaurants, health care, hotels, prisons, school systems, and other food operations.

Several hotel chains and catering contractors use their cook/chill equipment for their catering operations. Prior to cook/chill technology, food for large banquets would have to be prepared, cooked, and held hot for an extended period of time, usually hours before the actual meal service. With a cook/chill system, meals can be prepared days in advance and then chilled and held at controlled temperatures. This allows production to occur in a normal working shift. The meals can also be plated and stored in their chilled state during a normal working shift. Just prior to meal service, usually 20 to 60 minutes (depending on the product being served), the meals are reheated and served. Waiting to reheat the chilled plated foods provides the flexibility of adjusting service time in case a speaker extends the beginning of service.

Another example for cook/chill technology would be in the health care environment. Since patient hospital stays have grown increasingly shorter, menu cycles have also been reduced. Rather then cooking one menu item on every third or fourth day, that menu could be produced once in a larger batch using cook/chill production equipment and then chilled and stored for an extended period of time. The chilled menu item could then be reheated on an as-needed basis, thus reducing production time and decreasing food waste through overproduction. Cook/chill equipment also allows the chef to produce the day's production cycle in a single shift and leave the simple reheating procedure to a lower-paid cook or utilize a retherm system that reheats the food automatically.

RECEIVING AND STORAGE EQUIPMENT

Receiving Carts

Many foodservice operations use utility carts to transport foods from receiving to storage areas. Because utility carts are made of relatively light-gauge materials, using them to transport heavy cases of food causes the top shelf to bow and buckle. As a result, the utility cart loses its utility. A receiving cart made of heavy-gauge materials and designed to support heavy items is a good investment in a foodservice operation (see Figure 7.1).

Receiving Scale

Upon receiving incoming supplies, it is good practice to verify the shipment against the order for quantity, quality and integrity, product substitutions, and weight. A receiving scale will allow you to check the weight of product and compare it to the weight noted on the shipping label.

Shelving: Freestanding and Portable

Shelving systems can be purchased to solve almost any food storage problem or to fit almost all types of spaces. The efficiency of a storage space is influenced by the efficiency of the storage shelves used in the space. The wooden homemade shelves that are often used in dry storerooms are difficult to clean and are not allowed by many health departments in the United States. The cost of heavy-duty (14- or 16-gauge) stainless-steel shelves with wheels is very high, but the great durability of the equipment, its ease of cleaning, and its portability may offset the initial investment.

Figure 7.1. Receiving Cart. Courtesy of New Age Industrial Corporation, Inc.

Varieties of shelving include:

❑ Portable (on casters), freestanding (on posts), or wall-hung (cantilever)

❑ Multiple tiers (shelves), usually four or five for bulk storage

❑ Solid shelves with embossed, louvered, or flat shelf surfaces

❑ Shelves with removable plastic grids that can be cleaned in a dish machine

❑ Solid shelves constructed of stainless steel, galvanized steel, aluminum, high-impact plastic, or other materials

❑ Wire shelves constructed of stainless steel, galvanized steel, or high-impact plastic, chrome-plated or epoxy-coated

The accessories that can be added are almost limitless, but the most common ones are:

❑ Casters

❑ Stainless-steel posts (uprights)

❑ Rotating bumpers on the uprights

❑ Strip or wraparound bumpers

❑ Extra bracing for heavy products

❑ Wall-mounting clamps

❑ Wire enclosures (for security)

❑ Drawers and baskets

❑ Labeling clip-ons

High-density shelving allows for an increased storage capacity of 30 to 40 percent within a reduced square footage area. Shelving units constructed of stainless steel (because of its strength) move horizontally on casters guided by a track that is attached to fixed shelving units on the ends of the track. When leaving one mobile unit out for aisle space, the other units can slide back and forth to move the aisle to the space needed to access the stored goods (see Figure 7.2).

Dunnage racks are single-tier shelves designed to support stacks of heavy products, such as cases of canned goods, approximately 10 inches (250 millimeters [mm]) above the floor. They are frequently used in dry-storage and frozen-storage areas in large foodservice operations.

The sizes of shelving that are most often used in foodservice are:

Width: 12 inches (305 mm), 18 inches (460 mm), 21 inches (535 mm), 24 inches (610 mm), and 27 inches (685 mm) are the most common

Figure 7.2. High-Density Shelving. Courtesy of Eagle Group.

widths for use in dry storerooms, for use in walk-in refrigerators and freezers, and for general kitchen utensil storage.

Length: 36 inches (915 mm), 42 inches (1,070 mm), 48 inches (1,220 mm), 54 inches (1,370 mm), and 60 inches (1,520 mm) are the most popular sizes. These lengths should not be exceeded because of the loss of strength and rigidity beyond 60 inches (1,520 mm).

Height: The posts (uprights) can be purchased in many different heights. The most common are 33 inches (838 mm), 54 inches (1,370 mm), 63 inches (1,600 mm), 74 inches (1,880 mm), and 86 inches (2,184 mm).

General guidelines for shelving selection are:

- ❏ *Walk-in refrigerators.* The 27-inch (685-mm) shelf with the maximum height possible is a good selection to maximize storage capacity. Narrow walk-in refrigeration (less than 7 feet 6 inches [2.3 meters (m)] in width) will require narrow shelving.

- ❏ *Walk-in freezers.* Frozen foods are often shipped in boxes that are easily stacked. A combination of dunnage racks for case goods that can be stacked and four-shelf portable shelving units for odd-shaped items or small packages would be a good choice.

- ❏ *Dry storage.* Four- or five-shelf portable shelving units work well for spices, broken cases, or individual number 10 cans. For many larger foodservice facilities, the use of wooden pallets that are moved by forklift trucks may be appropriate, in combination with the standard shelving.

Shelving: Fixed or Attached to Equipment

Three kinds of attached shelving typically are found in a foodservice facility: elevated shelving, under-table shelving, and cabinet shelving.

Elevated shelving is attached either to a wall above the equipment or directly to the piece of equipment by stainless-steel tubular uprights. Wall-mounted shelving is preferable because of the elimination of the uprights from the table surface of the equipment. For equipment that is placed away from the wall, however, elevated shelving must be mounted onto the table or ceiling-hung. The most sanitary means for accomplishing this is to mount the uprights into the backsplash of the table.

Refrigeration (Coolers and Freezers, Walk-in and Reach-in)

The refrigeration equipment found in the modern foodservice facility may include:

- ❏ Reach-in refrigerators and freezers
- ❏ Walk-in refrigerators and freezers
- ❏ Undercounter refrigerators and freezers
- ❏ Roll-in refrigerators and freezers
- ❏ Pass-through refrigerators and freezers
- ❏ Refrigerated cold pans

❏ Soft-serve machines and ice cream cabinets

❏ Display refrigerators, such as deli counters, refrigerated grocery display cases, and other merchandising devices

The special features available for the many different types of refrigeration equipment are too varied to cover in this volume. This information can be found in any of the excellent reference books on foodservice equipment and refrigeration that are available. The four most commonly used refrigeration systems are walk-in refrigerators and freezers, reach-in refrigerators and freezers, display refrigerators, and blast chillers. Each is discussed in the text that follows.

WALK-IN REFRIGERATORS AND FREEZERS

Currently, the two primary types of walk-in refrigerators and freezers are prefabricated and built-in. The prefabricated walk-in is usually constructed from a series of 4-inch (10-centimeter)-thick modular panels. Each panel is made with urethane insulation material that is foamed into place between two sheets of metal. The kinds of metal that can be specified for prefabricated walk-ins include:

❏ Galvanized steel

❏ Painted galvanized steel

❏ Aluminum (embossed or plain)

❏ Painted aluminum

❏ Stainless steel

Walk-ins are often specified with several different finishes, such as white painted aluminum for the interior walls and ceiling, stainless steel on the exposed exterior walls, a galvanized steel on the unexposed interior walls, and galvanized steel on the interior floor so that quarry tile can be installed over it.

These panels are attached to each other (with a variety of latches and bolts) to form the outer walls, ceiling, partitions, and floor (optional) of the refrigerator. They can be purchased in many combinations of heights, lengths, and widths. A walk-in cooler is illustrated in Figure 7.3.

The specification of a prefabricated walk-in using the manufacturer's standard modular panels produces a refrigerator that is "nominal" in size. Each manufacturer determines the nominal widths, lengths, and heights of standard panels. A manufacturer's walk-in that is described as 8 feet by 12 feet (2.44 m by 3.66 m) may actually be 7 feet 6 inches by 11 feet 4 inches (2.32 m by 3.45 m) when built using standard panels of nominal size. Custom or full-size walk-in refrigerators are available and can be purchased, at an additional cost, in almost any size. The primary difference between nominal-size and full-size walk-ins is cost. Nominal-size units, because they use standard panels, are less expensive to manufacture than units requiring custom panel sizing. Knowing the difference between standard (nominal) and full-size walk-ins is critical when specifying these units.

Figure 7.3. Walk-in Refrigeration. Courtesy of THERMO-KOOL/Mid-South Industries, Inc.

Prefabricated walk-ins can be installed indoors using a number of different flooring systems, each with advantages and disadvantages:

Manufacturer's floor recessed into a pit. A pit about 4 inches (10 cm) deep and slightly longer and wider than the walk-in is built into the concrete subfloor of the building. The walk-in's floor panels are set into the pit. Then quarry tile (or a similar flooring system) is run continuously from the kitchen into the walk-in. The primary advantage of this approach is that carts and racks can be taken in and out of the walk-in across a level surface. This approach is ideal in new construction where the concrete subfloor can be poured with a pit at little additional expense. The disadvantage of this approach is that it may be impractical in a renovation, where cutting a pit in the existing floor is prohibitively expensive.

Manufacturer's floor with ramps. A ramp into the walk-in is necessary where the floor cannot be recessed. Ramps can be built either in the interior or the exterior of the walk-in. Interior ramps are furnished by the walk-in manufacturer. Exterior ramps often are built by the contractors who pour the floor and lay the tile. The disadvantage of this approach is that ramps can be steep enough to cause spillage as food items are carted up and down. The manufacturer's floor should be specified to be able to withstand the maximum point load of the object, cart, or shelving to be stored in the walk-in.

Installations without manufacturer's floor panels. Prefabricated walk-ins can be installed without the manufacturer's floor panels. In this approach the walls are anchored to the building floor on screeds that seal and support the structure. This approach provides a level passage from the kitchen into the walk-in. However, this approach requires insulating the floor under freezers to prevent the concrete from cracking due to temperature differences.

For many years, the working surfaces of walk-in coolers were made of galvanized steel. Despite the galvanizing treatment, steel floors proved to be vulnerable to pitting and rusting due to the moist conditions in coolers. The floors often wore out long before the rest of the unit, creating unsanitary conditions. The National Sanitation Foundation (NSF) now requires walk-in floors to meet substantially tougher standards for endurance. Stainless steel is an acceptable flooring material, as is aluminum tread plate provided that it is fully coved and integrated into the floor system. Galvanized steel can still be used in a walk-in cooler, but only if it is covered with another material that is acceptable as a working surface. Quarry tile is one such material.

A built-in refrigerator or freezer, which is more expensive than a prefab, is constructed of insulating foam walls, floors, and ceiling that are protected with structural glazed tile walls, quarry tile floors, and aluminum or stainless-steel ceilings. Large built-in refrigerators may also be constructed of fiberglass panels laid over the insulation. The built-in refrigerator has the advantage of lasting many years under conditions of heavy use but the disadvantage of being more expensive and more difficult to enlarge or move.

Walk-in refrigerators and freezers are usually specified with either self-contained (top- or side-mounted) or remote refrigeration systems. The self-contained units are usually hidden on top of the walk-ins by closure panels, but sufficient air space must be available to prevent the air-cooling units from building up heat in the space above the walk-in. If the large air mass in the space above the false ceiling is insufficient for removing the heat of the compressor, additional ventilation will be necessary. Remote refrigeration systems can be located some distance away either inside or outside the building, but the farther the distance, the greater the heat (efficiency) loss. Remote refrigeration has the advantage of keeping noise and heat away from the food production area. Refrigeration systems can be either air-cooled or water-cooled, depending on environmental conditions and utility availability. Heat recovery equipment is an important accessory to refrigeration systems because of high energy costs and can be effective for preheating water or heating space in the building. Preengineered refrigeration systems with multiple compressors are often specified for large food operations, providing greater energy efficiency and longer compressor life.

Common accessories and features that may be added to the walk-in specifications are:

❏ Outdoor, protected refrigeration systems
❏ Freezer alarm system that activates when the temperature reaches 15°F (−9.4°C)

❑ Extra interior vaporproof lights

❑ Roof caps for walk-ins located outdoors

❑ Wall protectors to prevent damage from carts (interior or exterior)

❑ Ramps for walk-ins not level with the floor

❑ Locks for doors

❑ Windows for doors

❑ Closure panels and trim strips for improving the outside appearance

❑ Thermoplastic strip curtains to reduce loss of cold air when door is open

❑ Foot treadle openers for doors

❑ Air vent to relieve pressure when doors are opened or closed

❑ Glass access doors for placing foods in the walk-in without the necessity of walking in

REACH-IN REFRIGERATORS AND FREEZERS

The word "refrigeration" refers to mechanically cooled refrigerators and freezers, and "refrigerator" means a refrigeration unit that maintains a temperature of 36°F (2.2°C) to 40°F (4.4°C). The most frequently used refrigerators in all types and sizes of food facilities are the reach-ins. The versatility, reasonable cost, and storage efficiency explain why this kind of refrigeration is popular. Figure 7.4 illustrates a reach-in refrigerator.

Figure 7.4. Reach-in Refrigerator. Courtesy of All True Photos.

Reach-in refrigerators can be purchased with one, two, or three compartments and are available with many different options and accessories. In selecting this type of equipment, consider these questions:

❑ Will space and budget permit the installation of one, two, or three compartments?

❑ Will the refrigerator be used for general storage or for special products that would fit better on interior tray slides?

❑ Should the refrigerator be adapted for roll-in carts, which eliminate all interior shelving?

❑ What capacities of storage are needed for reach-in refrigerators and freezers in the food production area?

❑ Is this refrigeration the primary cold storage capacity for the food facility, or is the refrigeration being used to augment walk-in refrigerators and freezers?

❑ What special features would the owner like to have specified for this refrigeration?

Typical specifications might include:

❑ Automatic condensate evaporator, which eliminates the need for a floor drain

❑ Adjustable shelving or tray slides to accommodate trays that are standard in the foodservice industry, such as 18-by-26-inch sheet pans, 12-by-20-inch steam table pans, or 530-by-325 mm gastronorm, a well-known pan size in Europe.

❑ Cam lift on spring-loaded hinges that cause the doors to close automatically

❑ Stainless-steel interior and exterior, or a combination of anodized aluminum and stainless steel, or all anodized aluminum

❑ Exterior thermometer

❑ Interior lighting

❑ Full-size door or half doors

❑ Doors with glass windows

❑ Pass-through (doors on both sides)

In summary, there are many options available to the food facilities planner in choosing refrigeration for a food operation. An excellent source of information is an equipment catalog from one of the leading refrigeration manufacturers. These can be seen in the offices of the food facilities consultant or at a dealer's showroom or can be obtained directly from the manufacturer.

Primary Use in the Food Operation

Reach-in and walk-in refrigeration must be provided within easy access of the primary food production areas. Many restaurants, hotel dining facilities, and institutions use a combination of walk-ins and reach-in refrigerators. Walk-ins are usually used to store bulk foods, while reach-ins provide convenient cold storage near the production area.

Size of Food Facility (Seats)	Walk-in Refrigeration				Reach-in Refrigeration†			
	Freezer		Refrigerator		Freezer		Refrigerator	
	Number	Size	Number	Size	Number	Size	Number	Size
Under 50	0	—	0	—	1	B	2	B
50–100	1	X	1	X	1	C	3	B
100–175	1	Y	2	X	2	B	3	C
175–250	1	Z	2	Y	2	B	3	C
250–500	1	Z	3	Y	2	C	4	C
500–750	2	Y	3	Z	2	C	5	C
More than 750	2	Z	4	Z	3	C	5	C

* Walk-in size key:
X: 9 by 12 feet (2.74 by 3.66 meters)
Y: 9 by 15 feet (2.74 by 4.57 meters)
Z: 9 by 20 feet (2.74 by 6.10 meters)

† Reach-in size key:
A: one-compartment
B: two-compartment
C: three-compartment

Figure 7.5. Refrigeration Requirements Based on Facility Size. Courtesy of Sandra Ley. *Foodservice Refrigeration* (New York: Van Nostrand Reinhold, 1980).

The method of calculating the capacity of walk-in refrigeration is included in Chapter 4. Reach-in refrigeration capacities are usually listed as net capacity in cubic feet (or cubic meters). This designation should mean that the available interior space for storage is the net cubic footage. However, in many instances, the interior space is not totally available for storage because of evaporators, lights, tray slides, and so on, and the net cubic footage may be somewhat less. Typical interior capacities are:

Determining Capacity and Size

> *One compartment:* 21.5 cubic feet (0.6 cubic m)
> *Two compartments:* 46.5 cubic feet (1.3 cubic m)
> *Three compartments:* 70.0 cubic feet (2 cubic m)

One interesting variation on refrigeration is the "refrigerator" that heats rather than cools. These heated cabinet units are used to hold hot foods and are an excellent application in food operations that need a large holding capacity.

Figure 7.3, which shows capacities, may be useful in estimating the needed refrigeration.

Because the refrigeration equipment in a foodservice facility will be operating 24 hours a day, it is wise to do everything possible to reduce the loss of energy through the purchase of the best equipment possible. Refrigeration is not the place to cut corners or to omit energy-saving accessories. Heat recovery from water-cooled refrigeration systems is easy to engineer and will bring a quick return on the investment. Also, medium-size and larger operations are likely to benefit from installing a central refrigeration system that supplies walk-ins, reach-ins, display units, salad bars, ice machines, and all of the other refrigerated systems in the facility.

HACCP (hazard analysis critical control point) guidelines dictates increasing time and temperature monitoring. A temperature monitoring system can automatically collect and retain pertinent and required data and can reduce the time, effort, and labor of having personnel walk around the kitchen collecting the same data manually. Because these systems use wireless technology, they can be easily installed into new kitchens or retrofitted into existing establishments.

Temperature

PREPARATION EQUIPMENT

A food facility's preparation area is where foods are processed before the meal is finally cooked and served. Typically, foods are mixed, seasoned, chopped, roasted, or cleaned in this part of the kitchen. The designer must group only the equipment that will be used for preparation in this area so that the highest level of efficiency can be achieved. The mixing of preparation equipment with final preparation equipment is a frequent layout mistake made by inexperienced designers.

Desirable features of the preparation area are sinks, worktables, utensil storage, access to refrigeration, and access to warewashing, as well as various kinds of food production equipment. The most commonly required equipment is discussed in some detail in this section.

Figure 7.6. Mixer. Courtesy of Hobart Corporation.

Mixers

DESCRIPTION

The mixer is a very versatile piece of preparation equipment that is found in nearly all kitchens. The specifier has many choices of sizes and accessories. Mixers are sized by bowl capacity, which ranges from 5 to 140 quarts. The mixer bowl normally is stationary, and the mixer head rotates inside the bowl with a dual circular motion so that all parts of the bowl are covered in the mixing process. The beaters usually furnished with the mixer include a flat beater for general mixing, a wire whip for light products such as whipped cream, and a dough hook for heavy yeast doughs. Large mixers (80 quarts or larger) are usually constructed with power lifts to raise the heavy mixer bowls to the proper position. Most mixers are equipped with a power takeoff for attaching optional equipment. Vegetable slicers, meat grinders, bowl dollies, and special dough mixer attachments are typical of the accessories that can be purchased for a mixer. A typical foodservice mixer is shown in Figure 7.6.

PRIMARY USE IN THE FOOD OPERATION

Mixers are used where large quantities of food are being mixed, where a variety of attachments are required, and where food processing is done.

DETERMINING CAPACITY AND SIZE

Figure 7.7 provides guidelines for determining the number and size of mixers necessary for a foodservice operation.

Meals Served per Day	MIXERS Bakery Not Included		MIXERS Including Bakery	
	Quantity	Size	Quantity	Size
Less than 100	1	5 quarts (4.7 liters)	1	12 quarts (11.4 liters)
100–200	1	12 quarts (11.4 liters)	1	12 quarts (11.4 liters)
			1	20 quarts (18.9 liters)
200–400	1	12 quarts (11.4 liters)	1	20 quarts (18.9 liters)
	1	30 quarts	1	30 quarts (28.4 liters)
400–600	1	20 quarts (18.9 liters)	1	30 quarts (28.4 liters)
	1	60 quarts (56.8 liters)	1	60 quarts (56.8 liters)
600–1,000	2	60 quarts (56.8 liters)	2	60 quarts (56.8 liters)
			1	80 quarts (75.7 liters)
1,000–1,500	1	60 quarts (56.8 liters)	2	60 quarts (56.8 liters)
	1	80 quarts (75.7 liters)	1	80 quarts (75.7 liters)
More than 1,500	2	60 quarts (56.8 liters)	2	80 quarts (75.7 liters)
	1	80 quarts (75.7 liters)	1	140 quarts (132.5 liters)

Figure 7.7. Mixer Requirements Based on Meals Served per Day.

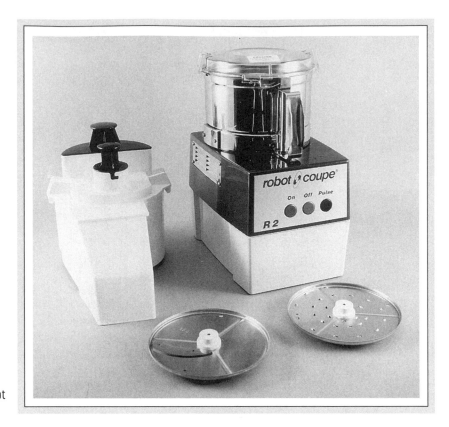

Figure 7.8. R2V Food Processor. Courtesy of Robot Coupe, USA, Inc.

Food Processors

DESCRIPTION

High-speed food processors, similar to the popular models designed for home use, have been used in the commercial foodservice industry for the last two decades. Prior to this, the most common food processors were the buffalo chopper and the vertical cutter-mixer (VCM). VCMs are still very much in use in large commercial kitchens, and each has its advantages. Figure 7.8 shows a typical food processor. The variety of food-processing machines available is far too great to list or describe in this text. The manager or owner might want to see a demonstration before choosing any kind of processor. The new, smaller high-speed food processors are made by several companies, offering a wide number of choices. The use of a small model in combination with a buffalo chopper or VCM might be a wise choice for the large food operation, especially if a wide variety of salads is included in the menu.

Buffalo Chopper

The buffalo chopper is illustrated in Figure 7.9. The food is chopped by a semicircular blade that rotates rapidly under a protective cover. As the food moves around the outside edge of the revolving bowl, it is chopped hundreds of times. The more often the food travels around the bowl, the more finely it is chopped. Vegetables, meats, and many other foods can be processed in a buffalo chopper.

Figure 7.9. Buffalo Chopper. Courtesy of Hobart Corporation.

Similar to a blender except that it is much larger and more expensive, the vertical cutter-mixer will cut, mix, and blend foods in seconds, and is used primarily for chopping meats and vegetables (see Figure 7.10). It is also an excellent piece of equipment for the bakery and will blend most doughs and frostings in two or three minutes. The VCM uses a high-speed stainless-steel curved knife that rotates on the inside of the bowl. It should be located in the kitchen beside a floor drain and near a source of hot and

Vertical Cutter-Mixer

Figure 7.10. Vertical Cutter Mixer. Courtesy of Hobart Corporation.

Product	Time	30-Quart VCM	45-Quart VCM
Bread crumbs	2 minutes	2–4 lb (.91–1.81 kg)	4–6 lb (1.81–2.72 kg)
Pie dough	1½–2½ minutes	2–6 lb (.91–2.72 kg)	3–8 lb (1.36–3.63 kg)
Hamburger	1–2 minutes	12–24 lb (5.44–10.89 kg)	18–36 lb (8.16–16.33 kg)
Lettuce	2–3 jogs of switch	4–6 heads	6–10 heads
Meat loaf	1–1½ minutes	12–25 lb (5.44–11.34 kg)	20–30 lbs (9.07–13.61 kg)
Cake batter	2½–4 minutes	15–30 lb (6.80–13.61 kg)	25–60 lb (11.34–27.22 kg)

Figure 7.11. Vertical Cutter-Mixer Capacities. Courtesy of Hobart Corporation.

cold water for ease in cleaning. The most common VCM bowl sizes range from 30 to 45 quarts. Typical capacities used for frequently processed foods are found in Figure 7.11.

Slicers

Slicers are motor-driven with a round carbon-steel or stainless-steel blade that is hollow- or bevel-ground. The blade and carrier are tilted at an angle of approximately 30 degrees from vertical so that gravity pulls the food product down the carrier into the path of the blade. A high-volume slicer can have a different configuration, with a horizontal cutting action and a device that stacks sliced product into portions with wax paper separators.

The diameter of the blade determines the size of the product that can be sliced. Most slicers have integral sharpeners to keep the blade in working condition. A wide variety of slicer sizes are available. Some, called automatic slicers, can be specified with a motor to move the carrier back and forth across the blade. As a safety device, most slicers have a hand grip and protective plate over the blade. Figure 7.12 shows a commercial slicer.

A wide variety of accessories are available for slicers, including:

❏ A food chute to hold different types of vegetables (tomatoes, cabbage, etc.) during slicing
❏ Variable speed control
❏ Gear-driven table adjustment for consistent slicing thickness
❏ Semi- or fully automatic slicing
❏ Removable or permanently mounted sharpener

A slicer often is mounted on a portable cart so that it can be used as needed in different areas of the kitchen. A cart with open shelves below the top and fold-down sides is ideal because it provides staging space for items to be sliced and short-term storage for finished products.

Slicers are dangerous pieces of equipment and should be used and cleaned only by trained employees. Although slicer manufacturers have done an excellent job of designing protective devices and safety features, accidents are still possible if the operator is careless.

Figure 7.12. Slicer Courtesy of Globe Food Equipment Company.

PRODUCTION/COOKING

The production/cooking area is physically located between preparation and the service area of a food facility. In the final production area, foods are cooked immediately before and during the meal period.

The production area should include refrigeration for storing foods that have been processed and are ready to be cooked. Most production equipment, such as grills and fryers, produces a large quantity of grease and soil and therefore should be installed in a manner that will permit easy cleaning. The production area should be adjacent to the warewashing area for easy access to the pot sink and a supply of clean dishes.

The production area should always include this equipment for storing and handling:

❑ Worktables or spreader plates
❑ Utensil racks and storage drawers
❑ Sinks
❑ A pickup station
❑ Hot- and cold-food holding equipment
❑ A storage place for raw ingredients

The production equipment for this area consists of:

- ❑ Ovens (standard, convection, deck, rotary, rack, conveyor, slow roasting, combi, microwave, and/or specialty ovens)
- ❑ Low- and no-pressure steamers
- ❑ High-pressure steamers
- ❑ Water filtration
- ❑ Tilting fry pan
- ❑ Kettle
- ❑ Bain-maries
- ❑ Griddle (grill)
- ❑ Grooved griddles
- ❑ Clamshell griddles
- ❑ Fryers
- ❑ Ranges
- ❑ Induction cooker
- ❑ Broilers
- ❑ Mongolian grill
- ❑ Rotisserie
- ❑ Cook/Chill

Ovens   There are many different types of ovens, and each has special advantages that must be carefully considered by the foodservice consultant or owner. The most popular ovens are classified as:

- ❑ Standard (under the range)
- ❑ Convection
- ❑ Deck
- ❑ Rack
- ❑ Conveyor
- ❑ Slow-roasting
- ❑ Combi
- ❑ Microwave

STANDARD OVENS

Description   The standard oven is typically built into a hot-top, open-top, grill-top, or other heavy-duty piece of range equipment. These ovens are popular because they are inexpensive and are conveniently located in the range (hot-food preparation) section of the kitchen.

Standard ovens have some disadvantages that have caused specifiers of equipment to look for better types of ovens. The primary disadvantages are:

- ❑ The location under the range makes it difficult for the cook to see or reach into the oven.
- ❑ The ovens are poorly insulated and thus energy-inefficient.

❑ Under conditions of heavy usage, standard ovens require frequent maintenance and repair of door hinges and thermostats.

❑ Cleaning under and behind standard ovens is extremely difficult.

❑ The capacity of the standard oven is relatively small in comparison to other oven designs.

Standard ovens are used for roasting and baking in the small- to medium-size foodservice operation. This type of oven should not be specified for a foodservice facility unless space and/or funds are severely limited. Other types of ovens discussed in this chapter offer superior choices for most foodservice operations.

Primary Use in a Food Operation

CONVECTION OVENS

Description   The most widely used oven in the foodservice industry is the convection oven. The convection oven is energy-efficient and occupies a small amount of space in the kitchen—characteristics that make it highly desirable. Figure 7.13 shows a convection oven. Convection ovens can be purchased in either single- or double-cavity units. A double-cavity convection oven measures approximately 36 inches (915 mm) wide by 40 inches (100 mm) deep.

In the convection oven, a fan circulates the heated air through the cooking cavity at a high rate. As the heat flows rapidly over the food product, heat transfer occurs more quickly than in a conventional oven, and cooking time is reduced. Because the rapidly moving air reaches all parts of the oven chamber, food can be placed in the convection oven on closely spaced shelves, thus increasing the capacity of the oven compartment.

The energy and space efficiency of the convection oven is primarily a result of rapid cooking and the utilization of almost all of the oven's interior space. Typical convection ovens will hold five full sheet pans of product in each of the oven chambers. Accessories for convection ovens

Figure 7.13. Convection Oven. Courtesy of Vulcan-Hart.

Number of Meals Served per Day	Single-Compartment Oven(s)	Double-Compartment Oven(s)
Under 100	1	0
100–200	1	0
200–400	1	1
400–600	0	2
600–1,000	0	3
1,000–1,800	0	4
1,800–3,000	0	5

Figure 7.14. Convection Oven Requirements Based on Meals Served per Day.

include removable liners for ease of cleaning, automatic timing devices, and a variety of exterior finishes.

Primary Use in the Food Operation

Convection ovens are excellent for cooking many products that will fit on a standard 18-by-26-inch sheet pan or standard gastronorm pans. Meats, baked potatoes, bakery products, and small roasts are products that can be easily prepared in this oven. The roasting of large pieces of meat, such as a whole turkey or ribs of beef, can be done in a convection oven, but the space utilization is not as effective, because the size of the meat does not permit the use of closely spaced shelves.

Determining Capacity and Size

The oven capacity selected will depend on the number of items on the menu that are normally cooked in an oven and whether there is a bakery in the operation or not. Figure 7.14 illustrates typical convection oven capacity needs for foodservice operations.

DECK OVENS

Description Often called a pizza oven because of its widespread use for making pizza, the deck oven is constructed of one, two, or three levels of oven space and can be either gas-fired or electric. A deck oven is illustrated in Figure 7.15. For many years, this was the most common oven in large restaurants or institutions for doing all types of baking and roasting. Because of the variety of foods that were cooked in these devices, manufacturers developed different sizes and capacities to handle different food products. One variation of the deck oven is the roasting oven. This is the same as a conventional deck oven except that the cavity is higher to accommodate large standing rib roasts, whole turkeys, or steamship rounds of beef.

The typical specifications for deck ovens include:

❏ Gas or electric energy

❏ Exterior finish of stainless steel or galvanized steel with black lacquer finish

❏ Number of decks

Figure 7.15. Deck Oven. Courtesy of G.S. Blodgett Corporation.

❏ Height of the cooking cavities
❏ Steel or brick hearth (a baker may prefer a brick hearth for French bread)
❏ High heat levels for pizza baking

The deck oven is a general-purpose piece of equipment that will handle a variety of roasting and baking needs. The deck oven's large footprint makes it impractical for the small food operation. A convection oven offers much greater cooking capacity with a smaller footprint. Many bakers continue to prefer the deck oven for the small- to medium-size bakery, however. Deck ovens are excellent for pizza because the interior cavity is large, permitting easy peeling (removal of pizza with a large spatula), and the oven can be heated to high temperatures.

Primary Use in the Food Operation

A standard 42-by-32-inch (1,067-by-813-mm) deck in a deck oven would hold 2 standard roasting pans, 2 18-by-26-inch sheet (bun) pans, 12 10-inch pies, or 4 1/1 (530-by-325-mm) gastronorm pans. Stacking the oven to three decks will increase these capacities accordingly.

Determining Capacity and Size

ROTARY OVENS

Description Rotary or revolving tray ovens are designed to increase airflow over the food. Unlike convection ovens, which move the air across the food with a fan, rotary ovens move the food itself within the cooking cavity. Trays holding food are mounted to large "wheels" that rotate like a Ferris wheel. The food is cooked while it moves around in a circular motion in the large, heated chamber. This method of roasting or baking is excellent because the heated chamber can be well insulated and is therefore energy-efficient. Moreover, the food can be cooked more evenly as a result of the airflow (convection) that is created when the food is in motion. Figure 7.16 illustrates a rotary oven.

The primary disadvantage of a rotary oven is its size. These ovens occupy a considerable amount of floor space as well as vertical space. The

Figure 7.16. Rotary Oven. Courtesy of Doyon Equipment, Inc.

small rotary ovens of one leading manufacturer measure 81 inches wide (2057.4 mm) by 44 inches (1176 mm) from front to back and 82 inches (2082.8 mm) high. Rotary ovens used for baking are much larger and are built on-site by the manufacturer.

Specifications that are typically used when purchasing this equipment include:

❏ Exterior finish (stainless steel or baked enamel on galvanized steel)
❏ Number of trays (capacity)
❏ Heating method (gas or electricity)
❏ Method of opening the door
❏ Insulation
❏ Adjustable revolving shelves
❏ Method of venting the oven cavity
❏ Temperature ranges
❏ Steam injection (for hard-crust breads)

Primary Use in the Food Operation

Rotary ovens are very popular with bakers because of their large capacity and even baking characteristics. These ovens often last many years under conditions of constant use, with only an occasional need for realignment or repair. Small rotary ovens are also excellent pieces of equipment for the production kitchen for roasting and are often used in conjunction with convection ovens.

REVOLVING RACK OVEN

Description Like the rotary tray oven, the revolving rack oven moves the food product while baking or roasting. This oven uses a rack that can be rolled inside the heated chamber (see Figure 7.17). The baker loads the rack with items ready for baking and wheels it into the oven. The rack is lifted and rotated in the oven chamber during the baking period and then wheeled from the oven to cool. There are two advantages to the revolving rack oven over the rotary oven. First, the revolving rack oven can match the capacity of the rotary oven while using substantially less floor space. Second, the baker does not have to remove the bun pans from the rack to set them in the oven. Instead, he or she simply rolls the entire rack into the oven and back out when baking is complete.

Figure 7.17. Rack Oven. Courtesy of Doyon Equipment, Inc.

Typical specifications for a rotating rack oven include:

❏ Size (capacity) in number of racks (one, two, or more)
❏ Energy source (gas, electric)
❏ Primary use (baking versus roasting) (This is very important due to product weight differentials.)
❏ Steam injection for crusty breads

Primary Use in the Food Operation

Rotating rack ovens are especially popular for baking breads, rolls, cakes, pies, cookies, and other items in large operations because of their high capacity. They also are used for roasting large quantities of meats and poultry. The primary advantages of rotating rack ovens are their ease of loading and unloading as well as their high capacity within a relatively small footprint.

CONVEYOR OVENS

Description The conveying of foods through a heated chamber is becoming more and more popular, especially in food operations that employ semiskilled and unskilled labor. A conveyor oven permits the food product to flow through the heated cavity at a predetermined speed while ensuring the same cooking time for each product prepared (see Figure 7.18). Conveyor ovens are in common usage in pizza operations.

There are two techniques for heating the product. In one method, the heating elements are located above and below the metal conveyor belt, so that the product can be cooked on both sides at once as it passes through the oven cavity. The second cooking method, called impingement, involves blowing hot air from a heating chamber through small orifices located above and below the conveyor belt. This second method removes the cold air layer surrounding the food, cooking the product more evenly and without the danger of scorching or overcooking the surface of the food product.

Figure 7.18. Conveyer Oven. Courtesy of Lincon/Wearever, Inc.

Baking Area, Square Feet/Square Meters	Belt Width, Inches/Millimeters)	Pizzas per Hour	Utility Requirements, BTUs/Hour
8/.74	24/610	30	135,000
10.7/1.0	32/810	60	135,000
21.4/2.0*	32/810	120	270,000

*The larger baking area and capacity are created by stacking two 32-inch-wide (812.8 mm) units.

Figure 7.19. Conveyor Oven Capacities.

The conveyor ovens are best used in high-volume foodservice operations. Once the conveyor speed is set, products can be cooked in rapid succession with consistent results. Pizza, cookies, muffins, hamburgers, and other products that are not too thick or dense cook uniformly in the conveyor oven. These are excellent merchandising ovens because they can be located where the customer can watch and smell food, such as pizza or cookies, being prepared.

Primary Use in the Food Operation

Conveyor ovens are sized by length, width of the conveyor belt, and speed of the belt. The length will in part determine the amount of heat that is applied to the food product as it passes through the cavity of the oven. The width of the belt will determine the amount of food that can be placed on the conveyor at one time, and the speed of the belt will determine the degree of doneness and amount of heat applied. These factors, plus other engineering features, determine the capacity of the oven. Figure 7.19 shows typical production capacities for conveyor ovens.

Determining Capacity and Size

SLOW-ROASTING OVENS

Description Experiments with low-temperature roasting have been in progress for many years. High heat applied to protein hardens the surface, removes too much moisture and fat, caramelizes any sugar in the product, and results in shrinkage. Low-temperature roasting of meats reduces the shrinkage and decreases the browning effect on the outside of the product. Ovens that are specifically designed to cook at temperatures of approximately 200°F (104°C) to 240°F (116°C) and hold the moisture from the meat within the oven cavity are classified as slow-roasting ovens (see Figure 7.20). Manufacturers claim a 30 to 40 percent reduction in shrinkage, which translates into significant savings for food operators who serve large amounts of roast meats. Some operators have claimed a savings large enough to pay for equipment in just one year.

Specifications for slow-roasting ovens might include low power requirements, double-stacked ovens, portability, and a hold feature. The hold feature automatically drops the temperature to approximately 140°F (60°C) at a certain time, so that the meat will remain at a proper serving temperature but will no longer cook. This is an important feature for foodservice operators who make a practice of cooking in the oven all night. (Ovens should not be set below 140°F because of the danger of bacterial growth.)

Figure 7.20. Slow-Cook Oven. Courtesy of Alto-Shaam, Inc.

The slow-roasting oven is primarily used for roasting meats. However, the oven can be very effective as a warming cabinet for holding hot foods and as a proof box for bakery products.

Primary Use in the Food Operation

A slow-roasting oven will hold between 80 and 120 pounds (36 to 54 kilograms [kg]) of raw meat per cavity. Where large food operations require additional capacity, these ovens can be stacked. The ovens are very space-efficient. For example, one leading manufacturer's slow-roasting oven takes up only 23 by 28 inches (560 by 750 mm) of floor space. The capacity of slow-roasting ovens is relatively less than convection ovens of similar size because they require long roasting periods, typically between three and a half and six hours, depending on the size of the meat and the degree of doneness (internal temperature) desired. In the same period, a convection or conventional oven could roast several times the amount of food.

Determining Capacity and Size

COMBI OVEN/STEAMER

The combi oven brings together oven and steamer in a single unit (see Figure 7.21). The combi oven uses both convected heated air and steam as energy sources for cooking. This combination allows the cook to use the equipment as a convection oven, a steamer, or both at the same time. The result is a highly versatile piece of equipment that can prepare a wide variety of food with excellent quality. When both sources of energy are used together, the combi oven cooks very rapidly, without drying out or overcooking the product. Other advantages of the combi oven are:

❑ Consistent flavor, color, and texture
❑ Multiple food items can be cooked at the same time without flavor transfer
❑ Reduced shrinkage when roasting
❑ Efficient use of kitchen space

Specifications for combi ovens typically include a stainless-steel exterior and interior, a self-contained steam boiler, an attached hose (used to wash out the interior), and a computer-controlled cooking program.

Description

The versatility of this equipment permits the cook to steam, braise, roast, bake, defrost, or reheat a wide variety of food products. Because these pieces of equipment are expensive, many operators question the use of a single piece of equipment that would cost as much or more than the combined prices of a separate convection oven and low-pressure steamer. If the food preparation staff is well trained in the use of a combi, then its many uses and space-saving feature seem to justify its high cost.

Primary Use in the Food Operation

Figure 7.21. Combi Oven/Steamer. Courtesy of Rational USA.

Determining Capacity and Size

The smallest combis hold six 12-by-20-inch steam table pans, and the largest hold 40 pans (or more). The larger combis will also accommodate full-size 18-by-26-inch bun pans. European versions offer similar capacities for cooking in gastronorm pans. The smaller combis tend to limit the use of the oven for baking, while the larger ovens can be adjusted to receive transport carts for the quantities typical of large institutions. Figure 7.22 lists the capacities of combi ovens from one leading manufacturer.

MICROWAVE OVENS

Description Raytheon Corporation first manufactured the microwave oven in the early 1940s. The name of this oven is derived from the short wavelength of the energy that radiates from the oven into the food. Microwaves are a part of the electromagnetic spectrum and are similar to radio waves. The microwave oven converts 110 volts of electricity from an

Size	Capacity in Servings	Number of Steam Table Pans*
Counter model	75–100	6
Small floor model	100–200	10
Large floor model	200–400	20
Mobile pan roll-in cart	400–600	40
*1/1 (325 by 530 mm) gastronorm pans have comparable capacities.		

Figure 7.22. Combi Oven Capacities.

energy form with long wavelengths to one of short wavelengths, and transmits this energy through the cooking cavity. This energy source causes water and fat molecules to vibrate at very high speeds, thus generating heat. The food product heats most rapidly where moisture occurs and where the density or thickness is minimal. Thus a product that is thick in the middle will not cook as uniformly as a flat or thin food product, and a liquid will heat more quickly than a solid of the same dimensions. Uniform cooking is accomplished when small amounts of foods are cooked at one time and the oven is equipped with two emitters (magnetrons). The greater the amount of power from each magnetron, the faster the foods will cook. Ovens with a rating of over 1,000 watts are recommended for commercial use; microwave ovens rated between 400 and 800 watts are not recommended for commercial use.

Primary Use in the Food Operation

Microwave ovens are widely used in restaurants to thaw and/or quickly cook small quantities of food. The chef can hold foods in the frozen or uncooked state until they are ordered and then prepare them rapidly. The oven has not been widely accepted for institutional use because it does not perform well for quantity cooking. As larger amounts of food are placed in the oven, cooking time increases.

Factors that affect cooking time are:

❑ Temperature of the food placed in the oven

❑ Amount of moisture in the food

❑ Density or thickness of the product

❑ Amount of food placed at one time in the oven

❑ Rated wattage of the oven

Typical uses of the microwave oven and the cooking times that can be expected from a 1,400-watt unit are found in Figure 7.23.

SPECIALTY OVENS

Wood-Burning Ovens

A popular trend for Italian or pizza restaurants is a custom-built wood-burning brick oven. These ovens are heated by a wood fire in a well-insulated brick-and-masonry enclosure with a stone or ceramic hearth. Pizzas and other dishes are placed inside the oven near the fire to give a pleasant smoky flavor to the food. These ovens require a skilled operator

Food Item	Weight Ounces (Grams)	Cooking Time
Roast beef	6 (170)	25 seconds
Steak (to be thawed)	12 (340)	20 seconds (each side)
Bowl of soup	8 (227)	45 seconds
Precooked bacon	2 (57)	15 seconds
Ham, sliced	3 (85)	30 seconds
Turkey, sliced	5 (142)	50 seconds
Meat loaf	5 (142)	50 seconds
Hot dog (2)	5 (142)	1 minute, 10 seconds
Stuffed lobster (thawed)	12 (340)	1 minute, 30 seconds
Fish fillet	5 (142)	30 seconds

Figure 7.23. Microwave Oven Cooking Times.

and a considerable amount of effort to build the fire, keep it burning, and clean it out (see Figure 7.24). Some oven companies have simplified this process with a gas burner that is similar in appearance to the wood-burning model.

Barbecue Ovens

A variety of ovens are available that will cook pork, beef, or poultry and impart a smoky flavor from either hardwood chips or logs. Small units are simple aluminum or stainless-steel boxes on wheels with a heating and smoke-providing device in the bottom of the oven. Large units use either hardwood logs or logs plus gas as a source of smoke and heat. Capacities can range from 24 half chickens or 16 slabs of baby back ribs up to 270 whole chickens and 800 pounds (360 kg) of ribs.

SPEED OVEN

Description   The turbo oven can have cooking times up to 12 times faster than convectional methods. The oven utilizes high-speed forced-air convection heating with microwave energy. The faster cooking times allows the operator to cook to order food products at faster speeds and quality standards comparable to convection cooking methods. Typically, turbo ovens do not require ventilation, which eliminates the need for expensive exhaust hoods and fire suppression systems.

Figure 7.24. Wood-burning Oven. Courtesy of Wood Stone Corporation.

The turbo oven can cook, bake, brown, broil, and roast a wide variety of fresh, frozen, or reheated products, such as pizza, toasted subs, frozen appetizers, and fresh-baked chicken.

Primary Use in the Food Operation

Small speed ovens are typically used at the point of service in a cafeteria setting. Due to the extremely fast cooking time, menu items can be quickly heated and immediately served to the customer. Larger speed ovens, which are just now coming onto the market, would be installed as part of the cooking battery similar to convection or combi oven. These larger ovens have the capacity to cook.

Determining Capacity and Size

Typically, smaller speed ovens are used at the point of service. Due to their cooking speed, orders can be filled in a very short period of time right in front of the customer. Therefore, one small oven would be sufficient at a given station in a cafeteria. Larger speed ovens are fairly new to the market, and specific capacity sizing information is not yet available.

Low- and No-Pressure Steamers

DESCRIPTION

Steaming is an extremely efficient cooking method because of the quick heat transfer between the steam and the food product. Steamers can be purchased in high-, low-, and no-pressure models. The low- and no-pressure models may also be considered preparation equipment because they can be used to prepare large quantities of food before the meal period begins. High-pressure steam cookers are used to prepare foods just before and during the meal period.

Low-pressure steamers (see Figure 7.25), which have been in use in commercial kitchens for many years, operate under a pressure of 5 pounds

Figure 7.25. Pressure Steamer. Courtesy of Vulcan-Hart.

Figure 7.26. Convection Steamer. Courtesy of Cleveland Range, Inc.

(2/25 kg) per square inch. One-, two-, and three-compartment models are available. Each compartment has a large capacity and can be specified to hold two large (12 by 20 inches [530 by 325 mm gastronorm]) perforated pans for cooking such items as boiled potatoes. The compartments can also be fitted to accommodate six full-size steam table pans. The capacity of this equipment makes it best suited to large institutions or restaurants.

No-pressure "convection steamers" (see Figure 7.26) have become popular in recent years because they are compact, will handle a large quantity of food, and are well liked by cooks and chefs. Since all steamers operate on the basis of convected heat, the term "convection steamer" is primarily a marketing device.

All steamers can be purchased with automatic timing devices, interior fittings to accommodate different sizes of pans, and special exterior finishes. Floor-mounted, wall-mounted, and modular units are available. The methods of producing steam and transferring the steam to the cooking cavity vary considerably from one model to the next. Many steamers are available with steam boilers located in a compartment under or beside the cooker.

Steamers and combi ovens are also available with and without boilers in most sizes. Once warmed up, boilers are essentially a reservoir of steam that is always available for use once the steamer is turned on with a product load. A steamer without a boiler will drop controlled amounts of water onto a heating element inside the steam compartment, thus providing instantaneous steam. The downside of boilerless steamers is when a heavy product load is continuously inserted into the steamer, it may have problems keeping up with the production schedule. However, boilerless steamers do not require deliming and regular boiler maintenance. They are also generally less expensive to purchase, operate, and maintain.

Primary Use in the Food Operation

Low- and no-pressure steamers are used in the preparation of vegetables, starchy items, seafood, and eggs. They cook these items quickly and thus support the batch cookery concept.

Determining Capacity and Size

The standard for judging the size of a steamer is the cooking time and the steam table pan capacity. Low- and no-pressure steamers will cook most vegetables in 8 to 15 minutes. Rice, spaghetti, and potatoes will cook in 20 to 30 minutes. Typical cooking times for low- and no-pressure steamers are found in Figure 7.27.

Water Filtration for Steam Boiler

In order to reduce deliming frequency as well as overall maintenance of the steamer's boiler, a specialized water filter should be installed on the water supply line going to the boiler. The water filter provides high-quality water with deliming capabilities. It also reduces chlorine and particulates while providing scale control. The filtration system should be specified with a shut-off flushing valve in order to change out the filter without turning off the water supply main. It should also be specified with a pressure gauge to verify the water pressure is high enough for proper operating standards of the steamer; low pressure would indicate the filter is dirty and needs to be replaced.

Food Item	Cooking Time in Minutes Fresh	Frozen
Chicken, 5–8 oz pieces	18–20	
Ribs, 3 lb and under	20–26	
Halibut, 6–8 oz portions	4–6	6–8
Asparagus, spears	4	6
Broccoli, spears	3	2–3

Figure 7.27. Convection Steamer Cooking Times. Courtesy of Cleveland Range, Inc.

Figure 7.28. Tilting Braising Pan. Courtesy of Vulcan-Hart.

Tilting Fry Pan (Braising Pan)

DESCRIPTION

The tilting fry pan is also called a tilting skillet or a tilting braising pan (see Figure 7.28). The advantage of this piece of equipment is versatility. Tilting fry pans can be used for grilling, steaming, braising, sautéing, or stewing. The piece of equipment has a long rectangular shape, with sides that are usually 6 to 10 inches (152 to 254 mm) high. The large, flat inside surface is good for grilling, and the tall sides give the added advantage of holding a large volume of food. Typical sizes range from 20 to 40 gallons (76 to 152 liters) and measure from approximately 36 inches wide by 30 inches deep (910 mm wide by 760 mm deep) up to 56 inches wide by 34 inches deep (1,420 mm wide by 860 mm deep). The fry pan tilts, as the name suggests, so that the liquids can be poured into a container. The tilting feature also permits easy cleaning if the pan is located over a floor drain. Accessories that are usually purchased with the equipment include a hot and cold filler faucet and/or spray rinse hose, as well as spreader plates for each side of the pan.

PRIMARY USE IN THE FOOD OPERATION

The tilting fry pan is very versatile and can be used as a:

- ❏ Bain-marie for holding foods in a hot-water bath
- ❏ Grill
- ❏ Braising pan
- ❏ Kettle for simmering or stewing
- ❏ Steamer with the lid in a closed position
- ❏ Fryer for foods cooked in small amounts of fat
- ❏ Poacher

DETERMINING CAPACITY AND SIZE

The tilting fry pan should be purchased in the largest size that space and funds permit. The smaller fry pans are difficult to use for grilling because of the high sides. The equipment is most useful when it is installed beside a steam-jacketed kettle or grill. This arrangement permits the cooks to have a choice of equipment to use, depending on the menu and/or volume of food that must be prepared.

Steam-Jacketed Kettles

The kettle is often described as the workhorse of the kitchen because of its versatility and popularity among cooks and chefs. The steam-jacketed kettle is heated from an inner jacket that contains the steam. This double-walled construction is very efficient because the heat from the steam is transferred directly into the food through the stainless-steel wall of the kettle.

DESCRIPTION

The American Society of Mechanical Engineers (ASME) has established safety codes that must be followed by manufacturers of steam equipment that is operated under pressure. The ASME requires that the inner jacket be able to handle from 5 to 50 pounds per square inch (psi) and that the kettle be constructed of heavy-gauge stainless steel. Steam-jacketed kettles should last many years in a kitchen unless they are dented or scratched through rough treatment. Most kettles use a simple steam valve that is opened slightly for simmering foods and more fully for cooking at higher temperatures.

Steam-jacketed kettles are usually furnished with a lid, and a large number of options are available to the equipment specifier. The most important of these is the selection of the method of mounting. Kettles can be mounted in a number of different ways:

- ❏ On legs
- ❏ On a pedestal base
- ❏ On a yoke (trunnion) for tilting
- ❏ Wall-hung
- ❏ Wall-hung and tilting
- ❏ On a tabletop

Figure 7.29 shows a kettle mounted on a pedestal; Figure 7.30 shows a wall-mounted kettle.

The price of the kettle increases dramatically as the mounting method becomes more complex. For example, a 40-gallon kettle mounted on legs will cost approximately one-third the price of the same capacity kettle wall-hung and tilting. The comparative advantages of the different mounting methods relate primarily to ease of cleaning and the convenience of pouring liquids from a tilting kettle.

Other accessories that are often specified to accompany a steam-jacketed kettle are:

- ❏ Hot- and cold-water flexible hoses for filling the kettles
- ❏ Spray rinse device for cleaning
- ❏ Water-metering device for measuring exact quantities to be added to the kettle

Figure 7.29. Steam-Jacketed Kettle, Pedestal-Mounted. Courtesy of Cleveland Range, Inc.

❑ Mixer attachments (these are very expensive)

❑ Cold-water attachments for rapid cooling of the product

❑ Large draw-off spigot

❑ Etched numbers on the inside of the kettle indicating the volume of liquid

❑ Self-contained gas or electric heaters that eliminate the necessity for a steam line

Figure 7.30. Steam-Jacketed Kettle, Wall-Mounted. Courtesy of Groen, a Dover Industries Company.

Meals Served per Day	Quantity	Capacity, Quarts (liters)
Under 100	1	10 (9.5), table-mounted
100–200	1	20 (19), table-mounted
200–400	1	20 (19)
	1	20 (76)
400–600	1	20 (76)
	1	40 (151)
600–1,000	1	20 (76)
	2	40 (151)
1,000–1,500	1	20 (76)
	1	40 (151)
	1	60 (227)
1,500–2,500	1	20 (76)
	2	40 (151)
	1	60 (227)
2,500 or more	1	20 (76)
	2	40 (151)
	2	60 (227)
	1	80 (303)

Figure 7.31. Kettle Selection Guidelines Based on Meals Served per Day.

PRIMARY USE IN THE FOOD OPERATION

The steam-jacketed kettle is most often used for bringing any liquid product up to a boiling temperature. Soups, stews, vegetables, stocks, sauces, boiled meats—any food product cooked in a liquid—can be efficiently handled in a steam-jacketed kettle.

DETERMINING CAPACITY AND SIZE

The menu and cooking procedures will have a direct influence on the number and type of kettles needed. The table-mounted kettles are small in capacity, ranging between 6 and 40 quarts, while floor models range in size from 20 to 150 gallons (75.8 L to 568.5 L). When considering the kettle capacity, allowance must be made for boil-over or foaming. Figure 7.31 may be used as a guideline for selecting kettles that will meet the needs of different types of food facilities.

Steam-jacketed kettles that are self-contained with either gas or electricity as a source of energy are large and expensive. Self-contained kettles are in common use, although the heating source increases the height and thickness of the kettle walls, making access to the kettle awkward for the cook.

Bain-Maries

DESCRIPTION

The bain-marie is a hot-water bath usually located in the cook's table or in the range area. For many years, bain-maries were very popular in large hotel and institutional kitchens as places to hold sauces, soups, and gravies at boiling temperature. The bain-maries were usually heated by a coil at the bottom of the bain-marie sink. As equipment manufacturers developed modern holding equipment, food facilities designers stopped specifying the bain-marie. In recent years, small bain-maries have become popular again because cooks find a double-boiler effect very convenient for making sauces without fear of scorching or burning.

Bain-maries can now be specified with small, attached water-circulating heating elements that connect to the side of the bain-marie sink. These heating devices maintain the water at 200° to 210°F (93.3° to 98.9°C).

PRIMARY USE IN THE FOOD OPERATION

The bain-marie is used for holding sauces, soups, and stock at near-boiling temperatures.

DETERMINING CAPACITY AND SIZE

Electrically heated stainless-steel tables and holding cabinets with humidity control are both excellent pieces of equipment for keeping foods at the proper temperature. Kitchens, therefore, may not need large bain-maries. A bain-marie sink approximately 2 feet by 2 feet (610 mm by 610 mm) would be sufficient for most restaurant kitchens, and 4 feet by 2 feet (1,220 mm by 610 mm) would work well for a large institutional kitchen.

Grills

DESCRIPTION

A grill (often called a griddle) has a flat, heated surface that is used to cook foods quickly in short-order, institutional, and restaurant food facilities. A grill can be purchased as a freestanding unit, as a part of a range top, as a table model, or in a modular unit for mounting on an equipment stand. Recently grills have been manufactured that can be dropped into a stainless-steel table, creating a smooth, easy-to-clean cooking area.

In institutions, grills are used to prepare a wide variety of food products, including steaks, chops, scrambled eggs, pancakes, and sautéed vegetables. The fast-food industry often uses a grill and a fryer for all hot-food preparation. Grills can be purchased for mounting on a stand with casters, permitting ease of cleaning after the grill is turned off at the end of the day. Fire regulations require automatic extinguishing devices because of the high temperature and the presence of flammable grease.

Accessories for grills are limited to the various methods for mounting the equipment, as discussed. Grills that are purchased as part of a range section should be specified with spreader plates on each side so that raw ingredients and cooked products can be handled easily by the cook. Chrome-plated grills are popular because of the ease of cleaning the surface after the grill is turned off (see Figure 7.32).

PRIMARY USE IN THE FOOD OPERATION

In the short-order restaurant, the grill is used for almost all breakfast menu items. At lunch, hamburgers, hot dogs, steaks, grilled sandwiches, and many other fast-food items are cooked quickly and efficiently on the grill.

Figure 7.32. Chrome-plated Griddle. Courtesy of Keating of Chicago.

In all types of food facilities, the grill is an extremely valuable piece of equipment that can prepare many different types of food.

DETERMINING CAPACITY AND SIZE

Grills are usually purchased in widths of 2, 3, 4, 5, or 6 feet (610, 915, 1,220, 1,525, or 1,830 mm). The distance from front to back of the grill top is usually between 21 and 34 inches (530 and 860 mm), less the narrow trough that is located along the front or back edge for collecting grease. Grills are rated by the number of hamburgers per hour that can be prepared. This cooking performance standard usually falls within a range of 400 hamburgers per hour for a 24-inch (610-mm) grill to 2,400 hamburgers per hour for a 6-foot (1,830-mm) grill.

Large grills usually have one control dial and thermostat for each 12 inches (305 mm) of grill surface. This feature permits the cook to have different surface temperatures at several points across the grill, so that different foods can be cooked at the same time. For example, fried eggs, sausage, and pancakes could all be cooked at the same time on a 4- or 6-foot (1,220- or 1,830-mm) grill.

Grooved Griddle

DESCRIPTION

The grooved griddle (grill) is constructed much in the same way as a conventional grill. Deep grooves are molded into the cooking surface of the grill, which give a dark, striped appearance to the meat as it is cooked. The grooved griddle is an excellent alternative to the overfired or underfired broiler for several reasons:

❏ Less energy is consumed.

❏ The amount of smoke produced is greatly reduced.

❏ Grease from the product is easily collected.

❏ The quality of the food product is more easily controlled because the temperature can be precisely set.

❏ Meat products are marked attractively, and the caramelizing effect adds a pleasant taste.

PRIMARY USE IN THE FOOD OPERATION

This type of grill is an excellent substitute for the conventional broiler. In addition, grooved griddles can be used for almost all the same foods that are normally prepared on a grill, except for eggs and pancakes.

Clamshell Griddle

DESCRIPTION

The clamshell griddle (grill) is also constructed much in the same way as a conventional grill with the addition of a top heating element. The additional heating element allows for cooking both the bottom and top surface at the same time without turning the product over. This increases production and decreases labor (see Figure 7.33).

PRIMARY USE IN THE FOOD OPERATION

Since the clamshell grill speeds up the rate of production, it is an excellent piece of equipment to install at the point of service. Menu items can be turned around very quickly, thus reducing the customer's wait time.

Fryers

DESCRIPTION

Fryers cook food by immersing it in hot fat. Frying temperatures range between 300° and 450°F (148.9° and 232.2°C). Fryers can be purchased as freestanding (see Figure 7.34), table-mounted, modular, or drop-in models. If the freestanding fryer is selected, gas can be used as an energy source.

Figure 7.33. Clamshell Griddle. Courtesy of Keating of Chicago.

Figure 7.34. Fryer. Courtesy of Vulcan-Hart.

If the modular or drop-in method for mounting the fryer is chosen, electricity is likely to be used because so few manufacturers offer gas-fired drop-in units. The design of the gas-operated fryer requires a greater amount of depth under the fat container, which must be enclosed in the floor-mounted cabinet.

Gas fryers are heated by a ring or straight "ribbon" burner located under the fat container or, in the newer high-capacity fryers, by a tube-fired system. Electric fryers are heated by resistance heaters enclosed in metal and immersed in the fat around the outside edges. Electric fryers are easy to clean because the immersion heaters can be raised out of the fat and the container can be removed and scrubbed in the pot sink. Gas fryers usually have a "cold" zone at the bottom of the fat container where crumbs and burned food particles can accumulate. Both types of fryers are popular, and neither type is recommended as more desirable than the other.

All fryers represent a safety hazard because the fat is kept at a very high temperature and can easily catch fire. Fire codes require that a fire extinguishing nozzle capable of automatically extinguishing a flash fire be located over each fryer. Fire codes also require a disconnect device that will cut off the source of energy from the device in the event that a fire does occur.

Accessories that are available for fryers include:

❑ Automatic fryer basket lifters

❑ Solid-state controls with timers

❑ Self-contained automatic fat-filtering device

❏ Stainless-steel frying chambers and exterior panels

❏ Semiautomatic loading systems

❏ Casters

Because of the extensive amount of grease that spills around fryers, sanitation is a major concern for the food facilities design consultant. Fryers that are portable or that are mounted in a modular bank and wall-hung are an excellent means of simplifying the sanitation problem. Both of these mounting methods permit frequent mopping under the fryer so that grease does not accumulate.

Pressure fryers seal the cooking cavity and introduce pressure. Pressurized frying results in a quicker cooking time. It takes more time, however, to load and seal products in a pressurized fryer than in a standard model.

PRIMARY USE IN THE FOOD OPERATION

Fryers are popular pieces of equipment because the public demands foods that are cooked in hot fat to a golden brown appearance. French fries, breaded meats, batter-dipped meats and vegetables, and French toast are foods typically cooked in the deep-fat fryer or pressure fryer.

Pasta Cookers

The pasta cooker is included in the fryer section of this text because these pieces of equipment are an adaptation of a fryer, using similar stainless-steel enclosures. Typically, two "fryer" units are placed side by side, and one side serves as the cooker and the second as a means of washing away excess starch. Automatic fryer lift baskets are used to lower and raise the baskets, so that cooking time is controlled. The basket of pasta is then placed into the second water bath for rinsing and holding, and a swing-away faucet is used to rinse away the starch. Cooking is stopped by the cold water, and the water drains into an overflow. Typically, 6 pounds (2.72 kg) of dry pasta become 15 pounds (6.80 kg) of cooked pasta, enough for about 24 servings. These cooked portions are placed into small containers, which can in turn be automatically lowered into water that has been set for a warming mode.

DETERMINING CAPACITY AND SIZE

Pasta cookers are rated by the capacity of the water container. Typical sizes range from 8.7 gallons (33 L) to 12.7 gallons (48 L). Specifications are also often used in which servings per hour are the standard of performance—typically, 1080 to 1440 10 oz. servings per hour.

Ranges

The range section of a foodservice facility is the most heavily used and often the most poorly designed section of the kitchen. Open-top (burner) and hot-top (solid) ranges are not energy-efficient to begin with, and they are usually turned on by the cooks when the operation opens and left on until it closes. Most food facilities would be better designed if the kitchen did not include open-top or hot-top ranges. The exception to this is the restaurant or club that includes a large number of sautéed foods or omelets on its menu. The open-top range is preferable for sautéing because

Figure 7.35. Range Sections. Courtesy of Vulcan-Hart.

the flame can be seen and adjusted. Figure 7.35 illustrates a range section with open burners.

DESCRIPTION

The types of ranges most often used in food-service facilities include:

- ❑ Open top with burners for sautéing
- ❑ Grill (or griddle) top of polished steel plate on which food can be cooked (e.g., pancakes, hamburgers, chops, scrambled eggs, etc.)
- ❑ Hot top of solid steel, on which pans are placed but not food
- ❑ Radial fin top, for large stock pots

Ranges can be ordered in combinations of these styles, such as a grill section placed adjacent to an open-burner section.

The ranges are often placed in the hot-food section of the kitchen in a bank or line of equipment to form a continuous range section (see Figure 7.36). Spreader plates can be placed between the equipment pieces to create convenient spaces for holding raw or cooked foods. The equipment can be specified with ovens under each piece or as modular with the equipment mounted on a stainless-steel stand. The modular version is much easier to clean but less space-efficient.

Ranges can be purchased that are only 1 foot (305 mm) wide with two hot-plate burners. These are very handy for small-volume range needs in a foodservice facility that does not have sautéed food items on the menu.

Many range manufacturers offer two (or more) lines of ranges, one described as being appropriate for restaurant use and the other for institutional or heavy-duty use. The nomenclature is not helpful to operators deciding which line of ranges to select because restaurants often place as many or more demands on their ranges than do institutional foodservice operations. The institutional line, though somewhat more expensive, generally is recommended for all commercial installations because it is more durable. In addition, restaurant ranges usually are offered in a

Figure 7.36. Range Lineup. Courtesy of Vulcan-Hart.

limited number of configurations, whereas heavy-duty ranges can be custom-configured to meet the exact needs of the operation. Restaurant ranges are appropriate in facilities where the demand is light, such as in a child care center where one simple meal is produced each day.

PRIMARY USE IN THE FOOD OPERATION

The small kitchen with a limited budget would probably include a range with an oven below it and an assortment of pots and pans for handling all of the cooking. The difficulty of cleaning, the inefficiency in energy usage, and the high labor costs in using and cleaning the pots and pans make the range an undesirable choice for a well-designed kitchen. The food facility that does a large amount of sautéing should include only one or two open-top ranges in combination with other, more efficient cooking equipment, such as steamers, steam-jacketed kettles, and convection ovens.

Induction Cooking

DESCRIPTION

Induction uses electromagnetic energy to heat cookware made of magnetic material (steel, iron, nickel or various alloys). When the unit is turned on, the coils produce a high-frequency alternating magnetic field, which ultimately flows through the cookware. Molecules in the cookware move back and forth rapidly, causing the cookware to become hot and cook the food. The cooktop's glass-ceramic surface is unaffected by the magnetic field since it contains no magnetic material. The heat of the pan will warm the glass; however, the cooktop will remain much cooler to the touch than other smoothtop surfaces.

Induction technology is comparable in transferable heat to gas even though it is an electric appliance. Also, induction has no open flame, red-hot coil, or other radiant heat source to ignite fumes or flammable materials. It has essentially no ambient heat since all the heat is being generated in the pan itself, thus providing a cooler working environment.

PRIMARY USE IN THE FOOD OPERATION

Induction cooking is an excellent means of producing cooked fresh product in front of the customer. This can take place on a cafeteria serving line or in a restaurant's dining room.

DETERMINING CAPACITY AND SIZE

The capacity of an induction cooker is very similar to a traditional range. When being used at the point of service, one or two induction elements are recommended.

Broilers

DESCRIPTION

A broiler is a final preparation piece of equipment that cooks rapidly from radiant or infrared heat. Most broilers cook either the top or the bottom of the food product, although some models cook the top and bottom at the same time. Broilers can be purchased as large freestanding pieces of equipment or can be table-mounted. Four types of broilers are typically used in the foodservice facility:

1. Freestanding top-burner broilers, often called hotel-style broilers
2. Charbroilers
3. Salamanders
4. Conveyor broilers

In broiling, the cooking time is usually controlled by the distance between the food and the source of heat. When using the heavy-duty hotel-style broiler (with heating elements above), as shown in Figure 7.37, the food is placed on a steel grate that can be adjusted up and down to control

Figure 7.37. Hotel Broiler. Courtesy of Southbend.

Figure 7.38. Charbroiler. Courtesy of Vulcan-Hart.

the temperature. The grate slides in and out also, so that food can be placed in or removed from the broiler.

Open-top charbroilers heat from below (see Figure 7.38); the product is placed on the cooking surface and can be watched during the broiling process. The distance from the heat source to the food product is usually fixed in charbroilers; the time the food is exposed to the heat controls cooking.

Conveyor broilers are excellent cooking devices because they can be operated by semiskilled personnel. One well-known hamburger chain uses a conveyor broiler to cook the hamburger on both sides at once at a predetermined speed. In this application, the employee does not need to judge the cooking time for preparing the hamburger.

Salamanders are small broilers that cook from above and are located above the range. This type of broiler is used by cooks and chefs for last-minute heating, browning, or broiling of food products such as fish and other seafood and food items that are topped with cheese or bread crumbs.

Accessories for broilers are limited to the type of exterior finish and the inclusion of small ovens under the broiler opening.

PRIMARY USE IN THE FOOD OPERATION

Dry-heat cookery is used for steaks, chops, hamburgers, and other meat products. Foods that have been broiled are popular because the fat content is reduced and the caramelization of the sugars in the food gives it an appealing taste.

DETERMINING CAPACITY AND SIZE

Broilers are often rated for performance on the basis of the number of hamburgers or steaks that can be prepared in one hour. One well-known manufacturer of overfired broilers lists a range of production capacities, from 100 12-ounce T-bone steaks per hour for a small model to 200 steaks per hour for a large double-section broiler. Determination of the correct size and number of broilers is based on estimates of the number of portions of each broiled item on the menu sold in a one-hour period.

A specialty broiler is available that uses wood (such as mesquite) as a source of heat, so that the flavor of the wood smoke is transferred to the food product. These broilers are popular for restaurants specializing in steaks or ribs because of the unusual flavor produced by the burning wood.

Mongolian Barbecue (Grill)

DESCRIPTION

The Mongolian barbecue is not only a piece of cooking equipment; it also enhances the dining experience. The Mongolian grill is used in conjunction with a refrigerated buffet counter offering a wide variety of raw, fresh ingredients. Guests fill bowls and select their sauce(s) and pass it to the chef. The chef then places the ingredients onto the Mongolian barbecue, which is essentially a round griddle that allows the cook to rotate the food in a circular fashion, giving guests the enjoyment of watching their food cooked fresh (see Figure 7.39).

PRIMARY USE IN THE FOOD OPERATION

Mongolian grills are installed not only for function but also for show. The grill is typically installed in a prominent location to add to the atmosphere of the dining experience. It is usually a focal point of the servery or dining room.

DETERMINING CAPACITY AND SIZE

Mongolian barbecues come in a variety of sizes, 36-, 42-, 48-, 60-, 72-, and 84-inch round models. The 36- to 48-inch models are used when one cook is used on the grill; the 60- to 84-inch models are used when two or more cooks will be cooking.

Figure 7.39. Mongolian Barbecue. Courtesy of Town Food Service Equipment.

Rotisseries

DESCRIPTION

Two styles of rotisseries are available, rotary and vertical. The rate of demand and the volume of cooked product needed would determine which of these two types is selected. Institutions and catering operations typically see most of their business during peak periods, while most restaurants require continuous service throughout the day.

Batch cooking versus continuous cooking dictates the type of rotisserie to use. For batch cooking, the rotary style is better. This rotisserie utilizes a rotary drum, in addition to rotary skewers, which creates a double rotation effect. As the product revolves, each piece is uniformly cooked and all are finished at the same time. The advantage is that a large volume of finished product is available at one time.

In vertical rotisseries (see Figure 7.40), skewers are lined up one above the other in front of a heat source. Since the product at the top cooks first, the skewers are moved as cooking progresses, with uncooked items added at the bottom and completely cooked product removed from the top.

Figure 7.40. Vertical Rotisserie. Courtesy of Henny Penny Corporation.

PRIMARY USE IN THE FOOD OPERATION

Rotisserie cookery is popular because it requires no added fat and offers the pleasant taste of chicken or other meats basted in their own juices. The appearance of rotating meats adds to the merchandising of the product, creating added sales.

DETERMINING CAPACITY AND SIZE

A variety of sizes are available, and most are designed for display cookery in clear view of the customer. Counter models with a total capacity of 12 to 15 chickens are popular, but the serious rotisserie restaurant will need a capacity of approximately 50 chickens. Cooking time is typically one hour for a 2½-pound chicken and 75 minutes for a 3½-pound chicken, so the total capacity needed is a function of determining the total needs for the peak meal and installing the number of units needed to handle the volume.

DESCRIPTION

Cook/Chill

As described at the beginning of this chapter, cook/chill is a method of production in which the food is cooked and then rapidly chilled and stored for later use. The two primary methods of cook/chill production systems are tumble chill and blast chill.

The tumble chill method cooks food in a kettle to at least 165°F, pumping and packaging food in oxygen impervious casings (bags) at pasteurization temperature, and rapidly tumble chilling to 41°F or less in an ice-water bath for an average of 45 minutes, depending on the viscosity of the product. It also includes a cook tank in which raw products are placed in casings, vacuum packed, cooked in a hot-water bath at pasteurization temperature and time, then chilled in a ice water bath. Since the food is pasteurized and held in a refrigerated state typically between 28°F and 32°F, most products can be held for up to six weeks.

A tumble chill food production system (see Figure 7.41) usually includes some of this equipment:

❑ *Mixer kettle.* Steam-jacketed kettles with agitator mixing arms—horizontal, vertical, or inclined agitators; tilting or stationary; ranging in sizes from 50 gallons (189.5 L) or more.

❑ *Metering filling station.* To empty kettle contents into casings.

❑ *Tumble chiller.* Ice-water bath with a drum that stirs casings continuously, horizontal or vertical.

❑ *Cook tank.* Hot-water bath cooking and cold-water chiller for products that have been vacuum packaged. Sizes range from 600 to 2,000 pounds (270 kg to 900 kg).

❑ Ice Builder: produces ice water for tumble chiller and cook tank.

DETERMINING CAPACITY AND SIZE

Determining the size and capacity of a tumble chill system is very complex and depends on many variables, such as shelf life, portion size, number of meals, menu frequency, storage capabilities at the central kitchen and

Figure 7.41. Tumble Chill Food Production System. Courtesy of Cleveland Range, Inc.

receptor kitchen, and more. Manufacturers of tumble chill equipment can help in the sizing of their equipment; however, it is critical to make sure that the entire central kitchen is appropriately sized by a professional food facilities consultant.

In the blast chill method, food is cooked in traditional cooking equipment then portioned into pans. The pans are placed into a blast chiller where they are cooled in less than 2 hours, depending on the thickness or viscosity of the product. The blast-chilled product can be stored for up to five days, which includes the day of production and the day of service.

BLAST CHILLERS

The blast chiller was developed to meet the challenge of food safety and to reduce the risk of food-borne illness. It certainly is not unusual for steam table pans pulled from the chef's table or cafeteria line to sit in the kitchen for hours before being put in the refrigerator. When this happens, the product stays for quite some time at a temperature that promotes rapid bacterial growth. A blast chiller is designed to prevent this problem by cooling food products rapidly. Figure 7.42 shows a blast chiller.

The blast chiller has three basic components that make it different from a conventional refrigerator. These are:

❑ High-capacity refrigeration system

❑ High velocity of forced chilled air

❑ Microprocessor controls that gauge either chiller internal temperature or (with a probe) product internal temperature

The microprocessor can include many other features, such as the ability to download time/temperature data to a computer for later review and analysis, a dual temperature mode for automatically switching from blast

Figure 7.42. Blast Chiller. Courtesy of Traulsen and Co., Inc.

chilling to normal temperature, and multibatch chilling for two or three different batches of food.

Recent emphasis in sanitation, brought about by HACCP regulation in which food handling and time/temperature considerations are emphasized, will undoubtedly create high levels of interest in blast chillers.

BAKERY EQUIPMENT

Bakeries that are designed as a part of a restaurant or institution can range in size from a table in the corner with a small oven to a full-size production bakery to serve multiple dining halls at a university or large hospital complex. The size of the bakery and volume of product produced will determine the type of equipment needed. Bakery equipment is typically more automated than conventional kitchen equipment because baked products are made in high volume with consistent processes. Automatic doughnut machines, roll dividers/rounders, and sheeter production tables are all highly specialized bakery equipment used for high-volume production.

As is the case with other preparation functions, the equipment selected for baking is determined by the menu. However, in selecting baking equipment, facility designers work closely with the owner to determine which items can be cost-justified. A family restaurant cannot bake sandwich bread (the usual white and wheat loaves) as inexpensively as it can be purchased from a large commercial bakery. But that same restaurant might be able to produce a signature sticky cinnamon bun at a cost that is justifiable. Similarly, a college that prepares 120 dozen cookies daily

Equipment Item	Small Bakery (Restaurant)	Medium Bakery (Institution)
Maple-top baker's table	✓	✓
Bench scale	✓	✓
Mobile flour and sugar bins	✓	✓
Mixer for dough preparation	✓	✓
Proofer, simple	✓	
Proofer, complex		✓
Roll divider/rounder		✓
Dough sheeter		✓
Steam-jacketed kettle		✓
Convection oven(s)	✓	
Rotary or rack oven(s)		✓
Dough retarder		✓

Figure 7.43. Comparison of Small (Restaurant) and Medium (Institutional) Bakery.

should invest in a cookie dropper, a machine that automates the process of forming balls of cookie dough on sheet pans.

Figure 7.43 compares the baking equipment that typically is used in small (restaurant) and medium (institutional) bakeries. The restaurant purchases bread, dinner rolls, and pies from a commercial bakery. It prepares breakfast muffins, sticky buns, and cakes from mixes. The institutional bakery purchases sandwich bread from a commercial bakery but makes dinner rolls, muffins, buns, cakes, pizza dough, and pies in its own bakery.

Specialized baking equipment shown in Figure 7.43 includes:

❑ *Sheeter.* A sheeter (see Figure 7.44) serves the function of a large metal rolling pin, driven by a motor. A small amount of flour falls onto the rolls to prevent the dough from sticking. Small pods of pie or pizza dough are placed between the rollers and stretched out into large thin sheets. Pizzas or pie crusts are made quickly, saving a considerable amount of handwork.

Figure 7.44. Sheeter. Courtesy of Rondo.

❏ *Roll divider/rounder.* A divider/rounder is suitable for dividing and rounding soft roll doughs, kaiser rolls, hoagies, pizza, and French rolls. The machine compresses a round of dough (about the size of a dinner plate) and divides it into 15 to 36 equal pieces. These pieces are then formed into round balls by a rotating action of the machine. A production capacity of 5,000 to 7,000 rolls per hour is possible. Labor savings for a food operation serving over 1,000 persons per meal would be significant.

❏ *Proofer.* A proofer is a heated cabinet with a means of maintaining moisture in which yeast doughs are placed to rise. The most common proofers are simple one-compartment portable cabinets with heating devices located in the bottom. The heating device has a container for water, which, when heated, distributes the steam through a small channel in the back of the cabinet to all of the shelves in the proofer. This type of proofer is inexpensive and will typically last for many years. For a medium to large restaurant or institutional bakery, a more complex proofer is desirable (see Figure 7.45), in which full racks of rolls can be rolled into a one-, two-, or three-section proofer, with highly controlled steam (humidity) and temperature.

❏ *Retarder.* A dough retarder is a special type of refrigerator. Cold temperatures slow fermentation of the yeast in the bread. Retarders are used to hold yeast-based doughs prior to baking.

SERVICE AND CAFETERIA EQUIPMENT

A wide variety of choices exist for the food facilities design consultant in developing the plans for service and cafeteria equipment. Service equipment usually includes those items that are located in or near the place where the food is presented to the customer. Typical kinds of equipment in these areas are:

❏ Food warmers of various configurations
  • Hot-food well
  • Heated cabinet
  • Portable hot-food warmer
❏ Cold-food holding
  • Cold-food well
  • Frost top
  • Pizza/sandwich prep
❏ Display cases
  • Sneeze guards
  • Soft serve
  • Condiment dispensing unit
  • Meal delivery cart

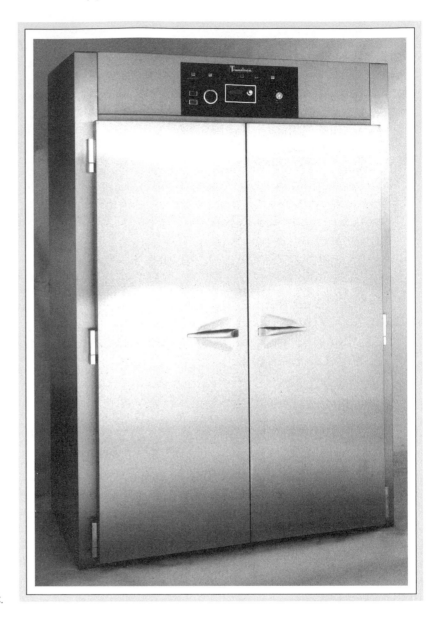

Figure 7.45. Proofer. Courtesy of Traulsen and Co., Inc.

Figure 7.46. Proofer Retarder. Courtesy of Doyon Equipment, Inc.

Information on some of these service items is included in other sections of this book. Certain kinds of equipment—cold beverage dispensers, for example—are furnished by beverage vending companies and therefore not included in this text. Service equipment provided by outside companies for equipment not included in the equipment contract should be carefully considered by the food facilities planner.

DESCRIPTION

Food Warmers

As the name suggests, food warmers heat and/or hold foods to a temperature that is just below the cooking temperature with little loss of moisture. The thermostat setting for this equipment is usually between 100°F and 300°F (38° and 149°C). Because a wide variety of bread and food warmers are available, the capacities of this equipment can best be determined by reading the information available in equipment catalogs.

One common type of food warmer is the steam table. In the early part of the nineteenth century, steam tables were large steam-heated, water-filled compartments (bain-maries, in effect) that kept foods hot in deep pans from either a hot-water bath or the evaporating steam. A modern "steam" table is not heated by steam. Instead, the wells are heated using electric elements. Many steam tables can be operated "wet" (with water in the wells) or "dry" (without water in the wells). The water in the wells is heated by the electrical elements, creating heated water vapor and giving the customer the impression of "steam" heat.

Steam table wells (see Figure 7.47) are designed for standard 12-by-20-inch pans. In countries using the metric system, steam tables are designed for standard sizes of gastronorm pans—325 by 530 millimeters. The heat level is controlled by a thermostat. The capacity of this food warmer is a function of the number of heated wells in the counter and the depth of the pans inserted into the wells.

The most popular bread warmers include one, two, or three stainless-steel drawers mounted in a cabinet. These warmers can be purchased as built-in or freestanding units. Capacities of the warmers vary with the height and width of the drawers and the number of drawers specified. Often these bread warmers are located in the service area of a restaurant so that the service staff can provide rolls without making a trip to the kitchen.

Another popular form of food warmer is the heated cabinet (see Figure 7.48). Some of these units are designed for countertop "grab-and-

Figure 7.47. Hot-Food Insert. Courtesy of Wells Bloomfield, a division of Carrier Commercial Refrigeration.

Figure 7.48. Holding Cabinet. Courtesy of Alto-Shaam, Inc.

go" service, whereas others are designed to hold food for later service. Food-warming and holding cabinets can be designed for portable use or for permanent installation. They include heated pass-through cabinets that are constructed to hold the standard 12-by-20-inch pan (325-by-530-mm gastronorm pan) and full-height pass-through warmers that are similar in appearance to a single-compartment refrigerator. Food-warming cabinets are available with a variety of options. Some simply heat the cabinet, while others introduce humidity and/or control the rate of evaporation within the cavity to preserve the quality and texture of sensitive foods such as eggs or biscuits.

The food facility design consultant should be conservative in specifying the number and capacity of food warmers because of the tendency of cooks to prepare food too early and then store it away in the food warmer well before the meal begins. To encourage last-minute and batch cookery, there should be enough food warmers to hold only a small proportion of the total food needed for the meal.

Cold-Food Holding

Cold-food holding equipment enables the user to safely hold food that needs to be held below 40°F (4°C) so that it can be displayed for the customer. Reach-in refrigerators with glass doors can be used, but it is difficult to serve food and diminishes the presentation. One common type of cold-food equipment is the cold pan or cold-food well (see Figure 7.49). Cold pans have a similar appearance to hot-food wells except that they keep the food cold by mechanical cooling or ice. Mechanical cooling allows for a longer holding period over ice pans. Some food wells also blow cold air around or over the top of the food product. It is critical to select a mechanical cold pan using air flow so that the air does not dry out the food, thus affecting presentation and flavor.

Another common type of cold-food holding equipment is the frost top (see Figure 7.50). Traditionally a stainless-steel plate would be mechanically cooled by refrigeration lines running through or just underneath the plate, allowing cold foods in serving crocks, containers, and the like to be displayed on a serving counter. Frost-top holding times are shorter in

Figure 7.49. Cold-Food Well. Courtesy of Wells Bloomfield, a division of Carrier Commercial Refrigeration.

Figure 7.50. Frost Top. Courtesy of Delfield Refrigeration.

length than cold-food wells; however, foods can be displayed in a much more appealing manner. To further enhance the eye appeal, frost tops are now being manufactured out of granite and other stone materials, increasing the attractiveness of the entire cold-food station.

Pizza and sandwich preparation tables provide easily accessible ingredients without having to open and close a refrigerator door frequently. These tables permit customers to view the ingredients they are ordering for their sandwich or pizza. Typically these preparation tables provide an elevated area in which one-eighth to full-size steam table pans full of ingredients can be placed. There is also a working-height section for making the sandwich or pizza. At the base of the table is a refrigerated section with backup ingredients for easy refilling of the refrigerated rail (see Figure 7.51).

Figure 7.51. Pizza and Sandwich Preparation Table. Courtesy of All True Photos.

DESCRIPTION

Many types of display cases are available including dry (bakery), refrigerated, and heated sections (see Figure 7.52). These cases can be configured for either employee service or self-service. Starbucks uses a display case with a self-service refrigerated section on the bottom and a served bakery section above. The majority of display cases are floor-mounted, similar to those seen in a grocery store, but countertop and "drop-in" units are available. Display cases are generally highly stylized with decorative finishes.

PRIMARY USE IN THE FOOD OPERATION

Display cases are primarily a decorative item designed to enhance the appearance of the food and market the food to the customer. Display cases have a wide variety of use in foodservice operations. Some are used to display raw food, which enhances the customers' perception of quality and freshness. High-end steak or fish houses may display the raw product in such a manner. Other cases are used to merchandise the food, such as in a bakery or deli application. The proliferation and popularity of convenience and "to go" items, such as prepackaged gourmet salads and specialty beverages, has led to open "air curtain" design that makes it easier for customers to see the product.

Display Cases

Figure 7.52. Display Case. Courtesy of Federal Industries.

Sneeze Guards

Sneeze guards, or breath protectors, are a necessary part of a serving area wherever the public can come into direct contact through breathing over open exposed food. The sneeze guard provides protection between the customer and the food and should be installed between 48 and 54 inches (121.9 cm and 137 cm) above the floor to provide protection for most individual heights. Sneeze guards can also be provided with lighting and heat lamps to help with the display and temperature maintenance of the food. They also can include additional accessories, such as end panels, bowl displays, signage, display shelves, and so on. Particular attention should be paid to the thickness of the glass based on the overall length of the sneeze guard (i.e., the longer the sneeze guard, the thicker the glass).

Condiment Dispensing Unit

Bulk condiment dispensers have become more common in today's cafeterias and fast-food restaurants. These dispensers can be operated either manually or by air, with each pump or push of a button respectively containing one portion size. Bulk condiments are much more economical than individual packets and much more sanitary than using a ladle placed inside a bucket of catsup. Food manufacturers are continuing to make more condiments and salad dressings available on the market for use in dispensing equipment, typically in 3-gallon (11.3 L) bags. Typically the condiment dispensing equipment is installed into a serving counter with the dispensing head exposed above the counter.

Soft-Serve Machines

A wide variety of soft-serve products can be made from a soft-serve machine (see Figure 7.53). Frozen yogurt, frozen custard, sorbet (sherbet), and ice milk are all popular desserts. Sundaes, cones, cups, and mixed flavors of product, either served by an employee or self-served, are all possible and are typically very profitable.

Small countertop models have a refrigerated container at the top for the liquid mix, which flows by gravity down into a cylinder that has refrigeration coils around the outside. When the liquid mix comes into contact with the freezing walls of the cylinder, a dasher of stainless steel or hard plastic scrapes the frozen product off the walls, incorporates air, and breaks down ice crystals. This produces a smooth product with a significant increase of volume because of air and freezing. The product is then deposited into a dish or cone. Large machines often hold the liquid mix in a bottom container for ease in filling and pump the proper amount of product into the freezing chamber.

Typical output volume can be determined by the number of hours per day that the machine is operated, since the production of frozen product is continuous. The size and capacity of a machine is determined by the horsepower of the motor and the capacity of the hopper that holds the liquid mix. Soft-serve machines should be sized carefully in large foodservice operations where the demand likely peaks immediately after lunch or dinner. Heavy demand may result in the product being drawn from the machine faster than the freezing cylinders can do their work. Pump machines, although more expensive initially, are desirable in high-demand

Figure 7.53. Soft-Serve Machine. Courtesy of Taylor.

settings bccause they inject more air into the finished product than do gravity machines.

Meal Delivery Cart

Meals that are consumed away from the point of production or establishments such as banquet halls or hospitals that do not have cafeterias require a meal delivery cart. There are many different ways to deliver meals to the consumer. Meals that are individually preplated for a banquet or wedding reception arc typically delivered in a banquet cart kept warm with the use of Sterno or electricity (see Figure 7.54). Meals that are assembled on trays for use in a hospital or nursing home would be delivered in a tray delivery cart (see Figure 7.55).

Current trends in available equipment allow meals and trays to be assembled, chilled and reheated directly in the cart. This method allows for the plating of meals during a single production shift while the rethermalization of the meal can occur just prior to service. This method typically saves on the quantity and cost of labor. Retherm methods include convection and conduction.

Carts should have clear visibility for pushing and also not be top-heavy. Meal delivery carts can be insulated to hold temperatures for longer periods or be noninsulated for shorter periods. When traveling long

Figure 7.54. Banquet Cart. Courtesy of Carter-Hoffman, a division of Carrier Commercial Refrigeration, Inc.

distances, large 8-inch (20.3 cm) casters are recommended with a wheel configuration that will allow the cart to turn tight corners. The travel path also needs to be considered to confirm that the cart can pass through all passageways needed.

BEVERAGE EQUIPMENT

❏ Soft-drink systems
❏ Ice machines and dispensers
❏ Coffee urns and dispensers
❏ Espresso/cappuccino machines
❏ Bar equipment
  • Beer systems
  • Wine storage and dispensing
❏ Water filtration

Figure 7.55. Tray Cart. Courtesy of Caddy Corporation of America, Inc.

A wide variety of beverage-related equipment is available to the food-service operator, and much of this equipment—especially coffee, juice, and soft-drink dispensing systems—is furnished by the beverage supplier. There are two reasons for this trend:

❑ Suppliers want the customer to use their product and to display the name of the product on the equipment. Providing the beverage equipment ensures an ongoing purchase of the product.

❑ Beverage suppliers are concerned about the quality of the product and typically provide equipment that will dispense the best drink possible.

Soft-drink companies typically offer dispensing equipment to food-service operations as part of their contract to provide syrup and carbon dioxide (CO_2). Thus, many small to medium-size food operators simply call the local soft-drink company and ask for their assistance in designing and installing the proper beverage equipment. However, soft-drink firms may be reluctant to provide equipment if the volume to be served is very high or if the owner desires specialized dispensing equipment. In these situations, the soft-drink dispensing equipment would be purchased as part of the overall equipment package for the foodservice facility rather than furnished by the beverage vendor.

Two specialized equipment pieces that should be considered in many food operations are "bag-in-box" soft-drink systems and espresso machines.

Soft-Drink Systems

There are two basic soft-drink systems: premix, in which the product is mixed and ready to drink and only needs to be chilled, and postmix, in which the product is shipped as a concentrate and water and carbon dioxide gas is added at the dispenser. Postmix systems are the most popular.

Depending on the volume, postmix systems can be as simple as a beverage-dispensing machine that is connected to a container of concentrate and a small tank of CO_2 plus cold water. The machine mixes, chills, and dispenses the beverage into a glass. The concentrate is typically held in a small (approximately 5 gallons, or 19 L.) metal tank or in a cardboard-and-plastic bag-in-a-box. Larger systems use a carbonator, a large CO_2 tank, a chiller, and plastic tubes that permit the beverage components to be located remote from the dispensing equipment. These larger systems permit the storage of the support equipment in a basement or nearby room, where cleaning and delivery access is simplified.

Ice Machines and Dispensers

DESCRIPTION

Ice machines and dispensers have become commonplace in the United States because of the high demand by American consumers for ice in almost all beverages. Also, ice not only keeps food cold but adds aesthetic appeal to salad bars and other food displays. Automatic ice makers and dispensers facilitate the use of ice in institutional and commercial foodservice operations.

In the early days of automatic ice making, the machine and storage bin were housed in one cabinet. That concept, however, was not adequate to the large variety of production and storage requirements across the industry. Manufacturers then separated the ice maker and the storage bin, allowing operators greater flexibility in sizing their equipment. With separate production and storage units, an operation can have the production capacity it needs to store ice for peak demand periods rather than producing it all at once. Today, the separate production and storage concept is the industry standard.

Another major trend has been toward increased customer self-service. Higher labor costs, more stringent sanitation requirements, and the overall convenience of self-service have made ice dispensers standard equipment in a growing number of foodservice operations.

Ice dispensers are total systems comprising three major components: production, storage, and dispensing. With respect to production, ice makers can be divided into two general types: flakers and cubers. Cubers produce clear, solid forms of ice that melt more slowly than flakes. However, the equipment required to produce cubes in high volume is more complex and expensive than flake-producing machines. Flakers produce ice on a continuous basis and require fewer moving parts and less energy than cubers. Their major disadvantages are that the quality of the ice is difficult to control, and flakes melt much faster than cubes.

Storage bins are available with varying capacities; 400 to 800 pounds (180 kg to 360 kg) is typical of one major manufacturer's line of dispensers. The bins can be refilled manually or automatically and are designed to stand on the floor or countertop or to be integrated into the service counter. Bins are insulated, equipped with a drain, and constructed of plastic, aluminum, galvanized steel, or stainless steel. A typical ice machine on a bin is shown in Figure 7.56.

Figure 7.56. Ice Machine. Courtesy of Hoshizaki.

Figure 7.57. Ice Dispenser with Under-Counter Ice Maker. Courtesy of Follett.

Dispensing mechanisms consist of all the components necessary to move the ice from the storage bin into the customer's glass. The most common (and least expensive) dispensers are gravity-fed, with the ice stored above the dispensing device. Such dispensers may combine production, storage, and dispensing functions into a single unit, or they may only store and dispense. In other systems suitable for large-volume operations, the ice maker is located below the service counter and fills a storage bin located adjacent to it. Ice is mechanically drawn up from the bin by means of a rotating "sweep arm" or auger and dispensed into the customer's glass (see Figure 7.57).

Dispensers with storage bins located above the counter generally give a more consistent quality of ice than those with storage compartments below and are mechanically simpler in design. However, when large quantities of ice must be stored, it is generally preferable to build the storage compartment into the serving counter and out of the customers' view.

PRIMARY USE IN THE FOOD OPERATION

The ice machine or ice-dispensing system is used to produce, store, and dispense ice for the various needs of the operation, such as beverage cooling and food displays.

DETERMINING CAPACITY AND SIZE

In choosing equipment to meet the requirements for ice in a foodservice operation, a number of factors need to be taken into consideration. Ice requirements include the amount needed for beverages and for other cooling/holding purposes, such as salad bars and seafood displays.

Beverage ice requirements can be determined using a rule of thumb based on the capacity of the glass. A glass typically requires one-half its capacity in beverage volume (fluid ounces) and one-half in the weight of the ice. For example, a 10-ounce (296 milliliters [ml]) glass filled to capacity will have approximately 5 fluid ounces (158 ml) of beverage and 5 ounces (1.4 milligrams [mg]) by weight of ice. If it is typical in the operation to fill the glass only halfway with ice, then the weight of the ice required would be 25 percent of the capacity of the glass.

The main problem in determining the total ice required for beverage service is the varying demand for beverages experienced in almost all food-service operations. During peak business hours, especially in the warmer months, the demand for ice is high; it drops off significantly at other times. Many operations experience peak demand for ice during lunch and dinner; hence the demand for ice is great between 11:30 A.M. and 9:00 P.M.

Ice machines are rated according to the amount of ice they can produce in a 24-hour period; ice storage bins are rated by the amount they can contain. Although an ice machine may have the rated capacity to produce, for example, 384 pounds (174 kg) of ice per day, this does not necessarily mean that this amount of ice will be produced. If the storage bin holds 200 pounds (91 kg) of ice, the machine will shut itself off when the bin is full. When the peak demand hits, the 200 pounds (91 kg) of ice in the storage bin plus the amount of ice that the machine can produce during the peak period is the total amount of ice available. To obtain the full amount that the ice maker can produce, a storage bin must be selected that is slightly larger than the machine's rated production capacity. With a very large bin, however, there is the risk of ice melting at the bottom.

Figure 7.58 may be helpful in determining the capacity needed in ice production and storage to meet requirements for beverage service. For the sake of illustration, it is assumed that one peak period of demand occurs during the day and that the glasses contain 50 percent ice by weight. Each guest is expected to be served two servings of iced beverages. For example, if the operation serves 500 guests, each with two 8-ounce (226 g) glasses, the minimum requirement would be 250 pounds)112.5 kg of ice per day.

Meals per Day	Glasses per Meal	Total Glasses	Glass Size			
			4 oz	6 oz	8 oz	10 oz
250	2	500	63	94	125	156
	Plus 25%		*78*	*117*	*156*	*195*
500	2	1000	125	188	250	313
	Plus 25%		*156*	*234*	*313*	*391*
750	2	1500	188	281	375	469
	Plus 25%		*234*	*352*	*469*	*586*
1,000	2	2000	250	375	500	625
	Plus 25%		*313*	*469*	*625*	*781*
1,500	2	3000	375	563	750	938
	Plus 25%		*469*	*703*	*938*	*1,172*
2,000	2	4000	500	750	1,000	1,250
	Plus 25%		*625*	*938*	*1,250*	*1,563*
3,000	2	6000	750	1,125	1,500	1,875
	Plus 25%		*938*	*1,406*	*1,875*	*2,344*

Figure 7.58. Ice Requirements Based on Demand.

The production and storage capacity of the ice machine selected should exceed the amounts indicated on the chart by 25 percent or more, depending on the operation, for these reasons:

❏ Ice is used for other purposes, such as salad bars.

❏ Ice is wasted.

❏ The production capacity of the ice-making unit may decrease during the summer months, when the air (or water) used to cool the refrigeration system is warmer.

❏ Employees may take ice out of the bin because they assume it is "free."

Figure 7.58 shows the result of adding 25 percent to the ice requirements. In the example just given, the operation should select an ice machine capable of producing and storing a minimum of 313 pounds (140.8 kg) of ice per day.

Coffee Urns

Although methods of brewing coffee have improved significantly over the chuck-wagon style of throwing a handful of grounds into a pot of boiling water, the basic method has been the same for many years. Boiling water is sprayed or poured over coffee grounds for a precise period of time so that the water carrying the coffee flavor and aroma drips through to the holding container. The coffee grounds are held in a cloth or stainless-steel basket, and the grounds are removed after the brewing process ends. This is done so that the bitter substance from the grounds does not continue to drip into the coffee. The formula for good coffee includes a clean urn, a good blend of coffee, and a fresh supply of water. The equipment is designed to hold the coffee at just below the boiling point by surrounding the coffee container with boiling water. This outer jacket of boiling water is used as the source of boiling water for the next batch of coffee and for making hot tea or other beverages. Figure 7.59 shows a commercial coffee urn system.

Figure 7.59. Coffee Urns. Courtesy of Cecilware.

DESCRIPTION

The most popular sizes are the 3-gallon (11.3 L) urn, twin 3-gallon urns (6 gallons), 6-gallon (22.7 L) urn, or twin 6-gallon urns (12 gallons, 45.4 L). Automatic coffee urns do not require the operator to pour the boiling water over the grounds or to measure the water. These urns usually are provided with a mixing device that forces a small amount of steam through the brewed coffee to prevent "layering."

DETERMINING CAPACITY AND SIZE

The standard cup of coffee is 5 to 6 ounces (.24 L), and the amount of coffee produced from 1 pound is usually $2\frac{1}{2}$ to 3 gallons (9.4 L to 11.3 L).

Although the coffee urn is frequently used in medium- and large-capacity foodservice facilities, one of the most popular coffee machines for restaurants, hotels, and small institutions is the automatic coffee brewer that deposits the coffee directly into a decanter. In this type of coffee maker, the water is heated as it flows through the device (rather than being stored) and is sprayed over a premeasured amount of coffee held in a paper filter. The coffee immediately pours in a small stream into a glass or stainless-steel container. The decanter can then be used by the server to pour coffee for guests. These units are less expensive than urns and produce an excellent quality of coffee. They are heated by electricity, and most can be plugged directly into a wall outlet.

PORTABLE COFFEE BREWING/SERVING SYSTEMS

A recent change to the popular automatic coffee brewer just described is the portable coffee brewing/serving unit (see Figure 7.60). These coffeemakers heat the water as it flows from the plumbing connection (cold water), and the boiling water is sprayed over the grounds in a paper filter. The coffee then flows into two portable containers, which are well insulated and attractive in appearance. The insulated containers of coffee are popular because of the interest in different flavored coffees and the ease of moving the "shuttle" units to different locations.

ESPRESSO/CAPPUCCINO MACHINES AND COFFEE BEAN GRINDERS

The popularity of espresso and cappuccino has created a high demand for equipment that will produce these drinks in an authentic manner. Espresso is a thick, dark coffee made by forcing hot water through finely ground coffee under pressure. Good espresso has a strong, flavorful coffee taste and aroma and shows a foam called *crema* at the top. Cappuccino is a combination of espresso and hot steamed or frothed milk. Cinnamon, chocolate, and whipped cream are often added but are not part of the true Italian formula.

High-volume espresso machines (see Figure 7.61) are expensive when compared to other coffee equipment, but the profit potential for a high-quality product may justify the expense. One-, two-, and three-unit brewing devices can be specified, and a variety of decorative domes and accessories are available.

Figure 7.60. Portable Coffee Brewers. Courtesy of Grindmaster.

Figure 7.61. Espresso Maker. Courtesy of Cecilware.

Coffee grinders are usually sold by the same companies that sell espresso machines and are available in a wide variety of sizes and appearances. Review of several manufacturers' products is recommended.

Bar Equipment

Bar design has two distinct components. The front of the bar and the bar top are typically decorative. Wood, copper, plastic laminate, and vinyl or leather bar rails are all popular. The underside of the bar—the area used by the bartender—is where design efficiency is important. Several leading manufacturers have developed modular components in which the various parts fit together to form a sanitary and efficient work space. Typical components would include:

- ❏ *Ice chest.* An insulated storage area for ice (does not make ice)
- ❏ *Drain board.* Both a work surface and a place to set glasses and utensils to air-dry
- ❏ *Blender station.* A space designed for blenders, including a small sink for sanitizing utensils
- ❏ *Refrigerated storage chest.* For holding condiments and cooling bottles
- ❏ *Hand sink, including soap and towel dispensers.* Required by the health department
- ❏ *Three-compartment sink.* Required by the health department for washing and sanitizing glassware
- ❏ *Storage bins.* Places to stack 20-by-20-inch (50.8-by-50.8 cm) racks of clean or dirty glasses
- ❏ *Bottle rails, often called "speed rails."* Used for storing open bottles of the bar liquor stock
- ❏ *Fruit drawer.* A special drawer to store fruit that will be used in mixed drinks

Although not widely used, small glass-washing machines are available for undercounter use. Storage cabinets for cooling bottles of beer and wine are often located on the wall behind the bar or out of sight under the bar. Figure 7.62 shows underbar units.

BEER SYSTEMS

There are two methods for dispensing beer from a keg (actually three methods if the British system of pumping beer from the cellar is used). The direct-draw beer coolers are simple and highly recommended for the small to medium-size bar. These systems have a small undercounter refrigerated cabinet that keeps the keg cold and dispenses the beer through the top of the cabinet. The simplicity and ease of moving the beer to the glass is reason enough for recommending this piece of equipment. Remote systems are much more complex, requiring insulated beer lines for short distances or complex tube-within-a-tube systems. In these systems, circulated saline in the outer tube chills the beer in the inner tube and delivers the cold beer at a remote location. Obviously, remote systems are

Figure 7.62. Underbar Units. Courtesy of Perlick.

expensive and can be cost-justified only in large-volume operations that require the location of the keg some distance from the bar.

WINE STORAGE AND DISPENSING EQUIPMENT

Wine storage is fairly easy to handle in the food operation of restaurants, hotels, and country clubs. Red wines need to be stored in a cool area, with the bottles on their sides so that the cork stays moist. White wines need to be refrigerated prior to service, and there are many opinions as to the proper temperature. If the white wine is too cold, some of the subtle flavors are not fully realized. However, many white wines sit in storage for some time and warm up considerably before they are consumed. Equipment commonly used for the storage of white wines includes small behind-the-bar refrigerators that merchandise the house wines very well or large single or double reach-in refrigerators with special racks for keeping the wine on its side. Another common wine display device permits the house wines to be opened and capped so that air does not destroy the flavors; this allows the bartender to save partially used bottles for several days.

Water Filtration

DESCRIPTION

Water filtration is a key element to both equipment longevity and taste of product. Filters on ice machines help inhibit scale buildup and have antimicrobial protection to inhibit any potential bacteria growth. Water filtration for coffee and other drinking water applications provide clear, fresh, quality drinking water. It reduces dirt and particles along with reductions in chlorine taste and odor. The filtration system should be specified with a shut-off flushing valve in order to change out the filter without turning off the water supply main. It should also be specified with a pressure gauge to verify the water pressure is high enough for proper operating standards of the steamer; low pressure would indicate the filter is dirty and needs to be replaced.

WAREWASHING EQUIPMENT

The warewashing machine in a foodservice facility usually represents the largest single cost of any piece of equipment. The purchase price of the machine plus the cost of the dish tables represents a substantial investment. In addition to the purchase price, the operating costs of the machine will include:

- ❏ Water
- ❏ Electricity for machine motors
- ❏ Electricity, steam, or gas for the wash/rinse tanks and water booster heater
- ❏ Ventilation
- ❏ Sewer charges
- ❏ Detergents
- ❏ Drying agents
- ❏ Labor
- ❏ Maintenance

Because of these costs, warewashing equipment is among the most expensive to operate in the foodservice facility. The dish machine must therefore be carefully selected, with consideration given both to the initial (capital) cost and to the ongoing cost of operation.

One common misconception is that the larger the warewashing machine, the higher the operating costs. In some instances the opposite is true. The smaller single-tank dish machine requires an employee to lift the doors and push the racks through manually, and it uses hot water and detergent far less efficiently. Moreover, since the low speed and small capacity require longer working hours, the cost per dish washed indeed might be higher.

The machine selected should wash the dishes at the lowest possible cost per dish, assuming that the needed funds and space are available.

For purposes of comparison, a university foodservice dining hall will be used as an example. The hall serves 800 students three meals per day with one-and-a-half-hour dining periods. The number of dishes to be washed per meal is estimated in this way:

800 persons × 6 dishes per person (includes glasses or cups)
= 4,800 dishes and glasses per meal

Because the dish operation cannot run continuously, an efficiency factor of 70 percent is assumed, so the rated capacity of any machine is multiplied by 0.7.

- ❏ A small single-tank door machine (rated capacity 1,500 dishes per hour) would wash these dishes in just over four and a half hours.

❑ A single-tank conveyor machine (rated capacity 4,000 dishes per hour) would wash them in under two hours.

❑ A two-tank conveyor machine (rated capacity of 6,500 dishes per hour) would complete the job in about one hour.

If students working part time were used for the one-hour period needed to wash the dishes with the two-tank conveyor machine, then the economy of the largest machine, in comparison to machines that require a full-time dishwasher, is clear. In other words, oversizing the machine results in a significant labor savings.

TYPES OF DISH MACHINES

Dish Machines

Warewashing machines all operate on the same principle. A spray of water is pumped over dishes and other utensils so that the soil is washed off by hot water and a detergent. The final rinse sanitizes the dishes either by spraying water at 180°F (82°C) or by using a chemical sanitizer. The dishes must be hot enough to dry without toweling when exposed to the air.

Single-Tank Door Machines

Single-tank door machines (see Figure 7.63) consist of a tank containing hot wash water and a detergent dispenser. The machine is provided with stainless-steel doors. Scraping, loading, and unloading are done manually. The operator opens the doors, slides the loaded dish rack into the machine, closes the door, and initiates the wash cycle. Water and detergent are recirculated by an electric motor-driven pump that pushes water through

Figure 7.63. Single-Tank Door-type Dish Machine. Courtesy of Hobart Corporation.

Figure 7.64. Single-Tank Conveyor Dish Machine. Courtesy of Stero.

spray arms or nozzles above and below the rack of dishes. The final rinse is sprayed onto the dishes at 180°F (82°C) after the wash cycle is complete. When the cycle is complete, the operator opens the door and slides the clean rack of dishes out of the machine and onto the clean-dish table for air drying.

Single-Tank Conveyor Machine

A single-tank conveyor machine (see Figure 7.64) consists of a tank of hot wash water held at a temperature of 140°F (60°C) mixed with a detergent. After the dishes have been manually racked and prescraped, the operator pushes the rack to the load end of the machine. A conveyor with pawls catches the leading edge of the rack and pulls it through the dishwasher at a preset speed. The water and detergent are circulated by a motor-driven pump through spray arms above and below the dishes. The dishes pass through a final rinse at 180°F (82°C) and air-dry on a clean-dish table after they emerge from the machine.

Two-Tank Conveyor Machine

Two-tank conveyor-type dishwashing machines (see Figure 7.65) are also available. The first tank contains hot wash water and detergent, and the

Figure 7.65. Double-Tank Conveyor Dish Machine. Courtesy of Stero.

second contains rinse water. The dishes go through a final rinse at 180°F (82°C). Motor-driven pumps circulate the wash water and spray rinse water over the dishes while they are carried through the machine by a conveyor. The addition of the extra rinse water tank permits dishes to be conveyed through the machine faster and results in a cleaner dish or utensil.

Flight, Rackless, or Peg-type Machines

A flight-type dish machine (see Figure 7.66) typically has two or three tanks. The two-tank machine consists of a wash tank and a rinse tank; the three-tank model has tanks for prewash, wash, and rinse. Both types provide a sanitizing final rinse. The flight machine uses a conveyor designed to hold most dishes and utensils without the need for racks. Dishes and trays are loaded directly onto the conveyor, which is equipped with rows of pegs approximately 4 inches (10 cm) high to hold trays and plates upright for proper washing, rinsing, and draining. The conveyor may be made of plastic and/or heavy-gauge stainless steel. Items such as cups, glasses, and silverware, however, must be racked in order to be conveyed through the machine.

Flight machines are frequently used in operations that wash dishes for 600 or more persons per meal. Smaller flight machines with two tanks may be economical for food facilities serving 600 to 900 persons per meal. Food facilities that serve more than 1,000 persons per meal would require a three-tank flight dish machine.

Figure 7.66. Flight-type Dish Machine. Courtesy of Champion Industries, Inc.

Circular Carousel or Continuous Conveyor Machine

A circular dish machine (see Figure 7.67) is a two- or three-tank machine attached to an oval-shaped dish table. The system uses a series of standard 20-by-20-inch (500-by-500-mm) dish racks that are conveyed around the oval. The circular dishwashing system is labor-efficient because the dishes are loaded directly onto the moving dish racks without first being stacked or accumulated. The second primary advantage is that the machine will continue to operate if left unattended for a few moments. (A flight-type machine will stop if a dish strikes the end of the conveyor without being removed.) The circular conveyor machine is especially labor-efficient in food operations that serve continuously over a long period of time or in high-volume foodservice operations.

DESCRIPTION

Once the appropriate size and type of dish machine has been selected, a number of additional considerations must be addressed:

❏ *Tank heat energy source.* Options typically include steam coils, steam injectors, gas, and electricity.

❏ *Final rinse heat source.* Final rinse water is usually heated to 180°F (82°C) by a dedicated booster heater. Booster heaters traditionally have used steam (large machines) or electric (smaller machines) heat. Gas-fired booster heaters have recently become available and represent a potential operational savings where natural gas is less expensive than electricity.

❏ *Direction.* Dish machines are designed to operate either left to right or right to left, depending on the layout of the dish area.

Many accessories and options are available for all types of warewashing machines and of course add to their cost. Some of the options are:

❏ Blower dryer for rapid air-drying of dishes and utensils

❏ Chemical sanitizing

Figure 7.67. Carousel Dish Machine. Courtesy of Adamation, Inc.

❏ Vent hoods for each end of the machine

❏ Stainless-steel legs and frames (standard on some machines)

❏ Stainless-steel enclosure panels to cover the motors and plumbing

❏ Automatic fill

❏ Energy-saving features such as automatic shut-off after dishes (or racks) pass through the machine

❏ Common water, steam, and electrical connection points

PRIMARY USE IN THE FOOD OPERATION

In addition to washing dishes, warewashing machines may be used to wash pots, pans, utensils, trays, sheet pans, and a variety of other items from the production areas. Unusual uses may include washing grease filters and ceiling tiles.

DETERMINING CAPACITY AND SIZE

Dish machines are rated by the number of dishes or racks per hour (at about 20 dishes per rack) that can be washed. Figure 7.68 illustrates the method for determining the dish machine size, assuming the standard efficiency factor of 70 percent. (It is always wise to err on the side of selecting a

Type of Food Facility	Dishes and Glasses per Person*
Restaurant with limited menu	5–8
Restaurant with extensive menu	12–14
Cafeteria	7–10
Luxury hotel dining	12–16
*Does not include silverware or stainless eating utensils.	

Figure 7.68a. Dish Utilization.

Dish Machine Type	Dishes per Hour	Racks per Hour
Single-tank door	1,550	62
Two-tank conveyor	5,850	234
Three-tank conveyor	6,650	265
Flight-type	12,000	

Figure 7.68b. Dish Machine Capacities.

machine that is too large rather than too small.) Using Figure 7.68a, the volume of dishes for a 100-seat restaurant with an extensive menu that turns over the dining room one and a half times per hour would be:

$$\text{100 seats} \times 1.5 = \text{150 persons per hour}$$

$$\text{150 persons} \times \text{13 pieces of dinnerware per person} = \text{1,950 dishes per hour}$$

Figure 7.68b shows typical dish machine capacities taken from the catalog of a leading manufacturer. Continuing the example, 1,950 dishes per hour at 70 percent efficiency would require a machine that would handle:

$$1950 \div .70 = \text{2,786 dishes per hour}$$

Following Figure 7.68b, a two-tank conveyor machine would be the appropriate selection for this operation.

Potwashing Machines

DESCRIPTION

There are two primary differences between a potwashing machine (see Figure 7.69) and a conventional dishwashing machine. First, the motor that pumps water under high pressure onto the pots and pans is larger than that normally installed on a dish machine. Dishwashing machines usually are manufactured with 2- or 3-horsepower motors, while potwashing machines are built with 5- to 10-horsepower motors that create a high-velocity water stream to strip off encrusted foods. Second, the internal size of the potwashing machine is large enough to accommodate large pots and standard 18-by-26-inch sheet pans or standard gastronorm pans.

The specifications of a pot machine are determined primarily on the basis of the volume of pots and pans to be washed. Many large foodservice facilities do not use potwashing machines at all. Managers often feel that a standard three-compartment sink with a garbage disposal and hand-operated prerinse is sufficient for washing pots, pans, and utensils. Very

Figure 7.69. Pot and Pan Washer. Courtesy of Insinger Dishwashers.

large institutions and large restaurants with complex menus can justify the expense of these machines.

The construction of potwashing machines is usually extremely rugged, with frequent use of 12-gauge stainless steel. Some of the larger machines employ a complete self-contained system in which the pots and pans are washed and rinsed on a large carousel. Smaller machines are designed to fit between soiled and clean tables in a simple layout similar to that used for a single-tank dishwasher.

PRIMARY USE IN THE FOOD OPERATION

The use of pot and pan machines is very much a matter of personal preference among foodservice managers. Most management people feel that the pans must be washed before being placed in the machine and that the only purpose of the machine is to sanitize and remove any greasy film that might remain. Other managers feel that the machine does an excellent job if encrusted materials are prewashed or scraped off before putting the pots into the machine. Many steam table pans and sheet pans do not have hard, encrusted food particles and therefore are easily washed by the machine.

The primary use in a food operation, and the decision to use this type of warewashing machine, may be based on:

❏ Number of persons being fed

❏ Complexity of the menu

❏ Type of equipment used in food preparation (e.g., a steam-jacketed kettle eliminates the need for many pots)

❏ Amount of money and/or space available for equipment

DETERMINING CAPACITY AND SIZE

Only a few companies manufacture potwashing machines, and the types of machines that are available do not fall into any standard classification. Because each of the machines is very different in construction and design, the best way to determine the size and capacity is to determine the number of pots, pans, or standard 18-by-26-inch or gastronorm pans that can be washed per hour. These numbers should then be compared to the volume of such pans used each day in the food operation.

Power Pot Sinks

DESCRIPTION

A relatively new and innovative method of washing pots and pans is through the use of a power potwashing sink (Figure 7.70). These devices utilize continuous, soil-removing water turbulence in which 115°F (46°C) water is circulated at a high rate to loosen and remove soil from pots and pans. The operator typically prerinses the pot or pan and places it in a large sink containing a mild detergent and rapidly circulating water. The pot or pan is then placed into a large sanitizing sink, which also circulates the hot water. Specifications include 14-gauge stainless-steel construction, a variety of sink sizes, built-in dispensers, drain boards, and a wide variety of lengths and shapes.

PRIMARY USE IN THE FOOD OPERATION

The power pot sink cuts down on the effort required to wash pots and pans, which clearly is one of the most demanding jobs in a food operation. The significant reduction in cost, when compared to the purchase of a powerful potwashing machine, may be a good reason to consider this piece of equipment.

DETERMINING CAPACITY AND SIZE

The primary decisions regarding power pot sinks involve the size of the tanks and the lengths of the soiled-item and clean-item drain boards. A moderate-size restaurant or club will be well served by a large (36 to 42 inches [915 to 1,065 mm] long) soak/wash sink, with 24-by-30-inch (610-by-760-mm) rinse and sanitizing sinks so that sheet pans can be fully

Figure 7.70. Power Potwashing System. Courtesy of PowerSoak.

submerged. However, the cost of increasing the length of the soak/wash sink is money well spent because of the greater capacity for pots and pans.

Conveyors and Accumulators

Once meals are consumed and taken to a cafeteria drop-off window, they need to make their way to the dish machine. Large institutions require either a soiled-tray conveyor or an accumulator. A conveyor (see Figure 7.71) automatically transports the tray to the scraping area on a horizontal conveyor belt. This belt could be made of plastic-type slats or a plastic/Kevlar material molded into a continuous cylindrical shape joined together, called a rubber band conveyor. The slat conveyor allows for the transport of small bowls and glasses since it is a relatively solid surface; the rubber band conveyor only provides two small bands to carry the soiled wear and only transports trays. Either type of conveyor should be specified with a belt washer for cleaning and sanitation.

The accumulator (see Figure 7.72) is usually revolving oval shape with tray carriers. These tray carriers provide for the vertical placement of trays, typically four high so that glasses can remain upright on the tray. The backside of the accumulator—the side not facing the drop-off window— is where the scraping of the tray occurs. The trays not removed by the

Figure 7.71. Dish Conveyor. Courtesy of Traycon Manufacturing Company, Inc.

worker simply continue around until the worker has time to remove it. Both conveying systems have their respective applications based on the number of meals per meal period, the square footage available, and the equipment budget.

WASTE-REMOVAL EQUIPMENT
The garbage can has long been the primary piece of equipment for removing waste from food production areas, and it continues to be used in

Figure 7.72. Accumulator. Courtesy of Caddy Corporation of America, Inc.

modern kitchens, in spite of the development of sophisticated machines that have improved waste-removal methods. However, waste removal through the use of garbage disposals and/or pulper/extractor systems has several advantages over the garbage can:

❑ The liquid part of the garbage is flushed into the sewer system, thus reducing the weight and volume of the garbage.

❑ The odors and vermin associated with garbage are greatly reduced.

❑ The waste material is transported through a soil pipe, eliminating the necessity of carrying a heavy can to a larger waste-disposal container.

❑ Pulpers process paper-based products, thus speeding the decomposition process and reducing the impact on landfills.

The advantage of the garbage can is that it can handle metal and glass objects, while the mechanical systems cannot.

DESCRIPTION

Disposals

Commercial disposals (see Figure 7.73) are specified primarily by motor size (see "Determining Capacity and Size," below). These accessories and features are frequently specified for disposals:

❑ Prerinse sprays

❑ Cones to direct the water and garbage into the disposal

❑ Electrical control panels for switching the disposal and water on and off

❑ Electrical overload and reversing mechanisms

❑ Silverware saver devices to prevent metal objects from entering the disposal

❑ Stainless-steel covers

PRIMARY USE IN THE FOOD OPERATION

Disposals grind food wastes and mix them with water so that they can be piped from the operation into the sewer system.

DETERMINING CAPACITY AND SIZE

Garbage disposals are usually specified by horsepower, with typical ranges being between $1/2$ and 7 horsepower. Many food facilities designers are of the opinion that the low-horsepower disposals are not a good buy. They do not have sufficient power to handle large quantities of refuse at one time, and therefore they often will cause clogging in the drain lines. Larger disposals, in the range of 2 to 3 horsepower, are recommended for general kitchen use. For dishwashing operations, particularly those that will require the disposal of both garbage and small quantities of paper, a 5-horsepower disposal is recommended. The installation of any type of disposal should provide adequate water intake to mix with solid particles, forming a slurry that will not clog the drain.

Figure 7.73. Disposer. Courtesy of InSinkErator.

Water-Recirculation Disposer Systems

Disposers often are built into soiled-dish tables to facilitate the scraping of dishes. In smaller operations, the disposer is mounted in an 18-inch (460-mm)-diameter stainless-steel cone that is integrally welded to the dish table. This approach is functional for smaller operations. However, in larger operations, where several employees are involved in scraping dishes, the soiled-dish table is fabricated with a trough (about 8 inches wide and 6 inches deep [200 mm wide and 150 mm deep]) through which water is circulated. The dish crew scrapes the waste from plates and dishes into the trough, where it is carried by the water flow to the disposer. The problem with this approach is high water consumption—as much as 9 gallons (34 L) per minute goes through the disposer. A water-recirculation system (Figure 7.74), integrated with a disposer, skims off the waste and sends it through the disposer and returns most of the water back to the trough. This saves a significant amount of water and is far less detrimental to waste treatment systems.

Figure 7.74. Water-Recirculation Disposing System. Courtesy of the Salvajor Company.

DESCRIPTION

The need for a waste disposal system that will not place large amounts of food or paper solids into the sewer system has increased dramatically. Many municipalities have ordinances against the use of commercial disposers because of the heavy load that they place on the sewer system. A pulping and extracting waste system (see Figure 7.75) is one of several alternatives available.

In a pulper, water and wastes are mixed together and ground into small particles (slurry). The grinding process is very similar to that of the conventional disposal, but the pulper does not wash the ground wastes into the sewer system. Instead, the water and slurry are piped to the extractor, where the solids are separated from the water. The water is returned to the pulper, mixed with fresh water, and reused in the grinding process. The solids from the extractor are conveyed to a conventional trash container. This material, which resembles wet sawdust or ground paper, is virtually odor-free.

Since much of the weight of garbage is the liquid, and the bulk of the garbage is reduced by grinding, the pulping and extracting process results in significantly less waste for a foodservice operation. However, the system costs considerably more than the conventional disposer and garbage

Pulper and Extractor Systems

Figure 7.75. Pulper/Extractor. Courtesy of Somat.

can. The high initial cost of the pulper/extractor is offset by savings from:

❏ A reduction in waste handling resulting from a smaller volume of waste

❏ Reduced water consumption

❏ Labor simplification, as the garbage does not need to be physically carried from the kitchen

An additional, important advantage of the pulper/extractor system is the reduction in odor in the kitchen and around the trash container. The specifications for the equipment options and accessories are limited because only a few manufacturers make the equipment. Systems can be specified that will:

❏ Operate under a soiled-dish table

❏ Operate with the extractor connected to a remote location (The slurry is piped from the pulper to the extractor.)

❏ Connect directly to the waste trough on a soiled-dish table

A foodservice facility with the kitchen and warewashing area located on the second floor is an ideal application for a pulper/extractor system. The pulper can be located on the second floor; the extractor is on the first floor near the garbage containers, and the slurry is piped from the pulper to the extractor downstairs. The need to carry heavy, smelly garbage down the stairs is eliminated.

PRIMARY USE IN THE FOOD OPERATION

The primary use of the pulper/extractor system is as an alternative method of garbage and paper disposal that does not place these waste materials into the sewer system.

DETERMINING CAPACITY AND SIZE

Pulper/extractor systems handle from 600 to 1,000 pounds (272 to 454 kg) of typical food waste per hour; higher capacity is available if multiple pulpers and extractors are installed. A facility considering a pulper/extractor system will need to estimate the quantity of waste produced. This type of waste system, unlike a garbage disposal, requires a significant quantity of pulp—that is, paper products—to work effectively. Ideal applications are in large-volume facilities using Styrofoam and paper plates, cups, and other containers.

Pulping and extracting systems are not cost-justified in the small restaurant or institution. A restaurant or institution serving under 500 meals per day probably would not have the funds necessary to purchase this equipment and probably would not have adequate space to house it. For larger foodservice operations, municipal codes, the amount of paper used in the operation, and the relative costs of using a conventional disposer and trash removal system are important considerations in determining whether to adopt the pulper/extractor system.

Trash Compactors

DESCRIPTION

Trash compactors are mechanical devices that compress waste materials so that the volume is greatly reduced. Compactors also permit wastes to be more easily transported out of the food production areas in portable carts or containers.

In recent years, the sale of compactors has dropped off considerably because their cost is high and they are difficult to clean (thus often creating sanitation and odor problems). In addition, many of the early designs had poor repair and maintenance records. The advantages of compactors in certain applications may outweigh the disadvantages, however. Large compactors may be installed at the back dock of large foodservice facilities, from which the garbage can be removed by trucks especially designed to lift and empty the compacted garbage from waste containers. Smaller compactors are often used in facilities that have a large accumulation of paper cups, plates, and glasses, boxes, and other types of trash.

Balers

DESCRIPTION

With more and more municipalities requiring recycling of cardboard, plastic, and glass, a baler can help reduce the size of the recycled material as well as reduce labor in breaking down cardboard boxes. Balers (see Figure 7.76) act much the same as compactors except that they can hold the recycled material together in plastic bags or plastic bandings. These bales can then be stored out of the way in a smaller space for future pickup.

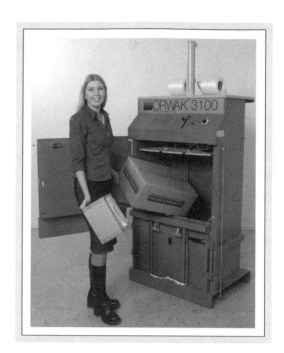

Figure 7.76. Baler. Courtesy of AB Orwak.

SUMMARY

Foodservice equipment should be selected based on necessity, the condition of current equipment, and the possibility of reducing energy and operating costs. The National Sanitation Foundation, which establishes sanitation and safety standards for equipment construction, is a good source of information. The NSF seal of approval is a recognized standard in the foodservice industry.

The types of equipment included in this chapter are the major pieces that foodservice consultants and their clients will consider purchasing. Comprehensive information about this equipment can be obtained from equipment catalogs, from manufacturer's representatives, or at any of the large equipment shows, such as those of the National Restaurant Association (NRA) or National Association of Foodservice Equipment Manufacturers (NAFEM). The foodservice consultant should be well versed in the many types of equipment available so that he or she can help the client make the best selection.

KEY TERMS

Cook-serve	Production/Cooking equipment
Cook-hold-serve	Bakery equipment
Cook/chill	Service and cafeteria equipment
Receiving and storage equipment	Warewashing equipment
Preparation equipment	Waste-removal equipment

QUESTIONS

1. List and describe the typical pieces of equipment that you would find in each of these areas:

   Receiving and storage
   Pre-preparation
   Final preparation
   Service
   Warewashing

2. What is the difference between a buffalo chopper and a vertical cutter mixer?

3. Why does a convection oven cook faster than a conventional deck oven?

4. Combi oven steamers, slow-cook ovens, rack ovens, and rotary ovens save energy. Why?

5. What is impingement?

6. Are broilers energy efficient? Why or why not?

7. How do gas and electric fryers heat the fat? Which method has the quickest recovery when a batch of frozen fries is cooked?

8. What is a sheeter?

9. What are the applications and advantages of cook/chill system?

10. How does a carousel dish machine save labor?

11. Why would an institution with a large number of customers need a pulper and extractor system? Where are the pulper and extractor typically located?

DISCUSSION QUESTION

Make a list of the kitchen equipment required for the menu that follows, keeping in mind that you must maximize the energy efficiency of the installation:

   Roast beef
   Variety of charbroiled steaks
   Baked potatoes
   French fries
   Salads and cold appetizers
   Baked breads
   Pies and cakes
   Hot and cold beverages
   A small service bar
   Grilled burgers (children's menu)
   Soup

Assume:

   100 seats
   All foods prepared "in house"

CHAPTER 8

Foodservice Facilities Engineering and Architecture

THIS CHAPTER

☑ Describes the primary considerations to be addressed by facilities planners to ensure the most economical use of energy in foodservice operations

☑ Provides a basic understanding of the primary utilities used in foodservice

☑ Describes the construction of hoods and ventilation systems in kitchens, dishwashing rooms, and service areas

☑ Lists the most commonly used finishes for floors, ceilings, and walls in foodservice operations

☑ Describes the methods for reducing sound in both public spaces and employee work areas

☑ Discusses the effects of lighting levels on productivity and safe food handling, and offers recommendations for minimum lighting levels in foodservice facilities

FOODSERVICE FACILITIES ENGINEERING

The engineering of a hotel dining facility, a complex restaurant, or a large institutional foodservice requires the expertise of both architects and professional engineers. The facility owner or manager who attempts to design and install electrical, plumbing, or heating, ventilation, and air-conditioning (HVAC) systems without professional assistance is courting disaster. Even the seemingly simple installation of a new warewashing system in a restaurant involves:

- ❏ Hot and cold water
- ❏ Floor drains
- ❏ Dish machine drains
- ❏ Electricity, steam, or natural gas
- ❏ Special ventilation to remove moist air

❑ Special floor, wall, and ceiling finishes

❑ Special lighting

The material in this chapter is not intended to be a do-it-yourself guide to complex engineering systems in foodservice facilities; rather, it is intended to offer a general overview and several useful ideas for resolving problems peculiar to the foodservice industry. For both students and foodservice planners, it will serve as a guide to the most accepted methods of engineering a foodservice construction or renovation project and provide an understanding of the basic language of the technical trades involved in electrical, plumbing, and HVAC systems.

Water Systems

The preparation of and service of food depend on a source of sanitary hot or cold water. Without water, vegetables could not be cleaned, soups prepared, dishes washed, or ice made. Hot water consumes about 13 percent of a restaurant's energy budget. Water use has an economic impact on the bottom line of a foodservice operation through the costs of:

❑ Supply: the metered cost of cold water

❑ Heating: the energy to heat water

❑ Waste disposal: the sewage costs of disposing of water

Although some foodservice facilities rely on wells, water is usually supplied through a municipal water system. Under most circumstances, these water sources are frequently checked and carefully monitored to keep out pathogenic bacteria or other harmful materials. The supply cost of municipal water is computed on the basis of gallons (liters) of consumption during a period ranging from one month to three months. When the water meter is read, the cost is then computed and a bill sent to the end user. Figure 8.1 shows the approximate consumption of hot water for typical uses in foodservice facilities.

Equipment Item	Hot-Water Consumption Gallons (Liters) Per Hour	
	Low	High
Vegetable sink	15 (57)	15 (57)
Triple-compartment pot sink	45 (170)	60 (227)
Prerinse spray for dishes	45 (170)	45 (170)
Prescraper for dishes, conveyor type		250 (946)
Prescraper for dishes, Salvajor type		180 (681)
Bar sink (three-compartment)	—	20 (76)
Bar sink (four-compartment)	—	25 (95)
Lavatory	3 (11)	5 (19)
Utility sink	3 (11)	5 (19)
Bain-marie	6 (23)	10 (38)
Coffee urn	3 (11)	5 (19)
Single-tank dish machine	45 (170)	50 (189)

Source: Adapted from *Guidelines for Hot Water Generating Systems for Food Service Establishments* (East Lansing, MI: State of Michigan.

Figure 8.1. Water Consumption in Foodservice Facilities.

WATER SUPPLY LOCATION AND HARDWARE

The location of water supply and drains are important considerations in the design and layout process. It is far less expensive to add a faucet during the design phase than after the facility has been opened. Supplying water to steam tables to fill the hot-food wells, to chef's tables, to kettles and tilting skillets, and to server stations is likely to save steps (and therefore labor costs).

A tremendous variety of faucets, drains, hoses, connections, and other hardware is available for foodservice applications. Taking the time to select the right hardware for the specific task is a smart idea, even though the hardware is only a small part of the overall equipment package for a new or renovated facility. As competitive pressures force fabricators and manufacturers to cut costs, operators and consultants who do not specify exactly what is needed are likely to be rudely surprised when inadequate hardware is delivered to the job.

WATER HEATING

Water-heating systems heat water to temperatures appropriate for dishwashing, food preparation, and lavatories. A water heater provides hot water to faucets in one of two ways: heating water at the faucet to the temperature at which it will be used, or heating it to a higher temperature, then storing it and tempering it with cold water before it reaches the faucet. Some foodservice establishments maintain separate water-heating systems for kitchen and lavatory use. One system generates very hot water to be piped to the kitchen, and the other warms water for the lavatories, where moderate temperatures are adequate.

All forms of energy can be used to heat water. Most foodservice establishments use electric or gas water heaters, although a few use oil or steam. Electric water heaters are efficient at converting electrical energy to hot water. However, they generally heat water more slowly than do other kinds of heaters and require a larger tank to keep an adequate supply of water available.

ENERGY CONSERVATION AND WATER USE

Even while maintaining the necessary high standards of sanitation, energy can be saved in water heating and dishwashing. Energy-saving procedures can be simple or exotic. Some foodservice operations now use rooftop solar collectors. The captured solar energy is used to warm the water before it enters the water heater, thus significantly reducing the energy expended by the water-heating system. Another popular idea is to use the waste heat from refrigeration cooling systems to heat dishwashing water. The concept of heat recovery is discussed in greater detail in the next section.

Significant energy and dollar savings can be achieved by keeping two basic objectives in mind. The first is to reduce the amount of hot water used, especially the amount wasted—every time water is used, some of it is wasted. The second goal is to reduce the temperature of the water to the lowest temperature appropriate for the use. Not only does it cost less to heat the water to a lower temperature, but heat losses from distribution pipes are related directly to the difference between the temperature of the water in the pipes and that of the surrounding air.

Specific recommendations for the design of energy-efficient foodservice facilities follow.

❏ A water heater uses less energy than a range top to heat the same amount of water. Hot tap water should thus be used for cooking whenever possible (an exception would be in localities where the water contains heavy concentrations of minerals). Cold water should be used only when required by the cooking method. Both cold and hot water should be supplied to the preparation areas.

❏ Water should be heated only to the temperature needed. Heating the entire supply of kitchen water to 180°F (82°C) is highly inefficient when only the final rinse of the dish machine needs water at such a high temperature. Booster heaters can be used to bring water to 180°F (82°C) where required for sanitizing. Similarly, heating the entire building's supply of hot water to 140°F (60°C) and then cooling it to 110°F (43°C) for hand washing is inefficient.

❏ Hot-water boosters should be located within 5 feet (30 cm) of equipment that needs 180°F (82°C) water for sanitizing. Longer distances cause heat loss in the pipes.

❏ Spring-operated valves on the kitchen and rest room faucets save water. One type is attached to hand levers, and another operates with a foot treadle. For kitchen sinks, spring-operated foot treadles are most effective because they leave the operator's hands free for other tasks. For lavatory faucets, a 15-second delay-action valve is required to satisfy health standards.

Hot-water usage can easily be determined for dishwashers, glass washers, potwashers, and silverware washers, as calculated in gallons per hour. These figures are established by the National Sanitation Foundation (NSF) and the manufacturer of the particular piece of equipment.

WATER-CONDITIONING SYSTEMS

Hard water contains mineral deposits in solution that subsequently precipitate in water heaters, boilers, and water lines. These deposits can decrease energy efficiency, clog the water supply pipes, and cause valves and other controls to malfunction. In addition, mineral deposits can leave unattractive spots on glasses and silverware, giving the impression of an unsanitary condition. Hard water increases the amount of detergent needed for proper cleaning and degreasing in dishwashers and pot sinks.

The hardness of water is usually measured in grains, expressed in terms of the amount of minerals (calcium carbonate and others) per million parts of water. One grain of hardness is equal to approximately 17 parts per million (ppm). If water contains less than 4 grains of hardness, it may not need to be softened. Water containing between 4 and 6 grains will leave deposits on pipes and on the walls of water heaters unless the water is treated by a water softener. Water softeners most commonly use a zeolite process in which a chemical reaction occurs between salt and a catalyst in the water softener. These systems are effective but are occasionally objectionable because of the small amount of sodium that remains in the water. An alternative to the zeolite process is the use of magnetic water treatment. These systems keep the minerals in water in suspension by passing the water through a multifield magnet, which helps prevent crystallization of the mineral substance.

Dish machines, steamers, combi ovens, coffee and beverage systems, and ice machines all are affected by the quality of the water supplied to them. Manufacturers of this equipment typically provide data on minimum water quality standards. When water that does not meet the manufacturer's standards is supplied to a piece of equipment, severe and expensive maintenance problems are likely to occur. Although conditioning systems rarely can eliminate water quality problems completely, they can reduce maintenance and repair costs substantially.

Small conditioning systems can be installed to improve the quality of the water supplied to individual equipment items. Or a large system can be installed to condition all of the water supplied to the kitchen. Each approach has advantages and disadvantages. Small systems condition only the water needed by a steamer, coffeemaker, or ice machine. They are easily installed and relocated as necessary. However, multiple small systems take more time to maintain. A single large conditioning system treating the water for the entire kitchen is relatively easy to maintain. The disadvantage is that the operation is paying to treat water that does not require conditioning. The decision about which approach is best depends on the overall quality of the water supply, how much equipment there is that needs conditioned water, and the capabilities of the maintenance staff.

Foodservice manufacturers often recommend simple water filters—as opposed to complex conditioning systems—for single-equipment items, such as ice machines, coffee makers, and steamers. These units are cost effective and are able to remove particulates and impurities from the water supply.

Electrical Systems

Electrical energy is one of the primary sources of energy for foodservice equipment as well as for lighting, air-conditioning, and ventilation. The basic unit of electrical energy is the *watt*. Foodservice equipment is rated in terms of *kilowatt-hours*, the number of watts (in thousands) consumed in an hour, abbreviated as kW or kWh. Building supplies of electricity are available in specific voltages, such as 110 volts, 208 volts, 230 volts, or 480 volts, and 1- or 3-phase. Higher voltages (e.g., 208, 230, or 480) and 3-phase connections are used for equipment that demands greater electrical energy.

Foodservice equipment must be selected to match the voltage and phase available in the facility. A dish machine designed for use with 208-volt 3-phase electricity will not operate if connected to a 110-volt 1-phase circuit. General guidelines for selecting the electrical characteristics of foodservice equipment follow.

❏ Determine the electrical characteristics of the building through discussion with the electrical engineer or building maintenance staff. The answer will typically be 110/240 volts, 110/208 volts, or 110/240~460/480 volts.

❏ Select the piece of equipment desired and use the highest electrical voltage possible. This will usually reduce the size of the copper wires that must be used in the building and so will reduce the cost of the installation.

❑ If electrical motors are involved, use the highest electrical voltage possible and 3-phase connections (which are more efficient).

❑ Select the method for connecting the electrical equipment to the power source. Equipment that will be permanently installed should be direct-wired. A male and female adapter (plug) can be used for equipment that will be moved or frequently disconnected.

❑ Ensure that the electrical characteristics and the type of connector appear on the mechanical drawing, in the equipment specification, and on the order for the equipment.

Adequate electrical connections for portable equipment such as slicers, toasters, food processors, hot-food warming carts, and coffee servers also should be provided. These items typically are designed to be connected to a duplex receptacle using a standard cord and plug. However, the standard electrical power supplied to a duplex receptacle may not be sufficient for commercial equipment—particularly if several pieces of equipment are plugged into the same circuit. For example, many of the hot-food holding carts used for banquets require more power than is available from a standard 15-amp circuit. The owner's representative should work carefully with the electrical engineer to ensure that adequate electrical power is available in all duplex receptacles.

ELECTRICAL ENERGY USE AND CONSERVATION

Electrical energy conservation requires an understanding of the rate structures employed by utility companies. Two basic rate structures are the step rate and the demand charge.

With step rates, utility rates are often based on a reduction in the cost per kilowatt-hour as the consumption increases. Recently objections have been raised to this method of billing because it rewards customers for excessive usage. However, the idea of getting a discount for the purchase of large quantities still exists in the business community, and electricity is usually no exception.

The step-rate schedule is often controlled by a local or state regulatory agency and may change as the cost of energy rises. A typical step-rate schedule is illustrated in Figure 8.2.

In demand-charge systems, a relatively large consumer of energy will probably have two charges on the electric bill: one charge for energy used and one for demand. While the energy billing represents the number of kilowatt-hours actually used, the demand charge reflects the cost to the utility of maintaining sufficient generating capacity to supply large, short-term energy demands put on the utility lines by consumers. The charge is based on the maximum energy demand imposed on the utility lines during a short interval, generally a 15-minute period, during the billing period. The maximum demand is measured by a demand meter, and the bill is based on the maximum demand (kWh) multiplied by the demand charge (cost per kWh) for the billing period. If the peak usage for a given billing period is 50 kilowatt-hours and the demand charge is $5 per kWh, the demand charge for that period will be $250,

Kilowatt-Hours	Rate per kWh
1–50	$0.150
51–100	$0.l00
101–200	$0.050
201–300	$0.040
301–500	$0.030
Over 500	$0.025
If the meter reading for a one-month period indicated that 750 kWh were used, the cost would be:	
50 kWh at $ 0.150	$7.50
50 kWh at $0.100	$5.00
100 kWh at $0.050	$5.00
100 kWh at $0.040	$4.00
200 kWh at $0.030	$6.00
250 kWh at $0.025	$6.25
Total	$33.75

Figure 8.2. Electrical Energy Step-Rate Illustration.

even if this peak is reached for only one 15-minute period during the month.

Demand charges may constitute a large percentage of the total electric utility bill. A serious energy management program needs to focus on demand as well as energy use because significant savings can be realized by lowering the peak demand. The food facilities consultant must be aware of the kilowatt-hour rating of each piece of equipment and give consideration to the total electrical demand created as a result of the kitchen design.

Gas

Natural gas, as well as other forms of refined fuels such as propane, is the primary source of energy for foodservice equipment. In fact, very few types of preparation equipment are not available with gas as the principal source of energy for cooking.

The decision to use gas-powered or electrical equipment often is based solely on the relative costs of operation for each energy source. A later section of this chapter discusses the procedure for comparing the cost of gas with alternative energy sources. However, several other factors are important to consider in the selection and specification of gas-fired equipment:

❑ *Operational practices and preferences.* A key factor in the selection of gas-fired equipment is the preferences of the employees who will use the equipment on a regular basis. Most chefs, for example, prefer a gas-fired range for sautéing because it offers a high degree of control over the heat applied to the pan. Preferences may not play as large a role in the selection of a gas-fired fryer or convection oven versus electric models.

❑ *Durability and maintenance.* Depending on the piece of equipment, electric heat may be a more durable source of heat over time. For example, gas-heated dish machines tended to suffer breakdowns because the high heat from the burner eventually damages the water tank. New dish machine burner designs are submerged in the water tank and are far more durable.

❏ *Initial cost.* The same equipment may be substantially more expensive in a gas-fired version than in the electric version (or vice versa).

❏ *Ventilation requirements.* Gas-fired equipment uses a combustion process, and the waste gases must be exhausted from the room. If the selection of gas-fired equipment would necessitate a separate ventilation hood and/or ductwork, those costs should be factored into the decision.

GAS VERSUS ELECTRIC EQUIPMENT: ENERGY COSTS

The efficient use of energy is important to the manager of a foodservice operation not only because everyone has a responsibility to conserve energy, but also because conservation can save money and increase profits. The average cost of energy for a restaurant exceeds 5 percent of the total sales. Food and labor usually are the only costs that exceed the cost of energy.

For those engaged in planning food facilities, the selection of the most economical fuel is a complex matter. The use of steam, for instance, has been mentioned as an economical cooking source under certain circumstances of availability, because of its ability to transfer heat efficiently to food. Figure 8.3 reports data provided by the American Gas Association regarding the relative energy requirements of gas versus electric equipment. These data suggest that a strong case can be made for the use of natural gas based on its efficiency.

The data presented in Figure 8.3 do not take into account two important considerations when comparing the cost and efficiency of natural gas versus electricity. First, the actual connected load and energy usage for a given type of equipment may vary significantly among manufacturers. Not all fryers, ovens, or grills require the same amount of electricity. Some are substantially more efficient than others.

Second, the data in Figure 8.3 do not reflect the amount of energy that is actually transferred to the food. Studies done by the author at Michigan State University indicate that the type of equipment selected is often more important in energy savings than the source of the energy. Frozen vegetables cooked on a hot-top range (gas or electric) will require much more energy than the same package of vegetables cooked in a pressure steamer. The reason for the difference is obvious. With stove-top cookery,

Figure 8.3. Estimated Energy Requirements for Foodservice Equipment (expressed in British Thermal Units, BTUs).

Equipment Item	Electrical Btus Required	Gas Btus Required
Kettle (40-quart)	41,000	52,000
Fryer	72,000	110,000
Convection oven	38,000	55,000
Combi oven	72,000	190,000
Steamer	61,000	90,000

most of the energy goes up into the hood and is wasted, whereas the closed cooking chamber of a pressure steamer holds the energy inside and allows it to be absorbed into the product being cooked.

Most of the energy used in a typical restaurant is used to prepare and store food. Cooking equipment is the greatest consumer of energy for these reasons:

❏ Heat-producing appliances require the highest consumption (flow of electricity or rate of use of gas).

❏ Cooking equipment is turned on for many hours during the day (often unnecessarily).

❏ Most of the heat produced is lost to the hood and is not recovered.

❏ The conversion of electricity or gas to heat is inefficient.

The answer to conservation is not easily found, but the foodservice operator can do certain things to reduce cooking energy loss:

❏ *Select equipment that is enclosed and insulated.* Closed cooking vessels contain the energy and permit it to be absorbed by the food. Rotary ovens, convection ovens, convection steamers, steam-jacketed kettles with lids, and microwave ovens are good examples of closed cooking vessels.

❏ *Cook foods in the largest quantity possible.* This cannot be done for vegetables and other foods that are cooked in small batches as the meal progresses. However, energy savings can be realized when certain foods (chili, soups, and casseroles) are cooked in large quantities all at once.

❏ *Cook at the lowest temperature possible.* The savings in shrinkage for low-temperature roasting of meats has been known to the food-service industry for years. However, cooks continue to roast meats at high temperatures (300° to 400°F, or 149-degrees to 204-degrees Celsius) to "seal in the juices," though in fact this method serves only to dry out the product. Slow cooking means lower energy consumption despite longer cooking time.

❏ *Carefully monitor preheating time for each piece of equipment.* It is all too common for cooks to turn on the main battery of cooking equipment first thing in the morning and allow the ranges, fryers, and ovens to go full blast all day long. Most modern cooking appliances have a quick recovery time and can be brought up to proper cooking temperature in only a few minutes.

❏ *Monitor the demand curve for electricity.* Electricity is sold in part on the basis of peak demand for the day. Be sure that the equipment is not turned on all at once during the opening hours of the food facility.

Steam

Steam is a primary source of energy in many foodservice operations, particularly large institutional facilities that use it as an energy source for other purposes as well. Smaller foodservice facilities rarely have steam available as part of the building's utility services. However, small steam generators for use solely in foodservice are available.

Steam cookery has a number of important advantages:

❑ Steam transfers energy to food rapidly.

❑ For cooking vegetables, steam is highly desirable because it prevents much of the loss of nutrients, color, and texture that occurs when vegetables are boiled in a stock pot.

❑ Because steam always remains at 212°F (100°C) when not under pressure, and at up to 250°F (121°C) under pressure of 15 pounds per square inch, it is a moderate, uniform cooking medium.

❑ Steam equipment requires little or no warm-up time; thus preheat time losses are minimal.

❑ Cooking times are usually much shorter using steam equipment than they are using range-top cooking or boiling.

Steam can be used to cook foods in two ways. Direct steam cookery involves introducing steam into a cooking compartment, where it comes into direct contact with food. Examples of direct steam cooking equipment include steamers and combi ovens. Indirect steam cookery uses steam to heat the metal walls of the cooking vessel, as in the case of steam-jacketed kettles. A third use of steam in the commercial kitchen is as a heat source for other purposes. For example, steam coils can be used to provide heat for hot water in dish machines and pot sinks and to provide heated makeup air in ventilation systems.

Reduced to its barest elements, a steam-heating system consists of a means of converting water to steam (the boiler or converter), piping to conduct the steam to where it is to be used, a coil or other surface for condensing the steam and transferring the latent heat from the steam to the air, a trap to prevent the steam from passing through the coil before it is condensed, and return piping to conduct the condensate back to the boiler.

LATENT HEAT

Steam is an efficient cooking medium because it contains and then releases a tremendous amount of energy. Raising the temperature of 1 pound of water from room temperature (70°F [21°C]) to the boiling point (212°F [100°C]) requires about 142 Btus. However, creating 1 pound of steam from boiling water demands almost an additional 1,000 Btus. A pound of steam thus is highly charged with energy, which it quickly transfers to cooler surfaces when it condenses (cools back to liquid form).

Figure 8.4 shows how the temperature of 1 pound of water would vary with time if subjected to a constant rate of Btu input. Notice that it would stay at 32°F (0°C) and 212°F (100°C) at sea level until, in each case, the latent heat conversions had taken place for the entire pound of water.

SATURATION

If a container of water is heated sufficiently at a constant pressure, the water temperature will rise until the boiling point is reached. While the water is boiling, the temperature will remain constant until all the water has been converted to steam. Then the temperature will rise again as the steam is further heated (see Figure 8.4). Steam at the temperature at which it coexists with water is called saturated steam, and the temperature

Figure 8.4. Latent Heat of Water When Converted to Steam.

is called the saturation temperature. The saturation temperature varies with the pressure. An increase in pressure increases the temperature at which the latent heat transfer takes place. The pressure at which the latent heat transfer takes place at a given temperature is called the saturation pressure.

STEAM PRESSURE

In the English-speaking world, steam pressures are measured in pounds per square inch (psi). There are, necessarily, two reference levels. One is the pressure above atmospheric pressure. This is the boiler's pressure, commonly called the gauge pressure and abbreviated *psi* or *psig*. Because of the variable nature of atmospheric pressure, steam pressures are more accurately described in terms of their absolute pressure, which is the total amount of their pressure above a perfect vacuum.

SUPERHEAT

As in the case of any gas, steam can be heated above the boiling point. Once steam has risen above the saturation temperature, each additional increase of 1°F (0.56°C) requires only about ~HF BTU per pound. The increase in temperature above the saturation temperature is called superheat. Steam that has a small amount of superheat is called dry steam. If heated more than a few degrees above the saturation temperature, it is referred to as superheated steam.

Obviously, neither dry nor superheated steam can coexist with liquid water. Since steam is a gas, it tends to expand in direct relation to increased temperature. The increased volume and small amount of extra heat value makes superheat a relatively worthless factor in steam heating. Its only real value is to ensure that there will be dry steam at the point where the steam is to be used. In other words, a few degrees of superheat at the boiler will minimize condensation in the supply lines to the steam coils.

CONDENSATION

When steam gives up its latent heat and changes from saturated steam to water at the same temperature, it condenses. The water is spoken of as condensate.

HEAT TRANSFER

Heat transfer usually occurs through a steam coil or by steam injectors. A steam coil is a heat exchanger, a metal tube into which steam is introduced and where it condenses, giving off its latent energy in the form of heat that radiates from metal tubes and/or fins on the outside of the coil. All steam coils are 100 percent efficient in the sense that the heat released by condensing steam within the coil has nowhere to go but into the air surrounding the coil. Tube and fin material, fin spacing, air velocity, and several other factors affect the rate at which the heat transfer (and therefore the condensation) takes place, but they cannot alter the fact that the steam's latent heat has only one place to go: into the coil, and from the coil into the surrounding air.

Steam injectors transfer heat by allowing the pressurized steam to escape into another medium, such as water or air. For example, steam injectors are sometimes used to heat the water in the wash tank of dish machines. The injectors are submerged in the tank and, when charged, expel steam directly into the water to heat it.

Steam coils generally are preferred over steam injectors for most heating purposes. Because coils are a closed system, there is no danger of contaminating food with "dirty" steam. Coils also are far quieter in operation than injectors.

SOURCES OF STEAM

Steam is generated for use in foodservice facilities in several ways. It can be:

❑ Purchased from a utility owned by a municipality or commercial company and piped to the kitchen
❑ Generated in a building boiler room and piped to the kitchen
❑ Generated in the kitchen by a small boiler located under or near the equipment
❑ Generated in the kitchen by a small boiler that is integral to the foodservice equipment

Of these sources of steam, the installation of small boilers for each piece of equipment is the least satisfactory because of the high maintenance costs and additional kitchen heat that they create.

In foodservice facilities, steam is an economical energy source, especially under these circumstances:

❑ The facility already has a source of steam.
❑ Several pieces of equipment are selected that are steam-heated. This helps to justify the cost of installing steam supply lines and condensate return lines.
❑ The steam source produces clean steam, with no unsafe impurities from rust inhibitors and antifoaming chemicals. Many hospitals

must have a source of clean steam because of the frequent use of steam in autoclaves for sterilizing equipment. These clean steam systems use chemicals that are approved by the United States Department of Agriculture and are also safe for direct injection on food products.

STEAM BOILER SIZING

If a new boiler is required to generate steam for the foodservice equipment, the size of the boiler is determined by the amount of steam needed by each piece of equipment. Steam is measured in terms of flow (pounds per hour) and pressure (pounds per square inch). Boilers typically are sized in terms of boiler horsepower (bhp), which equals approximately 34.5 pounds of steam per hour. Using data provided by the foodservice consultant, the mechanical engineer determines the bhp of the boiler required to supply the kitchen equipment. Because steam loses energy in pipes, boilers are located as close as feasible to the equipment they supply and are oversized to compensate for energy loss in the plumbing.

Utility Costs and Energy Conservation in Selecting Foodservice Equipment

An effective approach for selecting the energy source to be used for heating, cooling, and cooking purposes should compare all of the available alternatives for achieving the desired result, rather than simply pitting electric equipment against gas. The next simple, nine-step system can be used by any foodservice manager to determine the most economical fuel for heating, cooling, or cooking.

1. Identify the relevant equipment alternatives for achieving the desired result. For example, vegetable cookery can take place in a stock pot on a range, in a kettle, or in a steamer.
2. For each piece of equipment and each possible form of energy, determine the utility load. Electrical loads are rated in terms of kilowatt-hours (kW or kWh), gas loads in terms of cubic feet or Btu, and steam loads in pounds per hour. This information can be obtained from the equipment manufacturer's catalog sheets or, where the equipment itself is available, from the manufacturer's identification plate.
3. Convert the energy demand (usage) for each equipment alternative to a common unit of measurement, the Btu (British thermal unit), so that they can be compared. Use these conversion values:

$$\text{Electricity: Btus} = 3{,}413 \times \text{kilowatt-hours}$$

$$\text{Gas: Btus} = 1{,}000 \times \text{cubic feet}$$

$$\text{Steam: Btus} = 1{,}000 \times \text{pounds per hour}$$

4. Determine the cooking time for several typical products that would be prepared by the equipment. For example, a 5-pound (2.3-kilogram) box of green peas cooked on an open-top range might take 12 minutes to prepare but would take 6 minutes to cook in a convection steamer. Or a beef roast might take 4 hours to cook in a conventional deck oven but only 3 hours and 15 minutes in a convection oven.
5. Extend the cooking time to cover a meaningful period of time in the operation, such as a day or a week. This step is important to take account of variations in demand that occur by time of day or by day of the week.

6. Multiply the preparation time for the period (in hours) by the Btu consumption for each piece of equipment. Be sure to take into account the fact that employees run some kinds of equipment continuously even though they are actually used for cooking only intermittently (e.g., hot-top ranges). A steamer thus might be used for a total of 12 hours in a week, whereas a hot-top range might be consuming energy for 72 hours.

7. Determine the cost of each type of energy from the utility company rate sheet (or from recent bills). Multiply this cost by the consumption. A steamer using 96 kWh of electrical energy per week will cost $4.32 to operate for a typical week if electricity is billed at the rate of $0.045 per kWh.

8. Convert to Btus for comparison purposes. The steamer uses 27,304 Btus (8 kWh × 3,413) per hour at a rate of $0.27/hour (8 kWh × $0.045). Do this for each piece of equipment and energy source.

9. Compare the projected energy consumption and utility costs.

Ventilation — FOODSERVICE EQUIPMENT VENTILATION SYSTEMS

The successful removal of heat and air that is laden with grease particles and food odors requires a well-designed hood exhaust system. Many energy-saving hoods are now available, and each hood manufacturer claims to have come up with the most effective design. The buyer cannot hope to make an intelligent choice without understanding the principles of hood exhaust operation, including both the action of thermal air currents and the functions of the component parts of a hood system. Because of the high initial cost of the hood and the high ongoing costs of operation for the life of the entire system, time spent in acquiring such knowledge is a worthwhile investment.

Hoods remove air, water vapor, grease, and food odors from the kitchen range area and air and water vapor from dishwashing rooms. Electric ovens, steamers, and steam-jacketed kettles require hoods that remove only air, heat, and water vapor. If large quantities of grease from a broiler, charbroiler, fryer, or grill are present, the hood system must extract this pollutant before the air is drawn by fans to the outside of the building. To understand the most effective and energy-efficient means of removing hot air and airborne grease, it is necessary to outline the function of a simple hood system.

The basic functions of a kitchen ventilation system are to *capture* the air heated by the cooking process, *remove* as much grease from it as possible, *exhaust* the heated air to the outside, and *resupply* or make up the air removed from the kitchen. Ventilation systems typically capture air from cooking in stainless-steel canopies hung over the cooking equipment. The air rises into the canopy by means of convection (hot air rises). A fan, usually located on the roof of the building, is connected to the canopy by ductwork. The negative pressure (vacuum) created by the exhaust fan pulls the heated, grease-laden air from the cooking surface through filters or extractors designed to capture the grease. Because many kitchen ventilation systems exhaust a large quantity of air, it is often necessary to return air to the kitchen from outside the building. When a large amount of air is exhausted in the kitchen, a negative pressure condition is created that causes air to flow from other parts of the building. Makeup air systems are designed to offset this problem by introducing air at or near the hood to replace some portion of the volume of air lost to the exhaust process. Ventilation systems are designed to exhaust and/or supply a specific volume of air, measured in cubic feet per minute (cfm).

SIZING HOODS (COMPUTING EXHAUST VOLUME)

The volume of air to be exhausted and supplied by a ventilation system ideally is determined by two factors: the amount of heat generated by the equipment below the hood and the design of the hood itself. The amount of heat generated by cooking equipment varies tremendously. Ovens, steamers, and kettles generate relatively little heat because they enclose the cooking cavity; they produce approximately 20 to 25 cfm of thermal current per square foot of surface area. A hot-top range with a surface temperature approaching 800°F (426.6-degrees Celsius) may generate 100 cfm of thermal current per square foot. A gas-fired charbroiler, because of its open-flame burners, may generate as much as 175 cfm of thermal current per square foot. Exhaust fans must be sized to capture all the heat generated by the equipment.

The design of the hood itself also affects the exhaust requirements. For example, hoods mounted against walls with closed ends that extend down to the surface of the equipment (side curtains) contain the flow of hot, grease-laden air relatively well, whereas island-style hoods, open on all four sides, will require 30 to 50 percent greater exhaust cfm to capture the air effectively. This is because the exhaust fan is effectively drawing air up from all four sides of an island hood, but from only one side of a wall hood with side curtains. Also, because a single hood may have equipment of varying exhaust requirements beneath it, it is common practice to size hoods according to basic guidelines. Figure 8.5 provides an example of a manufacturer's sizing guidelines.

The table shows typical exhaust requirements in cubic feet per minute for each linear foot of hood for kitchen ventilation systems. Where systems have a UL (Underwriters Laboratories) listing, they are approved at the exhaust levels established by the manufacturer. Non-UL-listed hoods must comply with local building codes. Local codes typically adopt broader standards, such as those developed by the National Fire Protection Association and the Building Officials and Code Administrators International.

The exhaust requirements shown are for wall-mounted hoods. (Island-type hoods typically have higher exhaust requirements.)

Type of Hood/Filter	Equipment	cfm/Linear Foot
High-velocity grease extractor	Steamers, ovens, kettles	150–200
	Ranges, griddles, fryers	200–250
	Charbroilers, hot-top ranges	250–300
Baffle filters (UL-listed)	Steamers, ovens, kettles	250
	Ranges, griddles, fryers	300
	Charbroilers, hot-top ranges	350
Non-UL-listed hoods	Varies by municipality	300–500

Figure 8.5. Exhaust Requirements for Various Types of Foodservice Equipment.

In actual practice, the sizing of a hood system often deviates from the ideal process. The exhaust requirements for a hood system often are determined by looking to state and local building codes. Such building codes typically state the minimum requirements for ventilation quite conservatively in order to protect the public and the foodservice operator from the possibility of an unscrupulous "tin-knocker" building a hood system that is not functional. Most state and municipal codes offer exceptions to the rule for hoods that have met stringent performance standards and that have been tested by independent organizations, such as Underwriters Laboratories. However, foodservice operators rarely are aware of these exceptions and so are not in a position to take advantage of them. In addition, engineers who lack experience in the design of mechanical systems for kitchens—as well as some local code compliance officials—may not be aware of the relevant exceptions or understand how to apply them. As a result, the operator may end up with a hood system that moves far more air than is necessary. One of the advantages of working with a food facilities design consultant is his or her specialized knowledge and experience in the design and specification of kitchen ventilation systems.

CAPTURING GREASE PARTICLES: FILTERS AND EXTRACTORS

The two most commonly used devices for capturing grease from the air as it passes through the hood canopy are filters and extractors. In the past, filters were designed to trap grease in fine wire mesh (like steel wool) located in the path of the exhaust air. While these filters effectively captured grease, they retained it over the cooking surface and so represented a serious fire hazard. Contemporary filters force grease-laden air to move across baffles, changing direction rapidly, thus flinging grease particles onto the surface of the baffles. The baffles are designed to drain the grease into a trough for easy removal. Extractors operate on the same principle as baffle filters but force the air to make multiple reversals before entering the exhaust duct. Most baffles are 50 to 60 percent efficient, whereas extractors often remove more than 90 percent of the grease that passes through them. Figure 8.6 illustrates the difference between baffles and extractors.

The filters or extractors in most ventilation hoods need to be removed regularly and washed in the dish machine. However, systems are available that automatically wash the extractors and duct plenums, saving maintenance costs. These systems require a significantly greater initial investment because of the plumbing that must be built into the hood system.

MAKEUP AIR SYSTEMS

There are three basic approaches to introducing makeup air in a kitchen ventilation system (see Figure 8.7).

1. *Discharging air inside the hood.* Makeup air can be discharged inside the canopy itself; this approach is often referred to as a "short-cycle" design (see Figure 8.7a). A system of ducts connects the makeup air discharge to a supply fan located on the roof. Because the supply air is introduced into the hood cavity itself, these systems are designed to use untempered air (air brought directly from the outside without any heating during the winter months). Although the short-cycle design

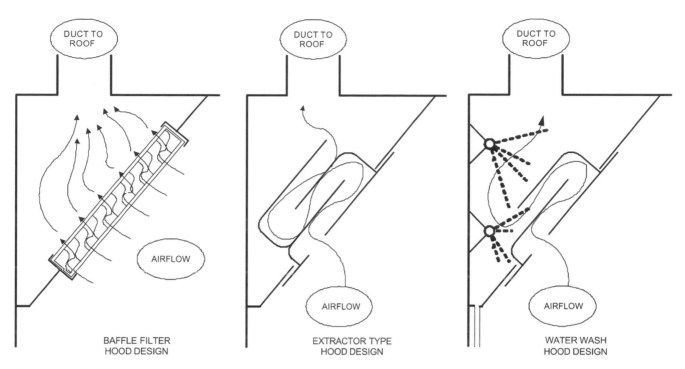

Figure 8.6. Baffle Filters versus Extractors in Removing Grease.

does not require the expense of tempered makeup air, it has two disadvantages.

   a. The amount of air that can be introduced directly into the hood cavity is limited to between 40 and 60 percent of the exhaust volume in most systems. This means that a large volume of indoor air is lost to the outdoors.

   b. On winter days, when the cold makeup air meets the moist heated air rising from the equipment, a tremendous amount of condensation is created under the hood.

2. *Discharging air along the face of the hood.* A second approach for introducing makeup air is to locate ducts and registers along the face of the

Figure 8.7. (a) Supply Air Discharged inside the Canopy (Short-Cycle Type. (b) Supply Air Discharged from the Face of the Hood. (c) Supply Air Discharged from a Separate Register in Front of the Hood.

hood (see Figure 8.7b). This approach can handle a far greater volume of makeup air—as much as 90 percent of what is exhausted. However, the supply registers direct the air out and down from the face of the hood, where it blows across the head and shoulders of the chef. For this reason, the supply air in front-discharge systems must be tempered to a level that is comfortable for the cooks (typically 55°F or 12.7-degrees Celsius). In addition, most manufacturers offer air registers that diffuse the high volumes of air over a relatively large surface area.

3. *Discharging air from separate registers.* Internal and front-discharge makeup air systems integrate the supply air registers and ductwork with the hood canopy. However, it is also feasible to use a completely separate duct and register system for introducing makeup air. Such systems tend to locate the registers in the ceiling just in front of the canopy (see Figure 8.7c).

Makeup air requirements typically are determined in relation to the volume of air exhausted by the hood as well as by the design of the makeup air system itself. In general, makeup air systems replace between 50 and 90 percent of the air removed by the exhaust system. The amount of air supply needed to make such a system effective is a matter of debate in the industry. The author's experience is that negative pressure is necessary to keep cooking odors in the kitchen and out of the dining room. A hood system using 80 percent or less makeup air seems to create a good balance between energy savings and a reasonable amount of negative air pressure in the kitchen.

FIRE-SUPPRESSION SYSTEMS

Kitchen ventilation hoods require fire-suppression systems. Traditionally, such systems consist of a pressurized tank filled with an extinguishing chemical and a series of pipes that terminate over the cooking equipment. If a fire develops, sensors (fusible links) open and the chemical is discharged. Once the fire has been put out, the operator cleans up the remaining extinguishing chemical, repairs any damage, and sanitizes the equipment before reopening for business.

Although these chemical systems continue to be widely used, they have several distinct disadvantages:

❏ If the fire is not completely extinguished and flares up after the canister has been emptied, the operation has no remaining protection.

❏ The chemical agent used to extinguish the fire must be completely cleaned from the equipment and the work area before the operation can reopen.

❏ The system must be inspected and regularly maintained in addition to the maintenance of other building fire suppression systems.

Several ventilation system manufacturers now offer fire suppression systems that are connected to the building's main sprinkler system. Although it seems counterintuitive to put out a grease fire with water, these systems actually do an excellent job. Water is sprayed in a very fine mist from nozzles over the equipment, effectively suffocating the fire. In addition, these systems are not limited in capacity, as the canister systems are, and require far less maintenance. Moreover, the installation cost of water-mist fire-suppression systems often is competitive with the cost of traditional canister systems in larger hoods.

The primary disadvantages faced by the operator who wants to realize the advantages of a water-mist fire-suppression system result from its relative newness in the design and construction industry. Unless engineers have had substantial experience dealing with kitchen mechanical systems, they are unlikely to be familiar with water-mist systems. Also, state and local building codes may make it difficult to install such systems. Some municipalities require water-mist systems to have sprinkler heads throughout the ductwork leading all the way to the roof—even though the traditional systems are not expected to meet a similar requirement. In a properly designed and installed water-mist system, there is no need for sprinkler heads beyond the duct collar; however, not all codes have caught up with this fact. The operator who desires the greater protection and lower maintenance costs of the water-mist system may need to advocate with the design team or, if a food facilities consultant is involved in the project, rely on the consultant to guide the team in this area.

AIR AND HUMIDITY CONTROL FOR THE DISHWASHING ROOM

Since warm air will hold more moisture than cool air, when moist warm air is cooled, water vapor condenses. Cool air containing less moisture increases the amount of moisture that can evaporate from the skin, and therefore is more cooling and comfortable for customers and employees. In foodservice establishments, the concern is that the air seems fresh and that humidity is low enough for comfort while the customers are sitting quietly in the dining room. For the employees, who are more active, a work space is comfortable if the temperature and humidity are slightly lower than in the dining room and if the air is moving rapidly.

Unfortunately, in the dishroom, the air is often very moist and the temperature extremely high.

Food facilities planners must insist that architects and engineers design into the HVAC system a sufficient amount of air supply and exhaust to keep the moisture level as low as possible in the dishwashing and pot-washing areas. Failure to create this condition will result in low productivity and high employee turnover among the warewashing personnel. A second problem arising from poor ventilation in the dishroom is a decrease in the effectiveness of air-drying as the dishes emerge from the washer. Wet dishes encourage bacterial growth, make a poor impression on customers, and, if towel-dried, are likely to be contaminated with organisms that cause illness.

HVAC SYSTEMS FOR DINING

The heating, ventilating, and air-conditioning systems for the dining room and other public spaces in a foodservice facility are beyond the scope of this text. The best heating source, the complexities of humidity and temperature control, and the environmental treatment of all spaces in both the front and back of the facility are technical matters that should be left in the hands of licensed and trained engineers.

Conveyor Systems

Conveyors have been used for many years in the industrial and manufacturing industries for moving materials from one place to another, at a maximum speed and with a minimum effort. In foodservice facilities, conveyors not only move objects but also can be designed to improve food quality (as in hospital tray makeup systems) and provide aesthetically pleasing dish tray areas in cafeterias and other self-service operations.

Although many conveyor systems are fabricated especially for the needs of a particular food operation, conveyors designed for general use in a foodservice facility can be purchased from a manufacturer's catalog. The general construction features of conveyors are:

❏ Conveyor transport or belt—the medium that moves the material (Many conveyors don't actually have belts; instead, they use different transport devices.)

❏ Conveyor bed—the part of the conveyor along which the belt travels

❏ Drive mechanism (if the belt is powered)—to move the belt along the bed

❏ Drive enclosure—a closed space, such as a cabinet, in which the motor and drive system are housed

❏ Return track for belt, with limit switch (a switch that will automatically cut the system off) and belt-washing system—typically located at the opposite end of the conveyor from the drive unit

❏ Drip pan—catches any liquids that fall from the conveyor belt

❏ Removable skirt panels—to enclose the structure of the conveyor bed

These parts vary, depending on the complexity of the conveyor system and the features desired by the foodservice owner or manager. Five transport systems are widely used in conveyors: belts, slats, rollers, pins, and links.

Flat, water-resistant conveyor belts were common during the early period of conveyor usage. Belts are still available, but are not as popular as slat conveyors because of their inability to "bend" around turns and corners.

Slat "belts" actually are composed of Delrin or other hard, flexible plastics. Each slat is 1 to 2 inches (25 to 50 millimeters [mm]) wide and 8 to 12 inches (200 to 305 mm) long. These slats are linked together at their centers to form a continuous flat transport surface. They are usually designed so that the belt can turn corners, and the slats overlap on the turns. Slat conveyor belts, with self-washing systems, are a clean and attractive solution for self-busing dish drop-off areas in cafeterias.

Roller conveyors may have "skate wheels" (about ½ inch [12.7 mm] wide and 2 inches [50.8 mm] in diameter) or rollers (as wide as the conveyor and about 2 inches [50.8 mm] in diameter). Roller conveyors are frequently used for gravity (nonpowered) conveyors or at the termination of a powered conveyor system. Gravity conveyors are less expensive and require little maintenance. However, in self-service applications, they are not as attractive and can cause accidents or dish breakage.

Pin conveyors are constructed of metal links with small pins protruding upward. The pins ensure that the tray or container being conveyed does not slip.

Link conveyor belts, constructed of a series of links made from Delrin or other hard but flexible plastics, are an excellent solution for conveying cafeteria trays. Installed in parallel pairs, these conveyors can be designed to move trays around sharp turns. The links are very strong and have been successful in self-service applications because they are attractive and do not break easily.

Conveying systems offer the potential for reducing labor costs in large foodservice operations, particularly in busing and warewashing areas. In operations that use trays and china, a well-designed conveyor system offers a far more attractive and sanitary solution than placing aluminum kitchen racks in the dining area to accumulate soiled trays. However, the design of conveying systems requires attention to detail, such as:

❏ Ensuring that the rate of conveyor travel is appropriate to the needs of the operation at *both ends* of the process. A conveying system that brings trays into the dishroom at twice the rate at which the crew can break them down and load them into the dish machine is clearly a poor solution.

❏ Providing a buffer at the unload end of a tray conveyor that runs into the dishroom, such as a gravity roller conveyor and accumulating table.

❏ Coordinating with the architects to provide a noise barrier shielding the tray drop area from the noise of the dishroom.

❏ Providing access to the conveyor for cleaning and maintenance, particularly at each end.

❏ Avoiding—at all costs—conveyor runs that are anything but horizontal. Vertical conveying systems are extremely difficult to keep clean and in good repair.

Utility Distribution Systems

Large foodservice operations typically require multiple ovens, kettles, steamers, grills, and fryers set adjacent to one another along a common wall. Gas, water, electric, and steam connections must be carefully routed through the interior structure of the wall to multiple rough-in points. When equipment is designed in two work areas, located back to back along a common wall, all of the utility connections for the equipment on each side must come through the common wall. As the type and number of utility connections required in a single wall increase, so also do the coordination demands and overall construction costs. An alternative approach is to locate the utility services in a stainless-steel raceway that is custom-fabricated according to the design of the facility. The raceway is nothing but a horizontal enclosure, 8 to 10 inches (203 to 254 mm) across and 12 to 18 inches (305 to 457 mm) high, that runs horizontally about 30 inches (762 mm) above the floor (see Figure 8.8). It contains pipes for hot and cold water, a gas supply pipe, an electrical conduit and "bus bars,"

Figure 8.8. Utility Distribution System. Courtesy of AVTEC Industries.

electrical bars that conduct electricity, and a steam supply (if needed). Connections to the equipment are made from the side or the bottom of the raceway.

Utility distribution systems offer three advantages:

1. Unlike connection points built into permanent walls, connections in the raceway can be added, removed, or relocated with relative ease should the equipment change.
2. Connections from the raceway to the equipment are well above floor level, making the cooking areas easy to clean.
3. Electrical and plumbing contractors at the job site need to make only one or two physical connections to the utility distribution system, rather than multiple connections for each piece of equipment.

Utility distribution systems generally are expensive. However, their cost needs to be weighed against the costs of engineering and constructing an array of complex utility services within a permanent wall. In large foodservice facilities, where sizable banks of equipment are required, a utility distribution system can prove to be a cost-effective alternative in comparison to traditional approaches.

Heat Recovery Systems

The cost of hot water is one of the biggest items on the foodservice energy bill. Hot water is used almost constantly during the normal operating hours of the facility, with peak usage when dishes are washed at breakfast, lunch, and dinner. Likewise, refrigeration equipment operates continuously during the normal operating hours of the foodservice facility. One way to save energy is to take the heat lost during refrigeration and use it for partial heating of dishwashing water.

Three common ways to remove heat are air cooling, water cooling, and use of a cooling tower. In all three methods, the heat is wasted unless it can be transported back to the food facility to be used for purposes such as heating water for kitchen or dishwashing use. With technology that has been in use for many years, heat from refrigeration can be easily transferred to water. Heat recovery systems were not widely used in the past only because fossil fuels were so cheap and abundant that such systems did not make sense economically.

The systems that are used to heat water as a by-product of refrigeration all operate on the same principle. Cold water that normally enters the hot-water heater first passes through the heat exchanger and removes the heat from the refrigeration system (water cooling of condensers). The formerly cold water is now slightly warm as it enters the water heater, and the cost of increasing the temperature of the water to acceptable levels (120–140°F [49–60°C]) is reduced. The equipment to accomplish the transfer of heat looks like a large domestic water heater. Figure 8.9 illustrates how this type of heat recovery system works.

Heat recovery systems can be designed for either an air-cooled heat exchanger, as described, or for a water-cooled refrigeration system, in which the water absorbs heat from the refrigerant as it leaves the compressor. Both approaches accomplish similar savings. Water-preheating heat recovery systems reduce energy costs, and the return on investment can be very dramatic.

Figure 8.9. Heat Recovery Systems.

Important factors to consider before purchasing a heat recovery system are:

❏ The hot-water needs of your operation
❏ Energy costs in your area
❏ Hot-water storage needs
❏ The location and condition of existing refrigeration equipment
❏ The amount of refrigeration in use

The most logical application for heat recovery systems in foodservice facilities is the large refrigeration system used for walk-in coolers and freezers. The compressors for these units are by themselves large enough to justify the cost for many heat recovery systems. Lesser, though significant, energy cost savings may be realized by connecting compressors for smaller pieces of equipment to the recovery system. Typically, reach-in refrigerators, display coolers, ice machines, and beverage dispensers are installed with self-contained refrigeration systems.

The compressors on these pieces are usually air-cooled, which means that the heat is dissipated into the kitchen, serving area, or dining room. If these areas are air-conditioned, each refrigeration unit adds to the air-conditioning load. Imagine the combined water-heating and air-conditioning savings that could be accrued by tying these smaller compressors into the heat recovery system. This is an excellent opportunity for energy savings that should not be overlooked when planning a new facility or renovating an existing one.

Other forms of heat recovery include solar heating and exhaust systems with heat exchangers. Systems for recovering heat from kitchen exhausts are designed to pull heat out of very hot air (from hoods over range sections and ovens) and recycle it into the water-heating system. Without some method of heat recovery, a tremendous amount of heat is lost "up the flue"; however, the air-to-water transfer that is used in these systems is much less efficient than other methods and requires a very large volume of hot exhaust air to justify the investment.

FOODSERVICE FACILITIES ARCHITECTURE

A complete treatment of architectural and interior design in relation to foodservice facilities lies beyond the scope of this text. However, there are several considerations in the architectural design of foodservice facilities that do need special attention because of their functional importance. These considerations include the construction of walls, floors, and ceilings; the provision of adequate lighting; and the control of noise.

Construction of Walls, Floors, and Ceilings in Foodservice Facilities

The specification and construction of building surfaces are usually the responsibility of the architect in new or renovated foodservice facilities. However, the architect often asks the foodservice consultant and/or the owner for recommendations on the types of finishes that are desirable.

The decision on the type of finish to be used may be based on budgetary limitations rather than the desirability of the surface. Ideally, the finishes that are recommended, especially for floors and walls, are chosen on the basis of ease in cleaning and resistance to damage or wear as well as aesthetics.

FLOORS

The floor surface in the kitchen and service areas should be easy to maintain, wear-resistant, slip-resistant, and nonporous. The most universally accepted floor material is quarry tile, which has an excellent record in the foodservice industry for not being slippery and for resisting grease absorption. The grout between the tile is slightly porous at first but quickly becomes sealed from the dirt and grease of the typical food operation. Grout can also be coated with commercial floor sealers before use. These sealers need to be reapplied at appropriate intervals. The use of a colored or tinted grout creates a better appearance and eliminates the need for bleaching or cleaning the grout joint. Quarry tile with embedded Carborundum chips has greater slip resistance and is recommended for use in wet or high-grease conditions such as are found in range areas and potwashing and dishwashing areas.

Floor finishes in dining rooms and public places can be of any material that is wear-resistant and easily cleaned. Carpeting in dining rooms is popular because it absorbs sound and provides a feeling of luxury. Carpeting is not recommended in high-soil areas such as:

- ❑ Servers stations
- ❑ Tray and dish drop-off areas
- ❑ Beverage stations
- ❑ Condiment stations
- ❑ Major traffic aisles
- ❑ Cashier stations

Ceramic tile is an excellent floor finish for public rest rooms or high-soil areas. Unglazed tiles are the best choice because of their slip-resistant qualities.

Vinyl tile is not recommended in dining rooms or public areas because it usually requires a high level of maintenance, especially waxing and frequent machine buffing. The amount of labor required over a few years will exceed the extra costs of an easy-care quarry or ceramic tile floor. A vinyl tile floor wears out quickly in a commercial kitchen, is slippery when wet, and is not grease-resistant. Vinyl tile can be used as an inexpensive floor covering in employee dressing rooms, employee dining areas, or offices.

Figure 8.10 lists recommended floor finishes for foodservice facilities.

WALLS

Wall finishes used in food storage and preparation areas include structural glazed tile, ceramic glazed tile, concrete block with epoxy coating or paint, plaster, and painted drywall as well as special materials, such as

Foodservice Area	Recommended Floor Finishes
Kitchen	Quarry tile
Dishwashing	Quarry tile with Carborundum
Storerooms, dry stores	Sealed concrete
Wash-down rooms for carts and trash containers	Quarry tile with Carborundum; quarry tile; sealed concrete
Receiving	Quarry tile; sealed concrete
Offices	Quarry tile; vinyl tile; carpet; wood
Employee rest rooms	Quarry tile; vinyl tile; unglazed ceramic tile; terrazzo
Corridors, back of the house	Vinyl tile; unglazed ceramic tile; sealed concrete
Corridors, public	Vinyl tile; unglazed ceramic tile; carpet; terrazzo
Dining rooms	Quarry tile; unglazed ceramic tile; carpet; terrazzo
Public rest rooms	Quarry tile; unglazed ceramic tile; terrazzo
Service areas	Quarry tile; unglazed ceramic tile; terrazzo

Figure 8.10. Recommended Floor Finishes for Foodservice Areas.

Marlite. However, not all of these finishes are ideal for foodservice applications. Figure 8.11 lists recommended wall finishes for different areas in a foodservice facility.

Budget limitations may dictate a less expensive finish over the more desirable ones. Such substitutions can result in costly problems in the end. For example, one approach to reduce costs is to use concrete block with epoxy paint behind the equipment in the range section of a kitchen. However, the high heat generated by fryers, ovens, ranges, and charbroilers

Foodservice Area	Recommended Wall Finishes
Kitchen, range section	Structural glazed tile; glazed ceramic tile
Kitchen, cold-food section	Structural glazed tile; glazed ceramic tile; concrete block with epoxy paint
Dishwashing	Structural glazed tile; glazed ceramic tile
Storerooms, dry stores	Concrete block with epoxy paint
Receiving	Concrete block with epoxy paint
Wash-down rooms for carts, etc.	Structural glazed tile; glazed ceramic tile
Offices	Painted drywall
Employee rest rooms	Glazed ceramic tile; concrete block with epoxy paint
Corridors, back of the house	Concrete block with epoxy paint; painted drywall
Corridors, public	Decorative wall selected by interior designer
Dining rooms	Decorative wall selected by interior designer
Public rest rooms	Glazed ceramic tile; decorative wall selected by interior designer
Service areas	Glazed ceramic tile; concrete block with epoxy

Figure 8.11. Recommended Wall Finishes for Foodservice Areas.

eventually causes the paint to discolor and flake off. Further, the grease generated by cooking is very difficult to remove from the small pits in the concrete block.[1] The ideal wall finishes in cooking areas are structural glazed tile or ceramic tile, either of which will resist damage from heat, grease, and frequent cleaning. The structural glazed tile is also highly resistant to impact when struck by a cart or other portable equipment.

CEILINGS

Ceilings in a foodservice facility are of two types: the structural ceiling, which supports the floors above, and the false ceiling, which may hide ducts and other architectural features or serve mainly to enhance the room's attractiveness.

New materials for ceilings are introduced so frequently and ceiling materials vary so widely that any list would be outdated in a short time. The most common ceiling materials are:

❑ Acoustical tile

❑ Drywall, painted

❑ Plaster, painted

❑ Wood, sealed or painted

❑ Exposed concrete

❑ Fiberglass

❑ Aluminum or other metal

The acoustical ceiling is the most common of those listed, because of its low cost and excellent sound-absorbing qualities. Special acoustical tiles have been developed that do not easily absorb moisture or grease from the air. The health department or local building codes usually have specific recommendations for the type of ceiling material that is acceptable for foodservice operations. Aluminum panel ceilings with perforations are often used because they can be easily removed for cleaning. Some aluminum ceiling panels can actually be put through the dishwashing machine.

If the ceilings in work areas are sound-absorbent, grease-resistant, moisture-resistant, and light-reflective, they will probably be acceptable to health officials. Ceilings in dining rooms and other public areas can be constructed of or covered with many types of material as long as they do not create either a fire safety problem or a health hazard.

Controlling Noise

Excessive noise in the workplace is of concern to managers because it can cause fatigue, irritability, and low productivity among workers. Noise control in the dining room and public areas of a foodservice facility is a significant consideration in creating a pleasant dining experience. Stopping the transfer of sound from areas adjacent to a banquet hall or private dining

[1] Our illustration deals with the use of standard epoxy paints applied over concrete block. There are two-stage epoxy-based materials, such as Sanitile by Carboline, that can be applied effectively to concrete block in a foodservice application.

room can mean the difference between a successful and an unsuccessful meeting or convention.

Architects, engineers, and foodservice consultants spend a significant amount of time seeking methods of creating a quiet environment. One of the problems with sound control in a typical foodservice operation is the nature of the operation itself. The activity and movement of workers, the noise of equipment, conversations between guests at the table, the speech of servers taking food orders and communicating with the kitchen, the clatter of glasses and dishes, and background music (when present) add up to a very high sound level.

Sound level (loudness) is measured in decibels. Noise above 130 decibels is painful to the normal ear and would seldom be encountered in a foodservice operation. Another characteristic of sound is the number of vibrations per second created from the sound source. The average human ear can only hear sound in the range from 15 to 20,000 vibrations per second.

In the dining environment, it is desirable to keep the decibel level low and to introduce low-frequency background music. High-frequency music or sound is generally less pleasant to the ear, especially in an eating place where conversation is encouraged among the guests.

SOUND-ABSORBING MATERIALS

Carpeting and draperies absorb sound and can create a pleasant appearance in the dining room. Glass and hard-surface floors, walls, and ceilings reflect sound and create reverberations that make table conversation difficult.

To control sound, the architect and interior designer generally mix these materials in the public spaces of a foodservice establishment. For example, glass, quarry tile, and terrazzo reflect 70 to 90 percent of sound, while carpet or cloth reflect only 40 to 65 percent (depending on the density and characteristics of the material). Generally, the use of some carpeting in the dining room and the selection of acoustical material for the ceiling will create the proper sound levels.

Noise in the kitchen and other support areas of a foodservice facility can be decreased but not eliminated. The use of quarry tile floors, ceramic tile, or other hard-surface walls and ceilings creates a sound-reflecting environment. Noises made by the use of dish machines, mixers, garbage disposers, metal pots and pans, stainless-steel tables, and other metal utensils add a considerable amount of sound to the kitchen. This list of sound-reduction ideas should be considered in the planning of the kitchen and other support areas:

❏ Acoustical ceilings

❏ Sound-deadening coatings on the underside of stainless-steel work surfaces

❏ Remote compressors for reach-in and especially for walk-in refrigerators and freezers

❏ Electronic transmittal of orders to display screens in the preparation areas, rather than by servers shouting out the orders to the cooks

❏ Low-volume background music in the workplace (such music tends to discourage radio owners from playing their sets full blast in the kitchen)

❏ Physical separation and/or enclosure of dishwashing and potwashing from other parts of the kitchen with walls designed to prevent sound transmission

Lighting

Well over 80 percent of our impressions are visual, and vision is essential to many elements of the foodservice business, such as preparation, service, and cash handling. When food workers cannot see accurately, errors and delays result, seriously affecting productivity.

Consider also the reasons people patronize foodservice operations: not only to eat, but also because of the quality of the physical environment. The difference between "eating" and "dining" depends on the ambience of the facility and the total experience—conscious and subconscious—of the customer. Properly directed light can help dissolve negative feelings and tensions. The goal is to provide guests with pleasant sensations designed to fit together into a complete dining experience. To create consistently positive experiences, control must be exerted over where the light goes, what its true color will be, and what effects it will have on the guests and workers, as well as the effects on the overall appearance of the interior design elements of the facility.

Each part of the eye sees a specific type of light. The cones of the retina allow one to see colors and details in bright sunlight. Studies have shown that cone color vision is improved by the stimulus of sound waves. The normal hustle and activity in a lunchroom, therefore, stimulate a keener perception of color. This may require the alignment of the color decor elements with the light levels and their direction to avoid assaulting the mind with a barrage of tension-producing stimuli. The effects work both ways. During evening dining, the sound waves from service activity will appear to warm up the colors in the room. This is an advantage, as the colors are otherwise perceived as being duller under the lower evening light levels. However, the efficiency of the retina rods, which allow one to see black and white under dim lighting conditions, is reduced by the stimulation of sound waves. Therefore, guests will experience greater difficulty in reading the black-and-white print of the menu, promotion cards, wine lists, charge slips, and checks. The room may appear to be well lighted to the manager when he or she sets the light levels during the quiet early evening hours. What happens is that the menu becomes harder to read as the *sound* in the dining room increases with the arrival of more guests. Ironically, unbalanced light levels can mean that when people are waiting to be seated and the operator wishes to turn the tables faster, the patrons already seated actually need more time to read printed materials and make a selection.

Although the eye can adapt to a wide range of lighting conditions, it does not always function with the same degree of efficiency. In order to establish light levels that can assist the eye in seeing more efficiently, five factors must be considered: time, size, contrast, brightness, and sound.

Time. One's level of comfort or discomfort, and therefore one's perception of time, is affected by the level and the tone of light. Waiting to be served and waiting for a check can be very tense experiences for a customer in a hurry. The degree of environmental comfort can mean the difference between the customer's being irritated or satisfied. Reading a menu under poor lighting conditions could take up too much time during a lunch or dinner rush and slow the turnover unnecessarily. Or if the customer is rushed into making a selection, he or she may not have time to read the entire menu.

Size. Light also affects space perception. Proper lighting can make a small room seem open and can make a large room feel cozy. In a darkened room, people seated a few feet apart feel much closer together than they would in a room with more light. On the menu, the size of the print has a direct relationship to the customer's ability to see efficiently at various light levels.

Contrast. The perceived difference between the detail of an object and its background is referred to as contrast. Spotlighting, in which light shines directly on a specific area, offers high contrast. The contrast between a coffee stain and a brown rug is low. Good contrast between the colors of the ink and paper can make a menu easier to read at any light level. In the kitchen, contrast comes into play when cooks work on highly reflective stainless-steel tables.

Brightness. The amount of light the eye sees on an object's surface is the brightness. This is the last controllable element of lighting, since time, size, contrast, and sound are often fixed before the acceptability of the light levels is evaluated. Putting more light on an object will improve the visibility of the object despite its small size, poor contrast, or the shortness of time allotted in which to distinguish the object.

Sound. As mentioned, light levels should be readjusted as the sound levels vary in the room. This can be done quite effectively with a light dimmer switch.

HOW MUCH LIGHT IS ENOUGH?

If you were in a dark cave with only a book of matches to light your way, you would be amazed at how efficient such a small amount of light can be. There is a rapid increase in the efficiency of light when moving from darkness into light, using as little as 3 foot-candles of light. (Note: A "foot-candle" measures the amount of light transmitted by one candle from one foot away.) In fact, when a task is illuminated, the available light may be as much as 90 percent efficient at a very low level. However, to move to 95 percent efficiency may require three times as much light and to be 100 percent efficient may require 10 to 100 times as much light. Close work involving very small objects, such as microcomputer chips, may require as much as 1,500 foot-candles of light, but only at the work surface.

Another factor in efficiency, similar in concept to contrast, is the reflective difference level of the task and the surrounding area. The comparative brightness of the light reflected off the object and off the background determines how easily the eye can distinguish the former. Ideal reflective levels would range from 40 to 60 percent at 40 foot-candles of light illuminating the task and the surrounding area. The surrounding area should reflect back 40 to 50 percent of the light, while the task should reflect back 50 to 60 percent. Except in a case such as reading, which normally requires a brighter background, there should be at least 10 percent more light reflected back from the task than from the surroundings. For example, as the illumination of a cash register keyboard is kept constant and the surrounding brightness of the countertop is raised gradually, the ability to see the keyboard improves. This improvement will be gradual and constant and will be at its maximum when the brightness of the surrounding counter is equal to or slightly less than the brightness of the keyboard. When the brightness of the surrounding counter exceeds the brightness of the keyboard, there is a radical falling off in the ability to see the keyboard without making computation errors.

Another example of reflectance difference would be a menu board on a bright wall. The bright wall competes for the eye's attention and would reduce the efficiency of reading the menu board.

One solution to this problem is found in the use of brightness ratios that mathematically compare the brightness of the task with the surrounding brightness. A 3 to 1 ratio is normal; 10 to 1 is the high limit. However, brightness ratios can be misleading. A work area could have a favorable brightness ratio but abnormally high levels of reflected glare from the task. If the brightness ratio of the menu board to the wall, for example, was 3 to 1 and the light on the menu board required to compete with the brightness of the stainless-steel wall was 1,000 watts, the excessive task light would reflect glare back into the customers' eyes and reduce their ability to see the board.

Glare is a common problem in poorly designed lighting systems. To reduce glare, one can reduce the reflectance of the surface or move the light out of the direct line of vision. Another solution is to build up a balanced intensity of brightness that absorbs and distributes the glare. For example, if the restaurant windows reflect glare from the perimeter lighting back into the eyes of the customer, shades may be hung in the windows, or the overall lighting level in the room may be increased so as to build a balanced intensity, which could be reduced as the sun sets. Figure 3.7 (Chapter 3) lists recommended light levels for various foodservice applications.

LIGHTING AND PRODUCTIVITY

Light is one of the many inputs that affect productivity. Its impact shows up most obviously in problems that can be traced to poor visibility. For example, low productivity may be revealed in sales figures that are not correctly transcribed or by a server's check that cannot be read under kitchen illumination, resulting in the preparation of the wrong item. But light has less noticeable effects. The level and kind of light can influence the way we function, both physically and psychologically. How motivated do we feel, for instance, when the weather is gray and cloudy, or when lighting is subdued rather than bright and warm?

Providing more illumination, however, is not the whole answer. In fact, reduced productivity often occurs in operations with high light levels that are merely running up utility costs unnecessarily. Better lighting and higher productivity are the result of knowledgeable planning, not merely adding wattage.

Studies show that a small increase in light levels can raise productivity significantly. Increases of 5 to 33 percent in productivity have been achieved by the proper placing of as little as 25 foot-candles of light. Better lighting reduces the time required to see and act on the task to be done. When speed increases, confidence grows, which further increases speed. Too little light or an unbalanced distribution increases the rate of error and reduces output.

The reduction of error is as important as increasing output. In a Federal Energy Administration test conducted at Ohio State University, a 12 percent reduction in errors in handwritten numbers occurred when light levels were properly adjusted. This reduction could be significant for restaurateurs in many ways, especially at the cash register.

Motivation is influenced by the way people perceive their environment. Workers seldom consciously consider the light falling on their tasks until strain, a headache, or fatigue sets in, but it affects them nonetheless. With better task visibility, work can be accomplished and high standards achieved with less effort. The right lighting also helps to create the impression of a comfortable work environment, in which employees are likely to approach their day with a more consistently positive attitude.

LIGHTING DESIGN

People tend to orient themselves and their activities according to the brightness levels of their environment. This visual aesthetic sense has a significant effect on what activities people consider proper in different levels of light. Overall, brightness is appropriate for spaces in which physical activity takes place, such as washing areas, receiving areas, stockrooms, assembly areas, and refrigerators. Lower light levels would be suitable for accounting, cash handling, counter sales, waiting areas, expediting stations, and access corridors. In either case, light levels should remain within a moderate range. When areas are too bright, colors and shapes appear jarring or distorted, and workers' concentration is affected.

Brightness also influences the mind's perception of the apparent weight of objects. Tote boxes, cases, trash cans, and trays will seem easier to lift if they are white or painted a bright color. It is a pity that most cardboard cartons remain a standard dull brown. If more manufacturers bleached or painted their containers white, workers would perceive the handling of cases of food off the truck and into storerooms as an easier task. In any event, to achieve a good level of reflectance, light levels should be high in areas where lifting and handling must be done.

The color of uniforms is another factor in lighting design, because of their visual impact. Uniforms for physical work should be bright.

Bacterial strains, especially those that cause odors and food poisoning, respond to light as well. Research has shown that streptococci of various strains (the kind usually found in food poisoning cases traced to poor employee hygiene) are killed by natural daylight, either direct or filtered through glass. The possibility of killing or preventing the growth of bacteria during food preparation, or of destroying odors without having to cover them up with equally obnoxious fumes, should interest any foodservice manager. Ultraviolet light also benefits employee health directly.

It has been found to increase the level of working capacity and resistance to infections, improve the stability of clear vision, and reduce respiratory infections.

SUMMARY

The owner, architect, foodservice consultant, and engineer must become involved in the engineering decisions affecting the foodservice facility. The quality of interior lighting, the HVAC system used, the energy efficiency of kitchen equipment, and the final cost of the project are all outcomes of engineering decisions.

A basic understanding of the types of energy sources available and the methods for designing high-energy-consumption equipment, such as hoods and dishwashing machines, is helpful in arriving at sound decisions regarding utility usage. Because floor, ceiling, and wall finishes have a great impact on the final cost of the project, the foodservice consultant must understand which ones will perform best. Trade journals, manufacturer's representatives, and professional engineers are good sources of information on foodservice facilities engineering.

KEY TERMS

Makeup air
HVAC

Utility distribution systems
Foot-candles

QUESTIONS

1. Since heating water is an extremely high consumer of energy, discuss methods for lowering the cost.

2. There has been a long-standing disagreement about which electric or gas (natural and propane) companies is most cost effective. How would you go about deciding which to choose? Does the design of the equipment bear on the question more than the cost per Btu for gas or electric?

3. Why is centrally generated steam a very economical heat source? Why are small steam boilers under each piece of equipment a problem?

4. Hood design is complex but very important to save energy (both heat and air-conditioning). Do hood systems that bring in outside air really save energy?

5. How would a utility distribution system save money?

6. The text mentions 13 wall finishes to help reduce noise. Can you name some of these?

7. What do 120, 220, 240, 460, and 480 mean? What are 1 phase and 2 phase?

8. Why should a disposer have a reverse and a silver saver? How does a silver saver work?

DISCUSSION QUESTION

Proper hood design is the most important method of conserving energy in a food facility. The hood will move large amounts of air, both heated (in winter) and air-conditioned (in summer). The source of the air is the important consideration. Discuss the advantages and disadvantages of the methods mentioned in this chapter for solving the energy usage problem in hood design.

APPENDIX 1

List of Associations and Industry Links

American Culinary Federation
    www.acfchefs.org
American Dietetic Association
    www.eatright.org
American Hotel and Motel Association
    www.ahma.com
American Institute of Architects
    www.e-architect.com
American Institute of Baking
    www.aibonline.org
American School Food Service Association
    www.asfsa.org
American Society for Nutrition
    www.nutrition.org
American Society of Healthcare Food Service Administrators
    www.ashfsa.org
Chef Magazine
    www.chefmagazine.com
Club Managers Association of America
    www.cmaa.org
Council of Hotel Restaurant Institutional Educators
    www.chrie.org
Dietary Managers Association
    www.dmaonline.org
Foodservice Consultants Society International
    www.fcsi.org
Foodservice Equipment and Supplies Magazine
    www.fesmag.com
Foodservice Equipment Reports Magazine
    www.fermag.com
Global Foodservice Online Site
    www.globalfoodservice.com
Institute of Food Technologists
    www.ift.org

International Association of Culinary Professionals
www.iacp.com

International Association for Food Protection
www.foodprotection.org

International Hotel and Restaurant Association
www.ih-ra.com

Manufacturers Agents for the Food Service Industry
www.mafsi.org

National Association of College and University Foodservices
www.nacufs.org

National Restaurant Association
www.restaurant.org

National Society of Healthcare Food Service Management
www.hfm.org

Nations Restaurant News Magazine
www.nrn.com

North American Association of Food Equipment Manufacturers
www.nafem.org

NSF International (National Sanitation Foundation)
www.nsf.org

Society for Foodservice Management
www.sfm-online.org

U.S. Food and Drug Administration
http://vm.cfsan.fda.gov

APPENDIX 2

Typical Foodservice Facility Designs

Layout of a Typical European Kitchen

Dining Hall (Kitchen and Servery) Serving 6,000 Meals per Day (University of Tennessee)

Hotel Kitchen

University Dining Hall

CLAIREMONT HOSPITAL

Hospital Kitchen

SECOND FLOOR PLAN
SCALE 1' / 4" = 1' – 0"

WEST STREET REDEVELOPMENT
167–175 WEST STREET.–Annapolis, MD 21401

THE METROPOLITAN

SHEET
A 3
OF 5

Restaurant Kitchen

EQUIPMENT SCHEDULE

MK.	QTY	DESCRIPTION
G-04	2	WARMER, COUNTERTOP
G-05	2	SNEEZEGUARD
G-06	1	HAND SINK
G-07	1	FRYER FILTER, MOBILE
G-08	1	FRYER, DRAIN CABINET
G-09	1	FRYER, DEEP FAT
G-10	1	CHARBROILER, COUNTERTOP GAS
G-11	1	GRIDDLE, COUNTERTOP GAS
G-12	1	REFRIGERATOR, LOWBOY
G-13	1	REFRIGERATOR, UNDERCOUNTER
G-14	1	WORK TABLE
H-01	1	EXHAUST VENTILATOR, WALL-MOUNTED
H-02	1	FIRE SUPPRESSION SYSTEM
H-03	1	EXHAUST VENTILATOR, WALL-MOUNTED
H-04	1	EXHAUST VENTILATOR, ISLAND
H-05	1	FIRE SUPPRESSION SYSTEM
I-01	1	SOFT SERVE MACHINE
I-02	1	TOPPINGS COUNTER
I-03	1	SOFT SERVE MACHINE
I-04	1	DESSERT COUNTER
I-05	4	SNEEZEGUARD, PORTABLE
P-01	1	REFRIGERATOR, 1 COMP
P-02	1	FREEZER, ONE COMPARTMENT
P-03	1	HAND SINK
P-04	1	WORK TABLE
P-05	1	OVEN, CONVEYOR
P-07	1	PIZZA PREP TABLE
P-08	1	SERVING COUNTER
P-09	1	WARMER, COUNTERTOP
P-10	1	SNEEZEGUARD
P-11	1	SNEEZEGUARD
P-12	1	SNEEZEGUARD
P-13	3	HEATED SHELF, ROUND
P-14	3	WARMER LAMPS, CONTEMPO
P-15	1	HOT FOOD UNIT, DROP-IN
P-16	1	SNEEZEGUARD, PORTABLE
P-17	1	COLD PAN, REFRIGERATED
P-18	1	COLD PAN, REFRIGERATED
S-01	2	SALAD BAR
S-02	2	REFRIGERATED COLD PAN
S-03	4	SNEEZEGUARD, 2 SIDED
T-01	1	SERVING COUNTER
T-02	-	- SPARE NUMBER -
T-03	2	SNEEZEGUARD, PORTABLE
T-04	1	COLD PAN, REFRIGERATED
T-05	1	HOT FOOD UNIT, DROP-IN

EQUIPMENT SCHEDULE

MK.	QTY	DESCRIPTION
A-01	2	SNEEZEGUARD, PORTABLE
B-03	1	JUICE OR BEVERAGE MACHINE
B-04	-	- SPARE NUMBER -
B-05	1	PREMIUM WATER DISPENSER
B-06	-	- SPARE NUMBER -
B-07	1	BEVERAGE DISPENSER, CARB & NON
B-08	1	DISPENSER, BEVERAGE, NON-CARBONATED
B-09	-	- SPARE NUMBER -
B-10	-	- SPARE NUMBER -
B-11	-	- SPARE NUMBER -
B-12	-	- SPARE NUMBER -
B-13	-	- SPARE NUMBER -
B-14	1	BEVERAGE COUNTER
D-01	1	SLICER, FOOD
D-02	1	DELI WORK TABLE
D-03	1	FREEZER, REACH IN
D-04	1	REFRIGERATOR, ROLL-IN
D-05	2	RACK
D-06	1	CABINET, HOLDING
D-07	1	HAND SINK
D-08	1	DELI COUNTER
D-09	1	SNEEZEGUARD
D-10	1	SNEEZEGUARD, PORTABLE
D-11	1	REFRIGERATOR, SANDWICH/SALAD
D-12	1	MOBILE WORK CART
D-13	1	BAKERY DISPLAY, MOBILE
D-14	1	SNEEZEGUARD, PARTITION
D-15	8	TRAY STAND/STATION SIGNAGE
E-01	1	SERVING COUNTER
E-02	-	- SPARE NUMBER -
E-03	-	- SPARE NUMBER -
E-04	-	- SPARE NUMBER -
E-05	-	- SPARE NUMBER -
E-06	-	- SPARE NUMBER -
E-07	1	SNEEZEGUARD
E-08	1	HOT/COLD PAN
E-09	2	HOT/COLD PAN
F-01	1	DISPLAY COUNTER
F-02	2	SNEEZEGUARD, PORTABLE
F-03	-	- SPARE NUMBER -
F-04	-	- SPARE NUMBER -
F-05	2	WARMER, COUNTERTOP
F-06	2	SNEEZEGUARD, PORTABLE
F-07	2	SNEEZEGUARD
F-08	2	HOT/COLD PAN
F-09	1	DISPLAY COUNTER
F-10	1	SNEEZEGUARD, PARTITION
F-11	1	DISPLAY COUNTER
F-12	1	CABINET, HOLDING
F-13	1	REFRIGERATOR, 1 COMP
F-14	1	HAND SINK
F-15	2	WARMER, FOOD
F-16	2	INDUCTION COOKER
G-01	1	SERVING COUNTER
G-02	1	COLD PAN, REFRIGERATED
G-03	1	SNEEZEGUARD, PORTABLE

Siena College Dining Hall

APPENDIX 3

Common Foodservice Design Symbols

PLUMBING

Water rough-in	●
Water rough-in connection	●○
Wastewater rough-in	○
Condensate drain or indirect waste	○--- IW
Wastewater rough-in and connection	○—○ w
Gas supply rough-in	⊗
Gas supply rough-in and connection	⊗—○
Steam supply	■
Steam supply stub-out	▶
Steam return	◪
Steam return stab-out	▷
Floor sink—open	□ FS
Floor sink—funnel grate	▤
Floor sink—funnel grate	▤
Floor drain	□ FD
Hose bib	⊤ HB
Hose rack	▭○ HR
Hot-water tank	○ HWT

Lavatories; wall, corner
    L1, L2, etc.   L1, L2, etc.

Grease trap
    GT

Can washer
    CW

Clean-out
    CO

Dishwasher
    DW

Sink
    S-1, S-2, etc.

Water heater
    WH

PIPING

Above-grade soil or waste
Below-grade soil or waste
Cold water
Hot water
Gas

ABBREVIATIONS

HW	Hot water
HSW	Hot soft water
CW	Cold water
PRV	Pressure reducer valve
AFF	Above finished floor
KEC	Kitchen equipment contractor
PC	Plumbing contractor
EC	Electrical contractor
C&P	Cord and plug
EF	Exhaust fan
AC	Air-conditioning
FD	Floor drain
FS	Floor sink
D.S.	Dimmer switch

LV	Low voltage
V.A.	4-inch vinyl base—cover type
E. PAINT	Epoxy paint
A.T.	Acoustical tile
C.T.	Ceramic tile
P.L.	Plastic laminate
Q.T.^{1}	6 × 6 quarry tile
Q.T.B.	6-inch covered bull-nose quarry tile
G.C.B.	Glazed concrete block
Q.T.^{2}	Six-sided quarry
M.P.	Metal pan-ceiling system
ML	Marlite fiberglass
S.P.	Stucco paint on drywall
E.M.U.	Exposed masonry units
C.B.	Concrete block
PT.	Paint
GL. BR.	Glazed brick base, recess ~HF inch
PART. BD.	Particleboard

ELECTRICAL SYMBOLS

Conduit stub flush couple with curb	▲
Flex tubing (36-inch minimum exposed)	♂
Waterproof conduit stub	●
Junction box, waterproof with final connection to equipment (36-inch minimum seal tight flex)	Ⓙ$_{WP}$
Junction box at ceiling	Ⓙ
Junction box at wall	⊸Ⓙ
Junction box above floor	Ⓙ
Junction box with final connection to equipment (36-inch minimum exposed)	Ⓙ
Junction box installed in equipment	⦙Ⓙ⦙
Single convenience outlet (wattage as shown)	⊖
Duplex convenience outlet (wattage as shown)	⬤
Single convenience outlet w/switch	⟿
Duplex convenience outlet (installed in equipment)	⊖

Single-purpose power outlet, 1 phase

Single-purpose power outlet, 1 phase
(installed in equipment)

Single-purpose power outlet, 3 phase

Single-purpose power outlet, 3 phase
(installed in equipment)

Floor outlet, flush or pedestal

Floor junction box

Recessed convenience outlct, single
(wattage as shown)

120 V motor

208-240 V 1-phase motor

208-240 V 3-phase motor

Clock outlet

Ground connection

Buzzer

Infrared warmer

Heat lamp

Incandescent light

Pull box (installed in equipment)

Switch S
3-way switch S_3
4-way switch S_4
Switch with neon pilot S_p
Vaporproof switch S_{vp}
Automatic door switch S_D
Double-pole waterproof switch S_{2wp}

Pull Switch	(P)
Push button switch	■

LIGHTING

Incandescent strip (number when scheduled)	
Fluorescent fixture (number when scheduled)	
Fluorescent strip (number when scheduled)	
Wall-washer light (number when scheduled)	
Neon tubing	- - - -
Exit light	⊗
Transformer	T
Lighting panel	
Power Panel	

REFRIGERATION

Thermostat	(T)
High-temperature alarm relay with red light and bell	
Safety alarm bell with red light	
Vaporproof light, 100 watts	
Evaporator (blower coil) with fan	
Liquid line solenoid	(S)$_L$
Conduit run for refrigeration, CO_2, gas, and carbonation lines	= = =
Pull box	

APPENDIX 4

Sample Documents

EXHIBIT A

SAMPLE
CONSULTANT PROPOSAL AND COVER LETTER TO THE
CONSULTANT/CLIENT AGREEMENT

(Note: Because of potential legal complexities which could involve this document, consultation with an attorney is suggested.)

Date

Addressee
Mr. John Smith
124 Central Avenue
Anytown, State, Zip

Re: Project Name:
    Location:
    Proposal No:

Dear:

Introductory Paragraph

1. Pleased about the opportunity to submit a proposal for (services) for (project) located at........

2. Brief description of project

Statement of Objectives
A brief statement of the work to be done on the project by the consultant.

Recommendation of Specific Services
(statement of scope of services pertinent to this project or requested by client)

Reference should be made to Exhibit B
Example: It is our opinion, based on your project objectives, that a phased proposal is the most prudent approach to accomplishing your goals. The phases are listed in the approximate chronological order they would be accomplished with a fee for each phase so that you can evaluate the overall project.

		Not to Exceed
Phase I	- Programming and Preliminary Planning	$ _____
Phase II	- Design Development & Engineering	$ _____
Phase III	- Preparation of Bid Documents	$ _____
Phase IV	- Coordination and Approval of Shop Drawings	$ _____
Phase V	- Final Inspection and Training	
	Total Fee	$ _____

This proposal and cover letter defines each of the phases in detail; it is upon the amount of work included in this detail that the fee has been computed. In addition to the fees set forth above, we will invoice for all reimbursable expenses incurred in the interest of the project as set forth in the Consultant/Client Agreement (Exhibit B) to which this proposal has been attached and made reference.

Additional Services Option
that can be provided by the Consultant (to be included unless specifically asked to omit)

Closing Paragraph
(assures follow-up)

1. Schedule follow-up or next step or arrange to call client at a certain time.

2. Tickler follow-up for a certain date to find out what is happening to proposal.

3. Thank client for consideration of our firm.

Respectfully submitted,

Writer's Name
Title

Initials: initials

Attached to this proposal and letter is:

Exhibit B: Consultant/Client Agreement

FOODSERVICE CONSULTANTS SOCIETY INTERNATIONAL

EXHIBIT B

SAMPLE
CONSULTANT/CLIENT AGREEMENT

(Note: Because of potential legal complexities which could involve this document, consultation with an attorney is suggested.)

Consultant:	(name and address of consultant)
	hereinafter called the CONSULTANT
Client:	(name and address of the client)
	(name of primary contact person, as designated by the client)
	hereinafter called the CLIENT
Project:	(official name of project)
	hereinafter called PROJECT.

REFERENCE DOCUMENTS:

Exhibit A.   Consultant Proposal and Cover Letter attached to the Consultant/Client Agreement
Exhibit B.   Consultant/Client Agreement

WHEREAS, the CLIENT desires, in connection therewith, to engage the CONSULTANT and the CONSULTANT desires to be retained by the CLIENT to perform consulting services as described in Exhibit A all upon the terms and subject to the conditions hereinafter stated;

NOW, THEREFORE, in consideration of the covenants herein contained, the parties agree as follows:

1. AGREEMENT

The CONSULTANT agrees to perform the basic services hereinafter set forth. Pursuant to the payment schedule, the CLIENT agrees to pay the CONSULTANT for their services the fees as set forth in Exhibit A herein made a part of this Agreement.

2. THE CONSULTANT'S SERVICES

The CONSULTANT's basic services shall include all those services as set forth in Exhibit A.

3. REIMBURSABLE EXPENSES

The CLIENT will reimburse monthly to the CONSULTANT for all actual expenditures made in the interest of the PROJECT for the incidental expenses apart from the fee set forth in Exhibit A including:

- expense of transportation
- traveling in connection with the PROJECT at actual cost for automobile rental and public transportation and the current U.S. Government approved allowance for automobile travel
- long distance telephone calls, telegrams, postage, delivery charges
- reproduction of drawings, specifications, programs, reports and manuals
- other normal disbursements and obligations incurred on the CLIENT's account. The CONSULTANT will request, in advance, the CLIENT's authorization and approval for any unusual or extraordinary expense

4. PAYMENT SCHEDULE OF FEES

The CLIENT will compensate the CONSULTANT for services performed in accordance with the schedule set forth in Exhibit A. Invoices are due and payable upon presentation monthly and a late charge of ____% will be added to all balances unpaid ____days after date of invoice and each month thereafter cumulatively. In addition, should it become necessary that an unpaid invoice be referred to our attorneys for collection, the CLIENT agrees to pay their reasonable fee for such work as well as any costs of suit which may be incurred.

Fee Retainer: The CLIENT shall pay to the CONSULTANT upon execution of this Agreement a retainer in an amount equal to ____% of the Fee, either estimated or actual, unless specified otherwise in Exhibit A. Said retainer shall be held by the CONSULTANT until the completion of the PROJECT, at which time it will be applied against the final invoice on the PROJECT.

(Note: Fees may be paid in several ways including, but not necessarily limited to, the following. CONSULTANT/CLIENT terms to determine which applies.)

a. Hourly Fee Basis: Invoices will be used monthly for the total number of hours expended during the month in the interest of the PROJECT in accordance with the Hourly Rate Schedule that is a part of this Agreement. The current rate schedule will remain in effect for this Contract for ____years after the date of this Agreement. After ____years, the then current schedule will be reviewed with the CLIENT and will become the effective rate schedule.

b. Fixed Fee Basis: Invoices will be issued monthly in accordance with the schedule set forth in Exhibit A.

5. DEFERRAL OR TERMINATION

This Agreement may be terminated by either party upon ____ days written notice should the other party fail substantially to perform in accordance with its terms through no fault of the other.

In the event the PROJECT is deferred for a period of more than ____ months during any stage prior to completion of the Scope of Work outlined in Exhibit A or there is more than one delay or deferral of ____ months or more, each during any stage prior to completion of the Scope of Work outlined in Exhibit A or the PROJECT is terminated or the CLIENT ceases to require services for any reason beyond the CONSULTANT's control, the CLIENT agrees to pay the CONSULTANT within ____days, in addition to any amount which may have been paid pursuant to the terms of this Agreement the following:

a. all fees which may be payable to the CONSULTANT as previously identified herein but are unpaid at the date the CLIENT notifies the CONSULTANT in writing of such deferral or termination (the date of such notification being hereinafter referred to as the "deferral date" or the "termination date" – whichever shall apply)

b. all expenses due to the CONSULTANT as previously identified herein for which the CONSULTANT has not been reimbursed as at the deferral or termination date;

c. all amounts representing compensation for extra services as identified hereinafter which have not been paid as at the deferral or termination date; or

d. in the case of deferral, all work necessary to reactivate the PROJECT and to make adjustments in design, equipment selection drawings, and all other data made necessary or desirable due to the deferral; in addition, the CONSULTANT shall be compensated on the basis of the rate schedule in use at the time of the resumption of work, and all other fees shall be adjusted to suit the revised rate schedule and any other changes.

6. OWNERSHIP OF DOCUMENTS

Drawings, specifications, reports, manuals and programs as instruments of service are the property of the CONSULTANT whether the PROJECT for which they are made be executed or not and are not to be used on other projects except by agreement in writing with the CONSULTANT.

(Note: The CLIENT and the CONSULTANT are free to agree to the above, or that the documents may become the property of the CLIENT. This is suggested language favoring the CONSULTANT.)

7. SUCCESSORS AND ASSIGNS

The CLIENT and the CONSULTANT each binds himself, his partners, successors, assigns and legal representatives of such other party in respect to all covenants of this Agreement. Neither the CLIENT nor the CONSULTANT shall assign, sublet or transfer his interest in the Agreement without the written consent of the other.

8. EXTRA SERVICES

If the CONSULTANT is caused extra services or other expenses due to change orders or revisions to documents previously approved by the CLIENT, the CONSULTANT shall be paid for such extra expense or services in accordance with paragraph 4.a Hourly Fee Basis. Such extras or changes shall be requested or confirmed in writing.

For the purpose of carrying out any special project requested by the CLIENT, the CONSULTANT agrees to prepare a written proposal covering the scope of the special project, which proposal shall be accepted or rejected in writing by the CLIENT.

9. PROFESSIONAL RECOGNITION

The CLIENT agrees to acknowledge the professional services provided by the CONSULTANT in detailed press releases, magazine articles and the like where reference is made to the planning, design or management consulting services performed by the CONSULTANT relative to the Hospitality Facilities for the PROJECT.

10. INDEMNIFICATION

It is further agreed by the CLIENT that, except for breach of the terms of this Agreement by the CONSULTANT and for losses and damages due to the gross negligence or intentional torts of the CONSULTANT, its officers, agents and employees, the CLIENT shall defend, indemnify against and save harmless the CONSULTANT, its officers, agents and employees from all losses, expenses, liabilities, demands, suits and other actions of every nature and description (including attorneys' fees and any liability imposed by an applicable law, ordinance, code, rule or regulation) to which any of the aforesaid may be subjected by reason of any act or omission of the CONSULTANT or officers.

agents, employees, licensees or invitees of the CONSULTANT, where such loss, expense, liability, demand, suit or other detriment directly or indirectly arises out of or in connection with the CONSULTANT or its successors' and assigns' activities on the premises of CLIENT or with this proposed Agreement.

(Note: The above suggested language favors the CONSULTANT, and may have to be modified under certain contractual conditions imposed by the CLIENT in order to obtain the project.)

11. Where the CONSULTANT is requested by the CLIENT to engage the services of other Subconsultant(s) in connection with the PROJECT, or to select Subconsultant(s) to render services to the CLIENT, the CONSULTANT shall obtain the CLIENT's written approval of the selected Subconsultant(s). The CONSULTANT shall not be responsible to the CLIENT or other persons for any losses, damage or other expenses incurred as a result of the errors, omissions or negligent acts of the selected Subconsultant(s).

12. This contract, by agreement of the parties, has been made in _____(City, County, State)_____ and the laws of the State of _____(State)_____shall govern this contract. In any action by either party to enforce the terms of this agreement, at the option of ____(Consultant firm)____the venue thereof shall be in (City, County, State named above).

13. This agreement shall not be binding upon either party hereto until the agreement is signed by the CLIENT and returned to and accepted by the CONSULTANT within ____ days of date of proposal. Such acceptance by the CONSULTANT shall be evidenced by the signature of the CONSULTANT on this agreement.

In WITNESS WHEREOF the parties hereto have made and executed this Agreement, the day and year indicated in the acceptance area below.

ATTEST: _____   CLIENT: _____

                                                                        By: _____

Date: _____

                                                                        Title: _____   Date: _____

ACCEPTED AT (Location) _____   (Name of Consulting Firm) _____

ATTEST: _____   By: _____

Date: _____   Title: _____   Date: _____

Foodservice Equipment Glossary

Au Gratin Oven. Enclosure with hinged door mounted on top of a broiler. Also called finishing oven.

Bain-Marie. Sinklike depression in a tabletop with a water bath heated by steam, gas, or electricity into which containers of food are placed to keep foods heated. Often used by chefs as a double boiler. Also called sandwich unit when used for refrigerated foods in sandwich preparation.

Baker's Stove. *See* Pot Stove.

Baker's Table. Table whose top has 4- to 6-inch-high (10- to 15.2-cm. high) curbing along the rear and sides to minimize spillage of flour onto floor during preparation. Often furnished with mobile or tilt-out ingredient bins under the top.

Banquet Cart. Insulated or noninsulated mobile cabinet with a series of interior shelves and/or racks to hold plates and/or platters of food. Usually equipped with an electric heating unit or refrigeration device.

Barbecue Grill. A live charcoal or gas-fired open-hearth horizontal grill having spits set across the top of the unit with rotisserie-type drive mechanism along the front working side.

Bar Workboard. Equipment below the top of a bar containing sinks, drain boards, cocktail mix stations, ice storage chests, beverage coolers, glass washers, and so on. Also called sink workboard.

Beef Cart. Mobile unit, with or without bottled gas, alcohol, or electric heating unit. Used for display and slicing of roast beef in the dining room.

Beer Cooler. Cooler in which kegs, cans, or bottles of beer are refrigerated. The direct-draw cooler is a low-counter type with self-contained tapping equipment and dispensing head(s).

Beer Dispenser or Tapping Cabinet. Refrigerated or ice-cooled insulated cabinet with beer-, soda-, and/or water-dispensing heads, drainer plate, and pan recessed flush with the bar top and a drain trough under. Usually built into a liquor bar top, between workboards.

Beer System. A method for tapping beer from remotely located refrigerated kegs and transporting it through pressurized, refrigerated, and insulated lines to dispensing heads located at one or more stations in the bar and/or backbar.

Beverage Carrier. *See* Carrier.

Bin. Semienclosed rectangular or round container, open on top, with or without lift-off, sliding, or hinged cover. Floor-type bins are usually mobile, of height to roll under a tabletop. Bins under a baker's table may be mobile or built in to tilt out. An ingredient bin may be used for flour, sugar, salt, beans, dry peas, and so on. A vegetable storage bin has a perforated or screened body. An ice storage bin is fully enclosed and insulated with hinged or sliding insulated door(s) at the front; it is normally stationary and set under an ice-making machine (head). A silverware (flatware) or cutlery bin is small and mounted in a holder set on or under countertop with other bins.

Blast Chiller. Quick-chill is the process of reducing the temperature of food rapidly to just above freezing (e.g., 34°F, 1.1-degree Celsius). Rapid cooling to low temperatures prevents the growth of microorganisms that cause food-borne illness. Blast chillers and quick-chill refrigerators have powerful cooling units that quickly bring food temperatures down.

Blender. Vertical mixing machine with removable cup or jar, having mixing and stirring blades in the bottom and mounted on a base with a drive motor. Normally set on a table or countertop. Used in preparing special diets in hospitals or in mixing cocktails in bars as well as to whip or puree food generally at home.

Blower-Dryer. Motor-driven attachment with a blower and electric- or steam-heated coil, mounted on top of a dishwasher for quick drying of ware at the end of the final rinse cycle.

Blower (Evaporator) Coil. *See* Unit Cooler.

Board. A rectangular or round board, small for easy handling, set on a hard surface or countertop, to prevent dulling of the knife blade when cutting food. It can be made of laminated or solid hard rock maple or of rubber or thermal plastic material. Usually furnished with a handle or grip. Sandwich and steam table boards are rectangular and narrow; they are mounted on a sandwich unit or the corresponding section of a countertop. Also called workboard in preparation areas of a kitchen.

Boil-in Bag. A clear plastic waterproof pouch containing foods that are heated by immersing the package in boiling water.

Bone Saw. *See* Meat and Bone Saw.

Booster. *See* Hot-Water Booster.

Bottle Breaker. Motor-driven device with revolving, horizontal, open-top pan in which empty glass bottles are safely flogged with steel bars.

Bottle Chute. Flexible cylindrical tubing to convey empty bottles from bar to bottle storage bin or breaking or crushing device. Load end is usually located at the cocktail mix station.

Bottle Crusher. Motor-driven device with rollers or reciprocating plate(s) to crush bottles, plastic containers, and cans. The unit is mounted on a stand with a waste receptacle beneath to receive crushed and broken articles. The loading chute is provided with a spring-loaded or gravity-hinged door.

Bottle Disposer. System consisting of bottle chute and storage bin, bottle breaker, or bottle crusher.

Bottle Trough. Trough suspended along the front of a bar workboard, usually at the cocktail mix station, to hold various bottles of liquor or mixer used often. Also called speed rail.

Bowl. A round-bottomed container open at top for mixing food. The salad bowl is a shallow type for mixing and displaying leafy vegetables. A coffee bowl is the lower of a two-piece, siphon-type coffeemaker, used as a decanter.

Braising Pan, Tilting. *See* Fry Pan, Tilting.

Breading Machine. Horizontal rotating cylinder set on a base with a drive motor and filled with breading mix. Food is placed in one end, carried through the cylinder by an internally mounted auger, and discharged at the other end. Food is tumbled in breading mix.

Bread Molder. Machine with a series of rollers and conveyor belts to shape a ball of dough to pan bread, hearth bread, or long rolls of varied length.

Bread Slicer. (1) Motor-driven machine with a multiple set of reciprocating knives in a single frame through which bread is pushed, or vice versa. (2) Motor-driven or hand-operated machine with a single revolving knife to slice single slices while a bread loaf is moved along in a chute by a gear-driven plate. Slice thickness may vary.

Breath Guard. *See* Display Case.

Briquette. One of the coal-size pieces of permanent refractory material used in open-hearth gas-fired grills to provide radiant broiling heat.

Broiler, Backshelf. Broiler with gas-heated ceramic radiants or electric heating elements, having an adjustable sliding grill. The unit is normally mounted on a panel and brackets above the rear of the range. Also called salamander broiler.

Broiler, Charcoal. Horizontal-type unit with removable bottom pan containing glowing charcoals to radiate high heat into the bottom of foods set on a grill above. Mounted on stand or enclosed cabinet or masonry base.

Broiler, Char or Open-Hearth. (1) Horizontal-type unit with gas-heated briquettes under a grill at the top. (2) Horizontal-type unit with non-glowing electric strip heaters at the top. May also be equipped with an adjustable electric grill above the top grill to broil both sides at once.

Broiler, Conveyor. (1) Horizontal-type unit with openings at both ends, using a motor-driven grill-type conveyor to transport food between or under gas-fired ceramics or electric heaters. (2) Horizontal-type unit, open at both ends, using a motor-driven, revolving, heated griddle to transport food under gas-fired ceramics or electric heaters.

Broiler-Griddle, Combination. (1) Unit with front opening with griddle plate set into top, equipped with gas-heated radiants under the griddle. Radiants heat food and griddle simultaneously. (2) Unit with front-opening door(s) having gas-heated radiants at the top of the cavity and food placed on a sliding or swinging type griddle plate set below.

Broiler, Pop-up. Enclosed horizontal-type unit with a slotted opening in the top and gas-heated radiants on both sides of the cavity. Food is placed in an elevating mechanism and broiled on both sides at the same time. Similar to a pop-up toaster.

Broiler, Pork and Spare Rib, Chinese. Counter- or stand-mounted narrow-depth broiler with two or three decks, each having gas burners and radiants, for cooking pork slices and spare ribs in metal platters.

Broiler, Upright. Vertical-type unit with an opening at the front and gas-heated radiant ceramics or electric heating elements at the top of the cavity. Food is placed on a sliding adjustable grill set under the radiants. May be mounted on countertop, oven or cabinet base, or stand.

Often aligns with ranges. May be equipped with removable charcoal pan.

BTU. A measurement of heat (British Thermal Unit).

Buffalo Chopper. A food preparation appliance that chops with a semicircular blade that rotates under a protective cover. The food is placed on a revolving bowl.

Buffet Unit One or more mobile or stationary counters having flat surfaces, with cold pans or heated wells at the top, on which chafing dishes, canapé trays, or other food displays can be placed for self-service.

Bun Divider. *See* Roll Divider.

Butcher Block. Rectangular or round shape—6, 10, 14, or 16 inches thick—consisting of hard rock maple strips, kiln-dried, hydraulically pressed together, glued, and steel-doweled through. The work surface of the block is smoothed surface of ends of strips. The block is mounted on open-type wood or steel legs.

Butter Chip Dispenser. Enclosed insulated unit with mechanical refrigeration or ice to hold tiers of butter pats placed on chips and dispensed one at a time. Normally set on a countertop. Also called butter chip cooler.

Cafeteria Counter or Serving Counter. In a cafeteria, top that is usually provided with recessed cold pans, recessed pans for hot-foods section, display and protector cases, and drain troughs for beverages; set on legs or masonry base with enclosure panels, semi- or fully enclosed cabinets with refrigeration or warming units beneath; all as required to accommodate foods to be served. Unit may be equipped with tray slide.

Can Crusher. Motor-driven machine with rollers or reciprocating plates or arms to crush cans and break bottles. Unit mounts on stand with space under for refuse receptacle to receive crushed articles. Also called can and bottle crusher.

Can Opener. (1) Hand-operated or motor-driven device fastened to the top of a table, wall, cabinet, and so on, to open individual cans. (2) Portable motor-driven device capable of opening cans while still in the case.

Can Washer. (1) Enclosed cabinet with spray heads for washing the interior and exterior of a can, mounted on open legs. (2) Round platform with a rotating spray head at its center for washing the interior of a can, mounted on a stand with foot-operated water valves. (3) Rinse nozzle built into a floor drain and connected to a hand-operated quick-opening mixing valve.

Can Washer and Sterilizer. Enclosed cabinet with spray heads for washing the interiors and exteriors of cans, mounted on open legs, provided with detergent dispenser and 180°F (82.2-degrees Celsius) hot-water rinse or steam-mixing valve for final rinse.

Carbonated Beverage System. *See* Soda System.

Carbonator. Motor-driven water pump, with tank and control valves, to combine cold water and carbon dioxide (CO_2) gas in a storage tank, producing soda water. Used for soda fountains, carbonated beverage dispensers, and dispensing systems.

Carrier. A unit for carrying food, beverages, and ware by hand for short distances, furnished with grip(s) or handle(s). Can be an enclosed cabinet, insulated, heated or refrigerated; or a wire basket or rack.

Cart. Mobile unit of varying structure: as an open shelf or shelves; a semi- or fully enclosed cabinet with single or multiple compartments that may be insulated. Used for transporting food or ware and for cleaning and storage.

Cash Drawer. Shallow drawer located under a countertop at the cashier end. Often provided with removable compartmented insert for currency and coins.

Cashier Counter. *See* Checkout Counter.

Cashier Stand. Mobile or stationary stand with solid top set on four legs, or semienclosed body open at bottom. May be provided with footrest, cash drawer, and tray rest on one or both sides.

Checkout Counter. Counter located between a cafeteria serving area or kitchen and a dining room, for use by checker and/or cashier. Also called cashier counter.

Chinese Range. Range with one or more large-diameter gas burners on an inclined top and a raised edge around each burner opening. Food is cooked in shallow bowls called woks. Range top is cooled by water flowing from a front manifold to a rear trough, with a strainer basket at one end. A swing-spout faucet mounted on a high splash guard at the rear fills the bowl when the spout is turned 90 degrees.

Chopping or Cutting Block. A heavy metal "L"-shaped device, embedded in the wall to carry the weight of heavy wall-hung equipment.

Chopping or Cutting Block. *See* Butcher Block.

Clam Opener. Device with hand-operated, hinged knife and fixed, V-shaped block attached to a tabletop.

Cleaning Cart. Mobile unit with one or more compartments for soiled linen, waste, and water for mops and wringer.

Cocktail Mix Station. Section of bar workboard where drinks are poured or mixed. Usually includes open-top ice storage bin and wells for mixer bottles and condiments.

Coffee Filter. Perforated metal container or disposable paper or muslin bag in coffeemaker or urn to hold bed of coffee grounds.

Coffee Grinder. (1) Bench-mounted hand- or motor-driven machine with bean hopper at the top, grinding mechanism, and discharge chute with holder for container or filter beneath. (2) Coffee-grinding attachment for a food machine.

Coffeemaker. (1) Hand- or automatically operated electric-heated unit in which a measure of hot water at the proper temperature is poured over a measured bed of coffee grounds contained in a filtering unit. The extracted beverage is discharged into a container and/or serving unit. (2) Hand- or automatically operated electric-heated unit in which a measure of hot water at the proper temperature is combined with a measure of instant coffee mix and discharged into a container. (3) Unit consisting of one or more sets of upper and lower bowls set on gas- or electric-heated range. The measure of water boiled in the lower bowl is forced by pressure into the upper bowl containing measured coffee grounds. When the set is removed from the heat source, the cooling lower bowl creates a vacuum, causing the liquid to flow back down through a filter in the bottom of the upper bowl. The upper bowl is then removed to permit use of the lower bowl as a server or decanter.

Coffee Mill. *See* Coffee Grinder.

Coffee Percolator. Covered cylindrical container with up to 120-cup capacity, electric- or gas-heated. Percolating device in center causes heated water to flow over a measured bed of coffee grounds contained in a filtering basket at top. Unit is normally hand-filled. Heating unit keeps coffee warm for serving. Bottom has draw-off faucet.

Coffee Range. Counter unit consisting of one to four low-rated gas or electric burners for making coffee with siphon-type coffeemakers.

Coffee Urn. Enclosed container of water with jar (liner) set into top. Urn water is heated by gas, electricity, or steam. A measure of hot water at proper temperature is poured over a measured bed of coffee grounds contained in a filtering unit. Beverage collects in jar and is discharged through bottom connection to draw-off faucet. Urn water is not used for coffeemaking. Equipped with water inlet valve to fill urn body.

Coffee Urn Battery. Assembly of units consisting of one or more water boilers and one or more coffee urns heated by gas, electricity, or steam. Battery is complete with piping, fittings, and controls between boiler(s) and urn(s).

Coffee Urn, Combination. (1) Coffee urn with water inlet valve and additional draw-off faucet for hot water, to make tea and instant beverages. (2) Pressure siphon type has sealed water and hot-air chambers with piping control between water jacket and jar. (3) Twin type has two coffee jars set into top of single container. Urn body is usually rectangular in shape. (4) Automatic type has electrically operated device to pump and measure hot water at thermostatically controlled temperature.

Coffee Warmer. Countertop range with one or more gas, electric, or canned heaters to maintain coffee at serving temperature, each with coffee bowl or decanter. Also called coffee server.

Cold Beverage Dispenser *or* Urn. *See* Iced Coffee/Tea Urn.

Cold Pan. Insulated depressed pan set into a table or countertop; provided with waste outlet; may be refrigerated with crushed ice, refrigeration coil fastened to the underside of the lining, or a cold plate. A perforated false bottom is provided when ice is used.

Combi Oven/Steamer. An oven that brings together oven and steamer in a single unit, which in turn cooks food rapidly.

Combination Steam Cooker and Kettle. *See* Cooker and Kettle, Combination.

Compactor. Mechanical device that compresses waste materials so that the volume is greatly reduced.

Compressor, Refrigeration. *See* Condensing Unit, Refrigeration.

Condensate Evaporator. Finned coil through which compressed refrigerant flows, absorbing the heat inside a refrigerator or freezer.

Condensing Unit, Refrigeration. Assembly consisting of mechanical compressor driven by electric-powered motor with either air- or water-cooling device. (1) Open-type unit has major components separate but mounted on same base. (2) Hermetic-type unit has major components enclosed in same sealed housing, with no external shaft, and motor operating in refrigerant atmosphere. (3) Semihermetic-type unit has hermetically sealed compressor whose housing is sealed and has means of access for servicing internal parts in field.

Condiment Cabinet. Semi- or fully enclosed cabinet, mobile or stationary, having several removable or intermediate shelves to store cook's or baker's condiments and spices in the cooking and preparation areas.

Condiment Shelf *or* Rack. Shelf or rack mounted above or under a tabletop to hold several condiment items for use by the cook or baker.

Condiment Stand. Standard-height mobile or stationary stand having a solid top with receptacle for holding condiment containers and a tray rest on one or both sides. May be open type with legs or enclosed type with cabinet base and shelves, or may have insulated cold pan and refrigerated base.

Confectioner's Stove. *See* Pot Stove.

Container, Food and Beverage. *See* Bin; Carrier.

Convection Oven. Gas- or electric-heated. Heat is circulated through the oven interior with a fan or blower system. Interior may be equipped with racks and/or shelves. Ovens may be stacked or set on a stand. Oven bottom may be constructed as part of the platform of a mobile basket rack cart.

Convenience Food. Any food item that has been processed by any method from the raw state and packaged for resale and/or further processing or use at later date.

Conveyor. A mechanized belt, often built into a stainless-steel cabinet, that transports materials from one location to another. In foodservice, conveyors are primarily used to move soiled trays from the dining area to the warewashing area. Conveyors can have a variety of types of belts. Usually they run horizontally, but they can also be designed to move trays vertically.

Conveyor Oven. Conveys food through a heated chamber at a predetermined speed. Often used to cook pizza.

Cooker and Kettle, Combination. One or more steam-jacketed kettles with one or more steam cookers mounted in top of single cabinet base or tops of adjoining cabinet bases. May be for direct steam operation or provided with steam coil or gas- or electric-heated steam generator in the base under the steam cooker(s).

Cooker-Mixer. Direct steam-heated, gas-heated, or electric-heated steam-jacketed kettle, with hinged or removable agitator mounted to supporting frame or brackets.

Cookie Dropper. Motor- or hand-driven machine used to portion and shape drops of cookie dough using dies. Unbaked cookies are dropped onto baking sheet pans or conveyor belt. Also called cookie machine.

Cook's Table. Table located in the cooking area of kitchen for cook's use.

Corn Popper. Enclosed unit with transparent front and ends, transparent doors on the working side, electrically heated popcorn popper suspended from the top, and warming heaters for storage of finished popcorn. May be mounted on counter or enclosed base.

Cotton Candy Machine. Machine with round tub and spinning unit and electric heating unit for converting sugar into cotton candy. May be set on countertop or stand.

Creamer. (1) Insulated container for cream, having ice or mechanical refrigeration, and provided with adjustable draw-off faucet for each cream measure. Often anchored to counter or wall. Also called cream dispenser. (2) Soda fountain unit with self-contained ice cream cabinet.

Creamer Rack. Rectangular basket of wire or plastic with compartments to fit glass creamers. Used to wash, fill, and store creamers.

Crusher. *See* Bottle Crusher; Can Crusher; and Ice Crusher.

Cryogenic Freezer. *See* Freezer.

Cubing Machine. *See* Dicing Machine.

Cutlery Box. Unit consisting of one or more compartments for storage and dispensing of flatware (knives, forks, spoons). Often set on a counter or tabletop, and sometimes built into the front of a cabinet under the top, or as a drawer.

Cutting Board. *See* Board.

Deep Fat Fryer. *See* Fryer.

Defrost System. Refrigeration system for a freezer consisting of a blower evaporator coil, heating unit, and controls. Electric type employs heating elements; hot-gas type uses heat exchanger to remove frost from the coil and allow condensate to flow to the drain pan under the coil.

Dessert Cart. Cart with several shelves for display and serving of desserts. May be equipped with mechanical or ice-refrigerated cold pan or plate and with transparent domed cover.

Detergent Dispenser. Device mounted on a dishwasher or sink for storage and dispensing of liquid detergent or mixture of powdered detergent and water into the wash tank of the unit through the pump manifold or incoming water line. Some units are equipped with a control device, electrically operated, to detect detergent strength in tank.

Dicing Machine. Bench-mounted hand- or motor-driven two-operation machine that first forces food through a grid network of knives in a square pattern and then slices the food the same length as the side of the square. May be attached to food mixing or cutting machine. Also called dicing attachment or cubing machine.

Dish Box. *See* Carrier.

Dish Cart. Cart for storage and dispensing of clean or soiled dishes. Usually of height to roll under counter or tabletop.

Dish Machine. Heated water is pumped over dishes and other utensils with enough pressure to remove soil and to sanitize with detergents. Clean dishes must be hot enough to air dry.

Dish Table. Work surface with raised sides and end(s) having its surface pitched to a built-in waste outlet, adjoining a sink or warewashing machine. There may be a soiled-dish table used for receiving, sorting, and racking ware, located at the load end of the sink or washing machine, and a clean-dish table at the unload end for draining of rinse water, drying, and stacking ware.

Disposals. Food waste grinding device mounted in tables and sinks and connected to soil pumping pipes to rid kitchens of soft waste materials.

Dispenser. Unit for storage and dispensing of beverages, condiments, food, and ware. May be insulated and refrigerated or heated. May be provided with self-leveling device. May be counter- or floor-mounted, stationary or mobile.

Display Case. A semi- or fully enclosed case of one or more shelves, mounted on countertop or wall, for display of desserts. Semienclosed types have transparent end panels and sneeze guards along customers' side to protect uncovered foods. Refrigerated types have insulated transparent panels and doors. Heated types are usually provided with sliding doors and electric heating units, with or without humidifier.

Dolly. Solid platform or open framework mounted on a set of casters, for storage and transportation of heavy items. May be equipped with handle or push bar.

Dough Divider. Motor-driven floor-type machine to divide dough (usually for bread) into equally scaled pieces. Pieces are removed from work surface by conveyor to next operation. Normally used for bread dough. Also called bread divider.

Dough Mixer. (1) Motor-driven machine with vertical spindle to which various whips and beaters are attached. Bowl is raised to the agitator. Mixers of 5- to 20-quart (4.75- to 19-L) capacity are bench-mounted. Mixers of 20- to 140-quart (19- to 133-L) capacity are floor type. (2) Motor-driven, floor-type horizontal machine with tilting-type bowl and horizontal agitator(s) for a large dough batch. Also called kneading machine or mixer.

Dough Molder. *See* Bread Molder.

Doughnut Fryer. *See* Fryer.

Doughnut Machine. Unit consisting of hand- or motor-driven batter dropper and shallow fryer. Doughnuts are conveyed through heated cooking fat or oil bath, turned over, and discharged out of bath into drain pan.

Dough Proofer. *See* Proof Box or Cabinet.

Dough Retarder. May be upright reach-in, low-counter bench-type, or walk-in refrigerator with series of racks or tray slides and/or shelves, in which dough is kept cool, to retard rising.

Dough Rounder. Motor-driven floor-mounted machine into which a piece of dough is dropped and rounded to ball shape by means of a rotating cone and fixed spiral raceway running from top to bottom. *See* Roll Divider.

Dough Sheeter. Motor- or hand-driven machine with a series of adjustable rollers to roll dough to sheets of even thickness. Also called piecrust roller.

Dough Trough. Large tub with tapered sides, usually mounted on casters, for storing and transporting large batches of dough. Some troughs have gates at the ends for pouring dough when the trough is lifted above a divider and tilted.

Drainer *See* Kettle Drainer.

Drink Mixer. Vertical counter-type unit with one or more spindles with motor at top. Switch is activated by drink cup when placed in correct position. Also called malted mixer.

Drop-in Unit. Any warming, cooling, cooking, or storage unit that is dropped into an opening in a counter or tabletop and is fitted with accompanying mounting brackets and sized flange.

Dunnage Rack. Mobile or stationary solid or louvered platform used to stack cased or bagged goods in a storeroom or walk-in refrigerator or freezer.

Egg Boiler. Electric-, steam-, or gas-heated unit with removable timed elevating device(s) to raise basket(s) or bucket(s) out of boiling water bath. Containers are lowered by hand. Ferris wheel–type unit automatically lowers and raises baskets through water bath. Also called egg timer.

Egg Timer. *See* Egg Boiler.

Espresso Machine. A machine that heats and holds hot water and pumps it under pressure through coffee in a sieve to make espresso. Many espresso machines also produce steam that is discharged through a wand for heating and frothing milk to make cappuccino and latte.

Evaporator. *See* Condensate Evaporator; Unit Cooler.

Extractor. (1) *See* Juice Extractor. (2) *See* Grease Filter *or* Extractor. (3) *See* Water Extractor.

Extruder. *See* French Fry Cutter.

Fat Filter. (1) Gravity type has disposable paper or muslin strainer set in holder on top of fat container. Unit is placed under drain valve of fat fryer. (2) Siphon type uses disposable paper or muslin strainer over fat container, attached to rigid siphon tube mounted on fat fryer, with other end of tube in fat tank. (3) Motor-driven pump type, portable or mobile, uses disposable paper strainer. Has flexible hose from fat tank to strainer. Strainer set on fat container.

Filter. (1) *See* Coffee Filter. (2) *See* Fat Filter. (3) *See* Grease Filter *or* Extractor.

Finishing Oven. *See* Au Gratin Oven.

Fire Extinguisher. Hand-operated, sealed with chemical inside, most commonly wall-mounted and provided with control and directional hose, or horn.

Fire Suppression System (Kitchen Hood). A system that senses a fire in the cooking equipment under the hood and then opens nozzles that spray a fire-retardant chemical, extinguishing the fire. Some fire suppression systems spray a fine water mist that suffocates the fire rather than (or in addition to) fire retardant chemicals.

Fish and Chip Fryer. *See* Fryer.

Fish Box. (1) Ice-refrigerated insulated cabinet with counterbalanced hinged or sliding door(s) at the top and drawer(s) at the bottom front. (2) Ice or mechanically refrigerated cabinet with tier(s) of self-closing drawers with insulated fronts. Also called fish file.

Fish File. *See* Fish Box.

Flatware. Knife, spoon, and fork used by the diner.

Floor Scale. (1) Unit fixed in a pit, its platform flush with finished floor. May have dial or beam mounted on top of the housing at the rear of platform framing, plus tare beam. Used for weighing heavy objects on mobile carriers. (2) Mobile type. *See* Platform Scale.

Food Carrier. *See* Carrier.

Food Cutter. (1) Motor-driven bench- or floor-mounted machine with a rotating shallow bowl to carry food through a set of rotating horizontal knives whose axis is perpendicular to the radii of the bowl. Knives are set under hinged-up cover. (2) Motor-driven floor-mounted high-speed machine with vertical tilting bowl having a vertical shaft with rotating knife. Also called vertical cutter-mixer or sold under various brand names.

Food Freshener. Electrically operated unit that introduces live steam to the exterior or interior of food, heating it to serving temperature without loss of moisture. Cabinet type has a hinged cover or drawer for warming the exterior of foods. Hollow-pin-type heats food interior through injection.

Food Merchandiser. Refrigerated, heated, or noninsulated case or cabinet with transparent doors and possibly transparent ends. Used for display and sometimes self-service of foods.

Food Processor. A food preparation appliance that chops, grates, and purees food into various sizes and shapes depending on the blade that is installed. Some food processors use a bowl that must be emptied into a pan when full; others are continuous-feed and empty directly through a chute into a pan.

Food Shaper. (1) Motor-driven unit with loading hopper, bench- or floor-mounted. Shapes food into rectangular or round patties of varying thickness. May be equipped with paper interleaving, removing, and conveying devices. (2) Attachment to meat chopper to shape ground food into rectangles of varied thickness. Also called food former.

Food Warmer. (1) Insulated mobile or stationary cabinet with shelves, racks, or tray slides, having insulated doors or drawers. May be electric, steam-heated or gas-heated and provided with humidity control. (2) Infrared lamp or electric radiant heating element with or without a glass enclosure, mounted above the serving unit in a hot-food section.

Freezer Reach-in, walk-in, and under counter freezers usually maintained at 15°F (−9.4°C) or lower.

French Fry Bagger. Motor-driven machine to convey, measure, and insert french-fried potatoes into paper bag blown open to receive product.

French Fry Cutter. Hand-operated or motor-driven machine or attachment to food machine that pushes potato through grid of knives set in square pattern in frame.

French Fryer. *See* Fryer.

Fryer. Floor- or bench-mounted unit heated by gas or electricity with tank of oil or fat into which foods are immersed. Common type has deep tank. Special types have shallow tanks for fish, chicken, doughnuts, and so on, and basket-conveyor type has a shallow tank for draining with baskets, arms, mesh-type belt, or rotating auger to move foods through the bath. Pressure type has a lift-off or hinged cover to seal the top of the fryer tank.

Fry Pan, Tilting. Rectangular pan with gas- or electric-heated flat bottom, pouring lip, and hinged cover. Floor-mounted on a tubular stand or wall mounted on brackets with in-wall steel carriers. A small electric pan may be table-mounted on legs. Also called braising pan, tilting griddle, or tilting skillet.

Fudge Warmer. Counter-mounted electrically heated insulated pot with hinged or lift-off cover and ladle.

Glass Washer. (1) Multitank horizontal machine with hand-activated rinse nozzle in one tank, revolving brushes in a second tank, and final rinse nozzles in a third. (2) Single- or double-tank door-type or rack-conveyor–type dishwasher.

Grater. (1) Bench-mounted hand- or motor-driven machine in which food is forced against the face of a revolving grater plate by a pusher or hopper plate. (2) Part of vegetable-slicing attachment to food machine.

Grease Filter *or* Extractor. (1) Removable rectangular or round frame having several layers of wire mesh or baffles and mounted in the exhaust equipment above or behind cooking units. (2) A series of baffles mounted in exhaust equipment, from whose surfaces grease deposits are flushed with wash water into a waste outlet. (3) Manifold-mounted water nozzles in exhaust equipment producing a fine spray mist that collects grease from laden air and drains through a waste outlet.

Griddle. Extra-thick steel plate with a ground and polished top surface, heated by gas or electricity. Surface edges are raised or provided with gutters and drain hole leading to catch trough or pan. May be set on countertop with legs, stand, or oven base.

Grill. Bench-mounted unit with fixed lower and hinged upper electrically heated plates. Plates have a waffle pattern for waffles and grooves for steaks, and are smooth for sandwiches.

Grill, Charcoal. *See* Broiler, Charcoal.

Grinder. (1) *See* Meat Chopper. (2) *See* Coffee Grinder.

Grooved Griddle. Much like a griddle, except has deep grooves molded into the cooking surface to give a striped appearance to the meat.

Hamper. *See* Linen Hamper.

Heat Exchanger, Steam. Boiler with coils to generate clean steam with possibly contaminated house steam. Used for steam-cooking units.

High-Speed Cooker. *See* Steam Cooker.

Hors d'oeuvre Cart. Cart with platforms on Ferris wheel having several food containers on each platform. Used for display and service.

Hot Chocolate Dispenser *or* Maker. (1) Counter-mounted electrically heated glass bowl with agitator or insulated tank with agitator for dispensing premixed hot chocolate. (2) Counter-mounted electrically heated unit that combines measure of heated water with measure of chocolate mix and dispenses mixture at touch of button.

Hot Dog and Hamburger Broiler. Semi- or fully enclosed cabinet with glass doors and panels for display. An electric heater under the top radiates onto hot dogs in baskets or on pins on wheel, or onto hamburgers laid on platforms mounted on motor-driven Ferris wheel. Food rotates while cooking.

Hot Dog Roller Grill. Counter-mounted unit with multiple steel rollers spaced about $1/4$ inch to $1/2$ inch apart. Hot dogs are placed between the rollers; as they spin, the hot dogs turn over the heating elements.

Hot Dog Steamer. Counter-mounted cabinet with transparent display panels and hinged covers or doors. The unit is electrically heated with a water bath and immersion device to generate steam for heating hot dogs and dry heat for warming rolls.

Hot Food Cabinet. *See* Carrier; Food Warmer.

Hot Plate. Countertop or floor-mounted unit with one or more open gas or tubular electric burners arranged left to right and/or front to rear. French hot plates are round or square solid steel plates, gas or electrically heated.

Hot-Water Booster. Electric-, steam-, or gas-heated insulated tank or coil used to raise the temperature of incoming hot water from house temperature to sanitizing temperature, as required by code. Booster may be mounted inside the housing or at the end of warewashing machine, under warewashing table, or remotely located.

Housekeeping Cart. Cart with one or more semi- or fully enclosed compartments for clean linen, a compartmented tray at the top for supplies, a cloth hamper for soiled linen, and a waste receptacle.

Humidifier. Electric-, steam-, or gas-heated unit used to evaporate and distribute water inside proofing equipment and hot-food warmers. May be fixed or removable attachment.

Ice Breaker. *See* Ice Crusher.

Ice Chest. *See* Ice Storage Bin.

Ice Cream Cabinet. (1) Mechanically refrigerated low-type chest with removable hinged flip-flop covers, used for storage and dispensing of ice cream. (2) Mechanically refrigerated upright cabinet with hinged door(s), for storage of ice cream.

Ice Cream Display Cabinet. Ice cream cabinet with sliding or hinged transparent doors or covers. Mostly used in self-service stores.

Ice Cream Freezer. Floor- or counter-mounted machine with mechanically refrigerated cylinder, having a dasher to mix and refrigerate an air–and–ice cream mix to a smooth consistency. The product is then placed inside a hardening cabinet.

Ice Cream Hardening Cabinet. Low cabinet with a lid(s) or upright cabinet with hinged door(s), insulated and refrigerated at a very low temperature to set ice cream hard.

Ice Crusher. (1) Motor-driven or hand-operated floor- or counter-mounted machine with spiked rollers, to crush large pieces of ice or ice cubes. (2) Attachment mounted between an ice-cube-making machine and an ice storage bin, having a damper for directing cubed ice to motor driven rollers with spikes to crush ice as required.

Ice Cuber. *See* Ice Maker.

Ice Dispenser. A floor-, counter-, or wall-mounted stationary ice storage bin with motor-driven agitator and conveyor mechanism or gravity feed that dispenses a measure of ice (cubed or crushed) through a discharge chute into a container at working level.

Ice Maker. Floor-, counter-, or wall-mounted unit containing refrigeration machinery for making cubed, flaked, and crushed ice. Maker may have integral ice storage bin. Larger-capacity machines generally have a separate bin in which ice is received via a connecting chute. Capacity is rated in pounds of ice per 24-hour day.

Ice Maker and Dispenser. Floor-, counter-, or wall-mounted ice maker with storage bin and dispensing mechanism. *See* Ice Dispenser; Ice Maker.

Ice Pan, Display. *See* Cold Pan.

Ice Plant. (1) An assembly consisting of a large-capacity ice maker that empties into a walk-in freezer or ice storage bin(s) on the floor below via directional chute(s). (2) A large-capacity, floor-mounted ice maker, having a small-capacity bin connected to vertical and horizontal conveyors with insulated sleeves for transporting ice to large-capacity bin(s).

Ice Shaver. Hand-operated or motor-driven floor- or bench-mounted machine whose rotating plate or wheel has a sharp knife that produces icelike snow when forced against the face of a cake of ice. Also called snowcone machine.

Ice Storage Bin. Insulated mobile or stationary cabinet of one or more compartments with hinged or sliding door(s) or cover(s). It is commonly mounted under an ice-making machine, with opening(s) in the top to receive product(s), and is fitted with a waste outlet in the bottom. Ice is normally scooped out of bin. Unit may be built into a counter.

Ice Vendor. Floor-mounted, mechanically refrigerated freezer with a coin-operated mechanism to release a measure of loose or bagged ice cubes at working level.

Iced Coffee/Tea Urn. Urn with stainless-steel or transparent glass jar and draw-off faucet. Stainless-steel type may be insulated. Glass jar may be equipped with ice compartment suspended from cover. Also called iced tea/coffee dispenser.

Induction Cooking. Electromagnetic energy to heat cookware made of magnetic material to produce a high-frequency alternating magnetic field causing the cookware to become hot. The cooktop's glass surface remains cool because it is not magnetic.

Infrared Heater *or* Warmer. Unit consisting of one or more lamps or electric strip heaters, with or without protective covering or reflector, mounted in a bracket or housing. Usually set over hot-food serving and display areas or inside enclosed displays. Unit produces infrared heat to keep food warm.

Infrared Oven. Oven having heat generated and radiated from electric infrared heating elements encased in a glass tube or from an exposed quartz infrared plate.

Injector, Rinse. *See* Rinse Injector.

Insert. Rectangular pan or round pot set into the top of a steam or hot-food table.

Juice Extractor. (1) Counter-mounted motor-driven ribbed cone having base with drain hole for juice. Half of fruit is pressed by hand, down onto cone. (2) Bench- or floor-mounted motor-driven machine that slices fruit in half and squeezes halves between nesting cones. (3) Hand-operated bench-type machine that squeezes fruit halves between inverted cones. Also called juicer.

Kettle Drainer. Mobile sink with screen or strainer basket, waste outlet with adjustable tailpiece, and push handle.

Kettle, Electric-heated. (1) Stationary or tilting two-thirds steam-jacketed or stationary fully steam-jacketed kettle with electric immersion heater in water between shells. Kettle is floor-mounted inside housing or attached to housing with tilting mechanism. Tilting device may be hand- or power-operated. Stationary unit is provided with water filler, hinged cover, and draw-off valve. Tilting type has pouring lip and may have draw-off valve, hinged cover, and water filler. (2) Stationary or tilting two-thirds steam-jacketed kettle set into top of cabinet base with remote electric-heated steam generator adjoining kettle. Kettle is provided with hinged cover, water filler, and draw-off valve.

Kettle, Flat-bottom. Rectangular pan with flat bottom having inner and outer shells. Live steam is introduced between shells, heating inner shell for cooking. Kettle is tilting type, floor-mounted on tubular stand or wall-mounted with brackets and in-wall steel chair carriers. Kettle front has pouring lip. Top has hinged cover.

Kettle, Gas-heated. (1) Stationary fully or two-thirds steam-jacketed kettle with a gas burner under the bottom of its outer shell to heat water between shells. The kettle is floor-mounted inside housing and provided with a water filler and hinged cover. (2) Stationary or tilting two-thirds steam-jacketed kettle set into the top of a cabinet base with remote gas-heated steam generator adjoining the kettle. Kettle is provided with hinged cover, water filler, and draw-off valve. (3) Stationary floor-type direct-fired kettle with a single shell, mounted inside insulated housing, with a gas burner under bottom of shell, draw-off valve, and hinged cover.

Kettle, Steam-jacketed. Kettle having live steam introduced between the inner and outer shell to heat the inner shell for cooking. Deep-type kettle generally is two-thirds jacketed. Shallow-type kettle generally is fully jacketed. May be mounted to the floor with tubular legs or pedestal base, or mounted to the wall with brackets and in-wall steel chair carriers. Tilting or trunnion type may be floor- or wall-mounted, having a worm gear device for hand operation. Stationary kettle has draw-off valve. Tilting kettle has pouring lip and may have draw-off valve. The kettle may be equipped with lift-off or hinged cover, filling faucet, water-cooling system, thermostat, and so on.

Kettle, Tabletop. Two-thirds steam-jacketed kettle, tilting type, with operating lever up to 20-quart capacity, or tilting worm gear device for 40-quart capacity; all direct-steam, electric-heated. All kettles have pouring lip. Tilting types have 20- and 40-quart capacity with a lever handle. Oyster stewing kettle is shallow tilting-type kettle.

Kettle, Tilting or Trunnion. *See* Kettle, Flat-bottom; Kettle, Steam-jacketed.

Kneading Machine *or* Mixer. *See* Dough Mixer.

Knife Rack. Slotted wood or stainless-steel bar set away and attached to edge of tabletop or butcher block. This forms a slot into which cutlery blades are inserted and held to create a safe and easily acessible storage place.

Knife Sharpener. (1) Bench-mounted motor-driven machine with rotating stones forming a V to grind edges on both sides of a blade. (2) Attachment to slicing machine. (3) Grinding-wheel attachment to food machine, having an attachment hub.

Linen Cart. Cart with several compartments for storage of clean linen. May be semi- or fully enclosed.

Linen Hamper. (1) Stationary or mobile metal cabinet with hinged metal cover. (2) Stationary or mobile framework with round cloth bag or cloth sides, ends, and bottom.

Lobster Tank. Transparent tank open at the top and with a water wheel at one end. Tank bottom is lined with special salt. Mounted on a stationary or mobile enclosed base with filtering and mechanical refrigeration system for tank water. Also called trout tank, with salt omitted.

Machine Stand. Mobile or stationary stand with solid or open-frame top, mounted on open legs or cabinet base, with adjustable dimensions to suit a specific machine or device.

Malted Mix Dispenser. Counter- or wall-mounted unit with a transparent covered hopper, having a lever for dispensing a measure of malted mix powder.

Meat and Bone Saw. Floor-mounted motor-driven band saw with upper and lower pulleys, stationary cutting table with gauge plate, and movable carriage.

Meat Chopper. Table- or floor-mounted hand- or motor-driven horizontal machine. Food placed in top-mounted hopper is fed by a stomper into cylinder with tight-fitting auger to drive food against rotating knife and perforated plate. Also called meat grinder.

Meat Grinder. *See* Meat Chopper.

Meat Hook Rack. One or more wood or metal bars mounted on a wall or floor stand, with fixed or removable sharp pointed metal hooks. Also called meat rail.

Meat Roaster, Steam-jacketed. Shallow steam-jacketed kettle with cover and draw-off valve.

Meat Tenderizer. Counter-mounted machine having two sets of round knives with spaced cutting edges, set apart on slow-speed rollers. Meats are inserted into a slot in the top, pass through the rollers, and are discharged at the bottom front.

Menu Board. Sign with fixed or changeable letters or removable lines listing the food items and prices.

Mexican Food Machine. Device used to hold a V-shaped tortilla when filling it to make a taco.

Microwave Oven. Stand- or counter-mounted oven in which foods are heated and/or cooked when they absorb microwave energy (short electromagnetic waves) generated by magnetron(s).

Milk Cooler. (1) Low insulated chest with mechanical or ice refrigeration, for storing and dispensing $\frac{1}{2}$-pint to 2-quart containers of milk. (2) Counter- or stand-mounted refrigerator with one or more 2- to 10-gallon containers equipped with sanitary tube connections that extend through flow-control handles for dispensing loose or bulk milk.

Milkshake Machine. *See* Drink Mixer; Shake Maker.

Mix Cabinet. Low counter-type or upright reach-in refrigerator in which the mix for frozen shakes or ice cream is stored.

Mixer, Dough. *See* Dough Mixer.

Mixer, Drink. *See* Drink Mixer.

Mixer, Food. Motor-driven machine with vertical spindle having several speeds on which various whips and beaters are mounted. Bowl is raised up to agitator. Mixers of 5- to 20-quart (19-L) capacity are bench type. Mixers of 20- to 140-quart (19- to 133-L) capacity are floor type.

Mixer Stand. Low-height stationary or mobile stand with four legs and a solid top to support a mixer up to 20-quart size. May be provided with undershelf and vertical rack for mixer parts.

Mixer, Vertical Cutter. *See* Vertical Cutter-Mixer.

Mixing Kettle. Vertical type has center-, bottom-, or side-mounted agitator assembly. Horizontal type has end-agitator assembly. All are floor-mounted and provided with removable or hinged cover and draw-off valve. Tank may be provided with recirculating pump and filtering system. This kettle is a part of a cook/chill system for mixing large volume liquid or semi-liquid product.

Modular Stand. Low-height open stationary stand with four or more legs, having an open framework top, to support heavy-duty modular cooking equipment.

Molder, Food. *See* Food Shaper.

Mongolian Grill. A round griddle that allows the cook to rotate the food in a circular fashion in front of the customer.

Napkin Dispenser. Countertop unit for storage and dispensing of folded paper napkins. Napkins are forced to headplate by spring out.

Order Wheel. Metal- or wood-spoked wheel with clips or hooks on its perimeter, located between cooks' and servers' areas, on which order slips are placed to maintain rotation and visibility.

Oven. Fully enclosed insulated chamber with wood-, gas-, electric-, or oil-fired heat, provided with thermostatic control or built-in thermometer. Deck-type units have chambers or sections stacked one above the other. Bake-type decks are approximately 7 inches (17.7 cm) high inside. Roast-type decks are 12 to 14 inches (30.5 to 35.5 cm) high inside.

Oyster Opener. *See* Clam Opener.

Pan and Utensil Rack. (1) One or more bars and braces suspended from a ceiling or mounted on posts or a wall, housing fixed or removable hooks for hanging pots, pans, and utensils. (2) Upright mobile or stationary unit, open or semienclosed, with tiers of angle- or channel-shaped slides to support pans. (3) Heavy-duty rectangular wire basket to hold pans and utensils upright in a pot washer.

Pan Washer. *See* Pot and Utensil Washer *or* Potwashing Machine.

Pass-through Window *or* Opening. Trimmed opening between kitchen and serving areas having a shelf for a sill. May be equipped with hinged or sliding door or shutter.

Pasta Cooker. An adaptation of a fryer, combining two fryer units (filled with water), one side for cooking and the second side for washing away the starch and holding the cooked pasta.

Pawls. A small metal device hat "grabs" a dish rack and helps to push the rack through a dishwashing machine.

Peanut Roaster. Electrically heated enclosed display case with hinged cover at the top.

Peeler. Floor- or bench-mounted machine having a vertical, stationary, abrasive-lined cylinder open at the top, a motor-driven agitator bottom plate, and an over-the-rim water supply. Product is discharged through a door in the cylinder side. Wastewater is discharged at the bottom. May be equipped with a peel trap basket that can be hung on a pipe over sink or set inside a cabinet base under the peeler. May also be equipped with a garbage disposal unit.

Peeler Stand. (1) Special-height mobile stand, open type, with four legs. (2) Special-height enclosed cabinet with adjustable legs, a door designed to house a trap basket, and a waste outlet.

Pellet Heater. Counter-mounted electric-heated, insulated cabinet having one or more vertical cylinders in which metallic discs, inserted at the top, are heated. Discs are dispensed at the bottom through drawer-type device. These heated pellets are often used in hospital foodservice to keep food hot when transported to the patient's room.

Pie and Pastry Case. *See* Display Case.

Pizza Oven. Baking-type oven of one or more decks, gas-, electric-, or oil-fired, having temperature range from 350° to 700°F (176.6- to 371-degrees Celsius). Deck(s) are of heat-retaining masonry material.

Pizza Sheeter. *See* Dough Sheeter.

Platform Scale. Mobile unit with a dial or beam, for weights up to 1,500 pounds (675 kg). May be floor- or stand-mounted.

Platform Skid. *See* Dunnage Rack.

Popcorn Machine. *See* Corn Popper.

Pot and Utensil Washer *or* Potwashing Machine. Machine of one or more tanks with hood or wash chamber above, inside which large ware is washed, using very big, high-pressure pumps. Water is pumped from tanks and sprayed over ware placed in racks or set on a conveyor or platform. One or more final fresh-water rinses sanitize ware. Machine has a 34- to 36-inch (86.3- to 91.6-cm) working height. (1) Door-type single-tank machine has power wash and final rinse only. (2) Door-type two-tank machine has power wash and power rinse tanks and final rinse. (3) Belt-conveyor machine is straight-through-type machine having one to three tanks plus final rinse. Ware is set directly on a belt. (4) Revolving tray-table type has two to three tanks plus final rinse. Ware is set directly on turntable platform.

Pot Filler. Faucet or valve with a hose mounted at a range, pot stove, or kettle to fill a vessel direct.

Pot Sink, Powered. A sink that circulates heated water around pots and pans in the soak compartment, loosening food waste.

Pot Stove. Low, floor-mounted single-burner stove with high Btu or kWh rating for use with large stock pots.

Pot Washing Machine. *See* Dish Machine.

Prefabricated Cooler. Walk-in refrigerator or freezer having insulated walls, ceiling, and floor fabricated in a shop and assembled on the job site. The insulated floor and base of the walls may be constructed as part of the building.

Preparation Table *or* Counter. Unit located in the preparation area of a kitchen, for cutting, slicing, peeling, and other preparation of foods.

Prerinse *or* Prewash Sink. Sink constructed as an integral part of a soiled-dish table, located near a dishwashing machine, and furnished with removable perforated scrap basket(s) and spray hose.

Pressure Cooker. *See* Steam Cooker.

Pressure Fryer. *See* Fryer.

Prewash. Separate machine or built-in section of a warewashing machine with tank and pump or fresh-water supply. Pump recirculates water over ware; fresh-water type sprays over ware, before pumped-wash section of machine.

Proof Box *or* Cabinet. Fully enclosed cabinet with gas, steam, or electric heater and humidifier. Sometimes unit may be insulated and have thermostatic and humidity controls. Box may be mobile. Traveling-type proofer has a conveying mechanism inside the overhead cabinet, as in large commercial bread bakery.

Protector Case. A single shelf mounted on posts with transparent shield at the front or at front and ends. Mounted over a countertop at hot-food or sandwich sections to protect uncovered food.

Pulper. Floor-mounted garbage and waste disposal machine with a vertical cylinder, grinder plate, knives, and sump compartment for non-grindable matter. Waste material is ground in a deep-water bath to form a slurry that is piped to a water extractor. Water from the extractor is recirculated to the pulper.

Quartz Oven. Oven that employs an electrically heated quartz plate or infrared quartz element inside a glass tube to generate heat. Also called infrared oven.

Quick Chiller. *See* Blast Chiller.

Rack: Cup, Dish, Glass, Plate, or Tray. (1) Rectangular or round basket of wire or plastic construction, with or without compartments or intermediate lateral supports, used for washing and/or storage of small ware. Racks are self-stacking for cups and glassware. (2) For upright unit, *see* Tray Rack.

Rack Pan. *See* Pan and Utensil Rack.

Rack Washer. Machine of one or two tanks with hood or wash chamber over, with one or two doors, using large-size high-pressure pumps and final sanitizing rinse. Steam- or electric-heated water is pumped from tanks and sprayed over racks wheeled onto tracks inside washer. Machine is made to recess into floor to have tracks set flush with finished floor.

Range. Unit with heated top surface or burners that heat utensils in which foods are cooked, or cook foods directly. Some ranges are equipped with an insulated oven base. Hot or even-heat tops and fry or griddle tops are gas- or oil-fired or electrically heated. Open or hot-plate tops have electric or gas burners.

Reel Oven. *See* Revolving Tray Oven.

Refrigerated Table. Tabletop-mounted on counter-type refrigerated base.

Refrigerator Shelves. Shelves of wire, solid, embossed, or slotted material with reinforced hemmed edges, mounted on tubular posts with adjustable sanitary brackets. May be in stationary or mobile sections.

Rethermalizer. A heated cabinet that brings food that has been quick-chilled up to serving temperature.

Revolving Tray Oven. Gas-, electric-, or oil-heated oven with a motor-driven Ferris wheel device inside having four or more balanced trays. Bake or roast pans are loaded and unloaded from a single opening with a hinged-down door. Steam may be added.

Rinse Injector. Device mounted to top or side of washing machine for storage and automatic dispensing of liquid water softener into the final rinse manifold.

Roast Oven. *See* Convection Oven; Oven; Revolving Tray Oven.

Roaster, Meat, Steam-jacketed. *See* Meat Roaster, Steam-jacketed.

Roll Divider. Hand- or motor-operated machine that divides a ball of dough into equal pieces. Hand-operated unit is stand or table mounted. Motor-driven unit is floor-mounted with a cabinet base and may be combined with a rounding device. Also called bun divider.

Roll Warmer. (1) Enclosed cabinet with a telescoping cover, heated by pellets or glowing charcoal under a false bottom. (2) Enclosed insulated cabinet with electric heating elements and humidity controls. The unit is provided with one or more drawers in a tier at the front; it sits on a countertop, legs, or a stand, or is built into a counter. Also called bun warmer.

Rotisserie. (1) Upright enclosed cabinet with a vertical grill having gas-fired ceramics or electric heating elements. A side-mounted motor drives revolving spits set in a tier in front of the heaters. The unit has hinged or sliding glass doors. (2) Upright enclosed cabinet containing a motor-driven Ferris wheel provided with food cradles or baskets passing under gas-fired ceramics or electric heating elements. (3) Enclosed, square, upright cabinet with meat suspended from top in center revolving motor-driven cradle, heated by four infrared lamps radiating from the corners. (4) *See* Hot Dog and Hamburger Broiler.

Salad Case. Unit consisting of a refrigerated counter with refrigerated food pans set into the top and a refrigerated or nonrefrigerated display case mounted on the countertop.

Salamander. A backshelf or cabinet mounted over the rear of a range or steam table, absorbing the heat to keep foods on it warm.

Salamander Broiler. *See* Broiler, Backshelf.

Saw, Meat and Bone. *See* Meat and Bone Saw.

Scale. *See* Floor Scale; Platform Scale.

Self-Leveling Dispenser. *See* Dispenser.

Service Stand. A stationary cabinet with a solid top at a working height used in a restaurant; may have shelves, bins, drawers, and refrigerated section for storage of linen, flatware, glassware, china, condiments, water, and ice.

Settee Bench. Bench with upholstered seat and upholstered back.

Shake Maker. Floor- or counter-mounted machine with one or two mechanically refrigerated cylinders, having dashers to mix and refrigerate an air-and-milk mixture to a flowing frozen dessert beverage. Unit may be equipped with syrup tanks and pumps and a mixing spindle to blend various flavors in shakes.

Shelving. Available in almost any style for storage of food or materials. Storage efficiency is determined by shelving efficiency.

Shrimp Peeler and Deveiner. Bench-mounted, motor-driven machine that removes vein and shell from shrimp and prawns.

Silver Burnisher, Holloware and Flatware. Machine with a tumbling barrel or vibrating open-top tub filled with steel balls and compound, in which silver-plated utensils are placed. Tumbling or vibrating action causes steel balls to rub tarnish from the surface of the utensils, exposing the base metal. Units may be bench- or floor-mounted or made mobile to roll under a tabletop.

Silver Washer and Dryer. Floor-mounted machine with a fixed or removable tumbling drum set inside a wash chamber with a hinged cover for washing, sterilizing, and electrically drying flatware. The removable drum has a perforated bottom and top cover. The fixed drum has a hinged cover and perforated ends. Machine has wash, rinse, and final sterilization rinse cycles. Electrically heated air is blown through wash chamber and drum to dry flatware.

Sink. (1) Preparation, cook's, or utility: one- or two-compartment type with drain board on one or both sides, each compartment averaging 24 inches (61 cm.) square. (2) Pot and pan or scullery: two-, three-, or four-compartment type with drain board on one or both sides, and possibly between, compartments. Each compartment should be minimum 27 inches (68 cm.) left to right and average 24 inches (61 cm.) front to rear.

Slaw Cutter. Floor- or bench-mounted machine with revolving slicer plate and hopper. Cored and quartered cabbage heads inserted in hopper are forced against slicer plate and discharge through chute below.

Slicer. Bench- or stand-mounted machine with a stationary motor-driven round knife and slice-thickness gauge plate and a reciprocating feed trough or carriage. Flat trough may have hand- and/or spring-pressure feed plate. Gravity trough may have hand- or automatic-feed plate. Trough may be hand-operated or motor-driven. Slicer can be equipped with automatic stacking and conveying device.

Slicer, Bread. *See* Bread Slicer.

Slicer, Vegetable. *See* Vegetable Slicer.

Slush Maker. Floor- or counter-mounted machine with one or two mechanically refrigerated cylinders having dashers to mix and refrigerate a water mixture to a flowing frozen dessert beverage.

Smokehouse, Chinese. Floor-mounted, enclosed, insulated roasting cabinet with gas burners and baffle plates, hinged door(s), duct connection, flue at top, and removable grease pan inside the bottom. Meat, fish, and poultry are mounted on skewers inside. Interior walls and door have deflector plates to direct drippings into the grease pan.

Sneeze Guard. *See* Display Case.

Snowcone Machine. *See* Ice Shaver.

Soda Dispenser. (1) Part of soda-making and refrigeration system: dispensing head attachment for mounting on a soda fountain, bar, counter, or at a server station, complete with drainer. (2) Enclosed cabinet, ice or mechanically refrigerated, to dispense premixed soda or combine soda water and syrup stored in a cabinet or remote tanks. (3) Floor- or counter-mounted cabinet with a self-contained soda and refrigeration system having remote or self-contained syrup tanks.

Soda Maker. Unit consisting of mechanical refrigeration system, carbonator, and soda storage tank.

Soda System. Assembly consisting of soda maker, syrup tanks, syrup, soda and refrigeration tubing, and soda-dispensing head(s) and/or cabinet(s). Also known as carbonated beverage system.

Soft Ice Cream Maker. Floor- or counter-mounted machine with one or two mechanically refrigerated cylinders having dashers to mix and refrigerate an air–and–ice cream mix to a flowing frozen dessert. Unit is equipped with hand or foot-operated dispensing head or control.

Soiled-Dish Pass Window. Trimmed opening in a partition between dishwashing and serving areas, having the soiled-dish table as a sill. The opening may be equipped with hinged or sliding door or shutter.

Soup Station. Section of cook's table or cafeteria counter with a hot-food receptacle, rectangular or round, set into the top.

Speed Oven. Utilizes high speed forced convected air combined with microwave energy to cook food rapidly.

Speed Rail. *See* Bottle Trough.

Spice Bench. Table with stationary cabinet above rear or below top, or mobile cabinet(s) under the top. Cabinet(s) have two or more spice drawers or bins.

Squeezer, Juice. *See* Juice Extractor.

Steam Cooker. Enclosed cabinet with one or more sealed compartments having individual controls into which clean steam is introduced for cooking or heating. Cooker may be direct-connected or equipped with gas-fired, electric, or steam coil generator in the base. (1) A cooker with compartments in tiers that cooks with low-pressure steam. Each compartment has a hinged door with a floating inner panel and a sealing gasket made tight with a wheel screw. Unit is floor-mounted or, if direct-connected, may be wall-mounted. (2) Cooker with high pressure has self-sealing door(s) with a gasket made tight by interior steam pressure. May be floor-, counter-, or-wall mounted. Also called high-speed cooker.

Steamer, Dry. *See* Food Freshener.

Steamer, Hot Dog. *See* Hot Dog Steamer; Steam Cooker.

Steam-jacketed Kettle. *See* Kettle, Steam-jacketed.

Stock Pot Stove. *See* Pot Stove.

Storage Rack. Unit consisting of one or more shelves mounted on angle, channel, or tubular posts, for storage of goods or ware.

Stove. Floor- or counter-mounted unit with one or more open gas or electric burners. Also called hot plate.

Swill Trough. (1) Depression in dish table approximately 6 to 9 inches (15.2 to 22.8 cm.) wide and 2 to 6 inches (5 cm to 15.2 cm) deep, equipped with waste outlet, strainer basket, and perforated cover. (2) Extra sink compartment of shallow depth located between compartments of potwashing sink, equipped with strainer basket.

Table. Top with solid flat surface, mounted on floor with legs, on wall with brackets and legs, or on semi- or fully enclosed cabinet. May be stationary or mobile. May have shelves under, shelves over, and tool drawer(s).

Tea Maker or Dispenser. (1) *See* Coffee Urn. Same as coffee urn with tea laid in strainer. (2) Counter-mounted unit used to combine instant tea mix with heated water for hot tea or cold water for ice tea.

Tenderizer. *See* Meat Tenderizer.

Timer, Egg. *See* Egg Boiler.

Toaster. (1) Counter-mounted pop-up type has two- or four-slice capacity. Electric only. (2) Counter-mounted conveyor type with a motor-driven conveyor carries the product between electric or gas-fired radiants. (3) Sandwich type: *See* Grill.

Tray Makeup *or* Assembly Conveyor. Motor-driven or gravity-type horizontal conveyor used to transport trays between various food loading stations.

Tray Rack. Upright mobile or stationary unit, open or semienclosed, having angle, channel, or tubular posts and one or more tiers of angle- or channel-shaped slides to support trays or pans. Rack may be built into cabinets or suspended from under tabletops.

Tray Slide *or* Rail. Horizontal surface that accommodates the width of a tray, extended out from, and running the length of, cafeteria countertop. May be constructed of solid material with or without raised edges and V beads; or of several tubular or solid rails or bars. Mounted on and fastened to brackets secured to countertop and/or counter body. Also called tray rest.

Tray Stand. Low-height, mobile or stationary four-legged stand with solid top. Top may have raised back and sides to prevent tray stacks from falling over.

Trough, Swill. *See* Swill Trough.

Trout Tank. *See* Lobster Tank.

Truck. *See* Cart.

Undercounter Sink Workboard. *See* Bar Workboard.

Unit Cooler. Semienclosed cabinet open at front and rear or top and bottom, depending on airflow, with a motor-driven fan blowing air through a mechanically refrigerated finned coil. Device is normally suspended inside a refrigerator or freezer. Also called blower (evaporator) coil.

Urn, Coffee/Tea. *See* Coffee Urn.

Urn Stand. Stationary stand with a solid top having raised edges all around, recessed drain trough(s) with waste outlet, and a drainer plate flush with the top. Raised, die-stamped openings are used to connect lines to an urn. Top is set on an open base with a shelf, semienclosed cabinet with a bottom (and intermediate) shelf, or enclosed cabinet with a bottom (and intermediate) shelf and door(s). May also be equipped with a fold-down step.

Vegetable Peeler. *See* Peeler.

Vegetable Slicer *or* Cutter. (1) Hand- or motor-driven counter-mounted machine having rotating removable plates with varied knives. Product is forced against plates and knives for slicing, dicing, grating, shredding, and the like. (2) Similar attachment to a food machine with rotating removable plates and knife arrangements.

Vegetable Steamer. *See* Steam Cooker.

Vertical Cutter-Mixer. Floor-type machine with a vertical tilting mixing bowl having a 25- to 80-quart (23.7- to 76 L) capacity. The bowl is equipped with a two-speed motor and a high-speed agitator shaft at bowl bottom with cutting-mixing knife. A hand- or motor-driven stirring and mixing shaft is fixed to the bowl's cover. A strainer basket may be included.

Waffle Baker. *See* Grill.

Water Boiler. (1) One or more urns of a coffee urn battery, heated by gas, steam, or electricity, to bring water to boil for making beverages. Usually connected to other urns with water piping and controls. Can be used separately. (2) Gas-, electric-, steam-, or oil-fired unit to heat water for use in kitchen.

Water Extractor. Floor-mounted machine located at the terminal of a waste-pulping system. The device augers pulp in a slurry out of the tank to a pressure head at the top, extracting water that is then recirculated into the system. The pulp is discharged into a chute to a waste receptacle.

Water Filtration. Important filter attached to coffee urns, ice machines, small boilers, steamers, and equipment that will operate best with clean bacteria-, chemical-, and scale-free water.

Water Heater. Counter-mounted instant electric heating device with faucet for making tea and hot chocolate drinks.

Water Station. Section of a counter or stand with a glass and/or pitcher-filling faucet and drain trough.

Window, Soiled-Dish Pass. *See* Soiled-Dish Pass Window.

Wine Rack. Fixed or portable folding unit with alternating stacked compartments open at front and rear to support wine bottles in a horizontal position for storage and display.

Wok. *See* Chinese Range.

Wood Top. Tabletop constructed of kiln-dried laminated hard rock maple strips, hydraulically pressed together, glued, and steel-doweled through.

Workboard. *See* Bar Workboard.

Worktable. *See* Preparation Table *or* Counter.

Bibliography

Alderman, Al. (2004). "The Changing Face of Custom Fabrication." *Consultant* 37/2: 97–100.

Arango, Jorge S., Cesar Rubio, and David Battenfield. (2005). "Sea and Shore." *Hospitality Design* 27/3: 156–59.

Austin, Tom. (2004). "Dining Alfresco." *Hospitality Design* 26/7: 102–5.

Bain, Kent. (2003). "What We Need from Facility Design." *Foodservice Equipment & Supplies* 56/7: 29.

Barista, Dave. (2004). "Recipe for Success." *Building Design & Construction* 45/9: 40–44.

Beamon, Kelly. (2003). "Naked Truth." *Hospitality Design* 25/5: 45.

Bean, Russell L. (2006)." Foodservice Buyer: Refrigeration." *Restaurant Business* 105/3: 72.

Bendall, Dan. (2004). "Cold Facts about Ice Makers." *Restaurant Hospitality* 88/2: 102–6.

Bendall, Dan. (2005). "Home on the Range." *Food Management* 40/10: 100–102.

Bendall, Dan. (2004). "The Money-Making Bar Setup." *Restaurant Hospitality* 88/7: 122–28.

Bendall, Dan. (2006). "A Perfect One-Two Punch." *Restaurant Hospitality* 90/1: 72–73.

Berta, Dina. (2004). "Well-Designed Kitchens Good for Business." *Nation's Restaurant News* 38/16: 16.

Bertagnoli, Lisa. (2004). "Built for Speed." *Restaurants & Institutions* 114/23: 51–58.

"Best New Servery Design." (2005) *Food Management* 40/4: 40.

Boss, Donna. (2003). "Vu Restaurant & Lounge." *Foodservice Equipment & Supplies* 56/5: 75.

Boss, Donna. (2003). "Rainwater Restaurant." *Foodservice Equipment & Supplies* 56/6: 39.

Boss, Donna. (2003). "Red Lobster's Coastal Home Design." *Foodservice Equipment & Supplies* 56/6: 50.

Boss, Donna. (2003). "The Lodge at Sea Island, Ga." *Foodservice Equipment & Supplies* 56/8: 45.

Boss, Donna. (2004). "Reflections." *Foodservice Equipment & Supplies* 57/11: 21–24.

Boss, Donna. (2005). "The Western Door: A Seneca Steakhouse." *Foodservice Equipment & Supplies* 58/5: 55–58.

Boss, Donna. (2005). "The Dining Room at Union Pacific Center." *Foodservice Equipment & Supplies* 58/8: 45–48.

Boss, Donna. (2006). "Facility Design Project of the Year." *Foodservice Equipment & Supplies* 59/5: 56–60.

Boss, Donna. (2006). "Colors." *Foodservice Equipment & Supplies* 59/7: 49–54.

Boss, Donna. (2006). "Café 37 at One South Dearborn in Chicago." *Foodservice Equipment & Supplies* 59/8: 37–42.

Brucker, Hilda J. (2006). "Creating a Signature Look?" *Pizza Today* 24/8: 33–34.

Buchthal, Kristina. (2006). "Richard Bloch." *Restaurants & Institutions* 116/3: 23.

Buchthal, Kristina. (2006). "This Old Front of the House." *Restaurants & Institutions* 116/12: 42–44.

Campbell, Liz. (2005). "Ask the Design Experts." *Consultant* 38/4: 58–62.

Campbell, Liz. (2006). "A Unique Design for Hospital Dining." *Consultant* 39/3: 58–63.

Carbonara, Joseph M. (2006). "Different by Design." *Foodservice Equipment & Supplies* 59/5: 15.

Carroll, Alisa. (2005). "Ship Ahoy." *Hospitality Design* 27/7: 176–79.

Catinella Orrell, Rita F. (2006). "Tasteful Kitchen Design." *Architectural Record* 194/10: 64–64.

Clarke, John. (2006). "Kitchen Design." *Grill* 1/6: 50–59.

"Clean Sweep." (2006). *Restaurants & Institutions* 116/17: 96–108.

"Common Kitchen Gaffes." (2003). *Nation's Restaurant News* 37/35: 46.

"Condiment Dispensing Systems Come of Age." (2003). *Nation's Restaurant News* 37/35: 40.

Craiger Hargesheimer. (2006). "A Builder's View." *Grill* 1/6: 55.

"Custom Stainless-Steel Fabrication." (2006). *Foodservice Equipment & Supplies* 59/9: 25.

"Deliver a Dining Experience." (2006). *Hotels* 40/4: 76–80.

"Design Trends: Non Commercial." (2006). *Restaurants & Institutions* 116/16: 50–51.

"Designing for Efficiency." (2003). *Nation's Restaurant News* 2/2: 7.

Ehrhardt, Ron. (2005). "Smaller Is Better in On-Site Foodservice." *Foodservice Equipment & Supplies* 58/1: 19.

"Equipment News." (2005). *Restaurant Hospitality* 89/2: 112.

"Equipment News." (2005). *Restaurant Hospitality* 89/4: 135.

"Fabulous Foodservice." (2006). *Appliance Design* 54/7: 7.

"Facility Design." (2006). *Foodservice Equipment & Supplies* 59/1: 36.

Frable, Foster Jr. (2003). "Never Underestimate the Importance of Facilities Design in the Success of a Foodservice Operation." *Nation's Restaurant News* 37/46: 18.

Frable, Foster Jr. (2004). "Well-Executed Commercial Kitchen Design Requires Step-by-Step Planning, Patience." *Nation's Restaurant News* 38/7: 18–60.

Frable, Foster Jr. (2004). "Construction Administration Lays Solid Foundation for Successful Design." *Nation's Restaurant News* 38/23: 26–28.

Frable, Foster Jr. (2005). "Well-Planned Transition between Front- and Back-of-House Cuts Down on Noise, Accidents." *Nation's Restaurant News* 39/26: 34,199.

Frable, Foster Jr. (2006). "Disoriented Customers Can Mean Lost Business for Operators." *Nation's Restaurant News* 40/20: 22.

Frable, Foster Jr. (2006). "Innovation Leads to a Better Way to Maintain Foods' Taste, Temperature on Holding Systems." *Nation's Restaurant News* 40/34: 18–64.

Gilstrap, Michelle. (2006). "Wood You Like." *Display & Design Ideas* 18/4: 18.

"Handsinks with Antimicrobial Protection." (2004). *Convenience Store News* 40/12: 83.

Huber, Douglas W. (2006). "Streamlining the Process." *Foodservice Equipment & Supplies* 59/6: 21–22.

Hume, Scott. (2004). "Open-Kitchen Designs." *Restaurants & Institutions* 114/9: 22–23.

"Innovations and Improvements in Working Kitchens: Keep 'Em Simple." (2003). *Nation's Restaurant News* 37/35: 48.

Jennings, Lisa. (2005). "FCSI Organizes Best-Practices Guidelines for Equipment Selection." *Nation's Restaurant News* 39/41: 8.

Jesitus, John. (2004). "Display Units Provide Options, Design Element." *Hotel & Motel Management* 219/9: 32–34.

Johnson, Michael O. (2006). "ADA—16 Years and Counting." *Foodservice Equipment & Supplies* 59/8: 21–23.

Katsigris, Costas, and Chris Thomas. (2006). *Design and Equipment for Restaurants and Foodservice: A Management View, Second Edition.* Hoboken, NJ: John Wiley & Sons.

Kooser, Ron. (2003). "Design for the Customers, Not the Designer." *Food Management* 38/9: 22.

Leberte, Mark. (2005). "A Good Installation." *Foodservice Equipment & Supplies* 58/10: 54.

Levere, Jane. (2003). "Aix en New York." *Hospitality Design* 25/3: 138.

Levin, Amelia. (2006). "Special Report: Energy Efficiency in Equipment and Practice." *Foodservice Equipment & Supplies* 59/10: 15–16.

Maclaurin, Donald. (2004). "Wise Design." *Foodservice & Hospitality* 37/5: 71–74.

Martin, Richard. (2006). "Chains Take Pains to Reinvent Themselves in Bids to Match Hipper Decor of Newer Rivals." *Nation's Restaurant News* 40/22: 21.

Mastrelli, Tara. (2006). "Don't Feed the Chefs." *Hospitality Design* 28/4: 45–46.

Mastrelli, Tara, and Douglas Fogelson. (2005). "Rustic Redefined." *Hospitality Design* 27/4: 66–69.

Mastrelli, Tara, and Michael Moran. (2005). "Horizontal Vertigo." *Hospitality Design* 27/3: 164–67.

Matula, Dennis L. (2003). "Air Balance Fundamentals for the Modern Restaurant." *Engineered Systems* 20/1: 58.

McPherson, John, Adrian Mitchell, and Andrew Ross. (2004). "Every Penny Counts: Operators Who Design Concepts for Value Get Biggest Bang for Buck." *Nation's Restaurant News* 38/33: 42–44.

"NRA Show Eyes the Future." (2005). *Restaurants & Institutions* 115/8: 18.

"On the Fry." (2006). *Restaurants & Institutions* 116/3: 60.

"Partners in Innovation." (2004). *Engineer* 293/7665: Special Section 6–7.

Perlik, Allison. (2004). "Setting the Stage." *Restaurants & Institutions* 114/1: 95–101.

Popp, Jamie. (2005). "What's Cooking?" *Restaurants & Institutions* 115/13: 50–58.

Powell, Peter. (2005). "Restaurant Refrigeration Tries Parallel Rack Approach." *Air Conditioning Heating & Refrigeration News* 224/2: 18.

Riell, Howard. (2003). "'Cleaning Up' a Corrections Kitchen." *Foodservice Equipment & Supplies* 56/3: 32.

Robson, Stephani K. A. (2004). "Designing for Dollars." *Restaurant Hospitality* 88/10: 72–74.

Russo, Bruce. (2006). "The Benefits of a Well-Designed Restaurant Pleasing to the Pocketbook as Well as the Eye." *Nation's Restaurant News* 40/23: 22–24.

Schechter, Mitchell. (2004). "An Architect of an Enduring Design." *Foodservice Equipment & Supplies* 57/6: 28–31.

Schechter, Mitchell. (2004). "United States: Equipment & Kitchen Design Update." *Consultant* 37/4: 23–29.

Seelye, Kathleen. (2006). "Thinking 'Green' Means Thinking Sustainably." *Food Management* 41/6: 32–34.

Seelye, Kathleen. (2006). "Energy Savings Are Green in More Ways than One." *Food Management* 41/9: 24.

Shea, Erin J. (2005). "Cool, Clean and Collected." *Restaurants & Institutions* 115/6: 93–94.

"Shelving." (2006). *Foodservice Equipment & Supplies* 59/9: 84–85.

Sheridan, Margaret. (2004). "Hungry Minds." *Restaurants & Institutions* 114/23: 69–70.

"Size Matters." (2006). *Caterer & Hotelkeeper* 196/4429: 54.

Soucie, Ray. (2005). "Serving Lines Create Theater." *FoodService Director* 18/10: 48.

Spata, Anthony J. (2006). "Great Facility Design Is More than Just a Pretty Face." *Foodservice Equipment & Supplies* 59/4: 29–30.

Stanford, Howard. (2005). "The Preferred Route." *Foodservice Equipment & Supplies* 58/8: 27–28.

Sweet, Kimberly. (2006). "Raising the Stakes." *Professional Remodeler* 10/4: 16–21.

"A Taste of Technology." (2006). *Restaurants & Institutions* 116/5: 75.

"25 Kitchenware Products That Changed the Industry." (2004). *Gourmet Retailer* 25/9: 102–7. Webb, Jim. (2006). "Kitchen Fundamentals." *Foodservice Equipment & Supplies* 59/2: 23–24.

Webb, Michael. (2003). "Perfectly Putman." *Hospitality Design* 25/3: 142.

Weber, Toby. (2004). "Beltram's Southern Designs." *Foodservice Equipment & Supplies* 57/5: 51.

Whitman, David C. (2003). "Organized Chaos." *Foodservice Equipment & Supplies* 56/8: 21.

INDEX